Fodor's 2019

WASHINGTON, D.C.

Welcome to Washington, D.C.

With its neoclassical government buildings and broad avenues, Washington, D.C., looks its part as America's capital. Majestic monuments and memorials pay tribute to notable leaders and great achievements, and merit a visit. But D.C. also lives firmly in the present, and not just politically; new restaurants and bars continually emerge, upping the hipness factor in neighborhoods from Capitol Hill to U Street. Fun museums and tree-shaded parks make it a terrific place for families. You may come for the official sites, but you'll remember D.C.'s local flavor, too.

TOP REASONS TO GO

★ **Cherry Blossoms:** For a few weeks in spring, D.C. is awash in glorious pink blooms.

★ **The White House:** 1600 Pennsylvania may be the best-known address in the United States.

★ **Memorials:** The lives of soldiers, presidents, and political figures are commemorated.

★ **Museums:** For every taste—whether you like spies, airplanes, history, or art.

★ **Globe-trotting Cuisine:** Diverse cultures support restaurants with authentic flavors.

★ **The Mall:** Ground zero for museums, picnics, festivals, and performances.

Contents

Fodor's Features

MAPS

Chapter 1

EXPERIENCE WASHINGTON, D.C.

26 ULTIMATE EXPERIENCES

Washington, D.C. offers terrific experiences that should be on every traveler's list. Here are Fodor's top picks for a memorable trip.

1 Cherry Blossom Festival

Every spring Washington is blanketed with a blizzard of little pink and white flowers, heralding the three-week-long National Cherry Blossom Festival. Many of the original trees (which were a gift from Japan in the early 1900s) stand around the Tidal Basin; come early or go out into the neighborhoods to avoid the crowds. *(Ch. 3)*

2 The NMAAHC

The National Museum of African American History and Culture chronicles the African American experience, from the journey of Africans taken into servitude through the Civil War, Jim Crow era, up to today. *(Ch. 3)*

3 White House

If there's one sight that says "America," it's the White House. The presidential estate at 1600 Pennsylvania Avenue offers selfie opportunities from both the street side and from the Ellipse. *(Ch. 6)*

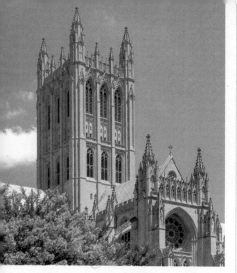

4 National Cathedral

With a prominent spot on the city's skyline, this stone church is built in a soaring 14th-century Gothic style and is the site of state funerals for presidents of every faith. *(Ch. 11)*

5 The Wharf

The District's newest neighborhood opened its first phase to great acclaim in late 2017, with a mix of residences, hotels, restaurants, shops, and nightspots along the Potomac southeast waterfront. *(Ch. 12)*

6 Georgetown

One of Washington's ritziest enclaves, Georgetown marries old-world charm with upscale dining and shopping, as well as a soupçon of college nightlife via Georgetown University. *(Ch. 7)*

7 14th Street and U Street

Historically, U Street was the focal point of early-20th-century African American culture in D.C. Today, it's a focal point of the District's dining and nightlife scene. *(Ch. 10)*

8 Smithsonian Museums

What do baby pandas, astronauts, and postage stamps have in common? They all make up the dizzying array of offerings at the Smithsonian's 19 museums. *(Ch. 3, 4, 11)*

9 Nationals Park

Washington isn't known nationally as a baseball town, but Nats games are one of the top things to do, with a waterfront setting, affordable tickets, and friendly fans. *(Ch. 12)*

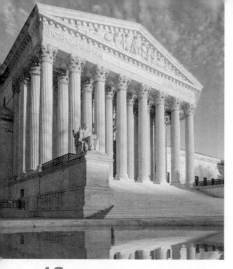

10 Supreme Court

The highest court in the country—and home of the third branch of government—is housed in a neoclassical white building a block from the U.S. Capitol. Oral arguments are open to the public. *(Ch. 5)*

11 Union Market and Eastern Market

D.C.'s market power couple (or are they frenemies?) set a high bar for discerning shoppers. Eastern Market is a little better known and more historic. Union Market offers high-end artisanal brands. *(Ch. 5)*

12 Kennedy Center

The pinnacle of performing arts in Washington, the John F. Kennedy Center for the Performing Arts has a prominent perch on the banks of the Potomac. It's worth a visit just for the views. *(Ch. 6)*

13 Mount Vernon

George Washington was always a farmer at heart, and you can visit his well-preserved colonial plantation home along the Potomac River, about 10 miles south of Alexandria. *(Ch. 14)*

14 Monuments and Memorials

If there's one place in Washington you need to visit, it's the National Mall. The 2-mile lawn between the Lincoln Memorial and the U.S. Capitol is home to most of the city's monuments and museums. *(Ch. 3)*

15 National Zoo

If you were to give Washington a signature animal, the giant panda would win. The National Zoo is home to three, as well as other animals, from elephants to lions to Amazonian frogs and monkeys. *(Ch. 11)*

16 Dupont Circle

Dupont has a little bit of everything: a mix of shops, restaurants, embassies and museums, including the Phillips Collection and the Heurich House Museum. It's also a popular residential area. *(Ch. 8)*

17 Potomac River

It won't attract swimmers or win "clean water" accolades anytime soon, but the Potomac swarms with kayakers, stand-up paddleboarders, rowers, and sightseeing cruises. *(Ch. 12)*

18 Arlington National Cemetery

A quick trip across the Memorial Bridge from the Lincoln Memorial brings you to this bucolic 624-acre plot of Virginia land that is the final resting place of two presidents and about 400,000 American veterans, including the Unknown Soldier. *(Ch. 13)*

19 Shaw

A decade ago, few visitors found themselves in this corner of Washington. Now it's the city's obsession, booming with artisanal bars, restaurants, and boutiques. Beer drinkers have plenty to cheer about, as do foodies looking for the newest D.C. hotspot. *(Ch. 10)*

20 U.S. Capitol

The seat of legislative power for the United States anchors one end of the Mall with a soaring dome, one of the tallest structures in the city. *(Ch. 5)*

21 The Newseum

At a time when the role of news in democracy is making headlines, this fascinating, state-of-the-art museum just up the street from the U.S. Capitol takes a deep dive into the First Amendment. *(Ch. 4)*

22 Holocaust Museum

You can't leave here without being moved. The brilliant museum is meant to evoke memories of Nazi-era Germany from the ghettos to the final solution. *(Ch. 3)*

23 Historic Hotels

The Watergate has been reborn and restored. Others, including the Mayflower, the Hay Adams, and Willard InterContinental have hosted everyone from Mark Twain to Martin Luther King Jr. *(Ch. 4, 6)*

24 H Street NE

It's a tad isolated and a little gritty, but the artsy H Street corridor is a good place to escape the capital's pomp and marble. Also called the Atlas District, it's home to many bars and restaurants. *(Ch. 5)*

25 Tidal Basin

One of the most photographed spots in Washington, this serene inlet lined with monuments, memorials, and cherry trees is just south of the National Mall. *(Ch. 3)*

26 Library of Congress

The world's largest library has about 838 miles of bookshelves. The catch: you can't actually check them out, but you can join a free tour of the of the grand building. *(Ch. 5)*

WHAT'S WHERE

1 The Mall and Federal Triangle. This expanse of green is at the heart of D.C., stretching from the Capitol to the Washington Monument, and is lined by some of America's finest museums. To the north, the Federal Triangle houses the National Archives and government offices.

2 Downtown, Chinatown, and Penn Quarter. Downtown is filled with hotels and restaurants. Penn Quarter attracts visitors to museums and galleries by day and notable restaurants by night. By night, crowds head to Chinatown's bars, restaurants, and movie theaters.

3 Capitol Hill and Northeast. The Capitol itself dominates this area, along with the Supreme Court and Library of Congress. Also explore the ever-growing H Street corridor.

4 Foggy Bottom, the West End, and the White House. There's great art at the Renwick Gallery, performances at the Kennedy Center, and a whiff of scandal at the Watergate. The world's most famous house sits at the eastern end of this area.

5 Georgetown. The capital's wealthiest neighborhood is great for strolling and shopping, with the scene centering on Wisconsin Avenue and M Street. The C&O Canal starts here too.

6 Dupont Circle and Kalorama. This hub of fashionable restaurants, shops, and embassies is also home to the most visible segment of the gay community.

7 Adams Morgan. One of D.C.'s most ethnically diverse neighborhoods has offbeat restaurants and shops and a happening nightlife.

8 U Street Corridor, Logan Circle, Shaw, and Columbia Heights. Revitalization has brought trendy boutiques and hip eateries to the area around 14th and U, which was a hotbed of African American culture in the early 20th century.

9 Upper Northwest. This mostly residential swath of D.C. holds two must-see attractions: the National Cathedral and the National Zoo.

10 Waterfront, Southeast, and Anacostia. The newly developing Waterfront district is D.C.'s liveliest new area, but the Navy Yard is not far behind.

11 Arlington and Northern Virginia. Technically the suburbs, this easy-to-reach region is home to the Pentagon and Arlington National Cemetery.

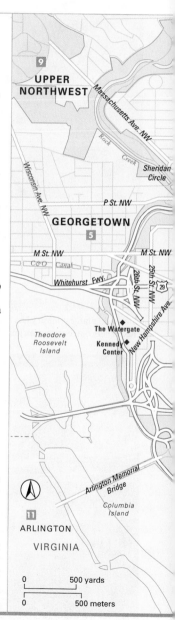

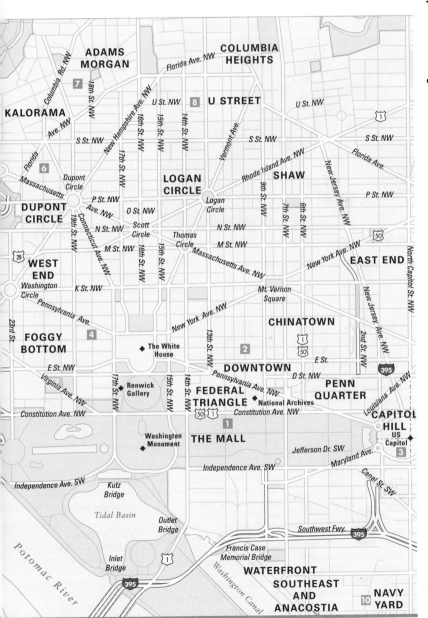

10 Things to Buy in Washington, D.C.

AN OFFICIAL WHITE HOUSE CHRISTMAS ORNAMENT
The White House has created a collectable Christmas ornament each year since 1981, each celebrating some aspect of presidential history. You can buy this year's—or any one that suits your fancy—at the White House Visitor Center Flagship Store at 1450 Pennsylvania Ave.

A UNIQUE MUSEUM GIFT
One thing the District has in abundance is spectacular museums—and along with museums come museum gift shops. These are some of the most underrated places for a shopping spree, with seriously curated wares including designer clothes, hangable art, coffee-table books, weird technology, and more. A few singular museum shops to check out are: the Renwick Gallery (contemporary American pottery, clothing, and jewelry), National Gallery of Art (books, clothes, and housewares featuring famous artworks), National Air and Space Museum (a favorite: astronaut ice cream), and the International Spy Museum (supercool decoder rings or a pen camcorder).

LOCAL FOOD PRODUCTS
D.C. has a lively food culture based on fresh ingredients, and local producers make delicious honey, jam, granola, beer, and more. Shop Made in D.C. at Dupont Circle has a fabulous selection of items (as well as art, clothing, and other locally made items) and primo signature gift boxes. Union Market in NoMa is another option. Salt & Sundry has foodie gifts as well jewelry, knits, and other works by local artists. And everywhere you go, keep an eye out for D.C.'s most iconic condiment, the sweet and tangy Capital City Mumbo Sauce.

A REAL-LIFE CHERRY TREE
Crowds flock to D.C. to view the ephemeral cherry blossoms, a traditional spring pilgrimage since the Japanese presented 3,000 of them as a gift to the capital city in 1912. If you'd like one of your own, you can order one through the DC Gift Shop; they'll spare you the trouble of having to shuffle it aboard the plane by sending it straight to your house. If a standard size cherry tree just isn't practical, what about a gemstone cherry blossom bonsai instead? The DC Gift Shop sells those, too.

LOCAL DESIGNER CLOTHING
Once upon a time (and not that long ago), the District was mostly about three-piece suits, with beach-sand tan being the most audacious color. These days, local fashion designers have quietly blossomed, creating and selling a variety of stunningly unique fashions that you won't find anywhere else. Mimi Miller, Amanda Casarez, and Maven Women by Rebecca Ballard are great places to start, but most don't have their own storefronts—yet.

BOOKS, BOOKS, AND MORE BOOKS
In a city with such integral ties to American history, you can bet your tricorn hat that you'll find a cornucopia of books

1

Experience Washington, D.C.   10 THINGS TO BUY IN WASHINGTON, D.C.

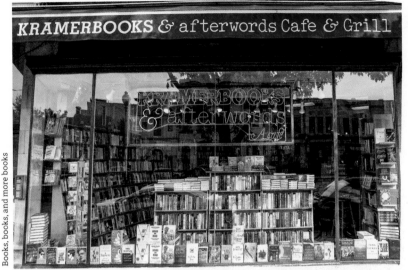

KRAMERBOOKS & afterwords Cafe & Grill

Books, books, and more books

covering every aspect of Americana. You'll find them in the shops of every museum and attraction—the shops at the Library of Congress, the National Building Museum, and the National Museum of American History are especially good. And while you're at it, there are several beloved independent bookstores with a local bent that are worth a peek as well, including Kramerbooks and afterwords café and the legendary Politics and Prose.

HANDCRAFTED SUNDRIES
Eastern Market on Capitol Hill has been a buzzing local market since 1873. It's still a viable food market, but these days, there's more. On weekends, artists and crafters take over the surrounding streets and the plaza, purveying colorful ceramic pitchers, aroma-therapy soaps, funky

fashion jewelry, cloth dolls, batik wall hangings, and a long list of other beautifully crafted items. Shop Made in D.C. and Union Market are other places you'll find the work of local makers.

A PLUSH PANDA
Perhaps there's no animal more beloved at the Smithsonian's National Zoo than the giant pandas—Mei Xiang, Tian Tian, and their son, Bei Bei. And many visitors will want to take one home. And you can. The zoo's gift shop sells plush pandas, plush panda backpacks, a plush panda children's chair, panda-adorned T-shirts, panda slippers, panda dessert plates—you get the idea. The good news? Stuffed pandas don't scratch or bite.

LOCALS SPORTS GEAR
D.C. has some serious sports teams, including the Nationals (baseball),

Wizards (basketball), Capitals (ice hockey), D.C. United (soccer), and Redskins (football). You can find good selections of caps, jerseys, T-shirts, and more at the stadiums themselves, if you happen to be there for a game. Or stop by any DICK's Sporting Goods, MODELL's Sporting Goods, even Target in the District.

DISTRICT-THEMED HOUSEWARES
You'll find one-of-a-kind boutiques selling super original items for your home, including artsy tea towels with D.C. motifs, D.C.-shaped cutting boards, and printed hand-drawn maps of D.C. neighborhoods. You can even find cookie cutters in the shape of the District. Check out Cherry Blossom Creative Workshop, HomeRule, and Hill's Kitchen for starters.

10 Things Not to Do in Washington, D.C.

DON'T TRY TO VISIT EVERY MUSEUM
The beauty of D.C.'s museums is that many of them are free, and there's a museum for every interest and taste, many concentrated in the Mall and Penn Quarter. Resist the impulse to see them all. Instead, pick a few that most interest you and focus on those.

DON'T DRIVE
D.C.'s traffic is worse than LA's, and parking is expensive, especially during the week. While Uber and taxis can be good options at night, the best solution to Washington gridlock is to buy a plastic SmartTrip card and use the Metro. Just don't stand on the left side of those long Metro escalators. That side's for walking.

DON'T STAY IN D.C.
Northern Virginia is practically an extension of the District and has some of the region's most excellent sights. Arlington National Cemetery is here, as is the iconic Iwo Jima memorial, Old Town Alexandria's historic waterfront, George Washington's estate at Mount Vernon, and cheaper hotels.

DON'T SKIP THE MALL AT NIGHT
D.C.'s monuments are open to visitors 24 hours a day, and touring them in the dark is simultaneously eerie and enchanting. Some, including the Korean War Veterans Memorial, are arguably more powerful when lit; others, like the Jefferson Memorial, are far more peaceful without the crowds. Join a guided tour or explore on your own.

DON'T STICK TO THE MALL
The 2-mile expanse between the Capitol and the Lincoln Memorial is ground zero for tourists. You'll want to spend some time here, but you need to get off the Mall and into D.C.'s colorful neighborhoods to really experience the city's energy and character. From the Georgetown restaurant booth where JFK proposed to Jackie to the food stalls at Union Market to the Chinatown house where the Lincoln assassinators conspired (now a karaoke bar).

DON'T DINE AT CHAINS
There's a Hard Rock Cafe here. Don't eat there. Washington's culinary scene is thriving—just ask the throngs who wait for hours to dine at Rose's Luxury. The city's strong international ties bring in a wealth of authentic international eats—try Ethiopian, Cuban, Lao, and more. And please don't buy an overpriced, underwhelming Mall hot dog; head to U Street for a chili-topped half-smoke at Ben's Chili Bowl.

1

Experience Washington, D.C. 10 THINGS NOT TO DO IN WASHINGTON, D.C.

Mall at night

DON'T VISIT IN SUMMER

Washington's flat topography, wide avenues, and sprawling Mall are perfectly suited for exploring by foot or bike (or even Segway). What's *NOT* fun is touring the city in 90-degree heat and face-melting humidity, which is what you could endure if you visit between June and August, also the busiest tourist season. In the fall, the temps are more comfortable, and the kids are back in school.

DON'T ASSUME YOU KNOW IT ALL

If you visited 5 to 10 years ago (or more), you haven't seen D.C. It's a safer and more interesting place now. You can drink locally brewed beer at hipster bars in Northeast, take in a waterfront concert or baseball game in Southeast, sip craft coffee made by former Marines, and go Instagram nuts at the new Renwick Gallery.

DON'T ASK WHERE HOUSE OF CARDS SCENES WERE FILMED

If you're looking for Frank and Claire Underwood's house—or Olivia Pope's office, for that matter—you're out of luck. House of Cards and Scandal may have put D.C. front and center on TV, but neither show is actually filmed in the District. However, you can see the locations from some classic TV shows and movies: the Lincoln Memorial and Reflecting Pool, where Forrest Gump reunited with Jenny; the treacherous staircase from The Exorcist; and various locations from The West Wing, to name a few.

DON'T "WING IT" WITH THE WHITE HOUSE

You can now take a selfie on a White House tour! What you can't do is check out the presidential digs on a whim. You must request a spot through your member of Congress at least 21 days to 6 months in advance, but you don't need to plan a visit to the White House Visitor Center.

Washington, D.C., Under the Radar

KENILWORTH AQUATIC GARDENS
Breathtaking water lilies and lotus flowers abound here. Spring and summer are the best times to visit, when the flowers and trees are in bloom. But fall at the park also has its charm, with leaves changing on cypress trees, calm waters, and lower temperatures. Stop by the gardens in early July for the annual Lotus and Water Lily Festival.

LINCOLN COTTAGE
Lincoln and his family lived in this cottage during the Civil War, and it's since become a museum and cultural center. Visitors can take self-guided tours through permanent exhibits that cover the history of the Civil War and the Lincoln family as well as frequent special exhibits.

PHILLIPS COLLECTION
Most visitors flock to the National Mall for art museums, but Dupont Circle's Phillips Collection offers a nice change of pace. Tucked away on a quiet residential street, the museum features modern and contemporary American and European art. Museum visitors can browse more than 4,000 works, including French impressionist paintings and American prints.

PEACOCK ROOM
Painted by American expatriate artist James McNeill Whistler, the Freer Gallery's most famous room's blue-and-gold-hued walls immediately catch visitors' eyes. Take a walk around the room to browse an extensive collection of Middle Eastern and Asian pottery. The blinds are drawn most of the year to preserve the painted walls.

WASHINGTON NATIONAL CATHEDRAL
Take in Gothic architecture, stained-glass windows, and gargoyles. In Northwest D.C., the cathedral boasts the highest point in the city. Book a ticket in advance to climb the 30-story central tower. A crypt level inside the cathedral holds the graves of President Woodrow Wilson, Helen Keller, and Matthew Shepard.

HILLWOOD ESTATE
Once the home of a D.C. socialite, Hillwood now holds collections of Russian imperial and French decorative art. Browse the Georgian-style mansion or roam neighboring gardens. A Japanese-style garden includes trickling streams and stone paths.

U.S. BOTANIC GARDENS
Often overlooked, the garden is a hidden gem, one of the oldest in the United States. It's home to a variety of rare and endangered plants. Don't miss Bartholdi Park, across the street from the main conservatory—it features colorful plants, flowers, and a photogenic fountain in the middle.

Meridian Hill Park

MERIDIAN HILL PARK
In Columbia Heights, the park is a good place to stop for a picnic or midafternoon stroll. Designed as an Italian garden, it has cascading water fountains, winding stone staircases, and plenty of green spaces.

SPANISH STEPS
Named for the famous staircase in Rome, D.C.'s steps, next to Embassy Row, aren't quite as grand but they do provide a tranquil reprieve from the hustle and bustle of the city.

ROOSEVELT ISLAND
Cross Key Bridge to get to Roosevelt Island, an 88-acre oasis in the middle of the Potomac River. Lush woods and miles of hiking trails offer views of Georgetown and the harbor.

WOODROW WILSON HOUSE
Take a step back in time at the sprawling estate near Embassy Row that was home to President Wilson and his wife after they left the White House in 1921. Walk up the grand staircase to browse stately rooms, including a parlor with the Wilsons' century-old Steinway piano.

Free Things to Do in D.C.

U.S. BUREAU OF ENGRAVING AND PRINTING
Everything from stamps to paper currency to military commissions is produced here. The Treasury Department prints up to 38 million notes a day. The free 40-minute tours (weekdays only, booked in advance) show you every step of currency production.

FREDERICK DOUGLASS HOUSE
One of the best views of the Capitol and the D.C. skyline can be found at this house perched on a hill in Anacostia. Douglass purchased the estate in 1877, named it Cedar Hill, and lived there until his death in 1895. You can tour the house and stroll the ground.

U STREET
The birthplace of Duke Ellington and an important hub of African American culture is known primarily for its theaters and live music venues. Miles Davis, Ella Fitzgerald, and Louis Armstrong all frequented the area, which is still full of popular restaurants, funky boutiques, and tons of nightlife.

SMITHSONIAN MUSEUMS
Thanks in large part to the Smithsonian Institution, Washington is absolutely stuffed with museums, 12 of which are connected with the institution endowed by James Smithson in 1846. But that's not all. Other free museums include the National Gallery of Art and the United States Holocaust Memorial Museum.

THE MEMORIALS
Forming the spine of the city, the National Mall is anchored by the Lincoln Memorial on the west, the Washington Monument in the middle, and the U.S. Capitol on the east. Other famous memorials remember Vietnam veterans, World War II, FDR, and Martin Luther King, Jr.

JOHN F. KENNEDY CENTER FOR THE PERFORMING ARTS
Opened in 1971, the Kennedy Center s one of the largest U.S. performing arts facilities, staging roughly 2,000 performances a year. Free tours include a stop at an exhibit about Kennedy's life and presidency and a walk through several of the main theaters. On your way out, catch a glimpse of the famous Watergate complex, just to the north.

THE PENTAGON
A building so big it requires six zip codes, the Pentagon houses the headquarters of the Department of Defense in its astonishingly large confines; at its widest point, the Pentagon is almost as wide as the Empire State Building is

National Gallery of Art

tall. Construction began in September 1941 and was finished in a remarkably quick 16 months. Tours are free but require advance reservations; check the Pentagon's website for details.

OLD STONE HOUSE
This otherwise unassuming house in Georgetown holds the distinction of being the oldest unaltered building in Washington. Christopher and Rachel Layman purchased the property in 1764 for about £1 and built the house the following year. The house, now a museum and public garden, was purchased and turned over to the National Park Service in 1953.

ROCK CREEK PARK
Rock Creek Park became the third national park ever created, signed into law by President Harrison in 1890. Just a 20-minute drive from the center of the city, it offers 1,754 quiet, beautiful acres for roaming, horseback riding, cycling, and inline skating.

EASTERN MARKET
Thomas Jefferson established the market in 1805, and it was moved to its current location in 1873, where it has remained for the last 142 years. Weathering the storm of competition from grocery store chains, Eastern Market has become a community staple and a great place to stock up or simply window-shop for food, crafts, or antiques. Weekends feature live music and local artists, and the farmers' market runs from 3 to 7 pm on Tuesdays.

NATIONAL ZOO
An act of Congress created the National Zoo in 1889. Designed by Frederick Law Olmsted, the 163-acre zoo is home to 300 animal species, nearly 60 of which are endangered or threatened, including three giant pandas.

WASHINGTON, D.C. BEST BETS

Fodor's writers and editors have chosen our favorites to help you plan. Search individual chapters for more recommendations.

🍴 RESTAURANTS

ASIAN
Sakuramen, *Ch. 09*
Teaism, *Ch. 04*
Thip Khao, *Ch. 10*
Yong Kang Street, *Ch. 13*

BREAKFAST
Farmers Fishers Bakers, *Ch. 07*
Jimmy T's Place, *Ch. 05*
Seylou Bakery and Mill, *Ch. 10*
Ted's Bulletin, *Ch. 05*

CAPITAL CLASSICS
Ben's Chili Bowl, *Ch. 10*
The Fourth Estate, *Ch. 04*
Old Edditt Grill, *Ch. 04*

COCKTAILS AND WINE
Jack Rose Dining Saloon, *Ch. 10*
Room 11, *Ch. 10*

FAMILY FAVORITES
Brasserie Beck, *Ch. 04*
City Tap House, *Ch. 04*
Crimson Diner, *Ch. 04*
Good Stuff Eatery, *Ch. 05*
The Market Lunch, *Ch. 05*
Millie's, *Ch. 11*
Rocklands, *Ch. 07*
Shake Shack, *Ch. 04*

GREAT HOTEL RESTAURANTS
Ashby Inn, *Ch. 13*
Blue Duck Tavern, *Ch. 06*
The Dabney, *Ch. 10*
Muze at the Mandarin-Oriental, Washington DC, *Ch. 03*

GREAT VALUE
Cafe Divan, *Ch. 07*
Chercher, *Ch. 10*
El Camino, *Ch. 10*
Full Kee, *Ch. 04*
Kabob Palace, *Ch. 13*
Lapis, *Ch. 09*
Parthenon, *Ch. 11*

ITALIAN
Fiola Mare, *Ch. 07*
Osteria Morini, *Ch. 12*

PIZZA
Comet Ping Pong, *Ch. 11*
Seventh Hill, *Ch. 05*
2 Amys, *Ch. 11*

PRETHEATER
Proof, *Ch. 04*
Zaytinya, *Ch. 04*

PRIX-FIXE
Little Serow, *Ch. 08*
minibar by Jose Andres, *Ch. 04*
Pineapple and Pearls, *Ch. 05*
2941 Restaurant, *Ch. 13*

ROMANTIC
NoPa Kitchen + Bar, *Ch. 04*
The Red Hen, *Ch. 10*
Siroc, *Ch. 04*
Tail Up Goat, *Ch. 09*

SEAFOOD
Hank's Oyster Bar, *Ch. 08*

SOUTHERN
Oohs + Aahhs, *Ch. 10*
Sweet Home Cafe, *Ch. 03*

SPANISH
Del Mar, *Ch. 12*
Estadio, *Ch. 10*

SPECIAL OCCASION
Inn at Little Washington, *Ch. 13*
Komi, *Ch. 08*
Marcel's by Robert Wiedmaier, *Ch. 06*
Rasika, *Ch. 04*
Rose's Luxury, *Ch. 05*

STEAKHOUSES
Bourbon Steak, *Ch. 07*

TRENDY RESTAURANTS
Cava Mezze, *Ch. 05*
Hazel, *Ch. 10*
Le Diplomate, *Ch. 10*
Momofuku CCDC, *Ch. 04*
Spoken English, *Ch. 09*

🛏 HOTELS

B&BS
Adam's Inn, *Ch. 09*
Embassy Circle Guest House, *Ch. 08*
Swann House, *Ch. 08*
Woodley Park Guest House, *Ch. 11*

FAMILY-FRIENDLY

Avenue Suites Georgetown, *Ch. 06*

Georgetown Suites, *Ch. 07*

Holiday Inn Capital, *Ch. 03*

The Mayflower Hotel Hotel, Autograph Collection, *Ch. 04*

Residence Inn Arlington Pentagon City, *Ch. 13*

Residence Inn Washington, D.C./Foggy Bottom, *Ch. 06*

HISTORIC

The Hay-Adams, *Ch. 04*

Morrison-Clark Historic Inn, *Ch. 04*

Omni Shoreham, *Ch. 11*

Ritz-Carlton Georgetown, *Ch. 07*

Willard InterContinental, *Ch. 04*

PET-FRIENDLY

The George Hotel, *Ch. 05*

Hotel Monaco, *Ch. 04*

The Line Hotel, *Ch. 09*

Palomar, Washington, D.C., *Ch. 08*

Park Hyatt Washington, *Ch. 06*

W Washington, D.C., *Ch. 04*

LUXURY

Four Seasons Hotel, Washington, D.C., *Ch. 07*

Mandarin-Oriental, Washington DC, *Ch. 03*

Ritz-Carlton Washington, D.C., *Ch. 07*

Sofitel Washington, D.C. Lafayette Square, *Ch. 04*

The St. Regis Washington, D.C., *Ch. 04*

ROMANTIC

The Fairmont, Washington, D.C., Georgetown, *Ch. 06*

The Jefferson, *Ch. 04*

TRENDY

The Dupont Circle Hotel, *Ch. 08*

VALUE

Comfort Inn Downtown D.C./Convention Center, *Ch. 04*

Courtyard Washington Capitol Hill/Navy Yard, *Ch. 12*

Fairfield Inn & Suites Washington DC/Downtown, *Ch. 04*

Glover Park Hotel, *Ch. 11*

Henley Park Hotel, *Ch. 04*

Hyatt Centric Arlington, *Ch. 13*

Pod Hotel DC, *Ch. 04*

Residence Inn Washington, D.C./Dupont Circle, *Ch. 08*

VIEWS

Hilton Washington DC National Mall, *Ch. 03*

Rosewood Washington D.C., *Ch. 07*

The Watergate Hotel, *Ch. 06*

🍸 NIGHTLIFE

BEST BARS

Barmini, *Ch. 04*

The Birchmere, *Ch. 13*

The Brixton, *Ch. 10*

Columbia Room, *Ch. 10*

The Dignitary, *Ch. 04*

Eighteenth Street Lounge, *Ch. 08*

The Morris, *Ch. 10*

P.O.V., *Ch. 04*

Tryst, *Ch. 09*

COMEDY CLUBS

Capitol Steps

DANCE CLUBS

Flash, *Ch. 10*

LIVE MUSIC

Black Cat, *Ch. 10*

Blues Alley, *Ch. 07*

9:30 Club, *Ch. 10*

Pearl Street Warehouse, *Ch. 12*

Rock and Roll Hotel, *Ch. 05*

PUBS

The Brighton SW1, *Ch. 12*

WINE BARS

Cork Wine Bar, *Ch. 10*

Washington, D.C. Today

Classically majestic and stunningly beautiful, the Capitol, the White House, and the Supreme Court stand at the heart of Washington, D.C., symbols of the enduring stability and strength of the nation, even during the most difficult times. But in recent years, D.C. has proven it's more than just a political town, emerging as a cosmopolitan, global city with world-class restaurants, hotels, and cultural events.

POLITICS

Donald Trump moved into the White House in 2017, but don't expect to find many fans among his Washington neighbors. The city is overwhelmingly Democratic (Trump won just 4% of the vote here) and many residents are still coming to uneasy grips with his arrival. On the day of Trump's inauguration, violent protesters set fire to trash cans near the White House. A day later, it was estimated that half a million people marched through the city to protest his views in the historic Women's March. Those dynamics may change, but for now the tensions still simmer, as visitors will likely find as they belly up to the bars around town. At one popular H Street haunt, the coasters read: "He may be the most powerful man on earth, but he'll never drink a beer in The Pug."

SPORTS

First and foremost, this is a football town, as the hordes of loyal Redskins fans demonstrate each fall Sunday at the city's many sports bars. Still, the team has struggled under billionaire owner Danny Snyder, who has shelled out big bucks to attract top players but has yet to return the team to the Super Bowl under his watch. Frustrated fans have noticed, and tickets are much easier to come by than they once were (though they still aren't cheap). Filling the void, the Capitals hockey team, led by perennial all-star Alex Ovechkin, finally snatched the long-evasive Stanley Cup in 2018. The Nationals baseball team has wowed D.C. in recent years with all-star talents like Max Scherzer, the 2016 Cy Young winner, leading the team to a string of playoff appearances; even though they don't seem to be able to get it together for the long-haul win, their fans remain loyal. The DC United soccer team, spearheaded by Wayne Rooney, one of the biggest names to play in the MLS, has a sparkling new stadium. And even the Wizards basketball team has shed its once-lowly reputation, joining the playoff ranks on the wings of scoring sensation John Wall.

MARIJUANA

D.C. has been on the cutting edge of the growing national movement to legalize marijuana, but with some complications. In 2014, D.C. voters overwhelmingly approved a measure permitting those over 21 to possess up to 2 ounces of marijuana, grow a small number of cannabis plants in their homes, and transfer up to an ounce of the drug to another adult—if no money accompanies the exchange. The law means you can smoke pot in private places, but you cannot buy it legally, which doesn't allow the pot tourism seen in states like Colorado. Still, that nuance has not dissuaded faithful users, and visitors should not be surprised if, on occasion, they encounter a whiff of pot smoke in the air.

DEMOGRAPHICS

Washington's postrecession economic boom has only accelerated the demographic face-lift that was already transforming the city. This shift is highlighted by several recent population milestones: an increase in residents, and a median age that has fallen below 34—almost four years younger than the country as a whole.

Hardly unrelated, the trends reveal that, after years of fleeing D.C. due to high crime rates and underperforming schools, more and more suburban families are opting to live in the city where they work. These younger professionals—mostly white, mostly drawn by the government and related industries—have helped bolster Washington's economy, but not without a price. Indeed, the gentrification—heightened by enormous stadium projects like Nationals Park—has reached deep into the traditionally black areas of Northeast and Southeast, stirring resentment, driving up costs, and pricing many longtime residents out of their childhood homes. Indeed, D.C. has one of the widest income gaps between rich and poor in the country, leaving local officials to seek ways to strengthen commercial interests without sacrificing community and culture.

FOOD

Washington has made great culinary strides in recent years. No longer known only for stuffy steak houses catering to lobbyists, D.C. now offers options to satisfy the most eclectic tastes. And top-tier chefs from around the country have taken notice, with many descending on D.C. to catch the wave. Most recently, 13 restaurants have been bestowed a coveted Michelin star, with two restaurants receiving two—and one (the venerable Inn at Little Washington) receiving three.

Wolfgang Puck's The Source, adjacent to the Newseum, wows visitors with its posh, three-story dining room and offbeat Asian-fusion menu. Jeremiah Langhorne aims to put mid-Atlantic cuisine back on the culinary map with The Dabney, with most of its cooking done on a central wood-burning hearth. Marjorie Meek-Bradley, a Top Chef alum, has made her mark with Roofers Union, featuring American fare, in Adams Morgan. And Johnny Monis, who won the 2013 James Beard award for the best chef in the mid-Atlantic region, is at the helm of the Michelin-starred Komi and Little Serow.

These relative newcomers join D.C. pioneers like Robert Wiedmaier, whose Belgian roots are on full display at the award-winning Marcel's in Foggy Bottom; and James Beard Foundatin Award–winning-chef turned humanitarian José Andrés, the culinary powerhouse behind Zaytinya, Oyamel, Jaleo, and the Michelin-starred minibar, all near Chinatown. He continues to expand his mini-empire with his newest endeavor, America Eats Tavern, which showcases historical takes on American favorites, including 19th-century mac and cheese and 1950s-era steak tartare.

FITNESS

Long agitated by D.C.'s unflattering designation as "Hollywood for ugly people," Washingtonians have fought back with a surging interest in fitness and health. In fact, the ACSM American Fitness Index recently ranked it as one of the nation's top three fittest cities. Quite aside from the numerous gyms popping up all over the city—and ignoring, for a moment, the countless joggers constantly circling the Mall—local residents have adopted a slew of activities to get outside and stay in shape. Like to play kickball? There are teams all over the city. Enjoy Ultimate Frisbee? There's a league for that, too. Rugby? Got it. Even bocce—the age-old Italian sport of lawn bowling—has inspired a passionate following and launched formal competitions around town. The District's many parks and green spaces cater perfectly to that game of pickup football (or *fútbol*), and the city's wild embrace of bike sharing has been complemented by the creation of bike-only lanes on some of its most traveled thoroughfares. Add a long list of burgeoning indoor crazes to the mix—everything from yoga and Pilates to Zumba and CrossFit—and you've got a city intent on shedding its wonks-only reputation.

Best Tours in D.C.

If ever there was a "do it yourself" city, it's D.C. The Metro system is safe and easy to navigate, and most major sights and museums are concentrated in a single area. Armed with a Metro map, a guide to the Mall, and a comfortable pair of shoes, you can do it all by yourself.

Nevertheless, the underground train is notably lacking in city views and driving tempts the fate of the parking gods, so sometimes a guided tour makes the most sense, especially if you're seeking the inside scoop from a local expert. Consider one of the following options if you're looking for chaperoned convenience.

For even more tours, please see the Tours section in the Travel Smart chapter.

Bike Tours

Bike and Roll. Based at both Union Station and L'Enfant Plaza, just off the National Mall, Bike and Roll offers a series of guided tours through D.C.'s top sites, including the Capitol, Supreme Court, and WWII Memorial. Bike rentals and Segway tours are also offered, and self-guided options stretch as far as Mount Vernon and even Pittsburgh. ☎ 202/842–2453 ⊕ www. bikeandrolldc.com ☞ From $44.

Capital Bikeshare. You can rent bikes by the hour with this bike-share scheme, and it's a great way to visit the memorials and monuments at your own pace, then return your bike to any of the 500 stations throughout the city. There are also stations in Alexandria and Arlington, VA, and neighboring Montgomery County, MD, if you want to venture farther afield. ☎ 877/430–2453 ⊕ www.capitalbikeshare.com ☞ Membership fee, from $8, includes first 30 mins before additional costs accrue.

Fat Tire Tours. Yet another option for touring the monuments on your own time, Fat Tire Tours offers guided day tours, sunset trips, Segway rentals, and packages that include entrance into the Newseum and Spy Museum. A typical tour is three hours of easy peddling. ⊠ 502 23rd St. NW, Foggy Bottom ☎ 877/734–8687 ⊕ dc.capitalcitybiketours.com ☞ From $39 Ⓜ Foggy Bottom–GWU.

⊙ Boat Tours

Capitol River Cruises. Sightseeing tours lasting 45 minutes are aboard the Nightingale and Nightingale II, former Great Lakes boats from the 1950s. Departures are hourly, 11 am to 8 pm, May through September, to 7 pm April and October. ⊠ Washington Harbor, 31st and K Sts. NW, Georgetown ☎ 301/460–7447 ⊕ www.capitolrivercruises.com ☞ $15.

Odyssey III. Specially built to fit under the Potomac's bridges, the Odyssey III departs from the Gangplank marina for daily dinner cruises, weekday lunch cruises, and weekend brunch cruises—elegant affairs with a dress code (jackets for men) at dinner. ⊠ 600 Water St. SW, D.C. Waterfront ☎ 202/488–6000, 800/700–0735 ⊕ www.odysseycruises. com ☞ From $65 Ⓜ Waterfront-SEU.

Potomac Riverboat Company. With docks in Alexandria, Georgetown, Mount Vernon, National Harbor, and The Wharf, this company offers a monuments tour, a Mount Vernon cruise, and a canine cruise. It also runs the sleek water taxi that connects The Wharf, Georgetown, Alexandria, and National Harbor. ⊠ Alexandria ☎ 877/511–2628 ⊕ www. potomacriverboatco.com ☞ From $15.

Thompson Boat Center. Another way to see the monuments from the Potomac River is through Thompson Boat Center in Georgetown, which offers canoe, kayak, and stand-up paddleboard rentals for self-guided tours. Pack a lunch and paddle over to Roosevelt Island for a picnic. A double kayak rents for $22 per hour, while a canoe goes for $25 per hour and a stand-up paddleboard for $22 per hour. Sculls are also available for certified rowers. ✉ *2900 Virginia Ave. NW, Georgetown* ☎ *202/337–9642* ⊕ *www.thompson-boatcenter.com* 🖾 *From $16.*

🚌 Bus Tours

Big Bus Tours. Brightly painted red and yellow open-top, double-decker buses provide a hop-on, hop-off service with different city loops. Discount ticket prices are sometimes offered online. ☎ *877/332–8689* ⊕ *www.bigbustours. com* 🖾 *From $49.*

City Sights. This bus tour offers double-decker fun for those seeking to take advantage of warmer weather and get an elevated view of Washington. The group runs multiple loops around the city, some of which extend well beyond the Mall to include Georgetown, the National Cathedral, Arlington National Cemetery, and the Pentagon. All trips offer hop-on, hop-off convenience, and several multiday options are available for those on longer stays. City Sights also offers night tours, boat trips, and guided bike tours. ☎ *202/650–5444* ⊕ *www. citysightsdc.com* 🖾 *From $44.*

DC Ducks. Ready for a unique take on Washington? DC Ducks takes the traditional jaunt through the city and adds a thrilling twist: the 90-minute guided tour ends with a splashdown in the Potomac River, where the amphibious Duck-mobile gives visitors a rousing water leg to their trip. Tours, which run from mid-March to November, begin at Union Station, leaving every hour between 10 am and 4 pm. ☎ *866/754–5039* ⊕ *www. dcducks.com* 🖾 *From $43.*

Gray Line. This venerable tour company specializes in lectured sightseeing tours of Washington. D.C., Mount Vernon, Gettysburg, and more. ☎ *202/779–9894* ⊕ *www.graylinedc.com* 🖾 *From $35.*

Old Town Trolley Tours. D.C.'s longest-running tour company offers one of the best narrated glimpses of the city's many historic wonders, with the option of hop-on, hop-off service at 24 different stops. Two loops are available: one wraps around the Mall and Capitol; the other extends from the Lincoln Memorial to Arlington National Cemetery in Virginia. (Transfers between the loops are part of the deal.) Visitors can begin their tour at any of the stops, and buses swing by every 30 minutes. ☎ *844/356–2599* ⊕ *www.trolleytours.com/washington-dc* 🖾 *From $57.*

OnBoard D.C. Tours. The daily six-hour "D.C. It All" tour lets you hop on and off with the guide at 12 locations, and from mid-March through October the tour includes a one-hour private Potomac River cruise. There's also a three-hour "D.C. The Lights!" nightlife tour. ☎ *301/839–5261* ⊕ *www.washing-tondctours.onboardtours.com* 🖾 *From $70.*

Best Tours in D.C.

👁 Segway and Scooter Tours

Rest your feet and glide by the monuments, museums, and major attractions aboard a Segway. Guided tours usually last between two and three hours. D.C. city ordinance requires that riders be at least 16 years old; some tour companies have weight restrictions of 250 pounds. Tours, limited to 6 to 10 people, begin with an instruction session.

CONTACTS Capital Segway. ✉ 818 Connecticut Ave. NW ☎ 202/682–1980 ⊕ www.capitalsegway.com Ⓜ McPherson Square **City Segway Tours.** ☎ 877/734–8687 ⊕ www.citysegwaytours.com. **Scootaround Inc.** ☎ 888/441–7575 ⊕ www.scootaround.com. **Segs in the City.** ☎ 800/734–7393 ⊕ www.segsinthecity.com.

👁 Specialty Tours

DC Metro Food Tours. Three-hour tours, on weekends year-round, explore the culinary heritage of a D.C. neighborhood, with 14 locales to choose from, including some in nearby Virginia. There's also a D.C. pub crawl around Old Town, Capitol Hill, and U Street, and private tours can be arranged. ☎ 202/851–2268 ⊕ www.dcmetrofoodtours.com ✉ From $60.

Smithsonian Associates. Experience D.C.'s art, history, and culture through the lens of the Smithsonian Associates. Tours of Arlington National Cemetery, nearby Civil War battlefields, and an Anacostia River hike are some of the excursions on offer. ☎ 202/633–3030 ⊕ www.smithsonianassociates.org ✉ From $135.

A Tour de Force. Local historian and author Jeanne Fogle will escort you via custom-designed limo or on walking tours of historic homes, diplomatic buildings, and

"the best little museums in Washington." You can opt for half-day, full-day, multiday, or evening tours. ☎ 703/525–2948 ⊕ www.atourdeforce.com.

Washington Photo Safari. Founder E. David Luria promises opportunities for photographers of all skill levels (even camera phones are fine) on his half-day and full-day "Monuments and Memorials" workshops, held every Wednesday and Saturday. Special themed tours, led by a team of professional photographers, are held on selected weekends. ☎ 202/537–0937 ⊕ www.washingtonphotosafari.com ✉ From $89.

🚶 Walking Tours

Capitol Historical Society. This group leads guided tours around the grounds of the Capitol weekdays at 5:30 pm, March through Memorial Day, 7 pm Memorial Day through Labor Day, and 5:30 pm Labor Day through October 31. The two-hour tour starts at Union Station. Reservations must be made at least 48 hours in advance. ☎ 800/887–9318 ⊕ www.uschs.org ✉ $30.

Cultural Tourism DC. This nonprofit group has 18 self-guided Neighborhood Heritage Trails, plus a citywide African American Heritage Trail, all of which are highlighted with historic markers. All the tours can be downloaded from its website. One week each fall, the group leads free guided walking tours that highlight the history and architecture of certain neighborhoods, from the southwest waterfront to points much farther north. You can also check out other cultural events happening around the city, many free, on the website. ☎ 202/661–7581 ⊕ www.culturaltourismdc.org ✉ Free.

DC by Foot. Dozens of tours, including the Tidal Basin and National Mall, Arlington National Cemetery, Capitol Hill, Georgetown, and U Street, are led by guides who work for tips, guaranteeing a highly entertaining experience. Tours last two to four hours, and are available year-round, but days and times vary by season and advance reservations are required. ☎ 202/370–1830 ⊕ www.free-toursbyfoot.com ✎ Guides work for tips.

D.C. Sightseeing. Well-known author Anthony Pitch, winner of a number of awards and with appearances on many TV programs, leads several D.C. sightseeing walking tours, including a full day highlights tour and a pair of two-hour excursions, "The Curse of Lafayette Square" and "The Lincoln Assassination." Tours can also be customized to your requirements. ✉ Washington ☎ 301/437–2345 ⊕ www.dcsightseeing.com ✎ $100 per hr (min 4 hrs) per individual or group (plus charge for driver, if one is used).

DC Walkabout. Download a tour to any mobile device and set off in your own time and at your own pace, guided by a narration, historical recordings, and even music and sound effects. Tours, ranging from 1 to 2 miles, include "American Scandal," "Capitol Hill," "Georgetown Ghost," "Haunted History," and "Lincoln Assassination." ☎ 202/421–4053 ⊕ www. dcwalkabout.com ✎ $9.

Historic Strolls. Step back in time on one of these interactive theatrical tours, which revisit Washington, D.C., during the Civil War, World War II, or in the 1960s. You can also sign up for a "Ghost Story Tour," on which Natalie Zanin dresses as Dolley Madison's ghost and shares stories of hauntings around the city, including Lafayette Square Park, where Edgar Allan Poe's spirit is said to wander. ☎ 301/873–3986 ⊕ www.historicstrolls. com ✎ $20.

History on Foot. Relive the night of President Abraham Lincoln's assassination with Detective McDevitt on this two-hour walking tour. From Ford's Theatre you'll follow the escape route taken by assassin John Wilkes Booth on the 1½-mile trek, ending at Lafayette Park. Tours are offered March through October. ☎ 202/347–4833 ⊕ www.fords. org ✎ $18.

Washington Walks. The wide range of tours offered by Washington Walks includes "Hamilton's D.C." and "Capitol Hauntings." ☎ 202/484–1565 ⊕ www. washingtonwalks.com ✎ From $20.

What to Read and Watch Before Your Trip

MOVIE: *MINORITY REPORT*
Based on a short story by Philip K. Dick, this Steven Spielberg blockbuster takes place in the year 2054, blending genres of sci-fi, action, and thriller. It's chock-full of dramatic chase scenes throughout a futurized D.C., as a "precrime" police force—backed by a team of surreal psychics—arrests people for crimes they're destined to commit in the future. It has all the special effects and over-the-top action sequences you could desire from a Tom Cruise protagonist and a Steven Spielberg budget.

MOVIE: *IN THE LOOP*
British filmmaker Armando Iannucci gives us the somewhat maddening, totally entertaining world of D.C. political missteps and blundered negotiations—that later inspired his HBO show *Veep*. The movie follows the political frenzy between Britain and the United States leading up to the Iraq War. Politicians and staffers race in circles around the conference rooms and hallways of D.C.'s government buildings, dropping dry gems of British humor along the way.

MOVIE/BOOK: *ALL THE PRESIDENT'S MEN*
This Academy Award–winning film follows Carl Bernstein and Bob Woodward—the two young *Washington Post* journalists responsible for the incredible investigation of the Watergate scandal—through their meetings with clandestine informant Deep Throat, the discovery of President Nixon's tapes, and the process of exposing it all to the American public. While a little less studly without the young Dustin Hoffman–Robert Redford combination, the nonfiction book of the same name (written by the journalists themselves) delves deeper into the details of a political detective story almost too good for fiction.

MOVIE: *LEGALLY BLONDE 2: RED, WHITE AND BLONDE*
Elle goes to Washington! Like many feature-film sequels, the second *Legally Blonde* takes everything that works in the original (when a young, ditzy Reese Witherspoon improbably makes her way through Harvard Law) and further satirizes itself, pushing the boundaries into ridiculous (but entertaining) content. Beyond the Barbie-like outfits, sorority cheer scenes, and one-liners, the movie does what political satire is meant to do: calls out some of the real farce and absurdity of American legislation.

BOOK/MOVIE: *ADVISE AND CONSENT*
Allen Drury's 1959 political thriller, following the tumultuous nomination process of a secretary of state with a Communist background, was both a *New York Times* bestseller and Pulitzer prize winner—a rare occurrence for any novel. Credited with creating a realistic yet racy tale about a could-be-boring political process, the book became a series and was followed by five sequels. The 1962 movie stars Henry Fonda, with many of the scenes shot in and around key Washington landmarks.

MOVIE/BOOK: *SEVEN DAYS IN MAY*
Kirk Douglas, Burt Lancaster, Frederic March, and Ava Gardner star in this 1964 film, where the Cold War hysteria of the times is condensed into a weeklong attempted takeover of the United States government. The 1962 *New York Times* best-selling book (by Fletcher Knebel and Charles W. Bailey II) served as the movie's inspiration. Both film and book follow the same structure, split into day-by-day chapters as the week's events unfurl.

MOVIE: *MR. SMITH GOES TO WASHINGTON*
In this 1939 black-and-white classic, a baby-faced, idealistic Jimmy Stewart comes to the nation's capital and is soon

wrapped up in the unscrupulousness of the U.S. Senate. Stewart's scene orating against greed and corruption on the floor of the Senate is still one of the most iconic cinematic performances ever about D.C. politics.

TV: *VEEP*

This HBO political comedy satirizes the personalities that make up American policy and power, with an Emmy-winning performance by Julia Louis-Dreyfus as the "Veep" (vice president, and on-again, off-again president hopeful), and a hilarious, hapless cast of political staffers. Scenes take you in and out of political press conferences, conspiratorial meetings in the VP's back rooms, the Oval Office, and halls of Congress, and many a limo drive through the streets of Washington.

VIDEO GAME: FALLOUT 3

The third edition of the popular action role-playing game takes place in the year 2277, following a terrible world war and other apocalyptic maladies. The hyperrealistic, multiperson, multiperspective game uses a postapocalyptic D.C. and surrounding area—complete with a bombed and charred White House, Capitol Building, and other famous landmarks—as its backdrop.

BOOK: *LONG DISTANCE LIFE*

Marita Golden's novel centers around one family's experience living in D.C. throughout the 20th century, but she vividly fills in the background with the complex history of black America as a whole. Naomi Johnson, the family's matriarch (and firstperson narrator of many chapters) moves from North Carolina to D.C. in 1926, and the novel continues from there to tell the hardships and joys of Naomi's family throughout generations in the capital city.

BOOK: *THE BEAUTIFUL THINGS THAT HEAVEN BEARS*

A refreshing break from the political circus of Capitol Hill, Dinaw Mengestu's novel exists instead within the stores, restaurants, and homes of Northwest D.C.'s Logan Circle neighborhood. In a city of monuments and memorials to America's (often constructed, embellished) past, and in a neighborhood on the brink of gentrification, Sepha, an Ethiopian refugee, moves through the daily grind of being an American while haunted by memories of his home country. Through Sepha's long talks and friendships with refugees from other African countries, Mengestu creates a gentle, moving portrait of the African diaspora in Washington.

BOOK: *MASTER OF THE SENATE: THE YEARS OF LYNDON JOHNSON*

Robert Caro traces Johnson's 1949 to 1960 career in the U.S. Senate as he faces all-too-familiar political challenges of policy making, across-aisle cooperation, and reconciling the desires of a rural Southern voter base with those of Washington's leaders. Caro aggrandizes Johnson as a leader and strategic winner of Congress, all the while describing the intricacies and power plays in America's legislative system.

MOVIE: *THE CONTENDER*

This 2000 thriller combines political process and sex-driven scandal, when the Republican opposition digs into the past and private life of a female candidate for vice president. Joan Allen, Jeff Bridges, Christian Slater, and Sam Elliott play characters ranging from affable to immoral. The political sexism, cutthroat party alliances, and invasion of privacy nod to the Clinton-Lewinsky scandal of the time—but the story still rings plenty true today.

Washington, D.C. with Kids

D.C. is filled with kid-friendly attractions. These sights are sure winners:

BUREAU OF ENGRAVING AND PRINTING

Any youngster who gets an allowance will enjoy watching bills roll off the presses. Despite the lack of free samples, the self-guided, 35-minute bureau tour is one of the city's most popular attractions.

DC DUCKS

What do you get when you cross a tour bus with a boat? A duck—DC Ducks, that is. Tour the city by both land and water without leaving your seats aboard these unusual amphibious vehicles: standard 2½-ton GM trucks in watertight shells with propellers.

DISCOVERY THEATER

Within the Smithsonian's Ripley Center on the Mall, this lively theater began as a low-key puppet show before expanding to feature more than 300 programs a year exploring art, science, and global heritage—everything from robots to the Wright brothers to African drums.

INTERNATIONAL SPY MUSEUM

This museum takes the art of espionage to new levels for junior James Bonds and Nancy Drews. Even the most cynical preteens and teenagers are usually enthralled with all the cool gadgetry. This museum is best for older tweens and teens—if you bring along a younger sibling, you could be in for a workout: there aren't many places to sit down, and strollers aren't allowed in the museum. Also, there is an entrance fee. The museum is slated to move to L'Enfant Plaza in 2019.

MOUNT VERNON

Farm animals, a hands-on discovery center, an interactive museum, and movies about the nation's first action hero make George Washington's idyllic home a place where families can explore all day.

NATIONAL AIR AND SPACE MUSEUM

There's a good reason why this place is one of the most popular museums in the world: kids love it. The 23 galleries here tell the story of aviation and space from the earliest human attempts at flight. All three gift shops sell freeze-dried astronaut food—not as tasty as what we eat on Earth, but it doesn't melt or drip. If you've never crunched into ice cream, it's worth the experience.

NATIONAL MUSEUM OF AMERICAN HISTORY

Oh, say, you can see … the flag that inspired "The Star-Spangled Banner," Oscar the Grouch, the ruby slippers from The Wizard of Oz, an impressive collection of trains, and more Americana than anyone can digest in a day.

NATIONAL MUSEUM OF NATURAL HISTORY

Say hello to Henry. One of the largest elephants ever found in the wild, this stuffed beast has greeted generations of kids in the rotunda of this huge museum dedicated to natural wonders. Take your kid to the O. Orkin Insect Zoo, home to live ants, bees, centipedes, tarantulas, roaches (some as large as mice), and other critters you wouldn't want in your house. Did we mention the dinosaurs?

NATIONAL ZOO

Known more for its political animals than its real animals, D.C. nevertheless has one of the world's foremost zoos. If your child is crazy about animals, this is an absolute must—it's huge.

PADDLEBOAT THE TIDAL BASIN

How better to see the Jefferson Memorial and the world-famous cherry trees—gifts from Japan—than from the waters of the Tidal Basin? The paddleboats get the kids and you off your feet and into the sun!

Chapter 2

TRAVEL SMART
WASHINGTON, D.C.

Updated by
Noe Kennedy

★ **CAPITAL**
Washington

👫 **POPULATION**
693,972

💬 **LANGUAGE**
English

$ **CURRENCY**
U.S. Dollar

📞 **AREA CODE**
202

⚠ **EMERGENCIES**
911

🚗 **DRIVING**
On the right

⚡ **ELECTRICITY**
120–220 v/60 cycles;
plugs have two or three
rectangular prongs

🕐 **TIME**
Same as New York

🌐 **WEB RESOURCES**
www.washington.org
www.nps.gov
www.si.edu

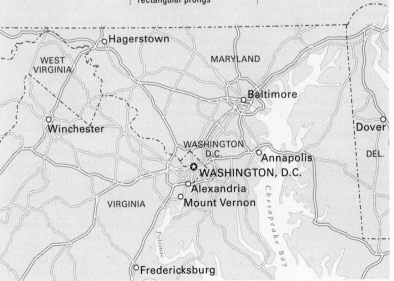

Know Before You Go: Washington, D.C.

BE AIRPORT SAVVY.

D.C. has three airports: Ronald Reagan Washington National (DCA), Dulles International (IAD), and Baltimore-Washington International Thurgood Marshall (BWI). DCA, located in Arlington, Virginia, about 4 miles from downtown D.C., is the closest and most convenient; it has its own Metro stop. BWI only serves shorter domestic flights (and some flights to the Caribbean and Canada). IAD is the main international airport, 25 miles west of downtown DC in Chantilly, Virginia. You can take the Silver Line as far as Wiehle—Reston East and hop on the Silver Line Express Bus from there. BWI is located just south of Baltimore, Maryland, about 45 miles north of D.C. You can take the MARC or Amtrak train from Union Station.

BE HOTEL SMART.

Hotels in downtown D.C. are expensive, though the rates typically drop during the weekend, after the business travelers leave. Arlington, Alexandria, and Bethesda are relatively nearby and may have better deals than downtown D.C. One thing to remember: Fairfax, Gaithersburg, and Vienna are not near downtown D.C., as some hotel advertising will have you thinking they are. The short of it: study the map before you book, to ensure you're staying relatively near the attractions you want to visit. And be sure to book a hotel near the Metro line if you don't have a car.

TAKE PUBLIC TRANS-PORT ... OR WALK.

Parking is expensive and traffic can be frightful, so relying on your car is not the best way to see the District. However, D.C. is a very pedestrian-friendly city, with many attractions within close range, so you may be able to walk to most of what you want to see. There's also has an excellent Metro system that can get you to most major sights as well (except Georgetown, which never installed a Metro stop). Another option is the DC Circulator bus, which costs $1 and has several routes past tourist sights.

KNOW WHAT STUFF IS FREE ... AND WHAT'S NOT AND STILL WORTHWHILE.

One beloved aspect of D.C. is that so many of its remarkable sights are free, including the Smithsonian museums and the national monuments and memorials. Even the blockbuster shows that sometimes stop by the National Gallery of Art are free. Check Visit D.C. or individual websites for free shows, concerts, lectures, and guided tours, especially at the National Gallery of Art and Library of Congress. That said, keep in mind that some of the city's best museums do come at a price that is still well worth your while, including the Phillips Collection, International Spy Museum, and Newseum.

THE EARLY BIRD CATCHES THE POPULAR-SIGHT TICKETS.

Get your tickets for popular sights long before your trip, including the White House and National Museum of African American History and Culture. For the White House, you'll need to contact your member of Congress several months in advance to request a self-guided public tour (citizens of foreign countries should contact their embassy in Washington, D.C.). If you miss out on the White House, the White House Visitor Center, across the street, is a good substitute, with its videos, artifacts, and displays delving into the life and times of America's most famous house. And if

2

Travel Smart Washington, D.C.   KNOW BEFORE YOU GO: WASHINGTON D.C.

you miss out on the National Museum of African American History and Culture, you can always try to get first-come, first-served tickets by going online day-of at 6:30 am, or stand in line for the walk-up passes available starting at 1 pm on weekdays.

BE A CAPITOL VIP.
Get a VIP Capitol staff-led tour by contacting your representative or senator up to 90 days in advance. Even if you miss out on the VIP tour, you can still visit the Capitol by making your own advance reservation online, or obtaining a same-day pass from the information desks located on the lower level of the U.S. Capitol Visitor Center. Note that same-day passes may have limited availability, especially during the spring, summer, and some holidays.

BEAT THE CROWDS AT STAR-STUDDED NSO PERFORMANCES.
The nation's capital celebrates the Fourth of July and Memorial Day with world-class perfor-mances starring the National Symphony Orchestra, which air around the world on PBS. Thousands of guests are invited to sit on the West Lawn of the Capitol and enjoy these spectacular concerts in person for free (bring a picnic—no alcohol allowed). But therein lies the problem—the thousands of people all vying to get in, requiring you to arrive hours early to stake your space on the grass (and possibly be turned away). You can see exactly the same shows (minus the fireworks) by attending the dress rehearsals in advance. A Capitol Fourth practices the evening before, normally at 6 pm, while the National Memorial Day Concert rehearsal takes place at 3:30 pm on the Sunday before Memorial Day. The host may be a tad improvisa-tional, and might not get all the lines on the first try, but the shows are enjoyable nonetheless. There's also a Labor Day concert on the Capitol's West Lawn showcasing the NSO (which is not aired on TV).

THINK SMALL.
While the Smithsonian museums get all the glory, remember that there are scores of excellent smaller museums, including the Clara Barton Missing Soldiers Office Museum, the President Woodrow Wilson House, the Society of the Cincinnati, and the National Museum of Women in the Arts. Plan ahead to know which ones suit your interests.

SAVE AT THE THEATER BOX OFFICE.
Washington, D.C., is a theater town, with well-reviewed theaters both large (Kennedy Center, Warner Theatre, National Theatre) and small (Woolly Mammoth Theatre Company, Shakespeare Theatre Company). Save on tickets by using a discount broker such as Goldstar, Groupon, and the TodayTix app. Also keep in mind that some theaters offer same-day tickets at a reduced price, including Arena Stage, Shakespeare Theatre Company, and Folger Shakespeare Theatre, while others offer pay-what-you-can-afford tickets, including Woolly Mammoth, Round House, and Constellation Theatre (arrive early and bring cash).

KNOW YOUR SEASONS.
Spring and fall have the best weather, with the added bonus of the famous cherry blossoms in spring and colorful changing foliage in fall. The holidays are another time when the nation's capital shines, with special events including the National Christmas Tree Lighting, ZooLights at Smithsonian's National Zoo, and the Downtown Holiday Market. House museums offer special candlelit tours that showcase colonial-era decorations, including Mount Vernon. D.C. also puts on an extravaganza of festivals, offering another reason to visit at a specific time of year. Some of the most popular include Day of Service on Martin Luther King Jr.'s birthday in January; Passport DC in May, when dozens of embassies open their doors to visitors; and St. Patrick's Day in March, with a parade down Constitution Avenue. But if you simply want to visit at a time with sunny weather and fewer crowds, early November is often prime.

Getting Here and Around

✈ Air Travel

A flight to D.C. from New York takes a little less than an hour. It's about 1½ hours from Chicago, 3 hours from Denver or Dallas, and 5 hours from San Francisco. Passengers flying from London should expect a trip of about 6 hours. From Sydney it's an 18-hour flight. Most major airlines fly into one of D.C.'s three major airports, but only Dulles and Baltimore airports are served by international carriers.

AIRPORTS

Ronald Reagan Washington National Airport (DCA) is in Virginia, 4 miles south of Downtown Washington.

Dulles International Airport (IAD) is in Virginia, 26 miles west of Washington, D.C.

Baltimore/Washington International–Thurgood Marshall Airport (BWI) in Maryland, about 30 miles to the northeast.

Reagan National Airport is closest to Downtown D.C. and has a Metro stop connected to the terminal. East Coast shuttles and shorter flights tend to fly in and out of this airport. Dulles is configured primarily for long-haul flights, although as a United hub, it's also well-connected regionally. BWI offers blended service, with its many gates for Southwest Airlines, as well as international flights. Although Metro trains don't serve Dulles or BWI, there is affordable and convenient public transportation to and from each airport. Be aware that the Mid-Atlantic region is prone to quirky weather that can snarl air traffic, especially on stormy summer afternoons.

AIRPORT TRANSFERS

Ronald Reagan Washington National Airport is the only regional airport reachable by the District's Metro system, a ride that takes about 20 minutes and costs between $2.30 and $2.65 (you must pay with a plastic SmarTrip card, available from machines in all stations); the Metro station is within easy walking distance of Terminals B and C, and a free airport bus shuttles between the station and Terminal A. Driving typically takes longer than the Metro (about 20 to 30 minutes, depending on traffic and where you start). If you are looking for a shared-ride shuttle, SuperShuttle is reliable and will take you to any hotel or residence in the city for around $16. A taxi will cost between $20 and $25 to Downtown, plus a $3 airport surcharge. Ride-share services like Uber and Lyft are allowed to pick up on the arrivals level.

Dulles International Airport is 27 miles from Downtown; the ride takes 45 minutes but can be considerably longer when traffic is heavy. Public transit will typically take an hour or more. If you take the Metro's Silver Line to the Wiehle-Reston East station (6 am to 10:20 pm); the 15-minute Silver Line Express bus ride from the station to the airport (every 15 to 20 minutes) is $5, payable with cash or credit card at the ticket counter in the Arrivals area. The Washington Metropolitan Area Transit Authority (WMATA) operates express bus service between Dulles and several stops in Downtown D.C., including the L'Enfant Plaza Metro station and Rosslyn Metro station in Arlington, Virginia, for $7.50 (every hour between 5:50 am and 11:35 pm); exact fare or a SmarTrip card is required. SuperShuttle costs $30 for one ($10 for each additional person) and takes about 45 minutes. Taxi fare to Washington, D.C., from Dulles is about $60 to $70 depending on traffic and takes about 45 minutes. Ride-share services like Uber and Lyft are allowed to pick up at the arrivals level.

Baltimore/Washington International Airport is 32 miles from Downtown; the ride takes 50 to 60 minutes but can be considerably longer when traffic is heavy. Both Amtrak and Maryland Rail Commuter Service (MARC) trains run between BWI and Washington, D.C.'s, Union Station from around 6 am to 10:30 pm; the ride takes 30 minutes and costs $15 and $45 on Amtrak, $7 on MARC's Penn Line; a free shuttle bus connects the airline terminals and the train station (which is in a distant parking lot). WMATA operates express bus service (Bus No. B30) between BWI and the Greenbelt Metro station from approximately 7 am to 10 pm (with more limited hours on weekends) for $7.50. SuperShuttle takes approximately 60 minutes and costs about $36. The fare from Downtown to BWI is about $90. Ride-share services like Uber and Lyft are allowed to pick up at the arrivals level.

Bus Travel

Most of the sightseeing neighborhoods (the Mall, Capitol Hill, Downtown, Dupont Circle) are near Metro rail stations, but a few (Georgetown, Adams Morgan) are more easily reached via Metrobus ($2 per ride, exact change payable in bills or coins or with a SmarTrip card; you can also buy a one-week pass for $17.50). Bus No. 42 travels from the Dupont Circle Metro stop to, and through, Adams Morgan.

The DC Circulator has six routes ($1 per ride, exact change payable in bills or coins or with a SmarTrip card; there are also one-, three-, and seven-day passes). The Eastern Market–L'Enfant Plaza, Woodley Park–Adams Morgan–McPherson Square, and Congress Heights–Union Station routes cut a path from

north to south; the Georgetown–Union Station and Rosslyn–Georgetown–Dupont Circle routes go east to west. And the National Mall route, which operates April to September only, stops at major sightseeing destinations around the Mall.

Several bus lines run between New York City and the Washington, D.C., area, including BoltBus, BestBus, Megabus, Peter Pan Bus Lines, TripperBus, Vamoose, and Washington Deluxe. Tripper and Vamoose routes run between NYC and Metro stations in Bethesda, Maryland, and Arlington, Virginia. All the buses are clean, the service satisfactory, and the price can't be beat. Believe it or not, with advance planning, you might be able to get a round-trip ticket for just $2. Megabus also has bus service from Toronto, Canada, and a handful of other U.S. cities. Several of the bus lines offer power outlets, Wi-Fi, and a frequent-rider loyalty program.

Car Travel

A car is often a drawback in Washington, D.C. Traffic is awful, especially at rush hour, and driving is often confusing, with many lanes and some entire streets changing direction at the beginning and end of rush hour. Most traffic lights stand at the side of intersections (instead of hanging suspended over them), and the streets often are dotted with giant potholes. The city's most popular sights are all within a short walk of a Metro station, so do yourself a favor and leave your car at the hotel. If you're visiting sights in Maryland or Virginia or need a car because of reduced mobility, time your trips to avoid D.C. rush hours, 7–10 am and 3–7 pm.

Getting Here and Around

With Zipcar, an urban car-rental membership service, you can rent a car for a couple of hours or a couple of days from convenient Downtown parking lots. A onetime application fee of $25, an annual membership fee of $70 (or $7 per month with a monthly plan option), plus hourly rates starting at $10, or $76 per day, buys you gas, insurance, parking, and satellite radio. Reserve online or by phone.

Another option is Car2Go, another car-sharing program featuring Smart cars and Mercedes-Benz, with a $5 application fee and no monthly fee. Rates are by the minute, starting at less than $0.50, which includes your parking charges, fuel costs, and insurance. The advantage of Car2Go is that you use the app to find the car closest to you, and you can drop it off at a different location, at any approved legal parking spot.

Like the comfort of a car but don't want to drive? Uber is your answer. You can request a ride through the mobile app or the Uber website. Drivers are available seven days a week, 24 hours a day. Once you request your ride, you'll be able to see exactly where the driver is and how long you'll have to wait. The fare for a Black (sedan) is $7 base charge, plus $3.46 per mile and $0.40 per minute; the SUV fare is $14 base charge, plus $3.71 per mile and $0.45 per minute; the economy option, uberX, charges a $1.21 base rate plus $1.13 per mile and $0.18 per minute. After registering, your credit card information is kept on file and your card is charged upon completion of your ride. When demand is high due to weather, holidays, or special events, rates can be considerably higher. Other ride-sharing apps like Lyft offer similar options.

PARKING

Parking in D.C. is a question of supply and demand—little of the former, too much of the latter. The police are quick to ticket, tow away, or boot any vehicle parked illegally, so check complicated parking signs and feed the meter before you go. If you find you've been towed from a city street, call 311 or the Department of Public Works Customer Service Center at 202/541–6083. Be sure you know the license-plate number, make, model, and color of the car before you call.

Most of the outlying, suburban Metro stations have parking lots, though these fill quickly with city-bound commuters. If you plan to park in one of these lots, arrive early.

Downtown private parking lots often charge around $5–$10 an hour and $25–$40 a day. Most of the streets along the Mall have metered parking. There is no parking at the Lincoln or Roosevelt memorials. If you don't find street parking nearby, try along Ohio Drive SW and in three lots in East Potomac Park, south of the 14th Street Bridge.

RULES OF THE ROAD

You may turn right at a red light after stopping if there's no oncoming traffic and no signs indicate otherwise, but D.C. has many such signs and one-way streets. When in doubt, wait for the green. The speed limit in D.C. is 25 mph. Beware of HOV express lanes on major highways during rush hours (you need an E-ZPass to use them, and costs are high).

🅜 Metro Travel

The Metro is a convenient way to get around the city—if you're staying near a Metro stop. It operates from 5 am weekdays, 7 am Saturday, and 8 am Sunday; it shuts down at at 11:30 pm Monday through Thursday, 1 am Friday and Saturday, and 11 pm Sunday. Keep in mind that service disruptions for weekend work are common. The Metro's base fare is $2 but can be much higher depending on the time of day and the distance traveled. All rides now require a SmarTrip card, a rechargeable fare card that can be used throughout the Metro, bus, and parking system. Buy your SmarTrip card at a vending machine in any station; they accept cash, credit cards, and debit cards. You can buy one-day passes for $14.75 and seven-day passes for $60.

🚕 Taxi Travel

Taxis are easy to hail in commercial districts, less so in residential ones. If you don't see one after a few minutes, walk to a busier street. If you call, make sure to have an address—not just an intersection—and be prepared to wait, especially at night. The base rate for the first one-eighth mile is $3.50. Each additional mile is $2.16, and each minute stopped or traveling less than 10 mph is $25 an hour ($0.40 per minute). A charge of $1 is tacked on for additional passengers, regardless how many. The telephone dispatch fee is $2. During D.C.-declared snow emergencies, there is an additional $15 fee. Cab rates in Virginia differ by county, but immediately surrounding D.C., riders should expect to pay $2–$3 for the first one-sixth mile and $0.36 for each additional one-sixth mile.

🚗 Ride-Sharing

Both Uber and Lyft operate in Washington, D.C., and may or may not be cheaper than a regular taxi depending on the time or day and distance traveled. Pooled rides are almost always cheaper for a single rider than a taxi but are almost always more expensive than the Metro. For a group of four people, however, a ride-share can be cheaper for a short trip than the Metro, since it has a base price of $2 per person.

🚆 Train Travel

More than 80 trains a day arrive at Washington, D.C.'s, Union Station. Amtrak's regular service runs from D.C. to New York in 3¼–3¾ hours and from D.C. to Boston in 7¾–8 hours. Acela, Amtrak's high-speed service, travels from D.C. to New York in 2¾–3 hours and from D.C. to Boston in 6½ hours, but can cost as much as a flight. Two commuter lines—Maryland Rail Commuter Service (MARC) and Virginia Railway Express (VRE)—run to the nearby suburbs. They're cheaper than Amtrak, but the VRE doesn't run on weekends or federal holidays. MARC's Penn Line does run on weekends, offering service to Baltimore for $8 each way.

Before You Go

🌐 Passport

All visitors to the United States require a valid passport that is valid for six months beyond your expected period of stay.

🆚 Visa

Except for citizens of Canada and Bermuda, most visitors to the United States must have a visa. If you are from one of the 38 designated members of the Visa Waiver Program, then you only require an ESTA (Electronic System for Travel Authorization) as long as you are staying for 90 days or less. However, some changes were made in the Visa Waiver Program in 2015, and nationals of Visa-Waiver nations who have traveled to Iran, Iraq, Libya, Somalia, Sudan, Syria, or Yemen no longer qualify for ESTA. Also, if you have been denied a visa to visit the United States, your application for the ESTA program most likely will be denied.

✒️ Immunizations

There are no immunization requirements for visitors traveling to the United States for tourism.

✒️ Embassies

All foreign governments have embassies in Washington, D.C., and most offer consular services in the embassy building.

📅 When to Go

LOW SEASON $

January through early March brings the fewest crowds to the District. However, since Congress is typically in session, hotels can still be more expensive during the week. Hotel prices can also drop after Christmas and in August, when Congress typically adjourns.

SHOULDER SEASON $$

If you aren't interested in cherry blossoms, late April through mid-May (before graduation season) and September (after Labor Day) can be good times to visit for fewer crowds and somewhat lower hotel prices, especially on weekends. Kids are back in school, so the tourist crowds are somewhat limited. Weekday nights are almost always more expensive, however.

HIGH SEASON $$$$

Spring is high season (particularly during cherry blossom season, which lasts about three weeks and can vary from late March through May). The highest hotel rates and occupancy levels tend to hit during the National Cherry Blossom Festival. Summer (June through August) is also typically busy with tourists, especially families.

Essentials

🧭 Addresses

Although it may not appear so at first glance, there's a system to addresses in D.C., albeit one that's a bit confusing for newcomers. The city is divided into the four quadrants of a compass (NW, NE, SE, SW), with the U.S. Capitol at the center. Because the Capitol doesn't sit in the exact center of the city, Northwest is the largest quadrant. Northwest also has most of the important landmarks, although Northeast and Southwest have their fair share. The boundaries are North Capitol Street, East Capitol Street, South Capitol Street, and the National Mall.

If someone tells you to meet them at 6th and G, ask them to specify the quadrant, because there are actually four different 6th and G intersections (one per quadrant). Within each quadrant, numbered streets run north to south, and lettered streets run east to west (the letter J was omitted to avoid confusion with the letter I). The streets form a fairly simple grid—for instance, 900 G Street NW is the intersection of 9th and G Streets in the NW quadrant of the city. Likewise, if you count the letters of the alphabet, skipping J, you can get a good approximation of an address for a numbered street. For instance, 1600 16th Street NW is close to Q Street, Q being the 16th letter of the alphabet if you skip J.

As if all this weren't confusing enough, Major Pierre L'Enfant, the Frenchman who originally designed the city, threw in diagonal avenues recalling those of Paris. Most of D.C.'s avenues are named after U.S. states. You can find addresses on avenues the same way you find those on numbered streets, so 1200 Connecticut Avenue NW is close to M Street, because M is the 12th letter of the alphabet when you skip J.

🍴 Dining

D.C. has always had a wide variety of international restaurants, but the general quality has improved, putting the city at the forefront of good eating.

DISCOUNTS AND DEALS

If you eat early or late you may be able to take advantage of prix-fixe deals not offered at peak hours. Many upscale restaurants offer great lunch deals with special menus at cut-rate prices designed to give customers a true taste of the place. At high-end restaurants ask for tap water to avoid paying high rates for bottled water.

PAYING

Most restaurants take credit cards, but some smaller places do not. It's worth asking. Waiters expect a 20% tip at high-end restaurants; some add an automatic gratuity for groups of six or more.

What it Costs

	$	$$	$$$	$$$$
AT DINNER	under $17	$17–$26	$27–$35	over $35

Prices in the reviews are the average cost of a main course at dinner or, if dinner is not served, at lunch.

RESERVATIONS AND DRESS

Always make a reservation at an upscale restaurant when you can. Some are booked weeks in advance, but some popular restaurants don't accept reservations. As unfair as it seems, the way you look can influence how you're treated—and where you're seated. Generally speaking, jeans and a button-down shirt will suffice at most restaurants, but some pricier restaurants require jackets, and some insist on ties. In reviews, we mention dress only where men are required to wear a jacket or a jacket and

Essentials

tie. If you have doubts, call the restaurant and ask.

MEALS AND MEALTIMES

Washington has less of an around-the-clock mentality than other big cities, with many big-name restaurants shutting down between lunch and dinner and closing by 11 pm. Many Downtown chain eateries close on weekends. For late-night dining, your best bets are restaurants near Dupont Circle and the U Street Corridor; for a late lunch, look for smaller places in Penn Quarter.

SMOKING

Smoking is banned in all restaurants and bars.

 Lodging

The District has some great hotels, but in general, hotel rates are very high, especially on weekdays.

RESERVATIONS

Always make a reservation in D.C. Hotels often fill up, and rooms in can be particularly hard to come by in late March or early April during the Cherry Blossom Festival, and in May, when students at the many local colleges graduate. Late October's Marine Corps Marathon also increases demand for rooms.

FACILITIES

You can assume that all rooms have private baths, phones, TVs, and air-conditioning, unless otherwise indicated. Breakfast is noted when it is included in the rate, but it's not a typical perk at most Washington hotels. There are a few hotels with pools, though some are indoors.

PARKING

Parking in D.C. is very expensive, and hotel parking fees can exceed $50. Independent garages may be slightly cheaper.

Street parking is free after 10 pm and on Sunday, but parking rules can be confusing, and tickets are expensive.

PRICES

Rates drop in August (during the Congressional recess) and in late December and January, except around inaugurations. Weekends are also more affordable. Travelers on a budget may find cheaper lodging in Virginia and Maryland suburbs, so long as the hotel is near a Metro line.

What it Costs			
$	$$	$$$	$$$$
FOR TWO PEOPLE			
under $210	$210–$295	$296–$400	over $400

Prices are for a standard double room in high season, excluding room tax (14.5% in D.C., 7% in MD, and 6.5% plus $1 in VA).

Shopping

Beyond the typical museum gift shops on the Mall, smaller one-of-a-kind shops, designer boutiques, and interesting specialty collections add to Washington's shopping scene alongside stores that have been part of the landscape for generations. Weekdays, Downtown street vendors add to the mix by offering funky jewelry; brightly patterned ties; buyer-beware watches; sunglasses; and African-inspired clothing, accessories, and art. Discriminating shoppers will find satisfaction at upscale malls on the city's outskirts. Not surprisingly, T-shirts and Capitol City souvenirs are in plentiful supply. Stores that cater to Downtown office workers may close on weekends, while stores in Georgetown, Adams Morgan, and the U Street Corridor may stay open late.

Where Should I Stay?

	NEIGHBORHOOD VIBE	PROS	CONS
The West End	Pleasant residential and office area along Pennsylvania Avenue. Stately early-20th-century buildings.	Safe area; close to Downtown's commercial sites and to halls of government, and the Mall.	Parking is always difficult and lots of traffic; older hotels with few budget rates.
Foggy Bottom	Bustling with college students most of the year. Its 18th- and 19th-century homes make for pleasant views.	Safe area; walking distance to Georgetown and the Kennedy Center; good Metro access.	Somewhat removed from other areas of city; paltry dining options.
Capitol Hill and Northeast D.C.	Charming residential blocks of Victorian row houses on Capitol Hill populated by members of Congress and their staffers.	Convenient to Union Station and Capitol. Stylish (if not cheap) hotels. Fine assortment of restaurants and shops.	Some streets iffy at night; parking takes some work; hotels are pricey. Blocks around Capitol and Union Station are chock-full of tourists.
Downtown	A vibrant, bustling, modern mix of commercial and residential properties, packed during the day and rowdy in places at night.	Right in the heart of the Metro system; easy access to the White House. Large selection of hotels, shops, and restaurants.	Crowded; busy; daytime street parking near impossible.
Georgetown	Wealthy neighborhood bordered by the Potomac and a world-class university. Filled with students, upscale shops, and eateries.	Safe area. Historic charm on every tree-lined street. Wonderful walking paths along river.	Crowded; no nearby Metro access; lots of traffic. Almost no parking. Lodging options tend to be expensive.
Dupont Circle	Cosmopolitan, lively neighborhood filled with bars and restaurants; beautiful city sights.	Plenty of modern hotels; easy Metro access; good selection of bars and restaurants.	Few budget hotel options; very limited street parking; crowded in summer months.
Adams Morgan	The center of late-night activity; eclectic and down-to-earth; languages galore.	Fabulous selection of ethnic bars and restaurants; vibrant, hip nightlife.	Few lodging options; 10-minute walk to Metro; very hard to park.
Upper Northwest	A pleasant residential neighborhood with a lively strip of good restaurants.	Safe, quiet; easy walk to zoo, Metro, restaurants; street parking easier than Downtown.	A long ride to attractions other than the zoo; feels like an inner suburb. Few new hotels.

Essentials

🍸 Nightlife

The District has a surprisingly busy night-life scene. Georgetown, the U Street Corridor, and Adams Morgan are popular destinations, but the Penn Quarter and Shaw are growing in popularity. Good happy hours abound during the week. Last call in D.C. is 2 am on weekends.

🎭 Performing Arts

Whatever you are looking for, Washington, D.C., has some of the most exciting and thought-provoking entertainment in the country. Since the opening of the John F. Kennedy Center for the Performing Arts in 1971, the city's performing arts culture has grown steadily. Washington now hosts the third-largest theater scene in the country, as well as a rich offering of nightly music opportunities featuring local, national, and international talent, and so much more. For up-to-date information, look for the *Washington City Paper* (⊕ *www.washingtoncitypaper.com*) or the *Washington Post's* Going out Guide (⊕ *www.washingtonpost.com/gog*).

🏃 Activities

Visitors to Washington can enjoy a wealth of outdoor attractions. Rock Creek Park is one of the city's treasures, with miles of wooded trails and paths for bikers, runners, and walkers that extend to almost every part of the city. The National Mall connects the Lincoln Memorial and the Capitol and is one of the most scenic green spaces in the world. Around the Tidal Basin you can run, tour the monuments, and rent paddleboats. Theodore Roosevelt Island, a wildlife sanctuary, has several paths for hiking and enjoyable spots for picnics. And these places are just a few among dozens.

BIKING

The numerous trails in the District and its surrounding areas are well maintained and clearly marked. Washington's large parks are also popular with cyclists. Plus, new bike lanes are on all major roads. The Capital Bikeshare scheme, with 400 stations around Washington, Arlington, and Alexandria, is also a great way to get around town.

SPECTATOR SPORTS

Washington, D.C., has several professional sports teams.

D.C. United. One of the best Major League Soccer teams has a huge fan base in the nation's capital, finding many of its fans in the international crowds who miss the big matches at home, as well as families whose kids play soccer. International matches, including some World Cup preliminaries, are often played on the grass field of Capitol Hill's RFK Stadium, the Redskins' and Senators' former venue, which is the home to D.C. United until mid-2018 when the new Audi Field in Southwest's Buzzard Point opened. Games are played March through October. You can buy tickets at the RFK Stadium ticket office or through the team's website, which offers special youth pricing. The D.C. Talon, the team mascot, entertains the crowd, along with enthusiastic, horn-blowing fans. ✉ *Robert F. Kennedy Stadium, 2400 E. Capitol St. SE, Capitol Hill* ☎ *202/587–5000* ⊕ *www.dcunited.com* ✉ *From $35* Ⓜ *Stadium–Armory.*

Washington Capitals. Stanley Cup winners in 2018, the Washington Capitals play loud and exciting home games October through April at the Verizon Center.

The team is led by one of hockey's superstars, Alex Ovechkin, and enjoys a huge, devoted fan base. Tickets are difficult to find but can be purchased at the Verizon Center box office, StubHub, or Ticketmaster. ✉ *Verizon Center, 601 F St. NW, Chinatown* ☎ *202/266–2222* ⊕ *capitals.nhl.com* 🚇 *From $45* Ⓜ *Gallery Pl.–Chinatown.*

Washington Mystics. This WNBA team plays at the Verizon Center in downtown Washington and perennially leads the WNBA in attendance, despite a losing record and having not yet made it even once to the WNBA Finals in two decades of operation. The games are loud, boisterous events. You can buy Mystics tickets at the Verizon Center box office or through Ticketmaster. The women's season runs from late May to August. ✉ *Verizon Center, 6th and F Sts., Chinatown* ☎ *202/432–7328* ⊕ *www.wnba.com/mystics* 🚇 *From $19* Ⓜ *Gallery Pl.–Chinatown.*

Washington Redskins. The perennially popular Redskins continue to play football in the Maryland suburbs at 82,000-seat FedEx Field. Under ongoing discussion is a name change for the team, since an increasing number of people deem it insensitive to Native Americans. Individual game-day tickets can be hard to come by when the team is enjoying a strong season. Your best bet is to check out StubHub (*www.stubhub.com,* the official ticket marketplace of the Redskins). ✉ *FedEx Field, 1600 FedexWay, Landover* ☎ *301/276–6000 FedEx Field* ⊕ *www.redskins.com* 🚇 *From $75.*

Washington Wizards. From October to April the NBA's Washington Wizards play at the Verizon Center and feature NBA All-Star John Wall. For showtime entertainment look for the G-Wiz, the G-Man, the Wiz Kids, and the Wizard Girls. Buy tickets from the Verizon Center box office, the Wizards' online, or Ticketmaster. ✉ *Verizon Center, 6th and F Sts. NW, Chinatown* ☎ *202/432–7328* ⊕ *www.nba.com/wizards* 🚇 *From $18* Ⓜ *Gallery Pl.–Chinatown.*

⊕ Health/Safety

Washington, D.C., is a fairly safe city, but as with any major metropolitan area it's best to stay alert. Keep an eye on purses and backpacks, and be aware of your surroundings before you use an ATM, especially one that is outdoors. Assaults are rare but they do happen, especially late at night in Adams Morgan, Capitol Hill, Northeast D.C., and U Street Corridor. Public transportation is quite safe, but late at night, choose bus stops on busy streets over those on quiet ones. If someone threatens you with violence, it's best to hand over your money and seek help from police later. Also be careful with smartphones and other electronics, as it's not uncommon for thieves to snatch those devices straight from the hands of unsuspecting pedestrians and Metro riders.

ⓢ Money

Washington is an expensive city, comparable to New York for hotels and restaurant prices. On the other hand, many attractions, including most of the museums, are free, though some can cost upward of $20 or more. Prices in this guide are given for adults. Substantially reduced fees are almost always available for children, students, and senior citizens.

Essentials

💲 Tipping

Tipping Guides for Washington, D.C.	
Bartender	$1–$5 per round of drinks, depending on the number of drinks
Bellhop	$1–$5 per bag, depending on the level of the hotel
Coat Check	$1–$2 per coat
Hotel Concierge	$5 or more, depending on the service
Hotel Doorstaff	$1–$5 for help with bags or hailing a cab
Hotel Maid	$2–$5 a day (in cash, preferably daily because cleaning staff may be different each day you stay)
Hotel Room Service Waiter	$1–$2 per delivery, even if a service charge has been added
Porter at Airport or Train Station	$1 per bag
Restroom Attendants	$1 or small change
Skycap at Airport	$1–$3 per bag checked
Spa Personnel	15%–20% of the cost of your service
Taxi Driver	15%–20%
Tour Guide	10%–15% of the cost of the tour, per person
Valet Parking Attendant	$2–$5, each time your car is brought to you
Waiter	15%–20%, with 20% being the norm at high-end restaurants; nothing additional if a service charge is added to the bill

📷 Packing

A pair of comfortable walking shoes is your must-pack item. This is a walking town, and if you fail to pack for it, your feet will pay. D.C. isn't the most fashionable city in the country, but people do look neat and presentable; business attire tends to be fairly conservative, and around college campuses and in hip neighborhoods like U Street Corridor, H Street, NoMa, or Adams Morgan, styles are more eclectic.

Winters are cold but sunny, with nighttime temperatures in the 20s and daytime highs in the 40s and 50s. Although the city doesn't normally get much snow, when it does, many streets won't be plowed for days, so if you're planning a visit for winter, bring a warm coat and hat and shoes that won't be ruined by snow and salt. Summers are muggy and very hot, with temperatures in the 80s and 90s and high humidity. Plan on cool, breathable fabrics, a hat for the sun, a sweater for overzealous air-conditioning, and an umbrella for afternoon thunderstorms. Fall and spring are the most enjoyable, with temperatures in the 60s and occasional showers. Pants, lightweight sweaters, and light coats are appropriate.

💲 Taxes

Washington's hotel tax is a whopping 14.8%. Maryland and Virginia charge hotel taxes of 5%–9.5%. The effective sales tax is 5.75% in D.C., 6% in Maryland and Northern Virginia.

D.C.'s Top Festivals

For a look at yearly events, visit ⊕ www.washington.org.

Winter

National Christmas Tree Lighting/Pageant of Peace (☎ 202/796–2500 ⊕ www.the-nationaltree.org, Dec.). Each year in early December, the president lights the tree at dusk on the Ellipse. Smaller decorated trees represent the states and territories, providing a festive setting. Concerts are held through the month.

Restaurant Week (⊕ www.ramw.org/restaurantweek, Jan. and Aug.). More than 200 top restaurants offer lunch and dinner menus for around $20 and $35, respectively—often a steal.

Spring

Georgetown French Market (☎ 202/298–9222 ⊕ www.georgetownfrenchmar-ketdc.com, late Apr.). Shop, eat, wander, and enjoy strolling mimes and live musicians in one of D.C.'s most beautiful neighborhoods.

National Cathedral Flower Mart (⊕ www.cathedral.org, early May). This long-standing free event on the cathedral grounds features food, music, kids' activities, and of course, flowers.

National Cherry Blossom Festival (☎ 877/442–5666 ⊕ www.nationalcherry-blossomfestival.org, late Mar.–mid Apr.). D.C.'s most eye-catching annual festival opens with an evening of world-class traditional and contemporary performances at the historic Warner Theater.

Washington Auto Show (⊕ www.washingtonautoshow.com, Apr.). Held at the Convention Center, this yearly event showcases the latest offerings from the world of automobiles.

Summer

Capital Pride Festival (☎ 202/719–5304 ⊕ www.capitalpride.org, early June). This weeklong festival with parade celebrates gay, lesbian, bisexual, transgendered, queer, and questioning citizens.

Independence Day Celebration (☎ 202/619–7222 ⊕ July4thparade.com, July). A parade sashays down Constitution Avenue, fireworks fly over the Washington Monument, and the NSO plays on the Capitol's West Lawn.

National Symphony Orchestra Labor Day Concert (☎ 202/416–8114 ⊕ www.kennedy-center.org, Labor Day weekend). This free concert is held on the grounds of the U.S. Capitol.

Smithsonian's Folklife Festival (☎ 202/633–6440 ⊕ www.folklife.si.edu, late June–early July). This two-week festival on the National Mall celebrates traditional dance and music, storytelling, and food from around the world.

Fall

National Book Festival (☎ 202/707–1940, early Sept.). This Saturday event attracts some of the world's top authors and poets to the Convention Center.

Veterans Day (☎ 703/607–8000 for Cemetery Visitor Center, ☎ 202/619–7222 for National Park Service, Nov. 11). Services are held at Arlington National Cemetery, Vietnam Veterans Memorial, and the U.S. Navy Memorial, with a wreath laying at 11 am at the Tomb of the Unknowns.

Washington International Horse Show (☎ 202/525–3679 ⊕ www.wihs.org, late Oct.). Held at Capitol One Arena, this annual show features jumping, dressage, barrel racing, and more.

Great Itineraries

One Day in D.C.

If you have a day or less in D.C., your sightseeing strategy is simple: take the Metro to the Smithsonian stop and explore the area around the Mall. You'll be at the heart of the city—a beautiful setting where you'll find America's greatest collection of museums, with the city's monuments and the halls of government a stone's throw away.

Facing the Capitol, to your left are the **National Museum of African American History and Culture, National Museum of American History, National Museum of Natural History,** and the **National Gallery of Art.** To your right are the **Freer Gallery,** the **National Museum of African Art,** the **Hirshhorn Museum and Sculpture Garden,** the **National Air and Space Museum,** and more. Head in the other direction, toward the **Washington Monument,** and you're also on your way to the **National World War II Memorial,** the **Lincoln Memorial,** the **Vietnam Veterans Memorial,** and more monuments to America's presidents and its past. A lover of American history and culture could spend a thoroughly happy month, much less a day, wandering the Mall and its surroundings.

If you're here first thing in the morning: You can hit monuments and memorials early. They're open 24 hours a day and staffed beginning at 9:30 am. The sculpture garden at the Hirshhorn opens at 7:30, and the Smithsonian Institution Building ("the Castle") opens at 8:30. In the Castle you can grab a cup of coffee, watch an 18-minute film about D.C., and see examples of objects from many of the Smithsonian's 19 museums and galleries.

If you have only a few hours in the evening: Experience the beauty of the monuments at dusk and after dark. Many people think they're even more striking when the sun goes down. National Park Service rangers staff most monuments until 10 pm.

Three Days in D.C.

DAY 1

With more time, you have a chance both to see the sights and to get to know the city. A guided bus tour is a good way to get oriented; a hop-on, hop-off tour will give you genuine insights without a lot of tourist hokum.

Because you can get on and off wherever you like, it's a good idea to use a bus tour to explore **Georgetown** and the **Washington National Cathedral,** neither of which is easily accessible by Metro. This is a good opportunity to visit **Arlington National Cemetery** as well.

In the afternoon, pick one or two museums located in Chinatown: the **International Spy Museum** (slated to move to L'Enfant Plaza), the **Smithsonian American Art Museum,** and/or the **National Portrait Gallery.**

DAY 2

Devote your next day to the Mall, where you can check out the museums and monuments that were probably your prime motivation for visiting D.C. in the first place. There's no way you can do it all in one day, so just play favorites and save the rest for next time. Try visiting the monuments in the evening: they remain open long after the museums are closed and are dramatically lit after dark.

Keep in mind that the **National Air and Space Museum** is the most visited museum in the country, while the **National Museum of Natural History,** the **National Gallery of Art,** and the **National Museum of American History** aren't far behind; plan for crowds almost any time you visit. If you visit the **United States Holocaust Memorial Museum,** plan on spending two to three hours. The National Museum of African American History and Culture is the newest museum on the Mall, with the lines to prove it; reserve timed tickets in advance, if you can. If you're with kids on the Mall, take a break by riding the carousel.

Cafés and cafeterias within the museums are your best option for lunch. Three excellent picks are the Cascade Café at the **National Gallery of Art**; the Mitsitam Café at the **National Museum of the American Indian,** where they serve creative dishes inspired by native cultures; and Sweet Water Café at the **National Museum of African American History and Culture,** showcasing the rich traditions of African Amerian cuisine. Just north of the Mall, the **Newseum,** while not free to enter, features a food court with a menu designed by celebrity-chef Wolfgang Puck. If you have more time (and more money to spend), drop by The Source, a ritzy Puck-owned restaurant behind the museum.

If the weather permits—and you're not already weary—consider the healthy walk from the **Washington Monument** to the **Lincoln Memorial** and around the **Tidal Basin,** where you can see the **Jefferson Memorial,** the **Franklin Delano Roosevelt Memorial,** and the **Martin Luther King Jr. National Memorial.** Nearby, nestled north of the Mall's reflecting pool, is the **Vietnam Veterans Memorial,** "The Wall," a sobering black granite monolith commemorating the 58,318 Americans who died in service of the Vietnam War—a design that's "not so much a tombstone or a monument as a grave," in the somber words of writer Michael Ventura.

DAY 3

Start your day on **Capitol Hill,** where you'll have the option of visiting the **Capitol,** the **U.S. Botanic Gardens,** the **Library of Congress,** the **Supreme Court,** and the **Folger Shakespeare Library.**

Call your senators or congressional representative (or your country's embassy, if you are a visitor from outside the United States) in advance of your trip for passes to see Congress in session. You can also venture into one of the congressional office buildings adjacent to the Capitol, where congressional hearings are almost always open to the public. (Visit ⊕ www.house.gov and ⊕ www.senate.gov for schedules.) Likewise, check the Supreme Court's website (⊕ www.supremecourtus.gov) for dates of oral arguments. If you arrive early enough, you might gain admission for either a short (three-minute) visit or the full morning session.

In the afternoon, hop on the Metro to bustling **Dupont Circle** for lunch, then visit the renowned **Phillips Collection** or head farther north on Connecticut Avenue to the **National Zoo** to say hi to the pandas.

Washington, D.C. Black History Walk

A walk along U Street and the eastern rim of Adams Morgan gives a taste of D.C. that most tourists never get. This tour through "Black Broadway" bounces from lively commercial streets brimming with hip bars, cafés, and boutiques to quiet, tree-lined, residential blocks, and highlights African American culture and history. This walk complements a visit to the amazing National Museum of African American History and Culture, which opened in 2016 on the National Mall.

"BLACK BROADWAY"— U STREET CORRIDOR

The Howard Theatre at T Street and Florida Avenue is a good place to start. Opened in 1910, this landmark of black culture found its way onto the National Register of Historic Places for hosting some of the greatest musical acts of the last century—a list that includes such notables as Ella Fitzgerald and native son Duke Ellington in the 1930s and, more recently, Lena Horne, James Brown, and Marvin Gaye. All but destroyed in 1968, following the assassination of Martin Luther King Jr., the theater was renovated beautifully in 2012 and now features live acts almost nightly. A short hike west, at 10th and U Streets, sits the **African American Civil War Memorial,** where the names of more than 200,000 black soldiers who fought for their freedom are inscribed. The adjacent **African American Civil War Museum** features wonderful photographs from the era and an extensive on-site database for searching individual soldiers. A block west at 2000 11th Street is **Washington Industrial Bank,** which thrived by offering African Americans a service that others in the city wouldn't: the option to borrow money. Next, grab a half-smoke at **Ben's Chili Bowl.** A D.C. landmark, Ben's refused to close its doors during the fierce riots that followed King's assassination. While most

Washington, D.C. Black History Walk

HIGHLIGHTS
U Street was the center of black culture before Harlem was Harlem. See where Duke Ellington played, indulge in a half-smoke at Ben's Chili Bowl, and learn a bit about African American history along the way.

WHERE TO START
Howard Theatre, just east of Metro's U Street/African-Amer Civil War Memorial/Cardozo stop on the Green or Yellow lines

LENGTH
About 1½ miles; 1–2 hours, with stops

WHERE TO STOP
All Souls Unitarian Church. The S2 or S4 bus lines on 16th Street will whisk you back Downtown.

BEST TIME TO GO
While the sun is up, though the nightlife on U Street is an attraction in itself.

WORST TIME TO GO
Avoid walking through Meridian Hill Park after dark.

EDITOR'S CHOICE
Check out the sprawling Miss Pixie's (*1626 14th St. NW*) for handpicked collectibles and browse Goodwood (*1428 U St. NW between 14th and 15th Sts.*) for antique wood furniture and estate jewelry.

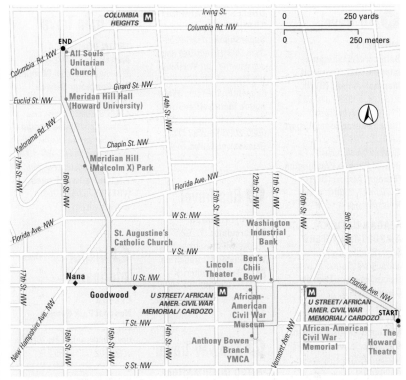

of U Street was being destroyed, Ben's fed the police officers and black activists trying to keep order. Next door is the **Lincoln Theater,** another exceptional jazz venue and, from 1922 until desegregation, one of the largest and most elegant historically black theaters. Two blocks north up 13th Street NW and a quick left will bring you to the **Anthony Bowen Branch YMCA,** the oldest black Y in the country (1853), recently completely overhauled.

NORTH OF U STREET
Venture north on 15th Street NW to marvel at **St. Augustine's Catholic Church**— a gorgeous, two-tower cathedral now home to a black congregation that seceded from its segregated church (St.

Matthews) in 1858. Feel free to walk inside to glimpse the striking stained-glass portrait of a black St. Augustine and St. Monica. A block farther north is sprawling **Meridian Hill (or Malcolm X) Park,** where a number of civil rights marches have originated over the years. Cutting through the park to 16th Street, you'll spot **Meridian Hill Hall,** Howard University's first coed dorm. Alumni of the elite African American school include Thurgood Marshall and Toni Morrison. Continuing north, past some beautiful working embassies, you'll find **All Souls Unitarian Church** at 1500 Harvard Street NW. Its pastor in the 1940s, Reverend A. Powell Davies, led the push to desegregate D.C. schools.

Contacts

✈ Air Travel

AIRPORTS
Baltimore/Washington International–Thurgood Marshall Airport (BWI). ☎ 800/435–9294, 410/859–7111 ⊕ www.bwiairport.com. **Dulles International Airport (IAD).** ☎ 703/572–2700 ⊕ www.flydulles.com. **Ronald Reagan Washington National Airport (DCA).** ☎ 703/417–8000 ⊕ www.flyreagan.com.

REAGAN NATIONAL (DCA) AIRPORT TRANSFERS
SuperShuttle. ☎ 800/258–3826, 703/416–7873 ⊕ www.supershuttle.com. **Taxicab Commission.** ☎ 311, 202/645–6018 ⊕ www.dfhv.dc.gov. **Washington Metropolitan Area Transit Authority.** ☎ 202/637–7000, 202/962–2033 TTY ⊕ www.wmata.com.

BALTIMORE/WASHINGTON (BWI) AIRPORT TRANSFERS
Amtrak. ☎ 800/872–7245 ⊕ www.amtrak.com. **Maryland Rail Commuter Service.** ☎ 410/539–5000, 410/539–3497 TTY, 866/743–3682 ⊕ www.mta.maryland.gov. **SuperShuttle.** ☎ 800/258–3826, 410/859–3427 ⊕ www.supershuttle.com. **Washington Metropolitan Area Transit Authority.** ☎ 202/637–7000, 202/962–2033 TTY ⊕ www.wmata.com.

DULLES (IAD) AIRPORT TRANSFERS
SuperShuttle. ☎ 800/258–3826, 703/416–7873 ⊕ www.supershuttle.com. **Washington Flyer.** ☎ 703/752–8294 ⊕ www.flydulles.com. **Washington Metropolitan Area Transit Authority.** ☎ 202/637–7000, 202/962–2033 TTY ⊕ www.wmata.com.

🚌 Bus Travel

D.C. CITY BUSES
DC Circulator. ☎ 202/671–2020 ⊕ www.dccirculator.com. **Washington Metropolitan Area Transit Authority.** ☎ 202/637–7000, 202/962–2033 TTY ⊕ www.wmata.com.

Ⓜ Subway Travel

METRO INFORMATION
Washington Metropolitan Area Transit Authority (WMATA). ✉ Downtown ☎ 202/637–7000, 202/962–2033 TTY, 202/962–1195 lost and found ⊕ www.wmata.com.

🚕 Taxi Travel

TAXI COMPANIES
Barwood. ☎ 301/984–1900 ⊕ www.barwoodtaxi.com. **Red Top.** ☎ 703/522–3333 ⊕ www.redtopcab.com. **Taxi Transportation.** ☎ 202/398–0500 ⊕ www.dctaxionline.com. **Yellow.** ☎ 202/544–1212 ⊕ www.dcyellowcab.com.

🚆 Train Travel

TRAIN CONTACTS
Amtrak. ☎ 800/872–7245 ⊕ www.amtrak.com. **Maryland Rail Commuter Service (MARC).** ☎ 866/743–3682, 410/539–5000 ⊕ www.mta.maryland.gov. **Union Station.** ✉ 50 Massachusetts Ave. NE, Washington ☎ 202/289–1908 ⊕ www.unionstationdc.com. **Virginia Railway Express (VRE).** ☎ 703/684–1001 ⊕ www.vre.org.

📍 Visitor Information

EVENTS
National Park Service. ☎ 202/208–6843 ⊕ www.nps.gov. **Smithsonian.** ☎ 202/633–1000, 202/633–5285 TTY ⊕ www.si.Edu. **White House Visitor Center.** ✉ 1450 Pennsylvania Ave. NW, Washington ☎ 202/208–1631 ⊕ www.nps.gov/whho.

THE DISTRICT
Destination DC. ✉ 901 7th St. NW, 4th fl., Downtown ☎ 202/789–7000, 800/422–8644 ⊕ www.washington.org.

VIRGINIA AND MARYLAND
State of Maryland. ☎ 866/639–3526 ⊕ www.visitmaryland.org. **Virginia Tourism Corporation.** ☎ 800/847–4882 ⊕ www.virginia.org.

Chapter 3

THE NATIONAL MALL

Updated by
Alison Thoet

👁 **Sights**   🍴 **Restaurants**   🛏 **Hotels**   🛍 **Shopping**   🍸 **Nightlife**

★★★★★   ★★☆☆☆   ★☆☆☆☆   ★★☆☆☆   ★☆☆☆☆

NEIGHBORHOOD SNAPSHOT

TOP EXPERIENCES

■ **Monuments at night:** For a unique (and less crowded) historical experience, tour the many monuments at night, when they are lit and beautiful.

■ **National Air and Space Museum:** Touch a moon rock, see the original *Spirit of St. Louis* and Apollo Lunar Module.

■ **National Archives:** Stand in awe as you read the Declaration of Independence, Constitution, Bill of Rights, and a 1297 Magna Carta.

■ **National Museum of African American History and Culture:** D.C.'s newest museum is also its most moving. Learn about when captive slaves were first brought to the New World and celebrate the many artists, writers, actors, and cultural leaders who have contributed to our country's history.

■ **National Gallery of Art:** Two massive buildings offer an extensive collection ranging from classics to modern art. Don't miss the only Leonardo da Vinci in the United States, the infamous *Ginevra de' Benci.*

■ **The Holocaust Museum:** This museum serves as a monument to those lost in the Holocaust and offers perspective on the effects of genocide across the world and decades to follow.

GETTING HERE

Federal Triangle (Blue and Orange lines) is convenient to the Natural History and American History museums. Smithsonian (Blue and Orange lines) is close to the Holocaust Memorial Museum and Hirshhorn Museum. Archives–Navy Memorial–Penn Quarter (Yellow and Green lines) takes you to the National Gallery of Art. L'Enfant Plaza (Blue, Orange, Yellow, and Green lines), is the best stop for the Hirshhorn and Air and Space Museum. Many visitors take advantage of the DC Circulator National Mall Route buses that cost just $1 and run daily up and down the Mall.

QUICK BITES

■ **Garden Café.** After marveling at the masterpieces in the National Gallery West Building, grab a quick bite on the ground floor at this full-service, sit-down café offering salads, house-roasted meats, and European-style desserts. ⊠ *National Gallery, West Building, 6th and Constitution* Ⓜ *Archives–Navy Memorial–Penn Quarter.*

■ **Mitsitam Cafe.** The quick-service food court offers stations with traditional and contemporary native dishes from five regional native cuisines, including seasonal offerings. The food here is meant to give visitors a deeper insight into the culinary history of Native American foods, including cooking techniques, ingredients, and flavors. ⊠ *National Museum of the American Indian, 4th St. SW and Independence Ave.* Ⓜ *Federal Center SW.*

■ **Sweet Home Café.** This cafeteria's menu offers traditional and authentic seasonally rotating dishes that showcase the rich history of African American cuisine from four distinct geographic regions. Many ingredients are locally sourced, and everything is cooked from scratch. ⊠ *Museum of African American History and Culture, 1400 Constitution Ave. NW* Ⓜ *Smithsonian or Federal Triangle.*

It could be said that the National Mall—the heart of almost every visitor's trip to Washington—has influenced life in the United States more than any other park. The National Mall is a picnicking park, a jogging path, and an outdoor stage for festivals and fireworks. People come here from around the globe to tour the illustrious Smithsonian museums, celebrate special events, or rally over the hot-button issues of the day.

Sights

Arthur M. Sackler Gallery

MUSEUM | The Smithsonian's second museum devoted to Asian art opened in 1987, having been inspired by the donation of 1,000 objects by Dr. Arthur M. Sackler. You can explore a dramatic collection of 12th- to 19th-century Buddhist art from South Asia, including a majestic stone image of Shiva Dakshinamurti (Lord of the South) and a fierce gilded bronze of Palden Lhamo, the deity that protects Lhasa, the capital city of Tibet. Through late 2020, a long-running exhibition will help you further your understanding of Buddhism with such immersive spaces as a Tibetan shrine, a Sri Lankan stupa, and an exhibition devoted to an 8th-century Korean monk. ⊠ 1050 Independence Ave. SW, The Mall ☎ 202/633–4880 ⊕ www.freersackler.si.edu ⛬ Free Ⓜ Smithsonian.

Bureau of Engraving and Printing

GOVERNMENT BUILDING | FAMILY | Paper money has been printed here since 1914, when the bureau relocated from the redbrick-towered Auditors Building at the corner of 14th Street and Independence Avenue. In addition to paper currency, military certificates and presidential invitations are printed here, too. You can only enter the bureau on tours, which last about 40 minutes. From March through early September (dates vary each year), free same-day timed-entry tour passes are issued starting at 8 am (plan on being in line no later than 7 am) at the Raoul Wallenberg Place SW ticket booth. For the rest of the year, tickets are not required, and visitors can simply wait in line. You also can also arrange a tour through your U.S. senator or representative. ⊠ 14th and C Sts. SW, The Mall ☎ 202/874–2330, 866/874–2330 tour information ⊕ moneyfactory.gov ⛬ Free Ⓜ Smithsonian.

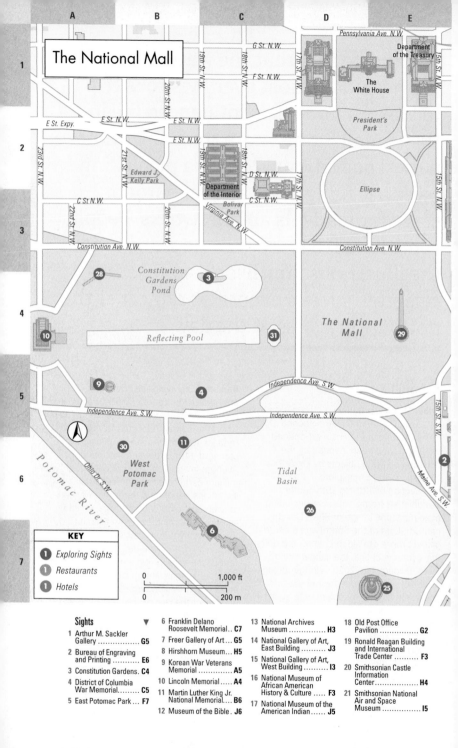

The National Mall

Pennsylvania Ave. N.W.

Department of the Treasury

The White House

President's Park

Ellipse

Edward J. Kelly Park

Department of the Interior

Bolivar Park

Virginia Ave. N.W.

Constitution Ave. N.W.

Constitution Ave. N.W.

Constitution Gardens Pond

The National Mall

Reflecting Pool

Independence Ave. S.W.

Independence Ave. S.W.

Independence Ave. S.W.

West Potomac Park

Potomac River

Tidal Basin

Ohio Dr. S.W.

Maine Ave. S.W.

KEY

- Exploring Sights
- Restaurants
- Hotels

0   1,000 ft
0   200 m

Sights ▼

1 Arthur M. Sackler Gallery **G5**
2 Bureau of Engraving and Printing **E6**
3 Constitution Gardens. **C4**
4 District of Columbia War Memorial........ **C5**
5 East Potomac Park ... **F7**
6 Franklin Delano Roosevelt Memorial.. **C7**
7 Freer Gallery of Art ... **G5**
8 Hirshhorn Museum... **H5**
9 Korean War Veterans Memorial **A5**
10 Lincoln Memorial..... **A4**
11 Martin Luther King Jr. National Memorial.... **B6**
12 Museum of the Bible . **J6**
13 National Archives Museum **H3**
14 National Gallery of Art, East Building **J3**
15 National Gallery of Art, West Building **I3**
16 National Museum of African American History & Culture **F3**
17 National Museum of the American Indian **J5**
18 Old Post Office Pavilion **G2**
19 Ronald Reagan Building and International Trade Center **F3**
20 Smithsonian Castle Information Center................. **H4**
21 Smithsonian National Air and Space Museum **I5**

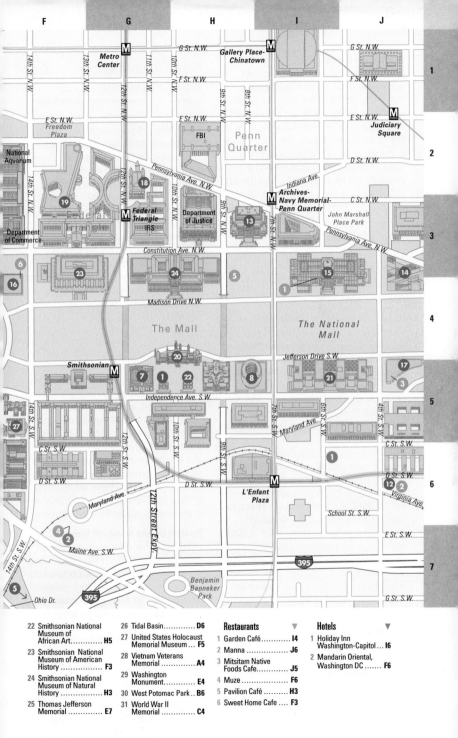

Restaurants ▼

Hotels ▼

Constitution Gardens

GARDEN | Many ideas were proposed to develop this 52-acre site near the Reflecting Pool and the Vietnam Veterans Memorial. President Nixon ordered temporary government office buildings on the site to be demolished in the early 1970s to make room for the gardens. Paths wind through groves of trees and a 1-acre island on the lake pays tribute to the signers of the Declaration of Independence, with all of their 56 signatures carved into a low stone wall. At the circular snack bar just west of the lake, you can get hot dogs, potato chips, candy bars, and soft drinks. ⊠ *Constitution Ave., between 17th and 23rd Sts. NW, The Mall* ⊕ *www.nps.gov/coga* Ⓜ *Farragut W or Foggy Bottom–GWU.*

District of Columbia War Memorial

GARDEN | Despite its location and age, visitors often overlook this memorial on the National Mall that President Herbert Hoover dedicated in 1931. Unlike the neighboring memorials on the Mall, this relatively small structure isn't a national memorial. The 47-foot-high, circular, domed, columned temple is dedicated to the 26,000 residents from Washington, D.C., who served in the Great War and the 499 men and women (military and civilian) who died in service. Unofficially referred to as the "World War I Memorial" in the District, the marble structure was restored through the American Recovery and Reinvestment Act of 2009 and is now maintained by the National Park Service. ⊠ *Independence Ave. SW, The Mall* ✛ *West Potomac Park, between the Reflecting Pool and Independence Ave.* ☎ *202/426–6841* ⊕ *www.nps.gov/nacc* Ⓜ *Foggy Bottom–GWU.*

East Potomac Park

CITY PARK | FAMILY | This 328-acre finger of land extends south of the Jefferson Memorial from the Tidal Basin, between the Washington Channel and the new Southwest Waterfront redevelopment neighborhood to the east

The FDR Memorial: Some History

Congress established the Franklin Delano Roosevelt Memorial Commission in 1955, and invited prospective designers to look to "the character and work of Roosevelt to give us the theme of a memorial." Several decades passed before Lawrence Halprin's design for a "walking environmental experience" was selected. It incorporates work by artists Leonard Baskin, Neil Estern, Robert Graham, Thomas Hardy, and George Segal, and master stone carver John Benson.

and the Potomac River to the west. Locals consider the park a retreat with its playgrounds, picnic tables, tennis courts, swimming pools, driving range, one 18-hole and two 9-hole golf courses, miniature golf, and pool. There's also a scenic riverfront trail that winds around the park's perimeter. Double-blossoming Japanese cherry trees line Ohio Drive and bloom about two weeks after the single-blossoming variety that attracts throngs to the Tidal Basin each spring. ⊠ *Ohio Dr. SW, The Mall* ☎ *202/426–6841* ⊕ *www.npca.org/parks* Ⓜ *Smithsonian.*

Franklin Delano Roosevelt Memorial

MEMORIAL | This 7.5-acre memorial to the 32nd president, on the west side of the Tidal Basin, includes waterfalls and reflecting pools, four outdoor gallery rooms—one for each of Roosevelt's presidential terms (1933 to 1945)—and 10 bronze sculptures. The granite megaliths connecting the galleries are engraved with some of Roosevelt's famous statements, including, "The only thing we have to fear is fear itself." A bronze statue of First Lady Eleanor Roosevelt stands in front of the United Nations symbol in the fourth room. She was a vocal spokesperson for human rights and one of the most influential women of her time. In consideration of Roosevelt's own disability, this was the first memorial designed to be wheel-chair-accessible, and several pillars include Braille lettering. The memorial was dedicated in 1997, but it wasn't until 2001 that a statue of a wheelchair-bound Roosevelt was added near the entrance after years of debate about whether to portray Roosevelt realistically or to honor his desire not to display his disability, as had been done throughout his presidency. ⊠ 400 W. Basin Dr. SW, The Mall ☎ 202/426–6841 ⊕ www.nps.gov/fdrm ⛽ Free Ⓜ Smithsonian.

Freer Gallery of Art

MUSEUM | The first art museum in the Smithsonian group of museums, donated by railroad tycoon Charles Lang Freer, is devoted to Asian and American art. A highlight is the Peacock Room, a jewel box of a space designed by James McNeill Whistler, with gold murals on peacock-blue walls, and a peacock-feather-pattern gold-leaf ceiling. At noon on the third Thursday of every month, the floor-to-ceiling shutters are opened, bathing the room in natural light. There are also works from around Asia, including China, Korea, and India, as well as the Middle East. ⊠ 12th St. and Jefferson Dr. SW, The Mall ☎ 202/633–4880 ⊕ www.freersackler.si.edu ⛽ Free Ⓜ Smithsonian.

★ Hirshhorn Museum and Sculpture Garden

MUSEUM | Conceived as the nation's museum of modern and contemporary art, the Hirshhorn is home to nearly 12,000 works by masters who include Alexander Calder, Andy Warhol, and Louise Bourgeois, as well as contemporary superstars Anish Kapor and Yinka Shonibare. The art is displayed in a circular poured-concrete building, designed by Gordon Bunshaft, that was dubbed the "Doughnut on the Mall" when it was built in 1974. Most of the collection was

The Freer|Sackler

The Smithsonian Institution has two museums of Asian art: the Freer Gallery of Art, which opened to the public in 1923, and the Arthur M. Sackler Gallery, which welcomed its first visitors in 1987. Both are physically connected by an underground passageway, ideologically linked through the study, exhibition, and sheer love of Asian art, and often referred to as the "Freer|Sackler." Free highlight tours are held regularly; the museums also regularly host films, concerts, talks, and other events.

bequeathed by the museum's founder, Joseph H. Hirshhorn, a Latvian immigrant who made his fortune in uranium mines.

The sculpture collection has masterpieces by Henry Moore, Alberto Giacometti, and Constantin Brancusi. Outside, sculptures dot a grass-and-granite garden. Among them is Yoko Ono's Wish Tree for Washington, DC, and on the plaza stands a 32-foot-tall yellow cartoon sculpture by pop-art iconographer Roy Lichtenstein that has become a beloved local landmark.

Inside, the third level's outer ring is the place to see thought-provoking conceptual art from the museum's permanent collection. The current exhibition, What Absence Is Made Of, which runs through spring 2020, offers the first chance for visitors to encounter new acquisitions by artists Annette Lemieux, Ed Atkins, and Huang Yong Ping, alongside well-known works by Felix Gonzalez-Torres, Ana Mendieta, and Hiroshi Sugimoto.

Inside, the third level is the place to see dramatic postwar art from the museum's permanent collection, displayed thematically, with works by artists such as Joseph Cornell, Isa Genzken, Alighiero

The view from inside the Lincoln Memorial captures its reflecting pool and the iconic Washington Monument.

e Boetti, and Sol LeWitt. Be sure to check out Cornell's *Untitled (Aviary with Yellow Birds)* and Yoko Ono's *Sky TV for Washington*. Large-scale text works by conceptual artist Lawrence Weiner round out the space.

The second level houses exhibits that rotate about three times a year, curated by museum staff and devoted to particular artists or themes. The lower level houses recent and experimental works from the permanent collection, while the sculpture garden makes an inspiring spot for a picnic. ⊠ *Independence Ave. and 7th St. SW, The Mall* ☎ *202/633–4674* ⊕ *www.hirshhorn.si.edu* 🎫 *Free* Ⓜ *Smithsonian or L'Enfant Plaza (Maryland Ave. exit).*

Korean War Veterans Memorial

MEMORIAL | At the west end of Mall, this memorial to the 5.8 million United States men and women who served in the Korean War (1950–53) highlights the cost of freedom. Nearly 37,000 Americans were killed on the Korean peninsula, 8,000 were missing in action, and more than

103,000 were wounded. The privately funded memorial was dedicated on July 27, 1995, the 42nd anniversary of the Korean War Armistice. In the *Field of Service,* 19 oversize stainless-steel soldiers toil through rugged terrain toward an American flag; look beneath the helmets to see their weary faces. The reflection in the black granite wall to their right doubles their number to 38, symbolic of the 38th parallel, the latitude established as the border between North and South Korea in 1953, as well as the 38 months of the war.

Unlike many memorials, this one contains few words. The 164-foot-long granite wall etched with the faces of 2,400 unnamed servicemen and servicewomen says, "Freedom is not free." The plaque at the flagpole base reads, "Our nation honors her sons and daughters who answered the call to defend a country they never knew and a people they never met." The only other words are the names of 22 countries that volunteered forces or medical support,

Introduction to the Smithsonian

Be amazed by the history of air and space travel, then explore the 1903 Wright Flyer that Wilbur and Orville Wright piloted over the sands of Kitty Hawk, North Carolina, in the National Air and Space Museum. Imagine yourself as Thomas Jefferson composing documents at his "writing box," or as Julia Child cooking in her perfect kitchen (both are on display at the National Museum of American History).

Thought-provoking modern art is on view at the constantly changing Hirshhorn Museum, where you'll see Roy Lichtenstein's 32-foot yellow cartoon sculpture in the outdoor sculpture garden and Yoko Ono's *Sky TV for Washington* inside the museum, or see the only Leonardo da Vinci painting in the United States at the National Gallery of Art West Building.

Visiting the Smithsonian

Most of the 19 Smithsonian museums are open daily between 10 am and 5:30 pm (with at least four or five closed days per year for major holidays), and all are free, though there are sometimes charges for special exhibits. During the spring and summer, many of the museums offer extended hours, closing as late as 7:30 pm. To get oriented, start with a visit to the Smithsonian building—aka the "Castle," for its towers-and-turrets architecture—which has information on all the museums. The museum also has a free app to help you explore the collections and buildings, but it has limited functionality.

Special Events

Smithsonian museums regularly host an incredible spectrum of special events, from evenings of jazz and dance nights to food and wine tastings, films, lectures, and events for families and kids. A full schedule is available at ⊕ *www.si.edu/events*. Popular events include live jazz on Friday evenings in summer at the National Gallery of Art sculpture garden and Take Five performances every third Thursday at the Smithsonian American Art Museum. The National Museum of the American Indian often holds weekend festivals that showcase the history and culture of native peoples from the around the world, complete with workshops, film screenings, hands-on activities for all ages, craft shows, and cooking demonstrations.

including Great Britain, France, Greece and Turkey. The adjacent circular Pool of Remembrance honors all who were killed, captured, wounded or missing in action; it's a quiet spot for contemplation. ✉ *Daniel French Dr. SW and Independence Ave. SW, The Mall* ☎ *202/426–6841* ⊕ *www.nps.gov/kwvm* ✍ *Free* Ⓜ *Foggy Bottom–GWU.*

★ Lincoln Memorial

MEMORIAL | Daniel Chester French's statue of the seated president gazing out over the Reflecting Pool may be the most iconic on the Mall. The 19-foot-high sculpture is made of 28 pieces of Georgia marble. The surrounding white Colorado-marble memorial was designed by Henry Bacon and completed in 1922. The 36 Doric columns represent the 36 states in the Union at the time of Lincoln's death; their names appear on the frieze above the columns. Over the frieze are the names of the 48 states in existence when the memorial was dedicated. At night the memorial is illuminated, creating a striking play of light and shadow across Lincoln's face.

Two of Lincoln's great speeches—the second inaugural address and the Gettysburg Address—are carved on the north and south walls. Above each is a Jules Guerin mural: the south wall has an angel of truth freeing a slave; the unity of North and South is opposite.

The memorial's powerful symbolism makes it a popular gathering place; in its shadow Americans marched for integrated schools in 1958, rallied for an end to the Vietnam War in 1967, and laid wreaths in a ceremony honoring the Iranian hostages in 1979. It may be best known, though, as the site of Martin Luther King Jr.'s "I Have a Dream" speech. ⊠ *2 Lincoln Memorial Cir. NW, The Mall* ⊹ *West end of Mall* ☎ *202/426–6841* ⊕ *www.nps.gov/linc* ⊠ *Free* Ⓜ *Foggy Bottom–GWU.*

Martin Luther King Jr. National Memorial

MEMORIAL | A "King" now stands tall among the presidents on the National Mall. For his dedication on October 16, 2011, President Barack Obama said, "This is a day that would not be denied." The memorial opened on August 28, 2011, 15 years after Congress approved it in 1996 and 82 years after the famed civil rights leader was born in 1929.

Located strategically between the Lincoln and Jefferson memorials and adjacent to the FDR Memorial, the crescent-shaped King Memorial sits on a 4-acre site on the curved bank of the Tidal Basin. There are two main ways to enter the memorial. From West Basin Drive, walk through a center walkway cut out of a huge boulder, the "Mountain of Despair." From the Tidal Basin entrance, a 28-foot-tall granite structure shows a likeness of King looking out toward Jefferson's statue. The symbolism of the mountain and stone are explained by King's words: "With this faith, we will be able to hew out of the mountain of

despair a stone of hope." The centerpiece stone was carved by Chinese sculptor Lei Yixin; his design was chosen from more than 900 entries in an international competition. Fittingly, Yixin first read about King's "I Have a Dream" speech at age 10 while visiting the Lincoln Memorial.

The themes of democracy, justice, hope, and love are reflected through quotes on the south and north walls and on the Stone of Hope. The quotes reflect speeches, sermons, and writings penned by King from 1955 through 1968. Waterfalls in the memorial reflect King's use of the biblical quote: "Let justice roll down like waters and righteousness like a mighty stream." ⊠ *1964 Independence Ave. SW, The Mall* ☎ *202/426–6841* ⊕ *www.nps.gov/mlkm* ⊠ *Free* Ⓜ *Smithsonian.*

Museum of the Bible

MUSEUM | Eight floors encompassing over 430,000 square feet are all dedicated to the history, narrative, and impact of the Bible on the world. The *illumiNations* exhibit displays Bibles in more than 2,000 languages, and visitors can touch, read, and explore them and other illuminated manuscripts. The museum includes exhibits focused on modern films, speakers, fashion, and technology to tell the story of the Bible's continuing influence today. Here you can also see the Dead Sea Scrolls, papyrus featuring early copies of the New Testament, designer clothing featuring religious idols, and even Elvis Presley's Bible. Stop by the Manna restaurant for biblically themed foods and other Mediterranean-inspired meals. This museum was founded and funded in part by Steve Green, CEO of the Hobby Lobby craft-store chain. ⊠ *400 4th St. SW, The Mall* ☎ *866/430–6682* ⊕ *www.museumofthebible.org* ⊠ *$20* Ⓜ *Smithsonian.*

★ National Archives Museum

LIBRARY | FAMILY | Monument, museum, and the nation's memory, the National Archives, headquartered in a grand

Continued on page 78

THE MALL
AMERICA'S TOWN GREEN

It could be said that the Mall—the heart of almost every visitor's trip to Washington—has influenced life in the U.S. more than any other expanse of lawn. The Mall is a picnicking park, a jogging path, and an outdoor stage for festivals and fireworks. People come here from around the globe to tour the illustrious Smithsonian museums, celebrate special events, or rally to make the world a better place.

The AIDS Memorial Quilt on the Mall in 1996.

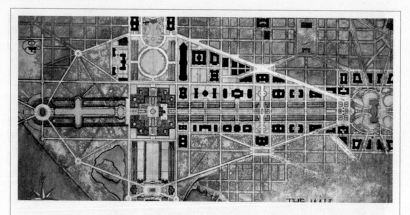

FROM TRASH HEAP TO TOURIST ATTRACTION: A BRIEF HISTORY OF THE MALL

Even before becoming the birthplace of American political protest, the Mall was a hotly contested piece of real estate. More than a century of setbacks and debate resulted not in Pierre L'Enfant's vision of a house-lined boulevard, but rather the premier green space you see today.

In 1791, Pierre Charles L'Enfant designed Washington, D.C., with a mile-long Grand Avenue running west from the Congress building. According to his plan, the boulevard would be lined with homes for statesmen and open green spaces, including a central garden bordered by a dense grove of trees.

L'Enfant's grandiose plan took more than 100 years to become a reality. By 1850, the area we now know as the Mall had not become a park, but was used instead as a storage area for lumber, firewood, and trash. With President Fillmore's permission, a group of businessmen hired landscape designer Andrew Jackson Downing to plan a national park featuring natural-style gardening. Sadly, Downing was killed in 1852, and his plan was never fully implemented.

Despite this setback, progress continued. The first Smithsonian museum on the Mall, the National Museum (now the Arts and Industries Building),

opened to the public in 1881, and after 35 years of construction, the Washington Monument was completed in 1884.

A victory for the Mall occurred in 1901, when the Senate Park Commission, or McMillan Commission, was created to redesign the Mall as the city's ceremonial center. The McMillan plan embraced L'Enfant's vision of formal, public spaces and civic art, but replaced his Grand Avenue with a 300-foot expanse of grass bordered by American elms. It also called for cultural and educational institutions to line the Mall. Finally, a modified version of L'Enfant's great open space would become a reality.

The National Park Service assumed management of the Mall in 1933. In the latter half of the twentieth century and into the twenty-first, new museums and monuments have opened on the Mall to create the public gathering place, tourist attraction, and tribute to our nation's heroes that we know today.

Above, McMillan Plan for the Mall, Washington, D.C., 1902.

Top, Martin Luther King Jr. delivers his I Have a Dream speech. Center, Vietnam War Veterans protest. Bottom, Million Man March.

HISTORIC RALLIES ON THE MALL

1894: Coxey's Army, a group of unemployed workers from Ohio, stage the first-ever protest march on Washington.

1939: Contralto Marian Anderson gives an Easter Sunday concert on the grounds of the Lincoln Memorial after the Daughters of the American Revolution bar her from performing at their headquarters.

1963: The Lincoln Memorial is the site of Martin Luther King Jr.'s inspirational I Have a Dream speech.

1971: The Vietnam Veterans Against the War camp out on the Mall to persuade Congress to end military actions in Southeast Asia.

1972: The first Earth Day is celebrated on April 22.

1987: The AIDS Memorial Quilt is displayed for the first time in its entirety. It returns to the Mall in 1988, 1989, 1992, and 1996.

1995: Nearly 400,000 African-American men fill the Mall, from the Capitol to the Washington Monument, during the Million Man March.

2009: The inauguration of President Barack Obama brings a record two million onlookers to the Mall.

2017: The Women's March on January 21, 2017, the day after President Donald Trump's inauguration, was the largest single-day protest in U.S. history.

WHAT ABOUT THE MONUMENTS?

Visitors often confuse the Mall with the similarly named National Mall. The Mall is the expanse of lawn between 3rd and 14th Streets, while the National Mall is the national park that spans from the Capitol to the Potomac, including the Mall, the monuments, and the Tidal Basin. To reach the monuments, head west from the Mall or south from the White House and be prepared for a long walk. To visit all the monuments in one day requires marathon-level stamina and good walking shoes. You're better off choosing your top priorities. Better may be to take a guided coach tour, or one at night.

TOP 15 THINGS
TO DO ON THE MALL

1. Ride the old-fashioned carousel in front of the Smithsonian Castle.

2. Watch the fireworks on the Fourth of July.

3. See the original Spirit of St. Louis, and then learn how things fly at the National Air and Space Museum.

4. Gross out your friends at the Natural History Museum's Insect Zoo.

5. Gawk at Dorothy's ruby slippers, Julia Child's kitchen, Abraham Lincoln's top hat, and Lewis and Clark's compass at the American History Museum.

6. Twirl around the ice skating rink in the National Gallery of Art's sculpture garden.

7. View astonishing wooden masks at the Museum of African Art.

8. Taste North, South, and Central American dishes at the National Museum of the American Indian's Mitsitam Café.

9. Exercise your First Amendment rights by joining a rally or protest.

10. Peek at the many-armed and elephant-headed statues of Hindu gods at the Sackler Gallery.

11. Pose with sculptures by Auguste Rodin and Henry Moore at the Hirshhorn Sculpture Garden.

12. Learn how you make money—literally—at the Bureau of Engraving and Printing.

13. Follow the lives of the people who lived and died in Nazi Germany at the Holocaust Memorial Museum.

14. Visit the newest museum, the National Museum of African American History and Culture.

15. Picnic and people-watch on the lawn after a hard day of sightseeing.

VISITING THE MUSEUMS ON THE MALL

MAKE THE MOST OF YOUR TIME

With 13 museums spread out along 11 city blocks, you can't expect to see everything in one day. Few people have the stamina for more than half a day of museum- or gallery-hopping at a time; children definitely don't. To avoid mental and physical exhaustion, try to devote at least two days to the Mall and use these itineraries to make the best use of your time.

Historical Appeal: For a day devoted to history and culture, start with the **National Archives,** grabbing lunch at its café. After refueling, the next stop is the **Smithsonian National Museum of American History.** Or, visit the **National Museum of the American Indian** or the **United States Holocaust Memorial Museum.** It takes planning, but a trip to the **National Museum of African American History and Culture** is a don't-miss experience.

Art Start: To fill a day with paintings and sculptures, begin at the **National Gallery of Art.** Enjoy the museum's sculptures while you dine in the garden's outdoor café. You'll find a second sculpture garden directly across the Mall at the **Hirshhorn.** If you like the

avant-garde, visit the Hirshhorn's indoor galleries; for a cosmopolitan collection of Asian and African art and artifacts, head instead to the **Sackler Gallery** and **Smithsonian Museum of African Art.**

Taking the Kids: The most kid-friendly museum of them all, the **Smithsonian National Air and Space Museum** is a must-see for the young and young-at-heart. There's only fast food in the museum, but the **Smithsonian Museum of the American Indian** next door has healthier options. If your young bunch can handle two museums in a day, cross the lawn to the **Smithsonian National Museum of Natural History.** This itinerary works well for science buffs, too.

THE BEST IN A DAY

Got one day and want to see the best of the Smithsonian? Start at the **Air and Space Museum,** then skip to the side-by-side **Natural History** and **American History Museums.** Picnic on the Mall or hit the museum cafeterias.

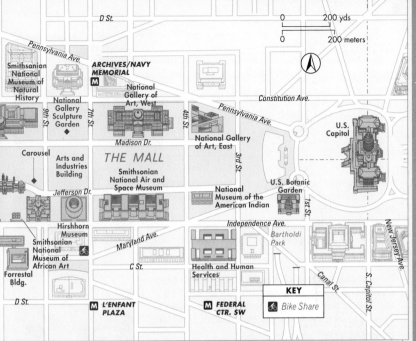

NOT ANOTHER HOT DOG! A Survival Guide to Eating Well on the Mall

Even locals wonder where to grab a decent bite to eat when touring the Smithsonian Museums. Hot dogs, soft pretzels, and ice cream from a cart don't make for a nutritious lunch. On a weekday, the streets north of Constitution Avenue offer easy-to-find lunch spots, but virtually all are closed on weekends.

Here are some places for better dining by the Mall, though several require a few blocks' walk.

On the Fly food carts offer eco-friendly, often organic snacks. Find one by the Sackler Gallery.

National Museum of the American Indian: The Mitsitam Café—the name means "let's eat" in the language of the Delaware and Piscataway people—is one of the best museum cafeterias on the Mall. Food stations serve native-inspired sandwiches, entrees, soups, and desserts from five regions of the western hemisphere.

Pavilion Café: Located in the **National Gallery's Sculpture Garden,** this eatery offers indoor and outdoor seating with views of the artwork and fountain/ice rink outside. The menu includes salads, sandwiches, and pizzas. You'll also find more food options inside the National Gallery.

Pennsylvania Avenue SE: If lunchtime finds you on the east end of the Mall, head past the Capitol to Pennsylvania Avenue SE. Between Second and Fourth Streets, you'll find plenty of pubs, cafés, and sandwich shops. It's a bit of a hike, but well worth the shoe leather.

Smithsonian National Museum of Natural History: Three high-quality restaurants focus on healthy, seasonal food, drinks, and desserts.

National Museum of African American History and Culture: Sweet Home Cafe, which serves diverse regional American cuisine, is among the best places to eat on the Mall.

ANNUAL EVENTS

The Mall's spacious lawn is ideal for all kinds of outdoor festivals. These annual events are local favorites and definitely worth a stop if you're in town while they're happening.

St. Patrick's Day Parade

WINTER

Ice Skating: Whirl and twirl at the outdoor ice rink in the National Gallery of Art's Sculpture Garden. *Mid-November through mid-March*

St. Patrick's Day Parade: Dancers, bands, and bagpipes celebrate all things Irish along Constitution Avenue. *Mid-March*

SPRING

National Cherry Blossom Festival: When the cherry trees burst into bloom, you know that spring has arrived. Fly a kite, watch a parade, and learn about Japanese culture in a setting sprinkled with pink and white flowers. *Late March through early April*

Cherry Blossom Festival

SUMMER

Smithsonian Folklife Festival: Performers, cooks, farmers, and craftsmen demonstrate cultural traditions from around the world. *Around July 4*

Independence Day: What better place to celebrate the birth of our nation than in the capital city? Enjoy concerts and parades on the Mall, then watch the fireworks explode over the Washington Monument. *July 4*

Screen on the Green: Film favorites are shown on a gigantic movie screen on Monday nights. Bring a blanket and picnic dinner to better enjoy the warm summer evenings. *Mid-July through mid-August*

Smithsonian Folklife Festival

Independence Day Reenactment

FALL

Black Family Reunion: D.C. celebrates African-American family values. Pavilions showcase businesses owned by African-Americans and events and performances feature black entertainers, celebrities, and experts. *September*

National Book Festival: Meet your favorite author in person at the Library of Congress' annual literary festival. Over 70 writers and illustrators participate in readings, live interviews, and events for kids. *September*

Marine Corps Marathon: The "Marathon of the Monuments" starts in Virginia but winds its way around the entire National Mall. It's as fun to cheer as it is to run. *Late October*

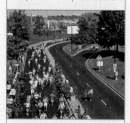
Marine Corps Marathon

PLANNING YOUR VISIT

National Cherry Blossom Festival Parade

KEEP IN MIND

■ All of the museums on the Mall are free to the public.

■ Since September 11, 2001 security has increased, and visitors will need to go through screenings and bag checks, which create long lines during peak tourist season.

■ Two museums require timed-entry passes: the Holocaust Museum from March through August, and the Bureau of Printing and Engraving. If you've got a jam-packed day planned, it's best to get your tickets early in the morning or in advance.

GETTING HERE AND GETTING AROUND

Metro Travel: You can access the Mall from several Metro stations. On the Blue and Orange lines, the Federal Triangle stop is convenient to the Natural History and American History museums, and the Smithsonian stop is close to the Holocaust Memorial Museum and Sackler Gallery. On the Yellow and Green lines, Archives/Navy Memorial takes you to the National Gallery of Art. The L'Enfant Plaza stop, accessible from the Blue, Orange, Yellow, and Green lines, is the best exit for the Hirshhorn and Air and Space Museum.

Bus Travel: Walking from the Holocaust Memorial Museum to the National Gallery of Art is quite a trek. Many visitors take advantage of the D.C. Circulator National Mall Route buses that cost just $1 and run daily.

Car Travel: Parking is hard to find along the Mall. You can find private parking garages north of the Mall in the Downtown area, where you'll have to pay to leave your car. If you're willing to walk, limited free parking is available on Ohio Drive SW near the Jefferson Memorial and East Potomac Park.

HELP, THERE'S A PROTEST ON THE MALL!

Since the 1890s, protesters have gathered on the Mall to make their opinions known. If you're not in a rallying mood, you don't have to let First Amendment activities prevent you from visiting the Smithsonian museums or enjoying a visit to the Mall.

■ **Use the back door:** All of the Smithsonian museums have entrances on Constitution or Independence Avenues, which do not border the Mall's lawn. Use these doors to gain admission without crossing the Mall itself.

■ **Know you're protected:** The Mall is a national park, just like Yosemite or Yellowstone. The National Park Service has a responsibility to visitors to make sure they can safely view park attractions. To this end, demonstrators are often required to keep main streets open.

■ **Avoid the crowds:** Even the biggest rallies don't cover the entire National Mall. If the crowd is by the Capitol, head west to visit the Lincoln Memorial. If protestors are gathered around the Washington Monument, visit the Jefferson Memorial on the opposite side of the Tidal Basin. There's plenty to see.

marble edifice on Constitution Avenue, preserves more than 12 billion paper records dating back to 1774 and billions of recent electronic records. The National Archives and Records Administration is charged with preserving and archiving the most historically important U.S. government records at its records centers nationwide and in presidential libraries.

Charters of Freedom—the Declaration of Independence, the Constitution, and the Bill of Rights—are the star attractions. They are housed in the Archives' cathedral-like rotunda, each on a marble platform, encased in bulletproof glass.

On display at the entrance to the David M. Rubenstein Gallery is a 1297 Magna Carta, the document of English common law whose language inspired the Constitution. This Magna Carta, one of four remaining originals, sets the stage for the *Records of Rights* exhibit in this interactive gallery that traces the civil rights struggles of African Americans, women, and immigrants. Highlights include the discharge papers of a slave who fought in the Revolutionary War to gain his freedom; the mark-up copy of the 1964 Civil Rights Act; and letters to the president from children who questioned segregation.

The Public Vaults go deep into the stacks. You can find records that give a glimpse into Federal investigations, from the Lincoln assassination to Watergate. Watch films of flying saucers, used as evidence in congressional UFO hearings, listen to the Nuremberg trials or Congress debating Prohibition. Reservations to visit the Archives are highly recommended. Reservations for guided tours, or for timed visit entries, should be made at least six weeks in advance. ⊠ *Constitution Ave., between 7th and 9th Sts., Federal Triangle* ☎ *866/272-6272, 877/444-6777 tours and reservations* ⊕ *www.archives. gov* ⊠ *Free; $2 fee for reservations* Ⓜ *Archives–Navy Memorial–Penn Quarter.*

National Gallery of Art, East Building

MUSEUM | The East Building opened in 1978 in response to the changing needs of the National Gallery, especially to house a growing collection of modern and contemporary art. The building itself is a modern masterpiece. The trapezoidal shape of the site prompted architect I.M. Pei's dramatic approach: two interlocking spaces shaped like triangles provide room for a library, galleries, auditoriums, and administrative offices. Inside the ax-blade-like southwest corner, the sunlit atrium is dominated by a colorful 76-foot-long Alexander Calder mobile. Visitors can view a dynamic 500-piece collection of photography, paintings, sculpture, works on paper, and media arts in thought-provoking chronological, thematic, and stylistic arrangements.

Highlights include galleries devoted to Mark Rothko's giant, glowing canvases, Barnett Newman's 14 stark black, gray, and white canvas paintings from *The Stations of the Cross, 1958–1966,* and several colorful and whimsical Alexander Calder mobiles and sculptures. You can't miss Katharina Fritsch's *Hahn/Cock, 2013,* a tall blue rooster that appears to be standing guard over the street and federal buildings below from the museum's roof terrace that also offers views of the Capitol. The Upper Level gallery showcases modern art from 1910–80 including masterpieces by Constantin Brancusi, Marcel Duchamp, Sam Gilliam, Henri Matisse, Joan Miró, Piet Mondrian, Jackson Pollock, and Andy Warhol. Ground-level galleries are devoted to American art from 1900–50, including pieces by George Bellows, Edward Hopper, Georgia O'Keeffe, Charles Sheeler, and Alfred Stieglitz. The concourse level is reserved for rotating special exhibitions.

The East Building Shop is located on the concourse level and Terrace Café looks out over the atrium from the upper level. You can access an audio tour on your mobile device, and docent-led tours are available most days at 1:30 pm. ⊠ *Constitution Ave., between 3rd and 4th Sts. NW, The Mall* ☎ *202/737–4215* ⊕ *www. nga.gov* ⊠ *Free* Ⓜ *Archives–Navy Memorial–Penn Quarter.*

National Gallery of Art, West Building

MUSEUM | The two buildings of the National Gallery hold one of the world's foremost art collections, with paintings, sculptures, and graphics dating from the 13th to 21st centuries. Opened in 1941, the museum was a gift to the nation from treasury secretary Andrew W. Mellon. The rotunda, with marble columns surrounding a fountain, sets the stage for the masterpieces on display in more than 100 galleries.

Ginevra de' Benci, the only painting by Leonardo da Vinci on display in the Americas, is the centerpiece of the collection's comprehensive survey of Italian Renaissance paintings and sculpture. Rembrandt van Rijn and Johannes Vermeer, masters of painting light, anchor the magnificent collection of Dutch and Flemish works. The 19th-century French Galleries house gorgeous French impressionist masterworks by such superstars as Vincent van Gogh, Paul Cézanne, Claude Monet, Auguste Renoir, and Edgar Degas.

Walk beneath flowering trees in the sculpture garden, located on the Mall between 7th and 9th Streets. Granite walkways guide you through a shaded landscape featuring works from the Gallery's growing collection, as well as loans for special exhibitions.

There are many free docent-led tours every day, and a recorded tour of highlights of the collection is available free on the main floor adjacent to the rotunda. For a quick tour, pick up the laminated "What to See in One Hour," which pinpoints 12 must-see masterworks. The Information Room maintains a database of more than 1,700 works of art from the collection. Touch-screen monitors provide access to color images, text, animation, and sounds to help you better understand the works. ⊠ *4th St. and Constitution Ave. NW, The Mall* ☎ *202/737–4215* ⊕ *www.nga.gov* ⊠ *Free* Ⓜ *Archives–Navy Memorial–Penn Quarter.*

★ National Museum of African American History and Culture

MUSEUM | Washington's newest, most powerful museum is perhaps best summed up with a quote by founding director Lonnie Bunch: "The African American experience is the lens through which we understand what it is to be an American." The museum serves as that lens, thanks to the 12 exhibitions that display nearly 3,000 historical artifacts, documents, photographs, memorabilia, and media.

The building's structure resembles nothing else on the Mall. The shape of its bronze-color corona was inspired by a Nigerian artist's carving, which is prominently displayed in one of the galleries. The corona's filigree design was patterned after railings made by enslaved 19th-century craftsmen. The museum's three tiers are hung at the same angle as the Washington Monument's capstone (it makes for a dramatic photo). Powerful quotes from African Americans are strategically placed throughout the space. The museum is divided into two parts: 60% of the museum is underground and the remaining 40% is aboveground. Exhibits underground share a somber and wrenching historical time line from slavery through civil rights. Aboveground, galleries celebrate the cultural contributions of African Americans.

To best experience this museum, start at the underground Concourse History Galleries. Here you'll see wreckage from a slave ship that broke apart off Cape Town, South Africa, in 1794 that drowned 212 people; a 19th-century slave cabin from Edisto Island, South Carolina, that was occupied until 1980;

I CHERISH MY OWN FREEDOM DEARLY,
BUT I CARE EVEN MORE FOR YOUR FREEDOM
NELSON MANDELA 199

Did You Know

Within the National Museum of African American History and Culture, you'll find a collection of the country's most moving and powerful exhibits. If necessary, visitors can take time to emotionally recharge within the contemplative space known as the reflection room, where a glass structure called the oculus allows light in from above, and a waterfall effect offers a quiet space for reflection.

the original casket of 14-year-old Emmett Till, who was murdered in Mississippi in 1955 for allegedly flirting with a white woman; a railcar with its very different first-class and "colored" sections; and a biplane used to train the Tuskegee Airmen who fought in WWII. Also on the main Concourse level is the 350-seat Oprah Winfrey Theater that hosts musical performances, lectures and discussions, film presentations, and other programming. The Center for African American Media Arts is on the second floor, where visitors can research their families in a genealogy center.

The third- and fourth-floor galleries have a more spirited vibe. Highlights include sports memorabilia like Jesse Owens's cleats, Michael Jordan's 1996 jersey, Joe Louis's gloves, Muhammad Ali's robe, Gabby Douglas's leotard, and nine Olympic medals won by Carl Lewis. Other collection gems include a lobby card from the 1967 movie *Guess Who's Coming to Dinner*; Louis Armstrong's trumpet; Michael Jackson's sequined jacket; and Marian Anderson's jacket and skirt that she wore when she performed a 1939 concert from the Lincoln Memorial, among many others.

You must have a timed pass to enter the museum. Same-day, timed passes are available online daily beginning at 6:30 am. A limited number of walk-up passes are given out weekdays beginning at 1 pm, but they go fast. Download the NMAAHC mobile app to further enhance your visiting experience. ⊠ *1400 Constitution Ave. NW, The Mall* ✛ *14th and Constitution Ave. NW* ☏ *202/633–1000, 844/750–3012 for timed-entry passes only* ⊕ *www.nmaahc.si.edu* ⊠ *Free* Ⓜ *Smithsonian or Federal Triangle.*

National Museum of the American Indian

MUSEUM | Visually and conceptually, the National Museum of the American Indian stands apart from the other cultural institutions on the Mall. The exterior, clad in Minnesota limestone, evokes a sense that the building was carved by wind and water. Inside, four floors of galleries cover 10,000 years of history of the native tribes of the Western Hemisphere. However, only 5% of the museum's holdings are on display at any one time. Touring with one of the "cultural interpreters" helps bring the history and legends to life. Live music, dance, theater, and storytelling are central to experiencing this museum. Tribal groups stage performances in the Rasmuson Theater and sunlit Potomac atrium. The most recent exhibition, *Americans,* runs through 2022, revealing the deep connection between Americans and American Indians, as well as how Indians have been embedded in unexpected ways in the history, pop culture, and the identity of the United States.

The Great Inka Road: Engineering an Empire explores the 20,000-mile road that crosses rivers, deserts, and mountains linking Cusco, the center of the Inca, to the farthest reaches of its empire. *Our Universe* exhibit tells the unique creation legends of eight different tribes, with carvings, regalia, and videos of tribal storytellers. *Nation to Nation: Treaties Between the United States and American Indian Nations* shares the history and legacy of U.S.–American Indian diplomacy from the colonial period to the present.

Visit between 11 and 2 on a sunny day to see the Potomac atrium awash in rainbows created by the light refracted through prisms in the southern wall, aligned to show the passage of time, with specific patterns marking the equinoxes and solstices. Free tours are offered weekdays at 1:30, and the museum's family-friendly imagiNATIONS Activity Center includes hands-on activities throughout the year. ⊠ *4th St. and Independence Ave. SW, The Mall* ☏ *202/633–1000* ⊕ *www.americanindian. si.edu* ⊠ *Free* Ⓜ *L'Enfant Plaza.*

Old Post Office Pavilion

CLOCK | Although the building is now the Trump International Hotel, the Old Post Office Tower (which is located within the hotel) is still available for tours to the public through the National Park Service. The building was a symbol of the modern American spirit when it was built in 1899 and was the first government building to have its own electric power plant. Now, tourists can see the 360-degree view from the top of the tower, the second-tallest building in D.C. Tours are free, but tour guests must enter through a specified entrance for the general public. Tours are from 9 to 5 daily with the last entry at 4:30. ✉ *Trump International Hotel, 1100 Pennsylvania Ave. NW, The Mall* ☎ *202/289–4224* ⊕ *www.nps.gov* Ⓜ *Federal Triangle.*

Ronald Reagan Building and International Trade Center

GOVERNMENT BUILDING | At more than 3 million square feet, this is the largest federal building in Washington, and the only structure used by both government and private entities. A blend of classical and modern architecture, it is also officially the World Trade Center, Washington, D.C. The Reagan Building hosts special events throughout the year, in addition to its permanent art collection including a section of the Berlin Wall and the Woodrow Wilson Presidential Memorial Exhibit and Learning Center. In summer, check out Live!, a free concert series, performed daily from noon to 1:30. A farmers' market takes over the plaza on Friday during the spring and summer. ✉ *1300 Pennsylvania Ave. NW, Federal Triangle* ☎ *202/312–1300* ⊕ *www.itcdc. com* 🖾 *Free* Ⓜ *Federal Triangle.*

Smithsonian Castle Information Center

MUSEUM | The original home of the Smithsonian Institution is an excellent first stop on the Mall to help you get your bearings and plan your exploration of the museums. Built of red sandstone, this Medieval Revival style building, better known as the "Castle," was designed by James Renwick Jr., the architect of St. Patrick's Cathedral in New York City. Although British scientist and founder James Smithson never visited America, his will stipulated that, should his nephew, Henry James Hungerford, die without an heir, Smithson's entire fortune would go to the United States, "to found at Washington, under the name of the Smithsonian Institution, an establishment for the increase and diffusion of knowledge." The museums on the Mall are the Smithsonian's most visible example of this ideal, but the organization also sponsors traveling exhibitions and maintains research posts in the Chesapeake Bay area and the tropics of Panama.

A 10-minute video gives an overview of the Smithsonian museums and the National Zoo, and the exhibition *The Smithsonian Institution: America's Treasure Chest* features objects representing all the museums, which reveal the breadth and depth of the Smithsonian's collections. James Smithson's crypt is in a small chapel-like room here. The Castle also has *Views from the Tall Tower*, an exhibit that lets you see how the Washington skyline has changed since 1863, a good café, brochures in several languages, and a museum store. Kids appreciate the historic carousel at the north entrance; at the south entrance you'll find the beautifully manicured Haupt Garden and copper-domed kiosk called the S. Dillon Ripley Center, which houses the Discovery Theater (delightful and affordable live, family-oriented shows on selected weekday mornings—usually geared for kids 2–12—are held here). ✉ *1000 Jefferson Dr. SW, The Mall* ☎ *202/633–1000* ⊕ *www.si.edu* 🖾 *Free* Ⓜ *Smithsonian.*

★ Smithsonian National Air and Space Museum

MUSEUM | This is the country's second-most-visited museum, attracting 9 million people annually to the world's largest collection of historic aircraft and spacecraft. The 22 galleries tell the story of aviation from the earliest human attempts at flight to supersonic jets and spacecraft. The museum has begun a multiyear renovation process to update and redesign all of the galleries by 2022, though it will remain open throughout the whole process, closing only construction areas.

Boeing Milestones of Flight Hall, which traces the evolution of air and space travel, captures visitors' excitement as soon as they enter the museum. Highlights include the Ryan NYP *Spirit of St. Louis*; North American *X-15*; Bell X-1 *Glamorous Glennis*; Mariner, Pioneer, and Viking planetary explorers; *SpaceShipOne* and Mercury *Friendship 7*. It's here where you can even touch a moon rock.

In the kid-friendly and very hands-on How Things Fly Gallery, exhibits explore the principles of gravity and air, supersonic flight, wing technology, aircraft and rocket propulsion, and space travel.

On the second floor, you can see the 1903 *Wright Flyer* that Wilbur and Orville Wright piloted over the sands of Kitty Hawk, North Carolina.

You can even climb into one of the museum's six motion simulators that let you experience the thrill of barrel rolls, space walking, and aerial combat. Or, immerse yourself in space by taking in an IMAX film. The movies—some in 3-D—employ swooping aerial scenes that make you feel as if you've left the ground and fascinating high-definition footage taken in deep space. ■ TIP→ **Buy IMAX theater and planetarium tickets up to two weeks in advance or as soon as you arrive (times and prices vary); then tour the museum.**

Free docent-led tours leave daily at 10:30 and 1 from the museum's welcome center.

The three-story museum store is the largest in all the Smithsonian museums,

and one of the best. You'll find souvenirs, clothing, books and movies, kites, and loads of collectors' items. A huge food court offers Boston Market, Donatos Pizzeria, and McDonald's fare. And if you have time, stop in at the Public Observatory on the museum's east terrace for a chance to peer through telescopes for a daytime look at the universe. It's open Wednesday through Sunday noon–3. ⊠ *Independence Ave. at 6th St. SW, The Mall* ☎ *202/633–1000, 866/868–7774 movie information* ⊕ *www.airandspace. si.edu* ✉ *Free; IMAX or planetarium $9; IMAX feature film $15; flight simulators $7–$8* Ⓜ *Smithsonian.*

Smithsonian National Museum of African Art

MUSEUM | FAMILY | This unique underground building houses stunning galleries, a library, photographic archives, and educational facilities that are dedicated to collecting, conserving, and studying Africa's arts and culture from a wide variety of media and eras. The rotating exhibits illuminate African visual arts, including sculpture, textiles, photography, archaeology, and modern art. *Currents: Water in African Art* showcases the power of art through pieces like intricately carved wooden masks and figures paying tribute to water spirits and deities. *African Mosaic: Celebrating a Decade of Collecting* presents a dynamic exhibition of paintings, sculpture, carvings, jewelry, clothing, and face masks, presented thematically so that visitors are encouraged to reflect on the connections between the artworks and what they communicate to the viewer. The museum's educational programs for both children and adults include films with contemporary perspectives on African life, storytelling programs, and festivals including Community Day. The hands-on workshops, such as traditional basket weaving, bring Africa's oral and cultural traditions to life. Workshops and demonstrations by African and African American artists offer a chance to meet and talk to practicing artists. ✉ *950 Independence Ave. SW, The Mall* ☎ *202/633–4600* ⊕ *africa.si.edu* 🎫 *Free* Ⓜ *Smithsonian.*

★ Smithsonian National Museum of American History

MUSEUM | FAMILY | The 3 million artifacts and archival collections in the country's largest American history museum explore America's cultural, political and scientific past, with holdings as diverse and iconic as Abraham Lincoln's top hat, Thomas Edison's light bulbs, Julia Child's kitchen, and Judy Garland's famed ruby slippers from the film *The Wizard of Oz*. The centerpiece of the **Star-Spangled Banner** gallery is the banner that in 1814 was hoisted to show that Fort McHenry had survived 25 hours of British rocket attacks and inspired Francis Scott Key to write the lyrics that became the national anthem. **American Stories** showcases historic and cultural touchstones of American history through more than 100 objects from the museum's vast holdings that rotate frequently: a walking stick used by Benjamin Franklin, a sunstone capital from a Mormon temple, Archie Bunker's chair, Muhammad Ali's boxing gloves, a fragment of Plymouth Rock, and a Jim Henson Muppet. Highlights tours are offered daily at 10:15 am and 1 pm. The Smithsonian Chamber Music Society and Smithsonian Jazz hold regular concerts at the museum. ✉ *Constitution Ave. and 14th St. NW, The Mall* ☎ *202/633–1000* ⊕ *www.american-history.si.edu* 🎫 *Free* Ⓜ *Smithsonian or Federal Triangle.*

Smithsonian National Museum of Natural History

MUSEUM | FAMILY | One of the world's great natural history museums offers 18 exhibition halls filled with giant dinosaur fossils, glittering gems, creepy-crawly insects, and other natural delights. There are more than 145 million specimens in all. Marvel at the enormous African bush elephant that greets visitors in the rotunda of the museum and learn about elephant behavior and conservation efforts. Discover **Q?RIUS**, a state-of-the-art, hands-on space featuring 6,000 objects, on-site experts, and an array of digital tools that focus on the natural world. Walk among hundreds of live butterflies in the **Butterfly Pavilion** ($). Check out giant millipedes and furry tarantulas in the **O. Orkin Insect Zoo** (don't miss the daily live tarantula feedings). See perfectly preserved giant squids, a jaw-dropping replica of a whale, and the ecosystem of a living coral reef in the **Sant Ocean Hall**. Watch as paleobiologists study the newest addition to the museum's collection of 46 million fossils, including the nation's T. rex found in Montana in 1988; a fully renovated Dinosaur and Fossil Hall is scheduled to reopen after renovations in 2019. ✉ *Constitution Ave. and 10th St. NW, The Mall* ☎ *202/633–1000* ⊕ *www.mnh.si.edu* 🎫 *Free; Butterfly Pavilion $6 (free Tues.)* Ⓜ *Smithsonian or Federal Triangle.*

★ Thomas Jefferson Memorial

MEMORIAL | In the 1930s Congress decided that Thomas Jefferson deserved a monument positioned as prominently as those honoring Washington and Lincoln. Workers scooped and moved tons of the river bottom to create dry land for the spot due south of the White House where the monument was built. Jefferson had always admired the Pantheon in Rome, so the memorial's architect, John Russell Pope, drew on it for inspiration. His finished work was dedicated on April 13, 1943, the bicentennial of Jefferson's birth. The bronze statue of Jefferson, standing on a 6-foot granite pedestal, looms larger than life. You can get a taste of Jefferson's keen intellect from his writings about freedom and government inscribed on the marble walls surrounding his statue. Check out the view of the White House from the memorial's steps—it's one of the best in the city. Learn more about Jefferson by visiting the exhibit called *Light and Liberty* on the memorial's lower level.

DC's Famed Cherry Blossoms

The first batch of cherry trees arrived from Japan in 1909, but they were infected with insects and fungus, and the Department of Agriculture ordered them destroyed. A diplomatic crisis was averted when the United States politely asked the Japanese for another batch, and in 1912 First Lady Helen Taft planted the first tree. The second was planted by the wife of the Japanese ambassador, Viscountess Chinda. There are 3,500 total trees around the Tidal Basin, some of which are considered original from 1912.

The ornamental Japanese cherry trees that line the Tidal Basin are now the centerpiece of Washington's three-week **National Cherry Blossom Festival**, held each spring since 1935. The festivities are kicked off by the lighting of a ceremonial Japanese lantern that rests on the north shore of the Tidal Basin, not far from where the first tree was planted in 1912 by First Lady Helen Taft. The celebration has grown over the years to include concerts, a running race, a kite festival, and a parade. The trees are usually in bloom for about 12 days in late March or early April. When winter will not release its grip, parade and festival take place without the presence of blossoms.

It chronicles highlights of Jefferson's life and has a time line of world history during his lifetime. ⊠ *Tidal Basin, south bank, off Ohio Dr. SW, The Mall* ☎ *202/426–6841* ⊕ *www.nps.gov/thje* 🎟 *Free* Ⓜ *Smithsonian.*

★ Tidal Basin

NATIONAL/STATE PARK | FAMILY | The Tidal Basin, a partially man-made reservoir between the Potomac and the Washington Channel, is part of West Potomac Park, adjacent to the Mall. It's the setting for memorials to Thomas Jefferson, Franklin Delano Roosevelt, Martin Luther King Jr., and George Mason. Two sculpted heads on the sides of the Inlet Bridge can be seen as you walk along the sidewalk that hugs the basin. The inside walls of the bridge also feature two other sculptures: bronze, human-headed fish that once spouted water from their mouths. Sculptor Constantin Sephralis modeled the fish after Jack Fish, the chief of the park, who retired at the time Sephralis made the sculptures. Once you cross the bridge, continue along the Tidal Basin to the right. This route is especially scenic when the famous cherry trees are

in bloom. The trees, a gift from the Japanese during the administration of William Howard Taft, are perhaps the Tidal Basin's most iconic feature beyond the memorials. ⊠ *Bordered by Independence and Maine Aves., The Mall* Ⓜ *Smithsonian.*

★ United States Holocaust Memorial Museum

MUSEUM | This museum asks visitors to consider how the Holocaust was made possible by the choices of individuals, institutions, and governments, and what lessons they hold for us today. The permanent exhibition, *The Holocaust*, tells the stories of the millions of Jews, Gypsies, Jehovah's Witnesses, homosexuals, political prisoners, the mentally ill, and others killed by the Nazis between 1933 and 1945. The exhibitions are detailed and sometimes graphic; the experiences memorable and powerful.

Upon arrival, you are issued an "identity card" containing biographical information on a real person from the Holocaust. As you move through the museum, you read sequential updates on your card. Hitler's rise to power and the spread of

European anti-Semitism are thoroughly documented in the museum's early exhibits, with films of Nazi rallies, posters, newspaper articles, and recordings of Hitler's speeches immersing you in the world that led to the Holocaust. Exhibits include footage of scientific experiments done on Jews, artifacts such as a freight car like those used to transport Jews to concentration camps, and oral testimonies from Auschwitz survivors.

Also on view is *Some Were Neighbors: Collaboration & Complicity in the Holocaust,* which examines how the Holocaust was made possible by decisions made by ordinary individuals. *I Want Justice* details the past and current judicial efforts to hold perpetrators accountable from the Nuremberg to Cambodia trials. *Genocide: The Threat Continues* looks at the people and places who are currently at risk. As part of this exhibit, visitors can speak in real time with people who have escaped genocidal and war crimes in northern Iraq and Syria.

After this powerful experience, the *Hall of Remembrance,* filled with candles, provides a much-needed space for quiet reflection.

Timed-entry passes (distributed on a first-come, first-served basis at the 14th Street entrance starting at 9:45 am or available in advance through the museum's website with a $1 per ticket service fee) are necessary for the permanent exhibition from March through August. Allow extra time to enter the building in spring and summer, when long lines can form. From September through February, no passes are required. ⊠ *100 Raoul Wallenberg Pl. SW, at 14th St. SW, The Mall* ☎ *202/488–0400, 800/400–9373 for tickets* ⊕ *www.ushmm.org* ✉ *Free; $1 per ticket service fee for advance online reservations* Ⓜ *Smithsonian.*

★ **Vietnam Veterans Memorial**
MEMORIAL | "The Wall," as it's commonly called, is one of the most visited sites in Washington. The names of more than 58,000 Americans who died in the Vietnam War are etched in its black granite panels, creating a powerful memorial. It was conceived by Jan Scruggs, a corporal who served in Vietnam, and designed by Maya Lin, a then 21-year-old architecture student at Yale.

Thousands of offerings are left at the wall each year; many people leave flowers, others leave the clothing of soldiers or letters of thanks.

In 1984, Frederick Hart's statue of three soldiers and a flagpole was erected to the south of the wall, with the goal of winning over veterans who considered the memorial a "black gash of shame." In 2004, a plaque was added to honor veterans who died after the war as a direct result of injuries in Vietnam, but who fall outside Department of Defense guidelines for remembrance at the wall.

The Vietnam Women's Memorial was dedicated in 1993. Glenna Goodacre's bronze sculpture depicts two women caring for a wounded soldier while a third kneels nearby; eight trees around the plaza commemorate the eight women in the military who died in Vietnam.

Names on the wall are ordered by date of death. To find a name, consult the alphabetical lists found at either end of the wall. You can get assistance locating a name at the white kiosk with the brown roof near the entrance. At the wall, rangers and volunteers wearing yellow caps can look up the names and supply you with paper and pencils for making rubbings. Every name on the memorial is preceded (on the west wall) or followed (on the east wall) by a symbol designating status. A diamond indicates "KIA." A plus sign (found by a small percentage of names) indicates "MIA." ⊠ *Constitution Gardens, 23rd St. NW and Constitution Ave. NW, The Mall* ☎ *202/426–6841* ⊕ *www.nps.gov/vive* ✉ *Free* Ⓜ *Foggy Bottom–GWU.*

The United States Holocaust Memorial Museum is the country's official memorial remembering those lost in the Holocaust.

Washington Monument

MEMORIAL | The 555-foot, 5 1/8-inch Washington Monument punctuates the capital like a huge exclamation point. The monument was part of Pierre L'Enfant's plan for Washington, but his intended location proved to be marshy, so it was moved 100 yards southeast. Construction began in 1848 and continued until 1884. Upon completion, the monument was the world's tallest structure and weighed more than 81,000 tons. Six years into construction, members of the anti-Catholic Know-Nothing Party stole and smashed a block of marble donated by Pope Pius IX. This action, combined with funding shortages and the onset of the Civil War, brought construction to a halt. After the war, building finally resumed, and though the new marble came from the same Maryland quarry as the old, it was taken from a different stratum with a slightly different shade. Inserted into the walls of the monument are 193 memorial stones from around the world. The Monument, undergoing an elevator modernization project, is scheduled to reopen in the spring of 2019. ⊠ *15th St. NW, between Constitution Ave. NW and Independence Ave. SW, The Mall* ☎ *202/426–6841* ⊕ *www.nps.gov/wamo* Ⓜ *Smithsonian.*

West Potomac Park

CITY PARK | **FAMILY** | Between the Potomac and the Tidal Basin, this park is known for its flowering cherry trees, which bloom for two weeks in late March or early April, and for a slew of memorials, including those of Abraham Lincoln, Martin Luther King Jr., Franklin Delano Roosevelt, Thomas Jefferson, and George Mason, as well as the World War II, Korean War, and Vietnam War Veterans memorials. It's a nice place to picnic and play ball, where families can relax and admire the views of the water. ⊠ *Bounded by Constitution Ave., 17th St., and Independence Ave., The Mall* ⊕ *www. npca.org.*

World War II Memorial

MEMORIAL | This symmetrically designed monument, in a parklike setting between the Washington Monument and Lincoln

Every Memorial Day, thousands flock to the Vietnam Veterans Memorial to pay their respects to those lost in the conflict.

Memorial, honors the 16 million Americans who served in the armed forces, the more than 400,000 who died, and all who supported the war effort at home. An imposing circle of 56 granite pillars, each bearing a bronze wreath, represents the United States and its territories of 1941–45. Four bronze eagles, a bronze garland, and two 43-foot-tall arches inscribed with "Atlantic" and "Pacific," representing victory on both fronts, surround the large circular plaza. The roar of the water comes from the Rainbow Pool, here since the 1920s and renovated to form the centerpiece of the memorial. There are also two fountains and two waterfalls. The Field of Stars, a wall of over 4,000 gold stars, commemorates the more than 400,000 Americans who lost their lives in the war. Bas-relief panels depict women in the military, medics, the bond drive, and V-J Day, all telling the story of how World War II affected Americans daily. ⊠ *17th St. SW and Home Front Dr. SW, between Independence Ave. SW and Constitution Ave. NW, The Mall* ☎ *202/426–6841* ⊕ *www.nps.gov/ nwwm* 🖃 *Free* Ⓜ *Smithsonian.*

🍴 Restaurants

Dining on the Mall is not what is used to be, with museums constantly upping the game for internal restaurants. The National Musum of African American History and Culture, the National Gallery of Art, and the National Museum of the American Indian are leading the charge for dining experiences on the Mall. For a quick bite, stop at one of the many food trucks sprinkled around the Mall, or head over to L'Enfant Plaza for fast food. If you are on the northeastern end of the Mall, it may be closer to walk north to the Penn Quarter.

Garden Café

$$ | AMERICAN | After marveling at the masterpieces in the National Gallery West Building, sit down in a lovely open courtyard, complete with a fountain and full dining service. This is not the usual museum cafeteria; you'll feast on delicately displayed seasonal salads and a sumptuous plate of chicken or fish. **Known for:** sophisticated menu; weekend brunch; serious desserts from an in-house pastry chef. $ *Average main: $20* ⊠ *National Gallery of Art, West Building, 6th and Constitution Ave. NW, The Mall* ✛ *Enter at 6th St.* ☎ *202/842–6716, 202/712–7453 reservations* ⊕ *www.nga.gov/visit/cafes/garden-cafe.html* ⊘ *No dinner* Ⓜ *Archives–Navy Memorial–Penn Quarter.*

Manna

$$ | **MEDITERRANEAN** | This museum restaurant is a foray into the past with a menu full of biblically inspired names like A Taste of Canaan, Revelations, and Exodus. The reality is that chef Todd Gray has created a menu filled with traditional falafel, lamb meatballs, and roasted eggplant over sides of marinated chickpeas and tabbouleh with pistachios and dates. **Known for:** Mediterranean-inspired cuisine with Biblical names; Sunday gospel brunch; open-seating concept. $ *Average main: $19* ⊠ *Museum of the Bible, 400 4th St. SW, The Mall* ☎ *855/554–5300* ⊕ *www.museumofthebible.org/museum/dining* ⊘ *No dinner* Ⓜ *Federal Center SW.*

Mitsitam Native Foods Cafe

$$ | **AMERICAN** | The food stations here offer both traditional and contemporary Native American dishes from throughout the Western Hemisphere. Executive chef Freddie Bitsoie offers seasonal menus from five regional native cuisines. **Known for:** seasonal cuisine from different native traditions; fry bread and corn totopos; cafeteria-style food stations. $ *Average main:* ⊠ *National Museum of the American Indian, 4th St. SW and Independence Ave. SW, The Mall* ☎ *202/868–7774* ⊕ *www.mitsitamcafe.com* ⊘ *No dinner* Ⓜ *Federal Center SW.*

Muze

$$$ | **ASIAN FUSION** | Hotel guests and visitors get a refreshing Asian twist on American favorites, blending the hotel's origins in China with modern-day D.C. Explore dim sum for breakfast, or try some of the well-known favorites for lunch and dinner, including grilled verlasso salmon, lobster pappardelle, and corn-crusted black grouper. **Known for:** Asian-Eastern fusion; all meals served; adjoining Empress lounge. $ *Average main: $33* ⊠ *Mandarin Oriental, Washington, DC, 1330 Maryland Ave. SW, The Mall* ☎ *202/787–6148* ⊕ *www.mandarin-oriental.com* Ⓜ *L'Enfant Plaza.*

Pavilion Café

$ | **CAFÉ** | At the edge of the National Gallery of Art's Sculpture Garden, you can sidle up to the counter and feast your eyes on the menu items before deciding what you'll order. From pastries to anything-but-ordinary salads to hot and cold sandwiches with Southwest or East Asian flavors, you'll have an array of choices. **Known for:** summer barbecue during Jazz in the Garden; boozy beverages during winter; pastries made fresh in-house. $ *Average main: $11* ⊠ *National Gallery Scultupre Garden, Constitution Ave NW and 7th St., The Mall* ✛ *At far end of National Gallery of Art Sculpture Garden* ☎ *202/289–3361* ⊕ *www.nga.gov/visit/cafes/pavilion-cafe.html/* ⊘ *No dinner* Ⓜ *Archives–Navy Memorial–Penn Quarter or L'Enfant Plaza.*

★ Sweet Home Café

$ | **AMERICAN** | The Mall's newest museum restaurant offers traditional and authentic dishes that rotate based on the seasons. Executive chef Jerome Grant infuses locally sourced ingredients and a from-scratch cooking style to showcase the rich history of African American cuisine from four distinct geographic regions. **Known for:** regional food stations; African American–style cuisine; rotating seasonal menus. $ *Average main: $13* ⊠ *National Museum of African American History, 1400 Constitution Ave. NW, The Mall* ☎ *202/633–6174* ⊕ *www.nmaahc.si.edu* ⊘ *No dinner* Ⓜ *Smithsonian or Federal Triangle.*

Hotels

The Mandarin Oriental stands out in luxury and experience for lodging near the Mall. However, other conveniently located chain hotels can be found in the area around L'Enfant Plaza, immediately south of the Mall, including a Hilton, Hyatt Place, and a Residence Inn.

Holiday Inn Washington-Capitol
$$ | **HOTEL** | **FAMILY** | One block from the National Air and Space Museum, this family-friendly hotel is in a great location for those bound for the Smithsonian museums, and, with Old Towne Trolley Tours stopping here, getting around town is a snap. **Pros:** rooftop pool and large deck area; kids eat for free; close to the best museums in town. **Cons:** limited dining options nearby; not much going on in the neighborhood at night; self-parking is available, but expensive. [$] *Rooms from: $210* ✉ *550 C St. SW, The Mall* ☎ *202/479–4000* 🌐 *www.hicapitoldc.com* 🛏 *536 rooms* 🍴 *No meals* [M] *L'Enfant Plaza.*

Mandarin Oriental, Washington DC
$$$$ | **HOTEL** | This luxury Asian chain made its way west to D.C. in 2004, offering the maximum in creature comforts on the Mall, a perfect place for luxury-seekers who want to visit the museums but also the Navy Yard and the Wharf along the southwest waterfront. **Pros:** plenty of luxury; reasonably close to both the Mall and waterfront; fantastic spa, pool, and fitness area. **Cons:** few nearby dining options outside the hotel itself; you'll need to take a car or taxi to get here; rates can be very high during much of the year. [$] *Rooms from: $495* ✉ *1330 Maryland Ave. SW, The Mall* ☎ *202/554–8588* 🌐 *www.mandarinoriental.com* 🛏 *397 rooms* 🍴 *No meals* [M] *L'Enfant Plaza.*

Performing Arts

FILM

★ **National Archives Film Series**
FILM | Historical films, usually documentaries, are shown here regularly. Screenings range from Robert Flaherty's 1942 coverage of the plight of migrant workers to archival footage of Charles Lindbergh's solo flight from New York to Paris. After catching a documentary, stroll by and inspect the Constitution and other world-changing documents in this solemn and impressive venue. ✉ *Constitution Ave. between 7th and 9th Sts. NW, Federal Triangle* ☎ *202/501–5000* 🌐 *www.archives.gov* [M] *Archives–Navy Memorial–Penn Quarter.*

National Gallery of Art Film Series
FILM | Free classic and international films, from Steven Spielberg's first feature-length film, *Duel*, to Béla Tarr's *Macbeth* that was filmed inside a Budapest castle, are usually shown in this museum's large auditorium each weekend. Sometimes films complement the exhibits. For more information about the specific films, pick up a film calendar at the museum or go online. ✉ *National Gallery of Art, East Building, Constitution Ave. between 3rd and 4th Sts. NW, The Mall* ☎ *202/842–6799* 🌐 *www.nga.gov* [M] *Archives–Navy Memorial–Penn Quarter.*

CONCERTS

Armed Forces Concert Series
MUSIC | In a Washington tradition, bands from the four branches of the armed services perform from June through August on weekday evenings on the U.S. Capitol West Front steps. Concerts usually include marches, patriotic numbers, and some classical music. Setup begins at 4 pm, but look out for scheduling changes or notices on individual bands' social media accounts. Food is permitted, but glass bottles and alcohol are not allowed. ✉ *U.S. Capitol, Capitol Hill* 🌐 *www.aoc.gov/*

news/2018-military-bands-summer-concert-series Ⓜ *Capitol S.*

★ National Gallery of Art Concert Series

CONCERTS | FAMILY | On Friday from 5 to 8:30 pm from Memorial Day through Labor Day, local jazz groups perform to packed crowds in the Pavilion Café at the Sculpture Garden. Listeners dip their feet in the fountain, sip sangria, and let the week wash away. From October to June free concerts by the National Gallery Orchestra and performances by visiting recitalists and ensembles are held in the West Building's West Garden Court on Sunday nights. Entry is first come, first served, with doors opening at 6 pm and concerts starting at 6:30 pm. On Wednesday, free midday performances of classical music begin around noon. Also be sure to check out its film series. ✉ *6th St. and Constitution Ave. NW, The Mall* ☎ *202/842–6941* ⊕ *www.nga. gov* Ⓜ *Archives–Navy Memorial–Penn Quarter.*

★ Smithsonian Institution Concert Series

CONCERTS | Throughout the year the Smithsonian Associates sponsor programs that offer everything from a cappella groups to Cajun zydeco bands; all events require tickets and locations vary. For an especially memorable musical experience, catch a performance of the Smithsonian Jazz Masterworks Orchestra in residence at the National Museum of American History. The Smithsonian's annual summer Folklife Festival, held on the Mall, highlights the cuisine, crafts, and day-to-day life of several different cultures. ✉ *1000 Jefferson Dr. SW, The Mall* ☎ *202/357–2700, 202/633–1000 recording, 202/357–3030 Smithsonian Associates* ⊕ *www.si.edu* Ⓜ *Smithsonian.*

🛍 Shopping

Museum Store in the United States Holocaust Memorial Museum

BOOKS/STATIONERY | This museum store offers a unique experience for visitors, offering a slew of books to further your knowledge of the Holocaust, memoirs from survivors, and other books centering on the plight of peoples in history. The shop also sells Jewish heritage items, such as mezuzah scrolls, menorahs, kiddush cups, and seder plates. You can also find secular items and souvenirs at the shop. ✉ *100 Raoul Wallenberg Pl. SW, The Mall* ☎ *202/488–0400* ⊕ *www.ushmm.org/museum-shop* Ⓜ *Smithsonian.*

National Air and Space Museum Store

GIFTS/SOUVENIRS | FAMILY | One of the world's most visited museums has a huge gift shop. The lower level of the three-floor, 12,000-square-foot store has tons of toys and games, plenty of souvenirs including T-shirts and totes, and an extensive selection of Star Wars and Star Trek licensed products for sci-fi fans. The upper level showcases a wide assortment of kites and books, but the largest selection of merchandise is on the middle level. Flight suits for both young and young at heart, space pens that work upside down, and freeze-dried "astronaut" ice cream are best sellers. The Einstein Planetarium Store has a fun array of Albert Einstein and space-related puzzles, games, and gadgets that especially appeal to teens and tweens. ✉ *Independence Ave. and 6th St. SW, The Mall* ☎ *202/633–4510* ⊕ *airandspace. si.edu* Ⓜ *L'Enfant Plaza or Smithsonian.*

★ National Archives Store and Gift Shop

CRAFTS | In a town full of museum shops, this store at the National Archives Museum stands out, with exclusive memorabilia, reproductions, apparel, books, gifts, and plenty of Founding Fathers gear that let you own a piece of history. Authentic-looking copies of the Constitution and other historical documents are printed in Pennsylvania. The popular "red tape" paperweights are crafted in the United States with real red tape that once bound government documents: hence the phrase "cut through the red tape." Other popular products feature Rosie the Riveter and Stars and Stripes bags; Teddy in Hat items for young children; and apparel featuring Franklin, Hamilton, and other Founding Fathers. Throughout the store, interactive games associated with special exhibits provide entertainment and education into history—of the United States and even you. Enter your last name into the computer and see how many people in the United States share your name and in which states they live. ⊠ *Constitution Ave. NW between 7th and 9th Sts., Federal Triangle* ☎ *202/357–5271* ⊕ *www. nationalarchivesstore.org* Ⓜ *Archives–Navy Memorial–Penn Quarter.*

National Gallery of Art West Building Shop
BOOKS/STATIONERY | This expansive shop, one of four in the National Gallery, offers a vast series of books, paper goods, apparel, fine jewelry, and knickknacks that all relate to or reflect the museum's art collection. Prices range from little over a dollar for a pencil, to well over $100 for designer jewelry. Some items were created by the museum, while the rest are curated and sourced by specific museum buyers to provide customers with a wide range of museum goods. Grab a Monet umbrella on a rainy day, or some Andy Warhol pop art crayons to pair with your favorite artist-themed coloring book. Here you can find whatever you need—and many things you didn't even realize you wanted. ⊠ *National Gallery of Art, West Building, 4th St. and Constitution Ave. NW, The Mall* ⊕ *shop.nga.gov* Ⓜ *Archives–Navy Memorial–Penn Quarter or L'Enfant Plaza.*

Pop-up Shop in the National Museum of African American History and Culture
GIFTS/SOUVENIRS | After traversing the many floors of the museum, you can shop here for merchandise from the many exhibits. Pick up a mug, T-shirt, or model of the museum's architecture to commemorate your trip. Many items here are handmade and inspired by the traditional histories woven into the museum, such as handmade sweetgrass baskets, African American dolls, jewelry, scarves, and even food items. ⊠ *National Museum of African American History and Culture, 1400 Constitution Ave. NW, The Mall* ☎ *844/750–3012* ⊕ *nmaahc.si.edu* Ⓜ *Smithsonian.*

USDA Farmers' Market
OUTDOOR/FLEA/GREEN MARKETS | Blueberry popcorn anyone? On Friday from May through October from 9 to 2, you can pick up fresh fruits, vegetables, breads, and other baked goods (and that flavored popcorn) across from the Smithsonian Metro station. Appropriately, the market is in the parking lot of the U.S. Department of Agriculture building. ⊠ *12th St. and Independence Ave. SW, The Mall* ☎ *202/708–0082* ⊕ *www.usda.gov/farmersmarket* Ⓜ *Smithsonian.*

Chapter 4

DOWNTOWN

Updated by
Bob Carden

◉ Sights	🍽 Restaurants	🛏 Hotels	🛍 Shopping	🍸 Nightlife
★★★★☆	★★★★☆	★★★★☆	★★★☆☆	★★★★☆

NEIGHBORHOOD SNAPSHOT

GREAT EXPERIENCES DOWNTOWN

- **CityCentre:** A high-end, open-air shopping district also has some good restaurants, including the acclaimed Momofuku.

- **International Spy Museum:** Indulge your inner James Bond with a look at 007's Aston Martin, along with more serious toys used by real spies.

- **Dining:** Penn Quarter is one of the city's best areas for dining, where José Andrés opened his first restaurant, Jaleo.

- **National Portrait Gallery and Smithsonian American Art Museum:** These masterful museums have something for everyone.

- **Newseum:** See parts of the Berlin Wall and play the role of a journalist. The roof-deck terrace provides postcard-perfect views of the Capitol.

- **Theater District:** Performances ranging from Shakespeare to contemporary dramas and musicals are mounted in Penn Quarter's theaters.

GETTING HERE

The Federal Triangle or Archives–Navy Memorial–Penn Quarter Metro stops serve the government buildings along Pennsylvania Avenue. Gallery Place–Chinatown gives direct access to the Capital One Arena, Chinatown, and the nearby museums. Judiciary Square has its own stop; Metro Center is the best choice for the National Theatre and Penn Quarter. Bus routes crisscross the area as well. Street parking on nights and weekends is limited.

PLANNING YOUR TIME

Downtown is densely packed with major attractions. Art lovers might focus on the **National Portrait Gallery** and **Smithsonian American Art Museum**; history buffs will enjoy the **National Building Museum**; families with kids may prefer the **International Spy Museum**; and media junkies will want to visit the **Newseum.** Come back at night to enjoy the many restaurants.

QUICK BITES

- **Nando's Peri-Peri.** For a quick lunch after visiting the National Portrait Gallery, this spicy Portuguese chicken restaurant can't be beat. ⊠ 819 7th St. NW ⊕ www.nandosperiperi.com Ⓜ Gallery Pl.–Chinatown.

- **Red Apron Butcher.** As its name implies, you can get a very meaty sandwich here, but there are excellent choices for vegetarians as well. The breakfast and lunch *tigelles* (crisp and chewy Italian flatbreads with assorted toppings) are especially good. ⊠ 709 D St. NW ⊕ www.redapronbutchery.com Ⓜ Archives–Navy Memorial–Penn Quarter.

- **Teaism.** The District's favorite Asian tearoom chain has a big location in Penn Quarter near the National Archives for tea, pastries, or a bento box or sandwich. ⊠ 400 8th St. NW ⊕ www.teaism.com Ⓜ Archives–Navy Memorial–Penn Quarter.

SAFETY

- Downtown's blocks of government and office buildings still become a bit of a ghost town when the working day is done, but a revitalized Penn Quarter remains energized late into the evenings, especially when there are events at the Capital One Arena.

Downtown, Penn Quarter, and Chinatown are a tale of three cities. Washington, D.C.'s, Downtown is staid, compact, and home to some wonderful hotels, though pretty quiet at night. Chinatown and the Penn Quarter jumps at night, there are loads of shops, bars, and restaurants. The Capital One Arena sits in the middle, and the nights are supercharged when the Capitals or Wizards are in town. There are also many great museums and theaters, including Ford's and the Warner.

⊙ Sights

There are loads of good museums and theaters here, most most of which are in Downtown, including the National Theater, the Warner, and Ford's, as well as most major museums. Chinatown and the Penn Quarter have the wonderful National Portrait Gallery.

American Veterans Disabled for Life Memorial

MEMORIAL | Located on a 2.4-acre tract adjacent to the Mall and within full view of the U.S. Capitol, this memorial illustrates the disabled veteran's journey, from injury and healing to rediscovery of purpose. The plaza, with a star-shaped fountain and low triangular reflecting pool, features bronze sculptures, glass panels, and granite walls engraved with quotations from 18 veterans describing their experiences. With its single ceremonial flame, the fountain is the focal point of this memorial. It's a powerful icon, expressing the healing, cleansing properties of water and the enlightenment, power, and eternal nature of fire. The needs of the disabled are front and center in the memorial's design. The low fountain can easily be surveyed by someone in a wheelchair; there are numerous benches in front of text panels and unobtrusive metal bars are placed strategically to help visitors who need assistance to sit or stand. Designed by Michael Vergason Landscape Architects, of Alexandria, Virginia, the memorial is a fitting reminder of the cost of human conflict. ✉ 150 Washington Ave. SW, Downtown ⊕ www.avdlm.org ✉ Free Ⓜ Federal Center SW.

Capitol One Arena

SPORTS VENUE | One of the country's top-grossing sports and entertainment venues, the 20,000-seat Capitol One Arena averages more than 200 events each year and has helped to turn the surrounding area into the most vibrant part of Downtown, where you'll find several of the city's best restaurants. But there are also decent food and beverage options inside the arena that go beyond the standard stadium fare of hot dogs, chicken fingers, and beer, including good local chili from Hard Times Café and Chesapeake Bay crab cakes, paired with craft beers and Angry Orchard Gluten-Free Hard Cider. Sporting events include hockey featuring the Stanley Cup champion Washington Capitals; basketball with the Washington Wizards, Washington Mystics, and Georgetown Hoyas; and figure-skating events. Outside, street musicians of all kinds and styles add to the experience. The Metro station is directly below the arena. ✉ *601 F St. NW, between 6th and 7th Sts., Chinatown* ☎ *202/628–3200* ⊕ *capitalonearena.view-lift.com* Ⓜ *Gallery Pl.–Chinatown.*

The FBI Experience

INFO CENTER | There have been no formal tours of FBI headquarters since September 11, 2001. Rather, visits can be arranged to see The FBI Experience. Located within the FBI headquarters building, it features interactive multimedia exhibits, artifacts from well-known cases, and large posters providing a history of the Bureau. The tour takes about 90 minutes and is self-guided, but there are typically both retired and active FBI agents on hand to offer information and answer questions. The Experience is open until 3 pm on weekdays, but you can't simply come in off the street. All visitors must arrange for tickets through their congressperson or senator. You can request a visit up to five months in advance but no less than four weeks before the desired date. You are generally notified two weeks prior to your date if you have been cleared for the visit, and you must arrive 30 minutes before your designated start time. ✉ *935 Pennsylvania Ave. NW, Downtown* ☎ *202/324–3447* ⊕ *www.fbi.gov/contact-us/fbi-headquarters/the-fbi-experience* ⊘ *Closed weekends* Ⓜ *Archives–Navy Memorial–Penn Quarter.*

★ Ford's Theatre

HISTORIC SITE | FAMILY | The events that took place here on the night of April 14, 1865, shocked the nation: during a performance of *Our American Cousin*, John Wilkes Booth entered the Presidential Box at Ford's Theatre and shot Abraham Lincoln in the back of the head; he died later that night. This block-long, Lincoln-centered cultural campus encompasses four sites. In the **Museum,** you'll explore Lincoln's presidency and Civil War milestones and learn about Booth and those who joined his conspiracy to topple the government. Artifacts include Lincoln's clothing and weapons used by Booth. The **Theatre,** which stages performances throughout the year, is restored to look as it did when Lincoln attended, including the Presidential Box draped with flags as it was on the night he was shot. During the spring and summer you can also watch a 30-minute one-act performance titled "One Destiny" that tells the story of the night from the eyes of those who were in the theater. In the restored **Petersen House,** you can see the room where Lincoln died and the parlor where his wife, Mary Todd Lincoln, waited in anguish through the night.

The centerpiece of the **Aftermaths Exhibits at the Center for Education and Leadership** is a jaw-dropping, three-story tower of 6,800 books written about Lincoln. Here, visitors take an immersive step back in time, entering a 19th-century street scene where they find a reproduction of Lincoln's funeral train car and see its route to Springfield, Illinois. Visitors also learn about the manhunt for John Wilkes Booth and his co-conspirators' trial, and

Kids love the International Spy Museum, where they can adopt a cover identity and try out being a spy in an interactive mission.

they interact with an "escape map" to the tobacco barn where Booth was captured. Exhibits also explore the fate of Lincoln's family after his death, explain the milestones of Reconstruction, and describe Lincoln's legacy and his enduring impact on U.S. and world leaders. A visit ends with a multiscreen video wall that shows how Lincoln's ideas resonate today.

Visits to Ford's Theatre require a free, timed-entry ticket. Same-day tickets are available at the theater box office beginning at 8:30 am on a first-come, first-served basis. You can also reserve tickets in advance at *www.fords.org* with a $3 fee per ticket. ✉ *511 10th St. NW, Downtown* ☎ *202/347–4833* ⊕ *www.fords.org* ✉ *Free; ticket reservations $3* Ⓜ *Metro Center or Gallery Pl.–Chinatown.*

★ International Spy Museum
MUSEUM | **FAMILY** | Fun for kids of all ages, the museum displays the world's largest collection of spy artifacts. *The Secret History of History* takes you behind the headlines, from Moses's use of spies in Canaan and Abraham Lincoln's

employment of the Pinkerton National Detective Agency as a full-scale secret service in the Civil War, to the birth of WWII's OSS. Check out the spy gadgets, weapons, vehicles, and disguises, and then see if you have what it takes to be a spy in *School for Spies. Exquisitely Evil: 50 Years of Bond Villains* brings you face-to-face with Bond villains. *Operation Spy*, a one-hour immersive experience, works like a live-action game, dropping you in the middle of a foreign intelligence mission. Each step—which includes decrypting secret audio files, a car chase, and interrogating a suspect agent—is taken from actual intelligence operations. Advance tickets (purchased at the museum or on its website) are highly recommended. All tickets are date- and time-specific. Tickets are most likely available on Tuesday, Wednesday, and Thursday or daily after 2 pm. ✉ *800 F St. NW, Downtown* ☎ *202/393–7798* ⊕ *www.spymuseum.org* ✉ *Permanent exhibition $21; Combo Museum and Operation $30 (when purchased online)* Ⓜ *Gallery Pl.–Chinatown.*

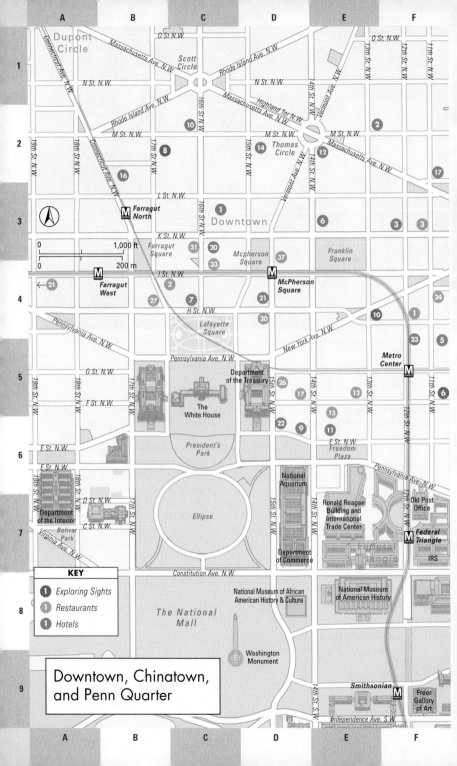

Madame Tussauds Washington DC

MUSEUM | This branch of the famous London-based waxworks franchise focuses on U.S. presidential history. You can see and pose for pictures (some for a small fee) with uncanny likenesses of the Founding Fathers or any of the presidents, including Barack Obama and his wife, or sit inside the Oval Office, painstakingly re-created in wax. The Civil Rights room features Martin Luther King Jr. and Rosa Parks. There are cultural icons, sports figures, and a behind-the-scenes exhibit where experts demonstrate wax sculpting. The Glamour Room is populated with waxen re-creations of George Clooney, Beyoncé, Zac Efron, and Taylor Swift, among others. ⊠ *1025 F St. NW, Downtown* ☎ *202/942–7300, 866/823–9565 to confirm hrs* ⊕ *www.madametussaudsdc.com* ⊠ *$22, with many extra additions possible* Ⓜ *Metro Center or Gallery Pl.–Chinatown.*

National Building Museum

MUSEUM | **FAMILY** | Architecture, design, landscaping, and urban planning are the themes of this museum, the nation's premier cultural organization devoted to the built environment. The open interior of the mammoth redbrick edifice is one of the city's great spaces and has been the site of many presidential inaugural balls. The eight central Corinthian columns are among the largest in the world, rising to a height of 75 feet. Although they resemble Siena marble, each is made of 70,000 bricks that have been covered with plaster and painted. The long-term exhibition *House and Home* features a kaleidoscopic array of photographs, objects, models, and films that takes visitors on a tour of houses both surprising and familiar, through past and present, exploring American domestic life and residential architecture. Among the most popular permanent exhibits is the *Building Zone,* where kids ages two to six can get a hands-on introduction to building by constructing a tower, exploring a kid-size playhouse, or playing with bulldozers and construction trucks. ⊠ *401 F St. NW, between 4th and 5th Sts., Downtown* ☎ *202/272–2448* ⊕ *www.nbm.org* ⊠ *$10; tool kits from $3; docent-led tour of building and entrance to Great Hall, shop, and café free* Ⓜ *Judiciary Sq. or Gallery Pl.–Chinatown.*

★ National Geographic Museum

MUSEUM | **FAMILY** | The National Geographic Museum is a small, hidden gem at the company's headquarters in the heart of downtown. There are two buildings separated by a large, airy courtyard. The permanent photographic exhibition in the back M Street building is free, and it offers a brief history of National Geographic expeditions, from Peary's South Pole adventure to finding the *Titanic*. Stories are told through lovely photography and poster boards. The changing exhibitions have an admission charge. Recent exhibits include *Treasures of Ancient Greece* and the *Tomb of Christ*. A bonus, National Geographic has one of the best—probably the best—cafeterias in town. It used to be restricted to employees but is now open to the public. Try it—you won't be disappointed. ⊠ *1145 17th St. NW, Downtown* ☎ *800/647–5463* ⊕ *www.nationalgeographic.com* ⊠ *$15; M Street Photographic Gallery free* Ⓜ *Farragut N.*

National Law Enforcement Officers Memorial

MEMORIAL | These 3-foot-high walls bear the names of more than 21,000 American police officers killed in the line of duty since 1791. On the third line of Panel 13W are the names of six officers killed by William Bonney, better known as Billy the Kid. J.D. Tippit, the Dallas policeman killed by Lee Harvey Oswald, is honored on the ninth line of Panel 63E. Other names include the 72 officers who died due to the events of 9/11. Directories here allow you to look up officers by name, date of death, state, and department. Call to arrange for a free tour. A National Law Enforcement

You'll find the famous portraits of President Barack Obama and first Lady Michelle Obama (among many others) at the National Portrait Gallery.

Museum is in the works; until then, a small visitor center (*400 7th St.*) has a computer for looking up names, a display on the history of law enforcement, and a small gift shop. ⊠ *400 block of E St. NW, Penn Quarter* ☎ *202/737–3400* ⊕ *www. lawmemorial.org* 🎟 *Free* Ⓜ *Judiciary Sq.*

National Museum of Women in the Arts

MUSEUM | This museum, in a beautifully restored 1907 Renaissance Revival building designed by Waddy B. Wood, brings to light remarkable female artists of the past, while promoting the best female artists working today. Founded in 1987, this is the only major museum in the world solely dedicated to recognizing women's creative contributions. In addition to hosting special exhibitions, the museum holds a collection of 5,000 artworks including paintings, drawings, sculpture, prints, videos, and photographs by Frida Kahlo, Camille Claudel, Mary Cassatt, Alma Thomas, Judy Chicago, Magdalena Abakanowicz, Nan Goldin, Louise Dahl-Wolfe, Helen Frankenthaler, and Élisabeth Vigée-Lebrun, among others. The installations highlight connections between historical and contemporary artworks. Gallery and artist talks, hands-on art workshops, and concerts are held regularly; check the museum's website for the calendar of events. ⊠ *1250 New York Ave. NW, Downtown* ☎ *202/783–5000* ⊕ *www. nmwa.org* 🎟 *$10* Ⓜ *Metro Center.*

★ National Portrait Gallery

MUSEUM | FAMILY | The intersection of art, biography, and history is illustrated here through images of men and women who have shaped U.S. history. There are prints, paintings, photos, and sculptures of subjects from George Washington to Madonna.

This museum shares the National Historic Landmark building Old Patent Office with the Smithsonian American Art Museum. Built between 1836 and 1863, and praised by Walt Whitman as the "noblest of Washington buildings," it is deemed one of the country's best examples of Greek Revival architecture.

America's Presidents shares the stories of the country's leaders and the times in which they governed. In this gallery, you'll see the only complete collection of presidential portraits outside the White House. Highlights include Gilbert Stuart's 1796 "Landsdowne" portrait of George Washington, Alexander Gardner's "cracked-plate" image of Abraham Lincoln from Lincoln's last formal portrait session before his assassination in 1865, a sculpture of Andrew Jackson on a horse, and political cartoonist Pat Oliphant's sculpture of George H.W. Bush playing horseshoes.

From portraits of World War II generals Eisenhower and Patton to Andy Warhol's *Time* magazine cover of Michael Jackson, the third-floor gallery, Twentieth-Century Americans, offers a vibrant tour of the people who shaped the country and culture of today. And, don't miss the *Bravo* and *Champions* exhibits on the mezzanine, especially if you enjoy the performing arts or are a sports buff. The displays of entertainers and American sports figures are dynamic and engaging.

There are free docent-led tours weekdays at noon and 2:30, and most weekends at 11:45, 1:30, 3:15 and 4:30. Check the website to confirm times. At the Lunder Conservation Center on the third and fourth floors, you can watch conservators restoring works. ⊠ *8th and F Sts. NW, Downtown* ☎ *202/633–8300* ⊕ *www.npg.si.edu* 🎫 *Free* Ⓜ *Gallery Pl.–Chinatown.*

★ **Newseum**

MUSEUM | FAMILY | The setting, in a dramatic glass-and-silver structure on Pennsylvania Avenue, smack between the White House and the Capitol, is a fitting location for a museum devoted to the First Amendment and the role of a free press in democracy. Visitors enter the 90-foot-high media-saturated atrium, overlooked by a giant breaking-news screen and a news helicopter suspended overhead. From there, 15 galleries display

500 years of news history, including exhibits on the First Amendment; global news; the rise of multimedia; and how radio, TV, and the Internet transformed worldwide news dissemination.

The largest piece of the Berlin Wall outside Germany, including a guard tower, is permanently installed in an exhibit explaining how a free press was a key contributor to the fall of the wall. One of only 19 copies of *The Pennsylvania Evening Post* from July 6, 1776, that published the Declaration of Independence is also here in an exhibit that explores how news of freedom led delegates in the 13 colonies to unite for independence.

Fifteen state-of-the art theaters, including an eye-popping "4-D" theater and another with a 90-foot-long screen, show features, news, sports, and documentaries throughout the day. In the Interactive Newsroom you can play the role of journalist, try your hand at investigative reporting to solve a mysterious animal breakout at the zoo, or step behind a camera and try to capture the most compelling photograph of a river rescue. Evocative press photos are on display at the Pulitzer Prize Photographs gallery.

There's a lot to take in here, but luckily tickets for the Newseum are valid for two consecutive days. ▪ **TIP**➔ **The Newseum will close at the end of 2019, but a new location in the District has not yet been found.** ⊠ *555 Pennsylvania Ave. NW, Downtown* ☎ *888/639–7386* ⊕ *www.newseum.org* 🎫 *$25* Ⓜ *Archives–Navy Memorial–Penn Quarter or Judiciary Sq.*

Smithsonian American Art Museum

MUSEUM | From Childe Hassam's *The South Ledges, Appledore* to Nelson Shanks's *The Four Justices,* the Smithsonian American Art Museum features one of the world's largest collections of American art that spans more than four centuries. Over the past few decades, the museum has broadened its collection to include modern and contemporary art,

On the exterior of the Newseum, the First Amendment is inscribed in its entirety.

too. Among the artists represented are Benny Andrews, José Campechi, Robert Indiana, Roy Lichtenstein, Isamu Noguchi, Robert Rauschenberg, Mickalene Thomas, and Charlie Willeto. The museum shares a National Historic Landmark building with the National Portrait Gallery.

On the first floor, you'll discover an enormous tinfoil altarpiece by James Hampton and more than 60 sculptures and paintings by Emery Blagdon that represent his thought-provoking and constantly changing *Healing Machine.* You can also experience American artwork from the 1930s, many created as part of New Deal programs. Highlights here include Marvin Beerbohm's *Automotive Industry,* Lily Furedi's *Subway,* and Edward Hopper's *Ryder's House.* Also on the first floor is the Direct Carving exhibit which showcases artists who work directly on a piece of stone or wood.

Art from the colonial period to the dawn of modernism is displayed throughout the galleries on the second floor. Discover masterpieces by Mary Cassatt,

Frederick Carl Frieseke, Thomas Moran, Harriett Whitney Frishmuth, George Catlin, Albert Bierstadt, Winslow Homer, and John Singer Sargent, to name just a few.

The museum's third floor features modern and contemporary paintings and sculpture and the Watch This! gallery, where you can see a selection of works from the museum's media art and film collection. Highlights include Nam June Paik's billboard-size piece with 215 monitors showing video images from the Seoul Olympics, Korean folk rituals, and modern dance.

At any given time, much of the museum's holdings are in storage, but you can view more than 3,000 artworks in its Luce Foundation Center, a visible storage space on the third and fourth floors, where visitors can also watch the museum's conservators at work. Free docent-led tours of the museum are available every day at 12:30 and 2. ⊠ *8th and G Sts. NW, Downtown* ☎ *202/633–7970* ⊕ *www.americanart.si.edu* ⊠ *Free* Ⓜ *Gallery Pl.–Chinatown.*

United States Navy Memorial

MEMORIAL | Although Pierre L'Enfant included a Navy Memorial in his plans for Washington, D.C., it wasn't until 1987 that one was built. The main attraction here is a 100-foot-diameter granite map of the world, known as the Granite Sea. It's surrounded by fountains, benches, and six ship masts. The *Lone Sailor*, a 7-foot-tall statue, stands on the map in the Pacific Ocean between the United States and Japan. The Naval Heritage Center, next to the memorial in the Market Square East Building, displays videos and exhibits of uniforms, medals, and other aspects of Navy life. If you've served in the Navy, you can enter your record of service into the Navy Log here. Bronze relief panels on the Pennsylvania Avenue side of the memorial depict 26 scenes commemorating events in the nation's naval history and honoring naval communities. ✉ *701 Pennsylvania Ave. NW, Downtown* ☎ *202/737–2300* ⊕ *www.navymemorial.org* ✆ *Free* Ⓜ *Archives–Navy Memorial–Penn Quarter.*

WWI Memorial

NATIONAL/STATE PARK | In late 2014 Congress redesignated this quiet, sunken garden, which was formerly named Pershing Park in tribute to General John J. "Black Jack" Pershing, the first—a century ago—to hold the title General of the Armies. An official unit of the National Park System, the World War I Memorial includes engravings on the stone walls recounting pivotal campaigns from World War I, when Pershing commanded the American expeditionary force and conducted other military exploits. Steps and small tables surround a fountain and duck pond, making for a pleasant midday respite. A new design for the memorial was selected in 2016 and groundbreaking has been mired in legal and technical issues. ✉ *15th St. and Pennsylvania Ave., Downtown* Ⓜ *McPherson Sq.*

🍴 Restaurants

Until recently, tourists who trekked north from the Mall hungry for something more than Smithsonian cafeteria food were stranded Downtown with little but high-end options. Now young Washingtonians are taking advantage of residential development and moving off Capitol Hill to Downtown, Penn Quarter, and Chinatown, where nothing short of a restaurant revolution has taken shape in the last decade.

Bibiana Osteria and Enoteca

$$ | ITALIAN | You might call this the Italian version of the uberpopular Indian spot Rasika, and you'd be correctly noting the modernist fingerprints of local impresario Ashok Bajaj. The 120-seat dining room, decorated in Bajaj's favored spare tones and metallic accents, specializes in hearty Italian cuisine dished out by uncommonly attentive and knowledgeable servers. **Known for:** being a Milan-inspired osteria; unexpected Italian dishes; affordable lunch specials. Ⓢ *Average main: $26* ✉ *1100 New York Ave. NW, entrance at 12th and H Sts., Downtown* ☎ *202/216–9550* ⊕ *www.bibianadc.com* ⊗ *No lunch Sat. Closed Sun.* Ⓜ *Metro Center.*

Bombay Club

$$ | INDIAN | One block from the White House, the beautiful Bombay Club tries to re-create the refined aura of British private clubs in colonial India. On the menu are unusual seafood specialties and a large number of vegetarian dishes, but the real standouts are the aromatic curries. **Known for:** great Indian curries; British colonial club vibe; upscale Sunday buffet brunch. Ⓢ *Average main: $24* ✉ *815 Connecticut Ave. NW, Downtown* ☎ *202/659–3727* ⊕ *www.bombayclubdc.com* ⊗ *No lunch Sat.* Ⓜ *Farragut W.*

Brasserie Beck

$$$ | BELGIAN | FAMILY | Give in to sensory overload at this homage to the railway dining rooms that catered to the prewar European elite. The food is just as rich as you'd expect: entrée-size salads with Belgian frites, *fruits de mer* platters with enough shellfish for a small army, and a dizzying lineup of artisanal beers. **Known for:** luxurious vintage-inspired interiors; excellent brunch that includes Belgian waffles and unlimited mimosas; great outdoor patio. $ *Average main: $32* ✉ *1101 K St. NW, Downtown* ☎ *202/408–1717* ⊕ *www.brasseriebeck. com* Ⓜ *McPherson Sq.*

Centrolina
$$$ | **ITALIAN** | This bright, airy Italian osteria has an adjoining market and a daily changing menu that is all about locally sourced meats and produce, as well as sustainable fish. Authentic and innovative, pastas and sauces are made fresh daily, and the specials change regularly. **Known for:** innovative pasta dishes; daily changing menu; fun option in CityCentre development. $ *Average main: $32* ✉ *974 Palmer Alley NW, Chinatown* ⬦ *Near Convention Center* ☎ *202/898–2426* ⊕ *centrolinadc.com* Ⓜ *Gallery Pl.–Chinatown.*

China Chilcano
$$ | **PERUVIAN** | The José Andrés formula is pleasantly familiar to D.C. diners who have visited his ever-growing empire of endlessly kicky small plate restaurants since Jaleo first opened in 1993. This hybrid of Peruvian and Chinese-Japanese styles, inspired by a 19th-century wave of migration to South America, is one of the newer additions to the stylish family. **Known for:** part of chef José Andrés's empire; Peruvian-inspired shareable small plates; pisco fruit cocktails. $ *Average main: $20* ✉ *418 7th St. NW, Penn Quarter* ☎ *202/783–0941* ⊕ *chinachilcano.com* ☾ *No lunch* Ⓜ *Gallery Pl.–Chinatown.*

★ City Tap House
$$ | **AMERICAN** | **FAMILY** | This upscale gastropub is just a block from the convention center, offering more than 40 beers on tap and loads of bottles. The ceilings are high, the walls all reclaimed wood, the bar copper, giving the large spot a warm,

rustic feel. **Known for:** standard American pub fare; great selection of beers; communal tables and big-screen TVs. $ *Average main: $18* ✉ *901 9th St. NW, Penn Quarter* ☎ *202/733–5333* ⊕ *pennquarter. citytap.com* Ⓜ *Gallery Pl.–Chinatown.*

★ Crimson Diner + Whiskey Bar
$ | **AMERICAN** | **FAMILY** | An upscale Southern-influenced diner with an open kitchen and lively bar, Crimson offers seating in booths to convey that diner feel. A huge breakfast menu is available all day, while dinner plates include shrimp and grits, rainbow trout, and, yes, meat loaf. **Known for:** Southern cooking; fine whiskey; great views. $ *Average main: $15* ✉ *627 H St. NW, Chinatown* ☎ *202/847–4459* ⊕ *www.crimson-dc.com* Ⓜ *Gallery Pl.–Chinatown.*

Daikaya
$ | **RAMEN** | This no-reservations, Sapporo-style ramen shop is one of the city's best bets for the tasty Japanese noodle soup. It offers five excellent types of ramen, with the vegan version a welcome option. **Known for:** small spot serving ramen; loud, local-friendly vibe; fancier Izakaya upstairs. $ *Average main: $14* ✉ *705 6th St. NW, Chinatown* ☎ *202/589–1600* ⊕ *www.daikaya.com* Ⓜ *Gallery Pl.–Chinatown.*

DBGB Kitchen and Bar
$$$ | **FRENCH** | After leaving D.C. in 1982, famed chef Daniel Boulud finally returned 32 years and 18 restaurants later to open this interpretation of a classic French brasserie in downtown D.C. The small plates of house-made sausage, coq au vin, and baked Alaska for dessert demonstrate the impressive culinary chops he picked up while away. **Known for:** world-famous chef's prodigal return home; variety of house-made sausages; fun cocktail menu. $ *Average main: $28* ✉ *931 H St. NW, Downtown* ☎ *202/695–7660* ⊕ *www.dbgb.com/dc* Ⓜ *Gallery Pl.–Chinatown.*

Del Frisco's Double Eagle Steak House
$$$$ | **STEAKHOUSE** | Del Frisco's is yet another upscale steak house in a city bursting with them. Like many others, the cuts of meat are tasty, generous, and pricey, but the overall atmosphere is nicer—or at least brighter—than many of its competitors. **Known for:** big, juicy steaks; floor-to-ceiling windows; large courtyard. [$] *Average main: $45* ✉ *950 I St. NW, Chinatown* ☎ *202/289–0201* 🌐 *www.delfriscos.com* [M] *Gallery Pl.–Chinatown or McPherson Sq.*

Dirty Habit
$$$ | **FUSION** | Inside trendy Hotel Monaco, Dirty Habit woos diners with a towering skylit space that until 1901 was the general post office. Homing in on globally inspired shared plates, the chef conjures up such satisfying dishes as poached hen dumplings and smoked Chilean sea bass. **Known for:** alfresco dining (and drinking) in the courtyard; popular happy hour; small plates in a historic space. [$] *Average main: $30* ✉ *Hotel Monaco, 555 8th St. NW, Penn Quarter* ☎ *202/783–6060* 🌐 *www.dirtyhabitdc.com* [M] *Gallery Pl.–Chinatown.*

District Taco
$ | **MEXICAN** | **FAMILY** | The line out the door at lunchtime is a dead giveaway that D.C.er's have taken to this fast-casual, Yucatán-style Mexican restaurant that got its start as a food truck in 2009. While you can customize the toppings of your tacos or burritos, ordering them the Mexican way (with cilantro and onion) is a sure bet. **Known for:** food truck origins; all-day breakfast tacos; extensive salsa bar. [$] *Average main: $8* ✉ *1309 F St. NW, Downtown* ☎ *202/347–7359* 🌐 *www.districttaco.com* [M] *Metro Center.*

Fadó Irish Pub
$ | **IRISH** | **FAMILY** | This classic Irish pub is in the middle of Chinatown, just a block or so from the Capital One Arena. "Fadó" is Gaelic for "long ago" or "once upon a time," and this homage to Irish pubs of old offers hearty traditional food like shepherd's pie, fish-and-chips, and an Irish breakfast. The "cottage" room in back resembles a turn-of-the-20th-century Irish dining room. **Known for:** fish-and-chips; good burgers; authentic Irish pub feel. [$] *Average main: $16* ✉ *808 7th St. NW, Chinatown* ✣ *1 block from Gallery Pl.–Chinatown Metro and Capital One Arena* ☎ *202/789–0066* 🌐 *fadoirishpub.com* [M] *Gallery Pl.–Chinatown.*

Fiola
$$$$ | **MODERN ITALIAN** | Chef Fabio Trabocchi's flights of fancy, such as oysters with granita and caviar or Nova Scotia lobster ravioli delight many area foodies but come with a hefty price tag. Happy hour and lunch menus offer more affordable small plates to go with inventive cocktails (head to the bar or patio for these à la carte options). **Known for:** upscale and innovative Italian dishes; date night crowd; encyclopedic beverage list. [$] *Average main: $47* ✉ *601 Pennsylvania Ave. NW, Penn Quarter* ✣ *Enter at 678 Indiana Ave.* ☎ *202/628–2888* 🌐 *www.fioladc.com* [M] *Archives–Navy Memorial–Penn Quarter.*

★ **The Fourth Estate**
$$ | **AMERICAN** | A hidden gem atop the National Press Building offers classic American cuisine (strong on seafood), beautifully prepared and presented in an elegant setting at surprisingly affordable prices. Although part of the National Press Club, which is private, the restaurant is open to the public. **Known for:** fresh seafood; great spot for pretheater dinner; opportunity to view National Press Club photos. [$] *Average main: $26* ✉ *529 14th St., Downtown* ☎ *202/662–7638* 🌐 *www.press.org/fourthestate* 🕒 *No dinner Mon. Closed Sun.* [M] *Metro Center.*

Full Kee
$ | **CHINESE** | Many locals swear by this standout from the slew of mediocre Chinese joints in the area. The style-free interior can be off-putting to some—reminiscent of the fluorescent-lit dives of Manhattan's Chinatown—but the cuisine

is better than most similar options within the city limits. **Known for:** rare good spot for Chinese food in Chinatown; Catonese-style roasted meats; no-frills decor. $ *Average main: $14* ✉ *509 H St. NW, Chinatown* ☎ *202/371–2233* Ⓜ *Gallery Pl.–Chinatown.*

The Hamilton

$$ | ECLECTIC | Formerly a Borders bookstore, the Hamilton (no relation to the hit musical) is now an enormous multiroom restaurant over a subterranean live music hall that can accommodate almost a thousand people. The menu is just as ambitious as the venue, offering burgers, sushi, pasta, steaks, salads, seafood, and one solitary vegetarian entrée. **Known for:** all-encompassing menu; huge space with live music; happy hour deals. $ *Average main: $26* ✉ *600 14th St. NW, Downtown* ☎ *202/787–1000* ⊕ *www.thehamiltondc.com* Ⓜ *Metro Center.*

Hill Country Barbecue Market

$$ | BARBECUE | FAMILY | Few who stop by this bustling hive of smoky brisket and gooey ribs can deny that it does Texas meat right. This is evident down to the pay-by-the-pound ethos that lets you sample one slice of lean beef and one scoop of gooey white shoepeg corn pudding alongside a succulent turkey breast, so tender it drips juice down your chin. **Known for:** Texas-style brisket—with the rub; cafeteria-style, pay-by-the pound ordering; country western karaoke night every Wednesday. $ *Average main: $18* ✉ *410 7th St. NW, Penn Quarter* ☎ *202/556–2050* ⊕ *www.hillcountrywdc.com* Ⓜ *Archives–Navy Memorial–Penn Quarter.*

Jaleo

$$ | SPANISH | Make a meal of the long list of tapas at chef José Andrés's lively Spanish bistro, although the five types of handcrafted paella are the stars of the ample entrée menu. Tapas highlights include the *gambas al ajillo* (sautéed garlic shrimp), tender piquillo peppers stuffed with goat cheese, and the grilled homemade chorizo, which also comes draped in creamy mashed potatoes. **Known for:** José Andrés original tapas eatery; sangria by the pitcher; different paella options. $ *Average main: $25* ✉ *480 7th St. NW, Penn Quarter* ☎ *202/628–7949* ⊕ *www.jaleo.com* Ⓜ *Gallery Pl.–Chinatown.*

Joe's Seafood, Prime Steak & Stone Crab

$$$$ | STEAKHOUSE | Just a couple of blocks from the White House, this gargantuan space (a century-old bank building), with a towering second-floor terrace, centers on a huge black granite bar adorned with marble columns and leather stools. Affiliated with the legendary Joe's Stone Crab in Miami, the D.C. Joe's distinguishes itself with steaks; sure they have seafood, but this is a steak house. **Known for:** primarily prime steaks but also fresh seafood; everything big: place, portions, prices; fun happy hour. $ *Average main: $52* ✉ *750 15th St. NW, Downtown* ✛ *On 15th St., a block from Treasury Building* ☎ *202/489–0140* ⊕ *joes.net* Ⓜ *Metro Center.*

Kaz Sushi Bistro

$$ | JAPANESE | Traditional Japanese cooking is combined with often inspired improvisations ("freestyle Japanese cuisine," in the words of chef-owner Kaz Okochi) at this serene location. For a first-rate experience, sit at the sushi bar and ask for whatever is best—you're in good hands. **Known for:** one of D.C.'s original sushi spots; unique Japanese dishes and small plates. $ *Average main: $26* ✉ *1915 I St. NW, Downtown* ☎ *202/530–5500* ⊕ *www.kazsushibistro.com* ✲ *Closed Sun. No lunch Sat.* Ⓜ *Farragut W.*

Kinship

$$$$ | MODERN AMERICAN | The unique menu divides Kinship's offerings into four categories; first there's craft, honoring a particular cooking technique, and then history, which offers a different take on a classic dish. The ingredients menu explores a certain product while the indulgence section is where you'll find

dishes like caviar with potato chips or lobster French toast. **Known for:** themed menu with diverse selections; Chesapeake Bay soft-shell crabs (when in season); warm yet chic ambience. $ *Average main: $50* ⊠ *1015 7th St. NW, Chinatown* ☏ *202/737–7700* ⊕ *www.kinshipdc.com* Ⓜ *Mt. Vernon Sq. 7th St.–Convention Center.*

★ minibar by José Andrés

$$$$ | CONTEMPORARY | For food fanatics who can afford it, a visit to chef José Andrés's cutting-edge culinary counter is as essential as a visit to the White House when visiting Washington. Here Andrés showcases his molecular-gastronomy techniques with the 20 or so courses on the tasting menu that vary regularly (no à la carte ordering allowed). **Known for:** hard-to-get reservations required; chocolate-covered foie gras; experimental cocktails. $ *Average main: $275* ⊠ *855 E. St. NW, Penn Quarter* ☏ *202/393–0812* ⊕ *www.minibarbyjoseandres.com/minibar.*

★ Momofuku CCDC

$$ | ASIAN | New York City legend David Chang made his D.C. debut with this outpost of his original Asian-street-food-inspired restaurant. As at the other Momofukus, the soft buns are a must—you won't regret ordering a few different types (be sure to include the pork, though). **Known for:** D.C's take on a NYC culinary legend; Asian street food like pork buns; delicious ramen noodles. $ *Average main: $17* ⊠ *1090 I St. NW, Downtown* ☏ *202/602–1832* ⊕ *ccdc.momofuku.com* Ⓜ *Metro Center.*

NoPa Kitchen+Bar

$$ | AMERICAN | It's hard to classify NoPa, which makes it such a fun place to hang. The food is, well, let's call it modern American fusion, with some French influences, a dash of Japanese technique, and a wonderful all-American Angus burger. **Known for:** creative menu with Asian, American, and European influences; excellent burger; just a block

from Capitol One Arena. $ *Average main: $25* ⊠ *800 F St. NW, Penn Quarter* ☏ *202/347–4667* ⊕ *nopadc.com* ⊗ *No lunch Sat.* Ⓜ *Gallery Pl.–Chinatown.*

Old Ebbitt Grill

$$$ | AMERICAN | People flock here to drink at the several bars, which seem to go on for miles, and to enjoy well-prepared buffalo wings, hamburgers, and hearty sandwiches (the Reuben is a must). A 160-year-old institution (it claims Teddy Roosevelt may have "bagged animal heads" at the main bar), Old Ebbitt also has one of Washington's best raw bars. **Known for:** one of D.C.'s oldest bars; standard bar menu, including great oysters; an institution that shouldn't be missed. $ *Average main: $27* ⊠ *675 15th St. NW, Downtown* ☏ *202/347–4800* ⊕ *www.ebbitt.com* Ⓜ *Metro Center.*

The Oval Room

$$$ | CONTEMPORARY | The city is full of established restaurants that cater to lobbyists and the government officials they're wining and dining, but the Oval Room is a rare example of one that also has great food. The menu is largely split between Southern-influenced dishes, like shrimp and grits, and Mediterranean-inspired ones, such as smoked yellowfin potato agnolotti. **Known for:** clientele of D.C. insiders; classy and intimate dining room; modern American cuisine like yellowfin tuna crudo. $ *Average main: $28* ⊠ *800 Connecticut Ave. NW, Downtown* ☏ *202/463–8700* ⊕ *www.ovalroom.com* ⊗ *Closed Sun. No lunch weekends* Ⓜ *Farragut W.*

Oyamel Cocina Mexicana

$$ | MEXICAN | The specialty at chef Jos🔲 Andr🔲s's Mexican stunner is *antojitos,* literally translated as "little dishes from the streets." But the high ceilings, gracious service, and gorgeous Frida Kahlo–inspired interior are anything but street, and even the smallest of dishes is larger than life when doused with chocolate mole poblano sauce or piquant lime-cilantro dressing. **Known**

D.C. Food Trucks

The nation's capital loves celebrity chefs and pricey bistros, but its latest romance is both affordable and accessible: food trucks. The mobile-food rush reached its peak several years ago when local brick-and-mortar restaurateurs attempted to fight the trucks' appeal by passing an ordinance to keep them from staying too long in one place. That battle continues, but visitors keen to try the best D.C. trucks can always take advantage of Twitter. Even those without a Twitter account are free to visit the trucks' pages to track their locations—and in many cases, check out menus to see whether chicken vindaloo or red-velvet cupcakes are on the docket at these favorite spots.

Arepa Zone (🌐 *www.twitter.com/arepazone*) is a celebration of Venezuelan cuisine; arepas, *cachapas* (cheese sticks), and *cachapas* (tacolike sweet corn pancakes) all feature heavily.

PhoWheels (🌐 *www.twitter.com/PhoWheels*) makes pho so delicious you'll want a cup even on a hot D.C. day (go for the eye-round steak). Soup can be a bit difficult to eat when sitting on a curb or park bench, but luckily PhoWheels also offers impressive bánh mì sandwiches and Vietnamese-style tacos.

Red Hook Lobster Pound (🌐 *twitter.com/lobstertruckdc*) is the Washington outpost of the popular Brooklyn, New York, spot that purveys rolls filled with überfresh shellfish from Maine (tossed with light mayo) and Connecticut (kissed by creamy butter) variations—or try the equally good shrimp roll for $7 less. Add a decadent chocolate homemade whoopie pie for dessert.

for: street-inspired Mexican small plates; grasshopper tacos; affordable lunch deals. [$] *Average main: $23* ✉ *401 7th St. NW, Penn Quarter* ☎ *202/628–1005* 🌐 *www.oyamel.com* [M] *Archives–Navy Memorial–Penn Quarter.*

The Partisan

$$$ | **MODERN AMERICAN** | Charcuterie is more than just salami at this wood-paneled homage to all parts of the pig. Sample servings of meat under headings like rich + earthy, herbal + floral, and boozy, and complement the taste with one of the vibrant small plates like grilled octopus and brussels sprout slaw. **Known for:** pig-focused charcuterie menu; late-night hot spot; great dessert menu including hazelnut mudpies. [$] *Average main: $30* ✉ *709 D St. NW, Penn Quarter* ☎ *202/524–5322* 🌐 *thepartisandc.com* [M] *Gallery Pl.–Chinatown.*

Paul

$ | **FRENCH** | **FAMILY** | This chic, quick café is the Parisian equivalent of Starbucks, but at a much higher level. The fluff of its cheese *gougeres* puffs, the heft of its salty-sweet croque monsieur sandwiches, and the delicate crunch of its almond-flour macaron cookies, will leave you craving for more. **Known for:** Parisian-style fast-casual chain; huge pastry selection; big crowds during lunch. [$] *Average main: $10* ✉ *801 Pennsylvania Ave. NW, Downtown* ☎ *202/524–4500* 🌐 *www.paul-usa.com* 🕘 *No dinner* [M] *Archives–Navy Memorial–Penn Quarter.*

P.J. Clarke's DC

$$ | **BURGER** | **FAMILY** | The D.C. branch of the venerable New York institution focuses on classic American comfort food, including burgers, oysters, rotisserie chicken, and steaks. Each day there's a blackboard special that could be tuna one

day, pasta the next. **Known for:** excellent burgers; great raw bar; energetic happy hour. [$] *Average main: $26* ✉ *1600 K St. NW, Downtown* ☎ *202/463–6610* 🌐 *pj-clarkes.com* [M] *Farragut N or Farragut W.*

★ Proof

$$$ | **CONTEMPORARY** | The name should make this spot's beverage-centric disposition clear: Proof has more than 1,200 different wine varieties in bottles and 40 by the glass, dispensed via a stainless-steel Enomatic machine. Food here is dictated by wine offerings. **Known for:** expansive wine menu; cheese and charcuterie boards; reasonably priced lunch prix-fixe on weekdays. [$] *Average main: $32* ✉ *775 G St. NW, Chinatown* ☎ *202/737–7663* 🌐 *www.proofdc.com* 🕓 *No lunch weekends* [M] *Gallery Pl.–Chinatown.*

Rare Steakhouse and Tavern

$$$ | **STEAKHOUSE** | **FAMILY** | Rare is two restaurants in one: a casual street-level tavern that will appeal to most diners and an upstairs high-end steak house. The Tavern is most accessible, with a large bar decorated with colorful murals, perfect if you are meeting friends or doing happy hour, and its menu takes pub grub to another level. **Known for:** dry-aged steaks; long, airy bar; upscale tavern downstairs, high-end steak house up. [$] *Average main: $27* ✉ *1595 I St. NW, Downtown* ☎ *202/800–9994* 🌐 *www.raresteaks.com* 🕓 *No lunch weekends* [M] *Farragut N, Farragut W, or McPherson Sq.*

★ Rasika

$$ | **INDIAN** | Adventurous wine lists, stellar service, inventive presentations that don't scrimp on the spice—this Indian kitchen would have been a local legend even without the romantic yet supersleek decor that drives date-night crowds to snap up reservations weeks in advance. The menu highlights unique tandooris and grills, from lamb to chicken, and uberpopular vegetarian dishes such as the fried spinach leaves with sweet yogurt sauce called *palak chaat*. **Known for:** upscale Indian with unique dishes; plenty of options for vegetarians; tables that book up weeks in advance. [$] *Average main: $25* ✉ *633 D St. NW, Penn Quarter* ☎ *202/637–1222* 🌐 *www.rasikarestaurant.com* 🕓 *Closed Sun. No lunch Sat.* [M] *Archives–Navy Memorial–Penn Quarter.*

Rosa Mexicano

$$ | **MEXICAN** | Big and vibrant, this Mexican restaurant and bar (a branch of the New York City original) sits directly across the street from Verizon Center. The menu focuses on "authentic" Mexican food, eschewing Tex-Mex and American-style burrito bombs, and prides itself on the tableside guacamole presentation. **Known for:** fresh guacamole prepared tableside; inventive margaritas; booming happy hour. [$] *Average main: $25* ✉ *575 7th St. NW, Penn Quarter* ☎ *202/783–5522* 🌐 *rosamexicano.com* [M] *Gallery Pl.–Chinatown.*

★ Shake Shack

$ | **AMERICAN** | **FAMILY** | Yes, it's a chain made most famous in Manhattan, but if you're craving a burger, there's no better place to address that problem than its D.C. Chinatown outpost. Juicy burgers with a special sauce, classic fries (get them with cheese), and tasty shakes make it worth the short wait—especially if you're looking for a tasty lunch between Downtown attractions at a reasonable price. **Known for:** classic Shack Burger (and that sauce!); vanilla milk shakes; long lines that go fast. [$] *Average main: $9* ✉ *800 F St. NW, Penn Quarter* ☎ *202/800–9930* 🌐 *www.shakeshack.com/location/f-street-dc* [M] *Gallery Pl.–Chinatown.*

★ Siroc Restaurant

$$ | **ITALIAN** | This wonderfully intimate Italian-Mediterranean restaurant sits in the heart of downtown D.C. Family owned and run, it's a rarity in downtown D.C., delivering top-notch food at very reasonable prices. **Known for:** fresh pasta made in-house; Italian-style seafood

presentations; intimate, candlelit dining. *Average main: $23* ✉ *915 15th St. NW, Downtown* ☎ *202/628–2220* 🌐 *www.sirocrestaurant.com* ⏲ *No lunch weekends* Ⓜ *Farragut N or Farragut W.*

The Smith

$$ | **AMERICAN** | **FAMILY** | Bright, loud, raucous, and fun, with a brightly lit bar and long, communcal tables, this branch of the New York City original makes it hard not to meet people. An "American" brassiere, it's a large space with an even bigger menu, so if you can't find something you like here, it might not exist. **Known for:** great bar scene; eclectic international menu; all-day breakfast. *Average main: $26* ✉ *901 F St. NW, Downtown* ☎ *202/868–4900* 🌐 *thesmithrestaurant.com* Ⓜ *Gallery Pl.–Chinatown or Metro Center.*

The Source by Wolfgang Puck

$$$$ | **ASIAN FUSION** | Iconic chef Wolfgang Puck's first foray into Washington offers two different dining experiences, both with a focus on Asian flavors and with some of the city's most dedicated servers. The downstairs area is home to an intimate lounge where guests can try small plates while upstairs the focus is all on haute cuisine. **Known for:** one of the world's most well-known chefs; upscale Asian-fusion cuisine; dim sum brunch. *Average main: $37* ✉ *The Newseum, 575 Pennsylvania Ave. NW, Downtown* ☎ *202/637–6100* 🌐 *www.wolfgangpuck.com/restaurants/fine-dining/3941* ⏲ *Closed Sun.* Ⓜ *Archives–Navy Memorial–Penn Quarter.*

Teaism Penn Quarter

$ | **ASIAN** | **FAMILY** | This informal teahouse stocks more than 50 imported teas (black, white, and green), and also serves healthy and delicious Japanese, Indian, and Thai food. You can mix small dishes—like udon noodle salad and grilled avocado—to create meals or snacks. **Known for:** impressive selection of teas; lunch dishes spanning several Asian cuisines; chocolate salty oat cookies. *Average main: $12* ✉ *400 8th St. NW, Downtown* ☎ *202/638–6010* 🌐 *www.teaism.com* Ⓜ *Archives–Navy Memorial–Penn Quarter.*

★ **Zaytinya**

$$ | **MIDDLE EASTERN** | This sophisticated urban dining room with soaring ceilings is a local favorite for meeting friends or dining with a group (and popular enough that reservations can still be difficult to get). Here chef José Andrés devotes practically the entire menu to Turkish, Greek, and Lebanese small plates, known as meze. **Known for:** variety of meze; roasted lamb shoulder to share; vegetarian-friendly options. *Average main: $26* ✉ *701 9th St. NW, Penn Quarter* ☎ *202/638–0800* 🌐 *www.zaytinya.com* Ⓜ *Gallery Pl.–Chinatown.*

Hotels

For those who have not stayed in Washington for a decade or so, throw away your expectations. Cutting-edge hotels, like Monaco in Penn Quarter and Donovan and Eaton Workshop closer to downtown, have joined the traditional luxury names like St. Regis and the Jefferson, with the steady but sure Marriotts and Hiltons still visible and growing.

Capital Hilton

$$$ | **HOTEL** | The choice of many celebrities and dignitaries since it opened in 1943, the Hilton has modern perks like a health club and spa and is well located for shopping and eating out. **Pros:** nice guest rooms; desirable location; great gym, however, there's a daily fee unless you're a silver, gold, or diamond Hilton Honors member. **Cons:** expensive valet parking; reports of street noise; fee for Wi-Fi. *Rooms from: $400* ✉ *1001 16th St. NW, Downtown* ☎ *202/393–1000* 🌐 *www.capital.hilton.com* *576 rooms* *No meals* Ⓜ *Farragut N.*

Comfort Inn Downtown DC/Convention Center

$ | **HOTEL** | There's nothing fancy at this hotel, and rooms tend to be on the small side, but the location, price, and daily hot breakfast buffet all add up to a good value. **Pros:** fresh afternoon cookies and popcorn and all-day coffee and tea; pleasant staff; decent hot breakfast. **Cons:** some street noise at night; a bit out of the way; valet parking is $30 per day. $ *Rooms from: $185* ✉ *1201 13th St. NW, Downtown* ☎ *202/682–5300* ⊕ *www.dcdowntownhotel.com* ⤶ *100 rooms* ⦿ *Free Breakfast* Ⓜ *Mt. Vernon Sq. 7th St.–Convention Center.*

Eaton Hotel, Washington, DC

$ | HOTEL | Eaton is a new, progressive hotel that not only provides a stylish, comfortable room but distributes digital content to its customers on hot-button issues of the day, including climate change and immigration. **Pros:** nice retro-chic design; makes a political statement; wellness center and bar on-site. **Cons:** you may not agree with the hotel's politics; valet parking only (costs extra); not particularly family-friendly. $ *Rooms from: $200* ✉ *1201 K St. NW, Downtown* ☎ *202/289–7600* ⊕ *eatonworkshop.com* ⤶ *209 rooms* ⦿ *No meals* Ⓜ *Metro Center or McPherson Sq.*

Fairfield Inn & Suites Washington DC/ Downtown

$ | HOTEL | Bold, contemporary design provides a soothing retreat in a busy part of town, near many of the top attractions like the Verizon Center, the National Portrait Gallery, and the Mall. **Pros:** complimentary hot breakfast buffet; lots of restaurants, entertainment, and attractions nearby; authentic Irish pub on-site. **Cons:** some complaints about street noise; small gym; part of town not for everyone. $ *Rooms from: $195* ✉ *500 H St. NW, Chinatown* ☎ *202/289–5959* ⊕ *www. marriott.com* ⤶ *198 rooms* ⦿ *No meals* Ⓜ *Gallery Pl.–Chinatown.*

Grand Hyatt Washington

$$$ | HOTEL | A city within the city is what greets you as you step inside the Hyatt's doors and gaze upward to the balconies overlooking the blue lagoon and the many conveniences within the atrium. **Pros:** great location for sightseeing and shopping; often has weekend deals; nice gym and indoor pool. **Cons:** often filled with conventioneers; chain-hotel feel; expensive valet parking. $ *Rooms from: $319* ✉ *1000 H St. NW, Downtown* ☎ *202/582–1234, 800/233–1234* ⊕ *www. hyatt.com* ⤶ *897 rooms* ⦿ *No meals* Ⓜ *Metro Center.*

Hamilton Hotel Washington, D.C.

$$$$ | HOTEL | A short walk from the White House and the Mall, this appealing art deco hotel, on the National Register of Historic Places, is a good choice for visitors doing the sights, as well as business guests who come for top-notch meeting rooms and the nearby Convention Center. **Pros:** central location near White House; well-equipped fitness center; personal service. **Cons:** some street noise; small rooms; expensive valet parking. $ *Rooms from: $440* ✉ *1001 14th St. NW, Downtown* ☎ *202/682–0111* ⊕ *www.hamiltonhoteldc.com* ⤶ *318 rooms* ⦿ *No meals* Ⓜ *McPherson Sq.*

★ The Hay-Adams

$$$$ | HOTEL | Given the elegant charm and refined style, with guest rooms decorated in a class above the rest, it's no wonder this impressive Washington landmark continues to earn international accolades for its guest experience. **Pros:** impeccable service; basically next door to the White House; complimentary bikes, helmets, locks, and cycling maps. **Cons:** expensive parking; no pool; small bathrooms for this price point. $ *Rooms from: $450* ✉ *800 16th St. NW, Downtown* ☎ *202/638–6600, 800/424–5054* ⊕ *www.hayadams.com* ▭ *No credit cards* ⤶ *145 rooms* ⦿ *No meals* Ⓜ *McPherson Sq. or Farragut N.*

Henley Park Hotel

$ | HOTEL | A Tudor-style building adorned with gargoyles, this National Historic Trust property has the cozy feel of an English country house, and the atmosphere extends to charming rooms that were once the choice of senators and notables from Washington society. **Pros:** centrally located; historic building; welcoming staff. **Cons:** some rooms are small with very tiny bathrooms; rooms can be noisy and not all have views; expensive valet parking. [$] *Rooms from: $175* ✉ *926 Massachusetts Ave. NW, Penn Quarter* ☎ *202/638–5200, 800/222–8474* 🌐 *www.henleypark.com* 🛏 *96 rooms* 🍴 *No meals* [M] *Mt. Vernon Sq. 7th St.–Convention Center.*

★ InterContinental The Willard Washington D.C.

$$$ | **HOTEL** | **FAMILY** | Favored by American presidents and other news makers, this Washington landmark only two blocks from the White House offers superb service, a wealth of amenities, and guest rooms filled with period detail and Federal-style furniture. **Pros:** major room renovation finished June 2018; impeccable service; exudes a real sense of history. **Cons:** expensive valet parking; no pool; street-facing rooms can be noisy. [$] *Rooms from: $399* ✉ *1401 Pennsylvania Ave. NW, Downtown* ☎ *202/628–9100, 800/827–1747* 🌐 *www.washington.intercontinental.com* 🛏 *376 rooms* 🍴 *No meals* [M] *Metro Center.*

★ The Jefferson

$$$$ | **HOTEL** | Every inch of this 1923 beaux arts landmark exudes refined elegance, from the intimate seating areas that take the place of a traditional check-in counter to the delicate blooms and glass atrium at the entryway to Plume, the fine-dining restaurant. **Pros:** exquisite historic hotel in a great location; impeccable service; the Quill is about the best hotel bar in the city. **Cons:** expensive; some rooms have views of other buildings; not at all family-friendly. [$] *Rooms from: $600* ✉ *1200 16th St. NW, Downtown* ☎ *202/448–2300* 🌐 *www.jeffersondc.com* 🛏 *119 rooms* 🍴 *No meals* [M] *Farragut N.*

JW Marriott Washington, DC

$$$$ | **HOTEL** | From the location near the White House to the views from the top floors, it's hard to forget you are in the nation's capital when you stay in one of the beautifully furnished rooms here. **Pros:** in the heart of town; lovely rooms with a luxurious, traditional feel; good views from top floors. **Cons:** very busy; charge for in-room Wi-Fi; pricey in-house restaurants. [$] *Rooms from: $449* ✉ *1331 Pennsylvania Ave. NW, Downtown* ☎ *202/393–2000, 800/393–2503* 🌐 *www.jwmarriottdc.com* 🛏 *772 rooms* 🍴 *No meals* [M] *Metro Center.*

The Kimpton Donovan

$$ | **HOTEL** | You won't find anything remotely close to a colonial reproduction at this Kimpton property amid the leather canopy beds, slick furniture, and spiral showers—perfect if you're seeking an out-of-the-box-style lodging. **Pros:** evening wine hour; hip rooftop pool; close to the White House. **Cons:** smallish rooms; 10-minute walk to Metro; nightly amenity fee of $23 per night. [$] *Rooms from: $250* ✉ *1155 14th St. NW, Downtown* ☎ *202/737–1200, 888/550–0012* 🌐 *www.donovanhoteldc.com* 🛏 *210 rooms* 🍴 *No meals* [M] *McPherson Sq.*

★ Kimpton Hotel Monaco Washington DC

$$$ | **HOTEL** | Elegance and whimsy are in perfect harmony at this popular boutique Kimpton hotel—Washington's first all-marble building—in the heart of the Penn Quarter. **Pros:** all the Kimpton extras like a nightly wine hour; amazing design throughout; historic charm. **Cons:** noisy part of town; no pool; expensive valet parking. [$] *Rooms from: $380* ✉ *700 F St. NW, Penn Quarter* ☎ *202/628–7177, 800/649–1202* 🌐 *www.monaco-dc.com* 🛏 *183 rooms* 🍴 *No meals* [M] *Gallery Pl.–Chinatown.*

The Madison Washington DC, A Hilton Hotel

$$$ | **HOTEL** | The signatures of presidents, prime ministers, sultans, and kings fill the guest register at this classic Washington address, noted for polite service and stylish comfort and now rebranded as a Hilton. **Pros:** central location; pretty guest rooms with plush furnishings and linens; staff goes the extra mile. **Cons:** 20-minute walk from the Mall; many rooms are a bit dark with no views; not enough plugs in the room for electronic devices. $ *Rooms from: $300* ✉ *1177 15th St. NW, Downtown* ☎ *202/862–1600* ⊕ *www.hilton.com* ⇥ *356 rooms* ⦿ *No meals* Ⓜ *McPherson Sq.*

Marriott Marquis Washington, D.C

$$$$ | HOTEL | This eco-friendly hotel, directly adjacent to the Washington Convention Center, spans an entire city block, and is capped with an enormous atrium skylight that accentuates the dramatic lobby sculpture. **Pros:** location near Metro; nicely designed building; within walking distance of great restaurants. **Cons:** rooms overlooking atrium have less privacy and can be noisy; expensive fee for in-room Wi-Fi; big and impersonal. $ *Rooms from: $450* ✉ *901 Massachusetts Ave. NW, Downtown* ☎ *202/824–9200* ⊕ *www.marriott.com* ⇥ *1224 rooms* ⦿ *No meals* Ⓜ *Mt. Vernon Sq. 7th St.–Convention Center.*

★ The Mayflower Hotel, Autograph Collection

$$$ | HOTEL | FAMILY | With its magnificent block-long lobby filled with antique crystal chandeliers, layers of gold trim, and gilded columns, there's little wonder that this luxurious landmark has hosted presidential balls since its opening in 1925, as well as historic news conferences and even, for a short time, the Chinese Embassy. **Pros:** near dozens of restaurants; a few steps from Metro; the setting of plenty of political history and scandal. **Cons:** rooms vary greatly in size; expensive parking and pet fees; charge for in-room Wi-Fi unless you're a Marriott rewards member. $ *Rooms from: $325* ✉ *1127 Connecticut Ave. NW, Downtown* ☎ *202/347–3000, 800/228–7697* ⊕ *www.marriott.com/hotels/travel/wasak-the-mayflower-ho-*

tel-autograph-collection ⇥ *731 rooms* ⦿ *No meals* Ⓜ *Farragut N.*

★ Morrison-Clark Historic Inn

$$ | HOTEL | A fascinating history makes these beautiful 1864 Victorian town houses an interesting as well as a comfortable and well-located choice. **Pros:** charming alternative to cookie-cutter hotels; historic feel throughout; near Convention Center. **Cons:** some street noise; room size and style vary considerably; some bathrooms are pretty small. $ *Rooms from: $249* ✉ *1015 L St. NW, Downtown* ☎ *202/898–1200, 800/332–7898* ⊕ *www.morrisonclark.com* ⇥ *114 rooms* ⦿ *No meals* Ⓜ *Metro Center.*

POD Hotel DC

$$ | HOTEL | If you're the type of traveler who doesn't spend a lot of time in your room because you'd rather be seeing the city, check out Pod Hotel in the Penn Quarter area of the city. **Pros:** affordable for this part of the city; on-site restaurant and rooftop lounge; some rooms on higher floors have views (and are quieter). **Cons:** very small rooms, but that's the point; not many amenities; some doubles have bunk beds. $ *Rooms from: $225* ✉ *627 H St. NW, Chinatown* ☎ *202/847–4444* ⊕ *www.thepodhotel.com* ⇥ *245 rooms* ⦿ *No meals* Ⓜ *Gallery Pl.–Chinatown.*

Renaissance Washington, D.C. Downtown Hotel

$$$ | HOTEL | Large rooms with views, extensive business services, such touches as fine linens, and a lavish fitness center and spa elevate this chain hotel into the luxury realm. **Pros:** convenient to Convention Center and Metro; nice lobby and rooftop terrace; great fitness center and spa. **Cons:** convention crowds; chain-hotel feel; expensive parking. $ *Rooms from: $379* ✉ *999 9th St. NW, Chinatown* ☎ *202/898–9000, 800/228–9898* ⊕ *www.marriott.com* ⇥ *794 rooms, 13 suites* ⦿ *No meals* Ⓜ *Gallery Pl.–Chinatown.*

★ Sofitel Washington, D.C. Lafayette Square
$$$ | HOTEL | Only a minute's walk from the White House, the French luxury chain could not have landed a better location, and its caring, multilingual staff offers a warm welcome and great service. **Pros:** prestigious location; highly rated restaurant; lovely rooms. **Cons:** lobby on the small side; expensive parking; many rooms have internal views. [$] *Rooms from: $360* ✉ *806 15th St. NW, Downtown* ☎ *202/730–8800* 🌐 *www.sofitel.com* 💳 *No credit cards* 🛏 *237 rooms* 🍴 *No meals* [M] *McPherson Sq.*

The St. Regis Washington, D.C
$$$$ | HOTEL | Just two blocks from the White House, this gorgeous 1926 Italian Renaissance–style landmark attracts a business and diplomatic crowd. **Pros:** close to White House; historic property; exceptional service. **Cons:** most rooms don't have great views; very expensive; some rooms noisy and in need of upgrading. [$] *Rooms from: $625* ✉ *923 16th St. NW, Downtown* ☎ *202/638–2626* 🌐 *www.stregiswashingtondc.com* 🛏 *172 rooms* 🍴 *No meals* [M] *Farragut N or McPherson Sq.*

★ W Washington, D.C
$$$$ | HOTEL | It's hip, sleek, very cool, and just steps from the White House. **Pros:** trendy ambience; individualized and attentive service; popular rooftop bar. **Cons:** pricey; might be too modern for some; no pool. [$] *Rooms from: $599* ✉ *515 15th St. NW, Downtown* ☎ *202/661–2400* 🌐 *www.starwoodhotels.com/whotels* 🛏 *349 rooms* 🍴 *No meals* [M] *McPherson Sq.*

Washington Marriott at Metro Center
$$$ | HOTEL | The big-chain feel is offset by a good location just steps away from the monuments and museums; attractive, comfortable guest rooms; and an indoor pool and health club. **Pros:** great location; Starbucks on property with outdoor patio; no surprises. **Cons:** generic decor; charge for in-room Wi-Fi; big and impersonal. [$] *Rooms from: $379* ✉ *775 12th St. NW, Downtown* ☎ *202/737–2200, 800/393–2100* 🌐 *www.marriott.com/wasmc* 🛏 *459 rooms* 🍴 *No meals* [M] *Metro Center.*

🍸 Nightlife

You'll find plenty of bars and lounges in the Downtown area, which has been wonderfully revitalized, compared to years past. Development around Chinatown and the Verizon Center has turned this into a lively neighborhood, especially when there's a sports or musical event at the arena. A few blocks south, the formerly quiet Penn Quarter is seeing larger evening crowds, thanks to the opening of several terrific new restaurants, cafés, bars, and a world-class theater scene. Conveniently, especially if you plan to imbibe, you can easily get to Downtown on the Metro, exiting at the Archives–Navy Memorial–Penn Quarter station (Green and Yellow lines) or at the Gallery Place–Chinatown stop (Green, Yellow, and Red lines).

BARS AND LOUNGES

Barmini
BARS/PUBS | Only a small plaque on a bland concrete wall in a nondescript block of Penn Quarter identifies one of Washington's most sophisticated experiences. Step inside to see José Andrés's cocktail lab for his acclaimed chain of restaurants that looks the part, with white-on-white furnishings and mixologists in lab attire often seen pouring smoking libations out of beakers. A metal notebook features a menu of more than 100 alcohol-centered liquid experiments, grouped by spirit. Make it a show with drinks such as the tequila-based Cedar and Agave, in which a glass and block of ice are infused with the smell of burning wood, table-side, or the Floral Cloud, a fruity gin-based beverage delivered in a hibiscus haze. Soak up the chemical reactions with snacks such as savory miniwaffles. Behind the bar you can peer

through a framed glass window to see a handful of foodies at the sister minibar taking a similarly science-inspired culinary tour. All comes at a cost (between $18 and $25). ⊠ *501 9th St. NW, Penn Quarter* ☎ *202/393–4451* ⊕ *www.minibarbyjoseandres.com/barmini* Ⓜ *Archives–Navy Memorial–Penn Quarter.*

The Dignitary

BARS/PUBS | Inside the shell of an art deco–inspired edifice that once housed a labor union is one of the newest and most comfortably elegant bars in D.C., the corner spot of the new Marriott Marquis. Deeper inside the hotel you'll find a bustling lobby bar as well as a large, noisy sports bar with 48 beers on tap. But the Dignitary attracts a more refined crowd with its focus on more than 50 types of bourbons and ryes poured by a crew of bartenders as experienced as they are friendly. Also features an outdoor patio in the warmer months. ⊠ *901 Massachusetts Ave. NW, Downtown* ☎ *202/824–9681* ⊕ *www.marriott.com/hotels/hotel-information/restaurant/wasco-marriott-marquis-washington-dc* Ⓜ *Mt. Vernon Sq. 7th St.–Convention Center.*

The Hamilton

MUSIC CLUBS | From the street, it looks like a swanky downtown D.C. restaurant with a high-ceilinged power bar to match. The magic really happens, however, with live shows in The Hamilton's cavernous basement space. Care in equal parts has focused on acoustics, comfort, and tiered seating that makes it hard to find a bad seat. There is secondary space above the bar-restaurant where the venue regularly hosts more intimate acts and "Free Late Night Music in the Loft." ⊠ *600 14th St. NW, Downtown* ☎ *202/787–1000* ⊕ *live.thehamiltondc.com* Ⓜ *Metro Center.*

★ P.O.V.

BARS/PUBS | For decades, the perfect way to end a night out in Washington was a trip up to the Sky Tavern on the Hotel Washington's 11th-floor rooftop. The W Hotel has replaced the Hotel Washington, and the Sky Tavern has been reincarnated as P.O.V. ("Point of View"), a trendy, hipster indoor lounge and outdoor terrace offering a tremendous view over D.C.'s low skyline. Enjoy the unique view of the Washington Monument and the White House while enjoying a pan-Mediterranean menu of cocktails, appetizers, and small plates. While the view here is no secret, meaning waits are common, P.O.V. does take reservations. Popping by in the late afternoon may be a more relaxed option. ■**TIP**➔ **After 5 pm, the venue only allows 21 and older.** ⊠ *515 15 St. NW, Downtown* ☎ *202/661–2400* ⊕ *www.povrooftop.com* Ⓜ *McPherson Sq.*

Quill

PIANO BARS/LOUNGES | At this *Mad Men* flashback fantasy bar tucked inside the Jefferson Hotel, the drinks are stiff and complicated, while the mood is a quiet celebration of all things civilized. The dimly lit, two-room, wood-paneled, art deco space provides an intimate atmosphere made even more welcoming by the friendly and expert service of the bartenders. A pianist quietly serenades patrons throughout the evening. Pricey, but worth it. ⊠ *The Jefferson, 1200 16th St. NW, Downtown* ☎ *202/448–2300* ⊕ *www.jeffersondc.com/dining/quill* Ⓜ *Farragut N.*

COMEDY CLUBS

★ Capitol Steps

COMEDY CLUBS | Putting the "mock" in democracy, the musical political satire of this group—many of whom are current or former Hill staffers—is presented in the amphitheater of the Ronald Reagan Building every Friday and Saturday at 7:30 pm and occasionally at other spots around town. This Washington classic is fun for the whole family, no matter on which side of the aisle you sit. Tickets are around $40 and available through Ticketmaster and online. ⊠ *Ronald Reagan Building and International Trade Center, 1300 Pennsylvania Ave. NW, Downtown*

☎ 703/683–8330 ⊕ www.capsteps.com Ⓜ Federal Triangle.

DC Improv

COMEDY CLUBS | Having just passed its 25th anniversary, the Improv is D.C.'s main spot for comedy, offering a steady menu of well-known and promising stand-up headliners—recent acts have included Judah Friedlander—as well as a bevy of funny amateurs. Tickets vary depending on the act. Typically, there's a two-item minimum from a full food and drink menu. ⊠ 1140 Connecticut Ave. NW, Downtown ☎ 202/296–7008 ⊕ www.dcimprov.com Ⓜ Farragut N.

DANCE CLUBS

The Park at Fourteenth

DANCE CLUBS | A high-end crowd includes visiting basketball players and R&B stars, who dance on four levels. The fancy and formal dress code is strictly enforced by the bouncers. Pricey perks include your own bottle service. You can arrange in advance to get a table or brave the long lines that develop later in the night. This is definitely a place to see and be seen. ⊠ 920 14th St. NW, Downtown ☎ 202/737–7275 ⊕ www.park14.com Ⓜ McPherson Sq.

🎭 Performing Arts

Several of Washington's most prestigious performance centers can be found in Downtown D.C. Woolly Mammoth Theater, the Shakespeare Theatre's Sidney Harmon Hall, and other venues are surrounded by a bustling nightlife where visitors have their choice of cuisines and after-performance conversation. You'll also be entertained by a host of street performers and musicians.

MAJOR VENUES

Capital One Arena

CONCERTS | In addition to being the home of the NHL Stanley Cup champion Washington Capitals and Washington Wizards basketball teams, this 19,000-seat arena also plays host to D.C.'s biggest concerts and other major events. Drivers need to park in one of the many underground garages close by, but there are several convenient Metro lines, too. During warmer months be sure to check out the frequent street concerts on the intersections surrounding the arena. ⊠ 601 F St. NW, Chinatown ☎ 202/661–5000 ⊕ capitalonearena.viewlift.com Ⓜ Gallery Pl.–Chinatown.

FILM

★ Landmark's E Street Cinema

FILM | Specializing in independent, foreign, and documentary films, this theater has been warmly welcomed by D.C. movie lovers both for its selection and its state-of-the-art facilities. The *Washington Post* has often declared it D.C.'s best movie theater in its annual assessments. Its concession stand is fabulous and it is also one of the few movie theaters in the city that serves alcohol. ⊠ 555 11th St. NW, Downtown ☎ 202/452–7672 ⊕ www.landmarktheatres.com Ⓜ Metro Center.

THEATER AND PERFORMANCE ART

Ford's Theatre

THEATER | FAMILY | Looking much as it did before President Lincoln was shot at a performance of *Our American Cousin,* Ford's hosts musicals as well as dramas with historical connections, and stages *A Christmas Carol* every year. The historic theater is now maintained by the National Park Service. Tours of the theater and accompanying museum are available for free, but timed entry tickets are required. Tickets to shows can range from $20 to $70 ⊠ 511 10th St. NW, Downtown ☎ 202/426–6925 ⊕ www.fords.org Ⓜ Metro Center.

National Theatre

THEATER | FAMILY | Though rebuilt several times, the National Theatre has operated in the same location since 1835. It now hosts touring Broadway shows, from classics like *Porgy and Bess* and *Chicago,* to contemporary punk like *American Idiot.* ■ **TIP→ From September through April,**

look for free children's shows Saturday mornings and free Monday night shows that may include Asian dance, performance art, and a cappella cabarets. Ticket prices vary with each show. ⊠ *1321 Pennsylvania Ave. NW, Downtown* ☎ *800/447–7400* ⊕ *thenationaldc.org* Ⓜ *Metro Center.*

★ Shakespeare Theatre

THEATER | This acclaimed troupe crafts fantastically staged and acted performances of works by Shakespeare and other significant playwrights, offering traditional renditions but also some with a modern twist. Complementing the stage in the Lansburgh Theatre is Sidney Harman Hall, which provides a state-of-the-art, midsize venue for an outstanding variety of performances, from Shakespeare's *Much Ado About Nothing* to Racine's tragic *Phèdre* for visiting companies like South Africa's Baxter Theatre and its production of *Mies Julie.* For two weeks in the summer the group performs Shakespeare for free at Sidney Harmon Hall. ⊠ *450 7th St. NW, Downtown* ☎ *202/547–1122* ⊕ *shakespearetheatre.org* Ⓜ *Gallery Pl.–Chinatown or Archives–Navy Memorial–Penn Quarter.*

Sixth & I Historic Synagogue

MUSIC | Known for its author readings and its comedy, with guests ranging from comedian Tina Fey to Nancy Pelosi, the Sixth & I Historic Synagogue has been named one of the most vibrant congregations in the nation. The intimate space, founded in 1852, hosts religious events as well. ⊠ *600 I St. NW, Chinatown* ☎ *202/408–3100* ⊕ *www.sixthandi.org* Ⓜ *Gallery Pl.–Chinatown.*

Warner Theatre

DANCE | One of Washington's grand theaters, the Warner hosts Broadway road shows, dance recitals, high-profile pop-music acts, and comedians in a majestic art deco performance space with wonderful acoustics. ⊠ *513 13th St. NW, Downtown* ☎ *202/783–4000* ⊕ *warnertheatredc.com* Ⓜ *Metro Center.*

★ Woolly Mammoth

THEATER | Unusual cutting-edge shows with solid acting have earned this company top reviews and 35 Helen Hayes Awards. The theater performs works for a decidedly urban audience that challenge the status quo. In recent years, they have welcomed Chicago's The Second City for an annual political comedy show as well as the works of Mike Daisey, the author of *The Agony and Ecstasy of Steve Jobs.* The troupe's talent is accentuated by its modern 265-seat theater in bustling Downtown D.C. The Woollies also create a unique lobby experience for each show; bring your iPhone and share the experience. ⊠ *641 D St. NW, Downtown* ☎ *202/393–3939* ⊕ *www.woollymammoth.net* Ⓜ *Gallery Pl.–Chinatown or Archives–Navy Memorial–Penn Quarter.*

⊖ Shopping

Downtown D.C. is spread out and sprinkled with federal buildings and museums. Shopping options run the gamut from the upscale CityCenter complex and Gallery Place shopping center to small art galleries and bookstores. Gallery Place houses familiar chain stores like Urban Outfitters, Bed Bath & Beyond, and Ann Taylor Loft; it also has a movie theater and a bowling alley. Other big names in the Downtown area include Macy's and chain stores like H&M, Target, and Banana Republic. With its many offices, Downtown tends to shut down at 5 pm sharp, with the exception of the department stores and larger chain stores. A jolly happy-hour crowd springs up after work and families and fans fill the streets during weekend sporting events at the Capital One Arena. The revitalized Penn Quarter has some of the best restaurants in town peppered among its galleries and specialty stores.

The worthwhile shops are not concentrated in one area, however. The Gallery Place–Chinatown Metro stop provides the most central starting point—you can walk south to the galleries and design shops, or west toward the Metro Center and Farragut North, though this trek is only for the ambitious. Although Gallery Place is a nightlife hot spot, the Metro Center and the Farragut area are largely silent after working hours.

CRAFTS AND GIFTS
★ Fahrney's Pens

CRAFTS | What began in 1929 as a repair shop and a pen bar—a place to fill your fountain pen before setting out for work—is now a wonderland for anyone who loves a good writing instrument. You'll find pens in silver, gold, and lacquer by the world's leading manufacturers. If you want to improve your handwriting, the store offers classes in calligraphy and cursive. And yes, the store still offers repair services for all writing instruments ⊠ *1317 F St. NW, Downtown* ☎ *202/628–9525* ⊕ *www.fahrneyspens.com* Ⓜ *Metro Center.*

JEWELRY
★ Tiny Jewel Box

JEWELRY/ACCESSORIES | Despite its name, this venerable D.C. favorite contains six floors of precious and semiprecious wares, including unique gifts, home accessories, vintage pieces, and works by such well-known designers as David Yurman, Penny Preville, and Alex Sepkus. The Federal Collection on the sixth floor features handmade boxes and paperweights with decoupages of vintage prints of Washington commissioned by the Tiny Jewel Box. *InStore Magazine* has named this family-run store "America's Coolest Jewelry Store." Even if you're not buying, come in and look around. It's like a shopping museum. ⊠ *1147 Connecticut Ave. NW, Downtown* ☎ *202/393–2747* ⊕ *www.tinyjewelbox.com* Ⓜ *Farragut N.*

MEN'S CLOTHING
J. Press

CLOTHING | Like its flagship store (founded in Connecticut in 1902 as a custom shop for Yale University), this Washington outlet keeps with the Ivy League traditions.

Harris tweed and classic navy blazers are the best sellers. ⊠ *1801 L St. NW, Downtown* ☎ *202/857–0120* ⊕ *www. jpressonline.com* Ⓜ *Farragut N.*

SHOPPING MALLS
CityCenterDC

SHOPPING CENTERS/MALLS | Downtown's newest shopping complex is an upscale gathering of high-end boutiques, restaurants, residential and office buildings, park, and open-air plaza, bordered by New York Avenue, 9th, 11th, and H Streets NW. It's all too easy to spend several hundred dollars in just a few minutes here, with leather goods from Longchamp, Louis Vuitton, and Salvatore Ferragamo; designer fashions and accessories from Burberry, Canali, CH Carolina Herrera, Kate Spade, Loro Piana, Paul Stuart, Zadig & Voltaire; outdoor clothing and sporting goods from Arc'teryx; Tumi luggage; and David Yurman jewelry. For a break from shopping or browsing, grab an indulgent treat from Momofuku Milk Bar, Rare Sweets, or a scrumptious gelato from Dolcezza and relax in the plaza with its benches, tables, and fountains. The 10-acre site will also have a luxury hotel, slated for completion in 2018. ⊠ *825 10th St. NW, Downtown* ☎ *202/347–6337* ⊕ *www.citycenter-dc.com* Ⓜ *Metro Center or Gallery Pl.–Chinatown.*

SPAS AND BEAUTY SALONS
Andre Chreky

SPA/BEAUTY | Housed in an elegantly renovated Victorian town house, this salon offers complete services—hair, nails, facials, waxing, and makeup. Because it's a favorite of the Washington elite, you might just overhear a tidbit or two on who's going to what black-tie function with whom. Adjacent whirlpool pedicure chairs allow two friends to get pampered simultaneously. ⊠ *1604 K St. NW, Downtown* ☎ *202/293–9393* ⊕ *www. andrechreky.com* Ⓜ *Farragut N.*

The Grooming Lounge

SPA/BEAUTY | Most spas are geared to women, but guys are pampered here. You can find old-fashioned hot-lather shaves, haircuts, massages, and business manicures and pedicures—everything a man needs to look terrific. The hair- and skin-care products—from Kiehl's, Billy Jealousy, and Malin+Goetz, to name just a few—are worth a visit even if you don't have time for a service. ✉ *1745 L St. NW, Downtown* ☎ *202/466–8900* ⊕ *www.groominglounge.com* Ⓜ *Farragut N.*

WOMEN'S CLOTHING

Coup de Foudre

CLOTHING | The name translates to "love at first sight," and that may be the case when you step into this inviting, elegant boutique. All the upscale lingerie hails from France, England, Belgium, and Italy, and the specialty is friendly, personalized bra fittings. Appointments accepted. ✉ *1001 Pennsylvania Ave. NW, Downtown* ☎ *202/393–0878* ⊕ *www.shopcdf.com* Ⓜ *Metro Center.*

Rizik's

CLOTHING | This tony, patrician Washington institution offers women's designer clothing, accessories, outerwear, bridal fashions, and expert advice. The sales staff will help you find just the right style from the store's extensive inventory from worldwide designers. If you're looking for a one-of-kind cocktail or evening dress, this is the place to get it. Take the elevator up from the northwest corner of Connecticut Avenue and L Street. ✉ *1100 Connecticut Ave. NW, Downtown* ☎ *202/223–4050* ⊕ *www.riziks.com* Ⓜ *Farragut N.*

Chapter 5

CAPITOL HILL AND NORTHEAST

Updated by
Mike Lillis

⊙ **Sights**
★★★★☆

🍴 **Restaurants**
★★★☆☆

🛏 **Hotels**
★★★☆☆

🛍 **Shopping**
★★★☆☆

🍸 **Nightlife**
★★★★☆

NEIGHBORHOOD SNAPSHOT

TOP EXPERIENCES

■ **The Capitol:** See where democracy is put into action. Start your tour at the visitor center, then walk among marble American heroes and gape at the soaring Rotunda.

■ **The Markets:** Eastern Market is the more traditional, offering fresh produce, baked goods, and locally made crafts. Union Market is an upscale version, featuring oyster bars and chic coffee. Both are beloved weekend destinations.

■ **The Library of Congress and Supreme Court:** Flanking the Capitol, both are architectural wonders offering a must-see window into the nation's history and the workings of government. At the court, you can watch live as the justices hear precedent-setting arguments.

■ **Union Station:** More than a train station, it's a stunning gem of classical architecture where the vaulted ceiling soars almost 100 feet above the massive marble floor. Shops and restaurants also await.

■ **Strolling and Dining:** The area boasts three lively commercial corridors: Pennsylvania Avenue, H Street, and Barracks Row, one of the city's oldest neighborhoods and a vital bulwark in wars past. All feature a wide array of bars, restaurants, and shops.

■ **United States Botanic Garden:** Wrinkle your nose at the corpse flower, explore the jungle, gawk at the orchids, or stroll the paths of the National Garden.

GETTING HERE

From the Red Line's Union Station, you can walk to most destinations on Capitol Hill. A new streetcar runs from behind the station along the full length of H Street—a good option for accessing the street's spirited nightlife. From the Blue and Orange lines, the Capitol South stop is close to the Capitol and Library of Congress, and the Eastern Market stop leads to the market and the Marine Corps Barracks. Bus Nos. 31, 32, 36, and Circulator buses run from Friendship Heights through Georgetown and Downtown to Independence Avenue, the Capitol, and Eastern Market.

SAFETY

■ While crime is rare around Capitol Hill, it does occur, particularly in fast-changing neighborhoods like the H Street corridor. Visitors can limit the risk with commonsense steps like keeping to well-populated areas and traveling with companions after dark. In short, stay alert—D.C. is relatively safe, but it's still a city.

QUICK BITES

■ **Library of Congress's Madison Building Cafeteria.** Steps from the Capitol, it gets raves for its varied breakfast and lunch (weekdays only). ✉ *Madison Building, Library of Congress, Independence Ave. SE, between 1st and 2nd Sts.* ⊕ *www.loc.gov* Ⓜ *Capitol S.*

■ **Union Station.** No matter the time of day or dining moods of your group, you'll find everything you might want here. ✉ *50 Massachusetts Ave. NE* ⊕ *www.unionstationdc.com/restaurants* Ⓜ *Union Station.*

■ **We, the Pizza.** *Top Chef's* Spike Mendelsohn flips specialty pies with creative ingredients. Closed Sunday. ✉ *305 Pennsylvania Ave. SE* ⊕ *www.wethepizza.com* Ⓜ *Capitol S.*

The people who live and work on "the Hill" do so in the shadow of the edifice that lends the neighborhood its name: the gleaming white U.S. Capitol. But beyond the area's grand buildings lies a vibrant and diverse group of neighborhoods with charming residential blocks lined with Victorian row houses and a fine assortment of restaurants, shops, and bars, where senators, members of Congress, and lobbyists come to unwind or to continue their deal making. This area includes the Eastern Market, the Atlas District (also known as the H Street corridor), Union Station, and Union Market.

 Sights

Belmont-Paul Women's Equality National Monument

HISTORIC SITE | Standing strong on Capitol Hill for more than 200 years, this house witnessed the construction of the U.S. Capitol and Supreme Court, and its early occupants participated in the formation of Congress. In 1929, the National Woman's Party (NWP), founded by Alice Paul, an outspoken suffragist and feminist, purchased the house, and it soon evolved into a center for feminist education and social change. For more than 60 years, the trailblazing NWP utilized its strategic location, steps from the U.S. Capitol and its Congressional offices, to lobby for women's political, social, and economic equality. Today, an expansive collection of artifacts from the suffrage and equal rights campaigns brings the story of the women's rights movement to life. The innovative tactics and strategies these women devised became the blueprint for women's progress throughout the 20th century. In 2016, President Obama designated the home as a national monument. ✉ *144 Constitution Ave. NE, Capitol*

Hill ✛ *Entrance on 2nd St., next to Hart Senate Office Building* ☎ *202/543–2240* ⊕ *www.nps.gov/bepa* 🖾 *Free* ⊙ *Closed Mon. and Tues.* Ⓜ *Union Station.*

Folger Shakespeare Library

LIBRARY | This Elizabethan monument, a white marble art deco building decorated with sculpted scenes from the Bard's plays, was designed by architect Paul Philippe Cret and dedicated in 1932. Inside, the design is Tudor England with oak paneling, high plaster ceilings, and ornamental floor tiles. Henry Clay Folger, the Library's founder, personally selected the inscriptions by and about Shakespeare that are found throughout the property. The Great Hall is simply stunning, and holds rotating exhibits from the library's collection. Terra-cotta floor tiles feature titles of Shakespeare's plays and the masks of comedy and tragedy while the First Folio of Shakespeare is always on view and may be thumbed through here digitally.

Visitors are greeted at the entrance to the Elizabethan Theatre with a marble statue of Puck from *A Midsummer Night's Dream*. With its overhead canopy, wooden balconies, and oak columns, the Theatre is a reproduction of a 16th-century inn-yard playhouse. This is the site for performances of Shakespearean plays, chamber music, readings, lectures, and family programs; check the website for a calendar of events. Understandably, the collection of works by and about Shakespeare and his times is second to none and both the Paster and New Reading Rooms are devoted to scholarly research. On Saturday at noon you can tour both rooms; advance reservations are required. A manicured Elizabethan garden on the grounds is open to the public, and the gift shop contains many collectibles featuring the Bard and English theater. ✉ *201 E. Capitol St. SE, Capitol Hill* ☎ *202/544–4600* ⊕ *www. folger.edu* 🖾 *Free* Ⓜ *Capitol S.*

★ **Library of Congress**

LIBRARY | Founded in 1800, the largest library in the world has more than 164 million items on approximately 838 miles of bookshelves. Only 38 million of its holdings are books—the library also has 3.6 million recordings, 14 million photographs, 5.5 million maps, 8.1 million pieces of sheet music, and 70 million manuscripts. Also here is the Congressional Research Service, which, as the name implies, works on special projects for senators and representatives.

Built in 1897, the copper-domed **Thomas Jefferson Building** is the oldest of the three buildings that make up the library. The dome, topped with the gilt "Flame of Knowledge," is ornate and decorative, with busts of Dante, Goethe, and Nathaniel Hawthorne perched above its entryway. The *Court of Neptune*, Roland Hinton Perry's fountain at the front steps, rivals some of Rome's best fountains.

The Jefferson Building opens into the Great Hall, richly adorned with mosaics, paintings, and curving marble stairways. The octagonal Main Reading Room, its central desk surrounded by mahogany readers' tables under a 160-foot-high domed ceiling, inspires researchers and readers alike. Computer terminals have replaced card catalogs, but books are still retrieved and dispersed the same way: readers (16 years or older) hand request slips to librarians and wait for their materials to be delivered. Researchers aren't allowed in the stacks, and only members of Congress and other special borrowers can check books out. Items from the library's collection—which includes one of only three perfect Gutenberg Bibles in the world—are on display in the Jefferson Building's second-floor Southwest Gallery and Pavilion. ■TIP→ **To even begin to come to grips with the scope and grandeur of the library, one of the free hourly tours is highly recommended.** ✉ *Jefferson Building, 1st St. and Independence Ave. SE, Capitol*

*Hill ☎ 202/707–9779 ⊕ www.loc.gov
⊠ Free ⊗ Closed Sun. Ⓜ Capitol S.*

Marine Barracks

HISTORIC SITE | In early 1801, President
Thomas Jefferson and the second commandant of the Marine Corps, Lt. Col.
William Ward Burrows, made a horseback tour through Washington, D.C.,
looking for a proper site for the Marine
Barracks. They selected "Square 927,"
and the commandant's house was completed in 1806, followed by the Barracks
in 1808. It was among the few buildings
left standing when the British burned
much of the Capitol in 1814. After years
of renovations and additions, the Geor-
gian-Federalist-style home now boasts
15,000 square feet of space and more
than 30 rooms. Still used for its original
purpose, the Home of the Commandants
on 8th and I Streets is said to be the oldest continuously occupied public building
in Washington, D.C. "Square 927," now
the block surrounded by 8th, I, 9th, and
G Streets SE, was designated a National
Historic Landmark in 1976. Although you
can't tour the home, you can see the
outside of this impressive home for the
commandant of the Marine Corps and
the historic Marine Barracks. ⊠ 801 G
St. SE, Eastern Market ☎ 202/433–6040
⊕ www.barracks.marines.mil Ⓜ Eastern
Market or Potomac Ave.

Smithsonian National Postal Museum

MUSEUM | FAMILY | The National Museum
of Natural History has the Hope Diamond, but the National Postal Museum
has the envelope wrapping used to mail
the gem to the Smithsonian—part of a
collection that consists of more than 6
million stamps. Exhibits, underscoring
the important part the mail has played in
America's development, include horse-
drawn mail coaches, railroad mail cars,
airmail planes, and a collection of philatel-
ic rarities. Learn about stamp collecting
and tour *Systems at Work,* an exhibit that
demonstrates how mail has gone from

the mailbox to its destination for the
past 200 years, featuring a high-def film
highlighting amazing technologies. The
William Gross Stamp Gallery, the largest
of its kind in the world, has an additional
20,000 objects never before on public
display, showing how closely stamps
have intertwined with American history.
The museum is housed next to Union
Station in the old Washington City Post
Office, designed by Daniel Burnham and
completed in 1914. ⊠ 2 Massachusetts
Ave. NE, Capitol Hill ☎ 202/633–5555
⊕ www.postalmuseum.si.edu ⊠ Free
Ⓜ Union Station.

★ **Supreme Court of the United States**

GOVERNMENT BUILDING | It wasn't until
1935 that the Supreme Court got its
own building: a white-marble temple
with twin rows of Corinthian columns
designed by Cass Gilbert. Before then,
the justices had been moved around to
various rooms in the Capitol; for a while
they even met in a tavern. William Howard Taft, the only man to serve as both
president and chief justice, was instru-
mental in getting the court a home of its
own, though he died before the building
was completed. Today you can sit in the
gallery and see the court in action. Even
when court isn't in session, there are still
things to see.

The court convenes on the first Monday
in October and hears cases until April
(though court is in session through June).
There are usually two arguments a day
at 10 and 11 in the morning, Monday
through Wednesday, in two-week
intervals.

On mornings when court is in session,
two lines form for people wanting to
attend. The "three-to-five-minute" line
shuttles you through, giving you a quick
impression of the court at work. The
full-session line gets you in for the whole
show. If you want to see a full session,
it's best to be in line by at least 8:30. For
the most contentious cases, viewers

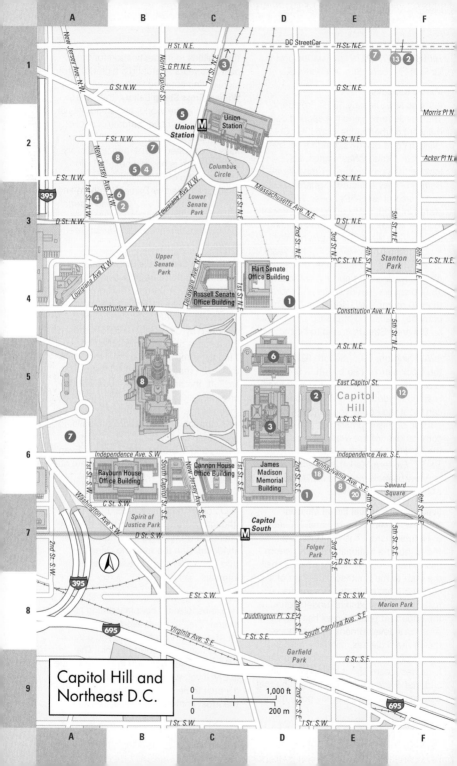

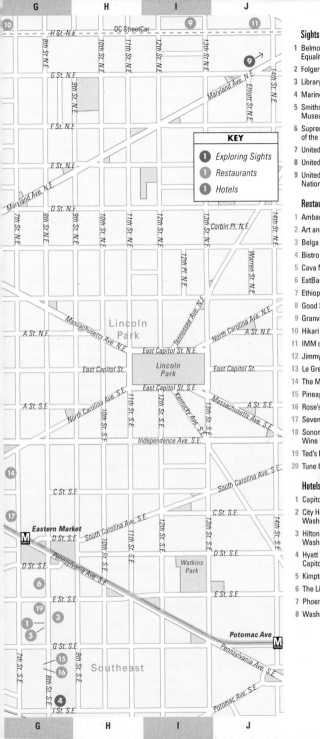

Sights ▼

1 Belmont-Paul Women's Equality National Monument..... **D4**
2 Folger Shakespeare Library...... **D5**
3 Library of Congress................ **D6**
4 Marine Barracks................... **G9**
5 Smithsonian National Postal Museum **C2**
6 Supreme Court of the United States **D5**
7 United States Botanic Garden ... **A6**
8 United States Capitol............. **B5**
9 United States National Arboretum **J1**

Restaurants ▼

1 Ambar Capitol Hill **G8**
2 Art and Soul **B3**
3 Belga Café......................... **G8**
4 Bistro Bis **B2**
5 Cava Mezze **G8**
6 EatBar............................. **G8**
7 Ethiopic Restaurant **E1**
8 Good Stuff Eatery.................. **E6**
9 Granville Moore's.................. **I1**
10 Hikari Sushi and Sake Bar........ **G1**
11 IMM on H.......................... **J1**
12 Jimmy T's Place................... **F5**
13 Le Grenier **F1**
14 The Market Lunch **G6**
15 Pineapple and Pearls **G9**
16 Rose's Luxury **G9**
17 Seventh Hill Pizza................. **G7**
18 Sonoma Restaurant and Wine Bar......................... **E6**
19 Ted's Bulletin **G8**
20 Tune Inn........................... **E7**

Hotels ▼

1 Capitol Hill Hotel **D6**
2 City House Hostel Washington DC **F1**
3 Hilton Garden Inn Washington DC/U.S. Capitol....... **C1**
4 Hyatt Regency Washington on Capitol Hill **A3**
5 Kimpton George Hotel............. **B2**
6 The Liaison Capitol Hill............ **B3**
7 Phoenix Park Hotel **B2**
8 Washington Court Hotel **B2**

have been known to queue up days before. In May and June the court takes to the bench Monday morning at 10 to release orders and opinions. Sessions usually last 15 to 30 minutes and are open to the public.

The *Washington Post* carries a daily listing of what cases the court will hear. The court displays its calendar of cases a month in advance on its website; click on "Oral Arguments." You can't bring your overcoat or electronics such as cameras and cell phones into the courtroom, but you can store them in a coin-operated locker. When court isn't in session, you can hear lectures about the court, typically given every hour on the half hour from 9:30 to 3:30. On the ground floor you can also find revolving exhibits, a video about the court, a gift shop, an information desk, and a larger-than-life statue of John Marshall, the longest-serving chief justice in Supreme Court history. ✉ *1 1st St. NE, Capitol Hill* ☎ *202/479–3030* ⊕ *www. supremecourt.gov* ✉ *Free* ⊙ *Closed weekends* Ⓜ *Union Station or Capitol S.*

★ United States Botanic Garden

GARDEN | FAMILY | Established by Congress in 1820, this is the oldest continually operating botanic garden in North America. The garden conservatory sits at the foot of Capitol Hill, and offers an escape from the stone-and-marble federal office buildings that surround it; inside are exotic rain-forest species, desert flora, and trees from all parts of the world. Walkways suspended 24 feet above the ground provide a fascinating view of the plants. Established in 2006, the National Garden emphasizes educational exhibits and features a Rose Garden, Butterfly Garden, Lawn Terrace, First Ladies' Water Garden, and Regional Garden. ✉ *1st St. at 100 Maryland Ave. SW, Capitol Hill* ☎ *202/225–8333* ⊕ *www.usbg.gov* ✉ *Free* Ⓜ *Federal Center SW.*

★ United States Capitol

GOVERNMENT BUILDING | Beneath the Capitol's magnificent dome, the day-to-day business of American democracy takes place: senators and representatives debate, coax, and cajole, and ultimately determine the law of the land. For many visitors the Capitol is the most exhilarating experience Washington has to offer. It wins them over with a three-pronged appeal: it's the city's most impressive work of architecture; it has on display documents, art, and artifacts from 400 years of American history; and its legislative chambers are open to the public, allowing you to actually see your lawmakers at work.

Before heading to the Capitol, pay a little attention to the grounds, landscaped in the late 19th century by Frederick Law Olmsted, famed for New York City's Central Park. On these 68 acres are both the city's tamest squirrels and the highest concentration of TV news correspondents, jockeying for a good position in front of the Capitol for their "stand-ups." A few hundred feet northeast of the Capitol are two cast-iron car shelters, left from the days when horse-drawn trolleys served the Hill. Olmsted's six pinkish, bronze-top lamps directly east of the Capitol are worth a look, too.

The design of the building was the result of a competition held in 1792; the winner was William Thornton, a physician and amateur architect from the West Indies. With its central rotunda and dome, Thornton's Capitol is reminiscent of Rome's Pantheon. This similarity must have delighted the nation's founders, who sought inspiration from the principles of the Republic of Rome.

The cornerstone was laid by George Washington in a Masonic ceremony on September 18, 1793, and in November 1800 both the Senate and the House of Representatives moved down from Philadelphia to occupy the first completed

Continued on page 137

ON THE HILL, UNDER THE DOME: EXPERIENCING THE CAPITOL

In Washington, the Capitol literally stands above it all: by law, no other building in the city can reach the height of the dome's peak.

Beneath its magnificent dome, the day-to-day business of American democracy takes place: senators and representatives debate, coax, and cajole, and ultimately determine the law of the land.

For many visitors, the Capitol is the most exhilarating experience Washington has to offer. It wins them over with a three-pronged appeal:

■ It's the city's most impressive work of architecture.

■ It has on display documents, art, and artifacts from 400 years of American history.

■ Its legislative chambers are open to the public. You can actually see your lawmakers at work, shaping the history of tomorrow.

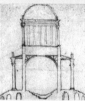

(Clockwise from top left) Moving into the new Capitol circa 1800; 19th–century print by R. Brandard; Thornton sketch circa 1797; the Capitol before the dome.

A Man with a Plan

1792–1807

William Thornton, a physician and amateur architect from the West Indies, wins the competition to design the Capitol. His plan, with its central rotunda and dome, draws inspiration from Rome's Pantheon. On September 18, 1793, George Washington lays the Capitol's cornerstone. In November 1800, Congress moves from Philadelphia to take up residence in the first completed section, the boxlike area between the central rotunda and today's north wing. In 1807, the House wing is completed, just to the south of the rotunda; a covered wooden walkway joins the two wings.

Washington Burns

1814–1826

In 1814, British troops march on Washington and set fire to the Capitol, the White House, and other government buildings. The wooden walkway is destroyed and the two wings gutted, but the walls remain standing after a violent rainstorm douses the flames. Fearful that Congress might leave Washington, residents fund a temporary "Brick Capitol" on the spot where the Supreme Court is today. By 1826, reconstruction is completed under the guidance of architects Benjamin Henry Latrobe and Charles Bulfinch; a low dome is made of wood sheathed in copper.

Domed if You Do

1850s–1880s

North and south wings are added through the 1850s and '60s to accommodate the growing government of a growing country. To maintain scale with the enlarged building, work begins in 1885 on a taller, cast-iron dome. President Lincoln would be criticized for continuing the expensive project during the Civil War, but he calls the construction "a sign we intend the Union shall go on."

(Clockwise from top left) The east front circa 1861; today the Capitol is a tourist mecca with its own visitor center; *Freedom* statue.

1960s–Today

Expanding the Capitol

The east front is extended 33½ feet, creating 100 additional offices. In 1983 preservationists fight to keep the west front, the last remaining section of the Capitol's original facade, from being extended; in a compromise the facade's crumbling sandstone blocks are replaced with stronger limestone. In 2000 the ground is broken on the subterranean Capitol Visitor Center, to be located beneath the grounds to the building's east side. The extensive facility, three-fourths the size of the Capitol itself, was finally completed on December 2, 2008 to the tune of $621 million.

Freedom atop the Capitol Dome

The twin-shelled Capitol dome, a marvel of 19th-century engineering, rises 285 feet above the ground and weighs 4,500 tons. It can expand and contract as much as 4 inches in a day, depending on the outside temperature.

The allegorical figure on top of the dome is *Freedom*. Sculpted in 1857 by Thomas Crawford, *Freedom* was cast with help from Philip Reid, a slave. Crawford had first planned for the 19½-foot-tall bronze statue to wear the cloth liberty cap of a freed Roman slave, but Southern lawmakers, led by Jefferson Davis, objected. An "American" headdress composed of a star-encir-cled helmet surmounted with an eagle's head and feathers was substituted. A light just below the statue burns whenever Congress is in session.

Before the visitor center opened, the best way to see the details on the *Freedom* statue atop the Capitol dome was with a good set of binoculars. Now, you can see the original plaster model of this classical female figure up close. Her right hand rests on a sheathed sword, while her left carries a victory wreath and a shield of the United States with 13 stripes. She also wears a brooch with "U.S." on her chest.

THE CAPITOL VISITOR CENTER

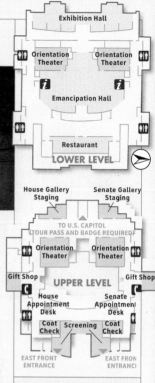

The enormous and sunlit Capitol Visitor Center (CVC) is the start for all Capitol tours, and brings a new depth to the Capitol experience with orientation theaters, an interactive museum, and live video feeds from the House and Senate. It also provides weary travelers with welcome creature comforts, including a 530-seat restaurant.

DESIGN

At 580,000 square feet, the visitor center is approximately three-quarters the size of the 775,000-square-foot Capitol. The center's belowground location preserves the historic landscape and views designed by Frederick Law Olmsted in 1874. Inside, skylights provide natural light and views of the majestic Capitol dome. The center opened in December 2008, three years late and $356 million over budget.

EMANCIPATION HALL

The center's largest space is a gorgeous sunlit atrium called Emancipation Hall in honor of the slaves who helped to build the Capitol in the 1800s. The plaster model of the *Freedom* statue, which tops the Capitol's dome, anchors the hall. Part of the Capitol's National Statuary Hall collection is also on display here.

MUSEUM

Other attractions include exhibits about the Capitol, historical artifacts, and documents. A marble wall displays historic speeches and decisions by Congress, like President John F. Kennedy's famous 1961 "Man on the Moon" speech and a letter Thomas Jefferson wrote to Congress in 1803 urging the funding of the Lewis and Clark Expedition.

KIDS AT THE CVC

The Capitol Visitor Center is a great place for families with children who may be too young or too wiggly for a tour of the Capitol. In the Exhibition Hall, the 11-foot tall touchable model of the Capitol, touch screen computers, and architectural replicas welcome hands-on exploration.

Challenge younger kids to find statues of a person carrying a spear, a helmet, a book, and a baby.

Tweens can look for statues of the person who invented television, a king, a physician, and a representative who said, "I cannot vote for war."

PLANNING YOUR CAPITOL DAY

LOGISTICS

To tour the Capitol, you can book free, advance passes at ⊕ *www.visitthecapitol.gov* or through your representative's or senator's offices. In addition, a limited number of same-day passes are available at the Public Walk-Up line on the lower level of the visitor center. Tours run every 15 minutes; the first tour begins at 8:50 and the last at 3:20, Monday through Saturday. The center is closed on Sunday.

Plan on two to four hours to tour the Capitol and see the visitor center. You should arrive at least 30 minutes before your scheduled tour to allow time to pass through security. Tours, which include a viewing of the orientation film *Out of Many, One,* last about one hour.

If you can't get a pass to tour the Capitol, the Capitol Visitor Center is still worth a visit. You can also take one of the free guided tours that do not require reservations.

To get passes to the chambers of the House and Senate, contact your representative's or senator's office. Many will also arrange for a staff member to give you a tour of the Capitol or set you up with a time for a Capitol Guide Service tour. When they're in session, some members even have time set aside to meet with constituents. You can link to the e-mail of your representative at ⊕ *www.house.gov* and of your senators at ⊕ *www.senate.gov*.

SECURITY

Expect at least a 30-minute wait going through security when you enter the Capitol Visitor Center. Bags can be no larger than 14 inches wide, 13 inches high, and 4 inches deep. View the list of prohibited items on ⊕ *www.visitthecapitol.gov*. (There are no facilities for storing prohibited belongings.) For more information, call ☏ *202/226–8000, 202/224–4049 TTY.*

BEAN SOUP AND MORE

A favorite with legislators, the Senate bean soup has been served every day for more than 100 years in the exclusive Senate Dining Room. It's available to the general public in the restaurant of the CVC (⊙ Open 7:30 AM–4 PM) on a rotating basis. You can also try making your own with the recipe on the Senate's Web site (⊕ www.senate.gov).

GETTING HERE—WITHOUT GETTING VOTED IN

The Union Station, Capitol South and Federal Center, SW Metro stops are all within walking distance of the Capitol. Follow the people wearing business suits—chances are they're headed your way. Street parking is extremely limited, but Union Station to the north of the Capitol has a public garage and there is some metered street parking along the Mall to the west of the Capitol.

RENOVATION

A complete renovation of the Capitol Dome was completed in late 2016, just before the presidential inauguration in January 2017.

TOURING THE CAPITOL

National Statuary Hall

Your 30- to 40-minute tour conducted by the Capitol Guide Service includes stops at the Rotunda, followed by the National Statuary Hall, the Hall of Columns, the old Supreme Court Chamber, the crypt (where there are exhibits on the history of the Capitol), and the gift shop. Note that you *don't* see the Senate or House chambers on the tour. (Turn the page to learn about visiting the chambers.) The highlights of the tour are the first two stops. . . .

THE ROTUNDA

You start off here, under the Capitol's dome. Look up and you'll see *Apotheosis of Washington,* a fresco painted in 1865 by Constantino Brumidi. The figures in the inner circle represent the 13 original states; those in the outer ring symbolize arts, sciences, and industry. Further down, around the Rotunda's rim, a frieze depicts 400 years of American history. The work was started by Brumidi in 1877 and continued by another Italian, Filippo Costaggini. American Allyn Cox added the final touches in 1953.

NATIONAL STATUARY HALL

South of the Rotunda is Statuary Hall, which was once the chamber of the House of Representatives. When the House moved out, Congress invited each state to send statues of two great deceased residents for placement in the hall. Because the weight of the statues threatened to make the floor cave in, and to keep the room from being cluttered, more than half of the sculptures have ended up in other spots in the Capitol. Ask your guide for help finding your state's statues.

ARTIST OF THE CAPITOL

Constantino Brumidi (1805-80) devoted his last 25 years to frescoing the Capitol; his work dominates the Rotunda and the Western Corridor. While painting the section depicting William Penn's treaty with the Indians for the Rotunda's frieze *(pictured above),* a 74-year-old Brumidi slipped from the 58-foot scaffold, hanging on until help arrived. He would continue work for another four months, before succumbing to kidney failure.

TRY THIS

Because of Statuary Hall's perfectly elliptical ceiling, a whisper uttered along the wall can be heard at the point directly opposite on the other side of the room. Try it when you're there—if it's not noisy, the trick should work.

ONE BIG HAWAIIAN

With a solid granite base weighing six tons, Hawaii's Kamehameha I in Statuary Hall is among the heaviest objects in the collection. On Kamehameha Day (June 11, a state holiday in Hawai'i), the statue is draped with leis.

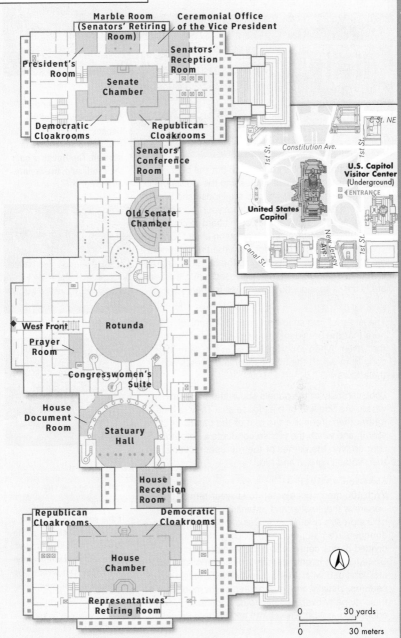

United States Capitol

Marble Room (Senators' Retiring Room)

Ceremonial Office of the Vice President

President's Room

Senators' Reception Room

Senate Chamber

Democratic Cloakrooms

Republican Cloakrooms

Senators' Conference Room

Old Senate Chamber

Constitution Ave.

1st St.

1st St.

C St. NE

U.S. Capitol Visitor Center (Underground)

ENTRANCE

United States Capitol

New Jersey Ave.

Canal St.

1st St.

West Front

Rotunda

Prayer Room

Congresswomen's Suite

House Document Room

Statuary Hall

House Reception Room

Republican Cloakrooms

Democratic Cloakrooms

House Chamber

Representatives' Retiring Room

0   30 yards

0   30 meters

GOING TO THE FLOOR

ONE IF BY LAND . . . ?

When flags fly over their respective wings of the Capitol, you'll know the House and Senate are in session. The House is on the south side, the Senate on the north.

A tour of the Capitol is impressive, but the best part of a visit for many people is witnessing the legislators in action. Free gallery passes into the House and Senate chambers have to be obtained from your representative's or senator's office. They aren't hard to come by, but getting them takes some planning ahead. Once you have a pass, it's good for any time the chambers are open to public, for as long as the current Congress is sitting. Senate chambers are closed when the Senate is not in session, but the House is open.

HOUSE CHAMBER

The larger of two chambers may look familiar: it's here that the president delivers the annual State of the Union. When you visit, you sit in the same balcony from which the First Family and guests watch the address.

Look carefully at the panels above the platform where the Speaker of the House sits. They're blue (rather than green like the rest of the panels in the room), and when the House conducts a vote, they light up with the names of the representatives and their votes in green and red.

SENATE CHAMBER

With 100 members elected to six-year terms, the Senate is the smaller and ostensibly more dignified of Congress's two houses. Desks of the senators are arranged in an arc, with Republicans and Democrats divided by the center aisle. The vice president of the United States is officially the "president of the Senate," charged with presiding over the Senate's procedures. Usually, though, the senior member of the majority party oversees day-to-day operations, and is addressed as "Mr. President" or "Madam President."

Judiciary Committee

House session

SWEET SPOT IN THE SENATE

In the sixth desk from the right in the back row of the Senate chamber, a drawer has been filled with candy since 1968. Whoever occupies the desk maintains the stash.

Visiting Government Buildings

You can visit many of Washington's government offices, but you have to do some advance planning in many cases. Here's a rundown of how far in advance you need to make arrangements.

No Advance Planning Required

Two of the most impressive places in Washington don't require advance reservations. The **Library of Congress** and the **U.S. Supreme Court** are architectural and political treasures.

With its murals, paintings, sculptures and statues, and, of course, millions of books and manuscripts, the Library of Congress is truly spectacular. Even if you're not a bookworm, the free docent-led tour is one of the best things going in the city. Revolving exhibits prevent the experience from ever getting stale. The Supreme Court does not offer guided tours, but visitors are welcome to amble through its public spaces, which include the courtroom itself. Other features include the John Marshall statue, a visitor film, and ever-rotating court-related exhibits. Court sessions are also open to the public, on a first-come, first-served basis.

Capitol Visitor Center

One of the most visited attractions, the **Capitol Visitor Center** is the starting point for tours of the Capitol and where you'll discover a plethora of historical treasures, including a table used by Abraham Lincoln during his 1865 inaugural address. Crowds in spring and summer can number in the thousands, so plan for at least three hours here. The five-football-fields-size underground complex is a destination in itself, with the model of the statue of *Freedom*, a 530-seat dining room that serves the famous Senate bean soup, and exhibits on the Capitol. A 13-minute orientation film lends some footing. The visitor center is open until 4:30 pm, Monday through Saturday, but the last time to catch a Capitol tour is 3:20. Allow extra time to go through security.

To visit the Capitol, you can reserve tickets online at ⊕ *www.visitthecapitol.gov*, contact your representative or senator, or gamble for a limited number of same-day passes.

section: the boxlike portion between the central rotunda and today's north wing. (Efforts to find the cornerstone Washington laid have been unsuccessful, though when the east front was extended in the 1950s, workers found a knee joint thought to be from a 500-pound ox that was roasted at the 1793 celebration.) By 1807 the House wing had been completed, just to the south of what's now the domed center, and a covered wooden walkway joined the two wings.

The "Congress House" grew slowly and suffered a grave setback on August 24, 1814, when British troops led by Sir George Cockburn marched on Washington and set fire to the Capitol, the White House, and numerous other government buildings. (Cockburn reportedly stood on the House speaker's chair and asked his men, "Shall this harbor of Yankee democracy be burned?" The question was rhetorical; the building was torched.) The wooden walkway was destroyed and the two wings gutted, but the walls were left standing after a violent rainstorm doused

The Supreme Court officially began meeting in this Corinthian-column-lined building in 1935.

the flames. Fearful that Congress might leave Washington, residents raised money for a hastily built, temporary "Brick Capitol" that stood where the Supreme Court is today. Architect Benjamin Henry Latrobe supervised the rebuilding of the original Capitol, adding American touches such as the corncob-and-tobacco-leaf capitals to columns in the east entrance of the Senate wing. He was followed by Boston-born Charles Bulfinch, and in 1826 the Capitol, its low wooden dome sheathed in copper, was finished.

North and south wings were added in the 1850s and 1860s to accommodate a growing government trying to keep pace with a growing country. The elongated edifice extended farther north and south than Thornton had planned, and in 1855, to keep the scale correct, work began on a taller, cast-iron dome. President Lincoln was criticized for continuing this expensive project while the country was in the throes of the Civil War, but he called the construction "a sign we intend the Union

shall go on." This twin-shell dome, a marvel of 19th-century engineering, rises 285 feet above the ground and weighs 4,500 tons. It expands and contracts up to 4 inches a day, depending on the outside temperature. The allegorical figure atop the dome, often mistaken for Pocahontas, is called *Freedom.* Sculptor Thomas Crawford had first planned for the 19.5-foot-tall bronze statue to wear the cloth liberty cap of a freed Roman slave, but Southern lawmakers, led by Jefferson Davis, objected. An "American" headdress composed of a star-encircled helmet surmounted with an eagle's head and feathers was substituted. A light just below the statue burns whenever Congress is in session.

The Capitol has continued to grow. In 1962 the east front was extended 33.5 feet, creating 100 additional offices. Preservationists have fought to keep the west front from being extended, because it's the last remaining section of the Capitol's original facade. A compromise was

Inside Congress: How Laws Are Made

Amid the grand halls of the Capitol building, members of Congress and their aides are busy crafting the laws of our land. It's not a pretty process; as congressional commentators have quipped, laws are like sausages—it's best not to know how they're made. But for iron stomachs, here's a brief tour through Washington's sausage factory.

The Idea Stage

Most laws begin as proposals that any of Congress's 535 members may offer in the form of bills. Many are trivial, such as renaming post-office branches. Others are vital, like funding the federal government. Once introduced, all proposals move to a relevant congressional committee.

Congressional Committees and Committee Hearings

Although thousands of proposals are introduced each year, almost all die in committee. Congress never has enough time to entertain each bill, so committee leaders prioritize. Some bills are dismissed for ideological reasons.

Others simply lack urgency. Efforts to rein in fuel costs, for instance, are popular when gas prices are high. Lobbying and special-interest money are other major factors influencing the content and even success or failure of individual bills.

For bills that advance, merits and drawbacks are debated in committee hearings. These hearings—staged in the congressional office buildings adjacent to the Capitol—are usually open to the public; check ⊕ *www. house.gov* and ⊕ *www.senate.gov*

under the "committee" headings for schedules. Committee members then vote on whether to move bills to the chamber floor.

Passing the House, Senate, and White House

A bill approved by committee still faces three formidable tests before becoming a law: it must pass the full House, the full Senate, and usually the White House.

Each legislative chamber has different rules for approving bills. In the House, proposals that clear a committee and have the blessing of House leaders need only a simple majority. In the Senate, legislation can be delayed by filibustering—a time-honored process of talking nonstop on the Senate floor—until at least 60 senators vote to end the delay. If the House and Senate pass different versions of the same proposal, then those differences are reconciled in a joint conference committee before returning to the respective floors for another round of voting.

A bill passed by both the House and Senate then proceeds to the White House. The president can either sign it—in which case it becomes law—or veto it, in which case it returns to Congress. Lawmakers can override a veto, but two-thirds of each chamber must support the override to transform a vetoed bill into law. When President George W. Bush twice vetoed a popular children's health care proposal, House supporters couldn't rally the two-thirds majority to override it. The bill enjoyed President Obama's support and became law after he took office.

reached in 1983, when it was agreed that the facade's crumbling sandstone blocks would simply be replaced with stronger limestone.

Free gallery passes to watch the House or Senate in session can be obtained only from your representative's or senator's office; both chambers are open to the public when either body is in session. In addition, the House Gallery is open 9 am to 4:15 pm weekdays when the House is not in session. International visitors may request gallery passes from the House or Senate Appointment Desks on the upper level of the visitor center. Your representative's or senator's office may also arrange for a staff member to give you a tour of the Capitol or set you up with a time for a Capitol Guide Service Tour. When they're in session, some members even have time set aside to meet with constituents. You can link to the home page of your representative or senator at *www.house.gov* and *www.senate.gov.*

Prior to entering the visitor center, allow about 45 minutes to go through security. Bags can be no larger than 14 inches wide, 13 inches high, and 4 inches deep, and other possessions you can bring into the building are strictly limited. (The full list of prohibited items is posted at *www. visitthecapitol.gov*) There are no facilities for leaving personal belongings, but you can check your coat. If you're planning a visit, check the status of tours and access; security measures may change. ⊠ *East end of The Mall, Capitol Hill* ☎ *202/226–8000* ⊕ *www.visitthecapitol. gov* ✉ *Free* ⊗ *Closed Sun.* Ⓜ *Capitol S or Union Station.*

★ United States National Arboretum

GARDEN | During azalea season (mid-April through May) this 446-acre oasis operated by the U.S. Department of Agriculture is a blaze of color. In early summer, clematis, peonies, rhododendrons, and roses bloom. At any time of year the 22 original Corinthian columns from the U.S. Capitol,

reerected here in 1990, are striking. All 50 states are represented by a state tree or flower. Since 2014, a pair of American bald eagles have made a home near the azaleas, and the nest can be seen via an unobstructed viewing scope. The arboretum has guided hikes throughout the year, including a Full Moon Hike, and dogs are allowed on the grounds as long as they're on a leash at all times. Check the website for schedules and to register. Visit the Cryptomeria Walk and Japanese Stroll Garden, which are part of the Bonsai and Penjing Museum. On weekends a tram tours the arboretum's curving roadways at 11:30 and on the hour 1–4. ⊠ *3501 New York Ave. NE, Northeast* ☎ *202/245–2726* ⊕ *www.usna. usda.gov* ✉ *Free* Ⓜ *Weekends: Union Station, then X6 bus (runs every 40 mins); weekdays: Stadium–Armory, then B2 bus to Bladensburg Rd. and R St.*

🍴 Restaurants

"The Hill," as locals know it, was once an enclave of congressional boardinghouses in the shadow of the Capitol building but is now D.C.'s largest historic district, with an eclectic mix of restaurants. Around the Capitol South Metro station, government offices end and neighborhood dining begins. Here, along tree-lined streets, some of the city's most acclaimed restaurants have joined the local bars and eateries that have long catered to lunch and happy-hour crowds during the week.

Neighborhood establishments and all-American pubs line historic Barracks Row, with Eastern Market anchoring the homey House side of the Hill; the Senate end is given a more hustle-and-bustle vibe with the chain dining and upscale boîtes of Union Station. The Atlas District, also known as the H Street corridor, is spilling with great restaurants, and a few blocks north is Union Market, where dozens of local food and beverage purveyors sell everything from arepas to Zinfandels.

The United States Botanic Garden, founded in 1820, is the oldest in North America.

Ambar Capitol Hill

$$ | **EASTERN EUROPEAN** | Never had Balkan comfort food? Ambar is your spot, a handsome, noisy, two-story restaurant-bar at the heart of Barracks Row that immediately wowed the critics after its opening in 2013. **Known for:** wonderful meats served nowhere else in town; all-you-can-eat small-plates; attentive and enthusiastic servers. $ *Average main: $20* ⊠ *523 8th St. SE, Eastern Market* ☏ *202/813-3039* ⊕ *www.ambarrestaurant.com* Ⓜ *Eastern Market.*

Art and Soul

$$$ | **SOUTHERN** | Best known as Oprah's longtime personal chef, Art Smith is now serving the Washington crowd at this funky Southern-fried spot that gives down-home cravings an upscale twist. The chic kitchen draws some of the city's biggest movers and shakers (including Michelle Obama), but still maintains a homey and welcoming atmosphere. **Known for:** the best biscuits in the city; Southern hospitality and the cuisine to go

along with it; dog-friendly outdoor patio (complete with menu for Fido). $ *Average main: $31* ⊠ *Liaison Capitol Hill, 415 New Jersey Ave. NW, Capitol Hill* ☏ *202/393-7777* ⊕ *www.artandsouldc.com* Ⓜ *Union Station.*

Belga Café

$$$ | **BELGIAN** | Belgium culture aficionados can go traditional with mussels and the crispiest of French fries or dabble in what the chef calls Eurofusion at this sleek café done up with dark wood and exposed brick. Classic dishes such as Flemish beef stew made with Corsendonk Brune beer sauce help capture that Belgian charm. **Known for:** 10 styles of mussels you can choose from; huge 12-page beer menu; waffle-centric brunch menu. $ *Average main: $28* ⊠ *514 8th St. SE, Eastern Market* ☏ *202/544-0100* ⊕ *www.belgacafe.com* Ⓜ *Eastern Market.*

Bistro Bis

$$$ | **FRENCH** | The zinc bar, cherrywood interior, and white tablecloths create

great expectations at Bistro Bis, where the seasonal menu serves a modern take on a French bistro. Thanks to its prime location, acclaimed menu, deep wine list, and classic cocktails, it's a popular spot for Washington power brokers and insiders. **Known for:** excellent steak frites and steak tartare; sophisticated ambience that attracts a powerful clientele; an elegant apple tart. $ Average main: $29 ⊠ Hotel George, 15 E St. NW, Capitol Hill ☎ 202/661–2700 ⊕ www.bistrobis.com Ⓜ Union Station.

★ Cava Mezze

$$ | GREEK | This modern mecca for mezes (small plates for sharing) delivers delicious, chic Mediterranean cuisine without the whiz-bang conceits of its pricier cousins. There are few surprises on the menu, save for the feta hush puppies, but the wood-and-brick interior and gallant service make the traditional dishes feel new again. **Known for:** crazy feta hush puppies and spicy lamb sliders; lots of vegan and gluten-free options; all-you-can-eat brunch with 25¢ mimosas. $ Average main: $24 ⊠ 527 8th St. SE, Eastern Market ☎ 202/543–9090 ⊕ www.cavamezze.com ⊗ No lunch Mon. Ⓜ Eastern Market.

EatBar

$ | CONTEMPORARY | A quintessential gastropub, EatBar has all the necessities for an easygoing dining experience: good beers, good tunes, and good eats. While the menu offers full-on entrées like smoked chicken and waffles and a double pimento cheeseburger, it mostly features shareable small plates like wild boar pâté and fried brussels sprouts with bacon (unsurprisingly meat-heavy since they were created by a butcher-cum-chef). **Known for:** ham fries, aka ham and potatoes whipped in ham fat; eclectic jukebox options; superb selection of beer, wine, and cocktails. $ Average main: $15 ⊠ 415 8th St. SE, Eastern Market ☎ 202/847–4827 ⊕ www.eat-bar.com Ⓜ Eastern Market.

Ethiopic Restaurant

$$ | ETHIOPIAN | The spongy rolls of sourdough *injera* bread (ubiquitous on Ethiopian plates) used in place of utensils can make traditional Ethiopian feel decidedly undelicate, but the bright surroundings and friendly service here make for a downright romantic experience. Venture off the well-beaten path of spicy lamb and lentils to try the spicy chickpea dumplings or fragrant simmered split peas, laden with garlic and served in a clay pot. **Known for:** minimalist yet friendly atmosphere; Ethiopian standards like beef tibs and injera; great Ethiopian coffee and beer options. $ Average main: $23 ⊠ 401 H St. NE, Capitol Hill ☎ 202/675–2066 ⊕ www.ethiopicrestaurant.com ⊗ Closed Mon. No lunch Tues.–Thurs. Ⓜ Union Station.

★ Good Stuff Eatery

$ | AMERICAN | FAMILY | Fans of Bravo's *Top Chef* will first visit this brightly colored burgers-and-shakes joint hoping to spy charismatic celebrity chef Spike Mendelsohn, but they will return for the comfort-food favorites. The lines can be long, as it's a favorite lunch spot of congressional aides, but Spike's inventive beef dishes are worth the wait. **Known for:** fun burgers like the "Prez Obama" (with bacon, onion marmalade, and Roquefort cheese); thick malted milk shakes; variety of dipping sauces for hand-cut skinny fries. $ Average main: $8 ⊠ 303 Pennsylvania Ave. SE, Capitol Hill ☎ 202/543–8222 ⊕ www.goodstuffeatery.com ⊗ Closed Sun. Ⓜ Eastern Market.

Granville Moore's

$$ | BELGIAN | This Belgian beer hall with a gourmet soul is worth a visit for both its intense beer list and mussels and frites, plus a few other unique salads and burgers. Snag a seat at the bar or at one of the first-come, first-served tables, and

linger over unfiltered artisanal brews that range from Chimay to obscure options from the reserve and limited-stock beer selection. **Known for:** steamed mussels served in five unique sauces; wide-ranging Belgian beer list; crunchy frites and homemade dipping sauces. $ *Average main: $20* ✉ *1238 H St. NE, Capitol Hill* ☎ *202/399–2546* ⊕ *www.granvillemoores.com* ⊗ *No lunch Mon.–Thurs.* Ⓜ *Union Station.*

Hikari Sushi and Saki Bar

$ | SUSHI | Blink and you'll miss it, but this family-owned gem that sits at the heart of H Street has been serving up its delicious version of Japanese fusion since well before the neighborhood became hipster central. The seafood menu is extensive, featuring an affordable selection of traditional sushi and sashimi, as well as 50 different roll options. **Known for:** reliably good sushi and unique rolls; a generous selection of both traditional sake and Japanese beers; a quiet dining area where you can hear your companions. $ *Average main: $16* ✉ *644 H St. NE, Capitol Hill* ☎ *202/546–0523* ⊕ *www. hikarirestaurant.com* Ⓜ *Union Station.*

IMM on H

$$ | THAI | "IMM" in Thai means "pleasantly full," and this tiny newcomer at the eastern edge of the H Street corridor will get you there happily. The spicy curries and other traditional entrées like pad Thai come in heaping servings, all but ensuring you'll have leftovers for tomorrow's lunch. **Known for:** intimate dining with attentive service; heaping curries, spiced hot as you like; happy hour sushi deals. $ *Average main: $18* ✉ *1360 H St. NE, Capitol Hill* ☎ *202/748–5536* ⊕ *www. immthai.com* Ⓜ *Union Station.*

Jimmy T's Place

$ | AMERICAN | This D.C. institution is tucked in the first floor of an old row house only five blocks from the Capitol where talkative regulars and the boisterous owner pack the place daily.

Enjoy favorites like eggs Benedict made with a toasted English muffin, a huge piece of ham, and lots of hollandaise sauce. **Known for:** classic greasy-spoon atmosphere; breakfast combos like grits and pumpkin pancakes; absolutely no substitutions and cash only. $ *Average main: $7* ✉ *501 E. Capitol St. SE, Capitol Hill* ☎ *202/546–3646* ▭ *No credit cards* ⊗ *Closed Mon. No dinner* Ⓜ *Capitol S.*

Le Grenier

$$ | FRENCH | Le Grenier's slogan is "the French on H," and the name is no joke. This cozy spot not far from Union Station has every bit the feel of a Parisian neighborhood bistro, with a menu of traditional favorites to match. **Known for:** traditional French comfort food in a cozy setting; signature cocktails like the "H for Hipster"; affordable brunch with a superb Bloody Mary. $ *Average main: $20* ✉ *502 H St. NE, Capitol Hill* ☎ *202/544–4999* ⊕ *www.legrenierdc.com* ⊗ *Closed Mon.* Ⓜ *Union Station.*

The Market Lunch

$ | AMERICAN | FAMILY | Digging into a hefty pile of pancakes from this casual counter in Eastern Market makes for the perfect end to a stroll around the Capitol. Favorites include eggs, grits, and pancakes in the morning and crab cakes, fried shrimp, and fish for lunch. **Known for:** blueberry buckwheat pancakes; long lines and lots of kids; cash-only policy. $ *Average main: $14* ✉ *Eastern Market, 225 7th St. SE, Eastern Market* ☎ *202/547–8444* ⊕ *www.marketlunchdc. com* ▭ *No credit cards* ⊗ *Closed Mon. No dinner* Ⓜ *Eastern Market.*

★ Pineapple and Pearls

$$$$ | CONTEMPORARY | For his follow-up to the smash hit Rose's Luxury, chef Aaron Silverman opened this reservation-only dining room next door that offers only an expensive 12-course (give or take) tasting menu (the price includes beverages and tips). Bar seating is also available for a lower price that doesn't include

the drinks. **Known for:** expensive (but all-inclusive) tasting menu; fun and low-key dishes with zero pretension; intense reservation process. $ *Average main: $325* ⊠ *715 8th St. SE, Eastern Market* ☎ *202/595–7375* ⊕ *www.pineapplean-dpearls.com* ☾ *Closed Sun., Mon., and (usually) Sat.* Ⓜ *Eastern Market.*

★ Rose's Luxury

$$ | MODERN AMERICAN | A darling of both diners and the media, Rose's Luxury lives up to the hype as one of the city's most welcoming and groundbreaking dining destinations. The dishes are as delightful as they are shocking, and cause visitors to wait in line for hours to visit the supremely stylish re-creation of a hipster's dream dinner party. **Known for:** innovative small plates; the sausage, lychee, and habanero salad; long waits for a table (with reservations only for big groups). $ *Average main: $20* ⊠ *717 8th St. SE, Eastern Market* ☎ *202/580–8889* ⊕ *www.rosesluxury.com* ☾ *No lunch.*

Seventh Hill Pizza

$ | PIZZA | The breezy charm of this casual bistro quickly vaulted its pizza to the top of the list of D.C.'s best places for pies. Each is named for a nearby neighborhood—the zesty mating of basil and anchovies on the "Southwest Waterfront" pie is matched only by the creamy goat cheese of the "Eastern Market." Pizzas match well with the small cast of bottled beers available. **Known for:** locally named wood-fired pizzas; bright and welcoming atmosphere; Nutella calzone for dessert. $ *Average main: $16* ⊠ *327 7th St. SE, Eastern Market* ☎ *202/544–1911* ⊕ *www.montmartredc.com/seventhhill* ☾ *Closed Mon.* Ⓜ *Eastern Market.*

Sonoma Restaurant and Wine Bar

$$ | WINE BAR | This chic multilevel wine bar has pours aplenty (in both tasting portions and full glasses) along with well-thought-out charcuterie boards piled with prosciutto and fluffy, grill-charred focaccia. There's more-filling fare, too,

like potato gnocchi with mushrooms. **Known for:** hip and vast wine menu; happy hour catering to a congressional crowd; house-made charcuterie and thin-crust pizzas. $ *Average main: $22* ⊠ *223 Pennsylvania Ave. SE, Capitol Hill* ☎ *202/544–8088* ⊕ *www.sonomadc.com* ☾ *No lunch Sat.* Ⓜ *Capitol S.*

Ted's Bulletin

$$ | DINER | FAMILY | This cheeky homage to mid-20th-century diners is styled after a newspaper office, with menus printed in broadsheet format and specials mounted on the wall in mismatched plastic lettering. But one bite of the grilled cheese with tomato soup or the "'Burgh" burger, served on Texas toast with coleslaw, French fries, and a runny egg, will convince you that the kitchen's skills are no joke. **Known for:** fun newsroom-meets-diner ambience; milk shakes with clever names (with or without alcohol); homemade Pop-Tarts. $ *Average main: $17* ⊠ *505 8th St. SE, Eastern Market* ☎ *202/544–8337* ⊕ *www.tedsbulletin.com* Ⓜ *Eastern Market.*

Tune Inn

$ | DINER | Part bar, part diner, part happy-hour haunt for Hill staffers, this Capitol Hill tradition is one of the neighborhood's last great dives. Opened in 1947, and still run by the same family, the space was upgraded after a fire in 2011 but retains its lodgelike decor, including a healthy display of taxidermied animals staring down from the walls. **Known for:** cheap beer and greasy grub; an utter absence of pretension; breakfast served all day. $ *Average main: $8* ⊠ *331 Pennsylvania Ave. SE, Capitol Hill* ☎ *202/543–2725* Ⓜ *Capitol S.*

Hotels

To be sure, politics and commerce, like oil and water, don't mix, but they sure make for a great neighborhood to spend a few nights. Fortunately, there's no lack of options when it comes to lodging on Capitol Hill. From modernist luxury suites, to comfy boutique settings, and even a hideaway hostel for the most thrifty travelers, the neighborhood offers plenty of choices to base your visit at the hub of some of Washington's best political, commercial, and cultural sights.

Capitol Hill Hotel
$$ | HOTEL | FAMILY | A great choice if you want to stay on the Hill and need some extra room to spread out: all Federalist-chic-style units are suites, with kitchenettes, large work desks, flat-screen TVs, and spacious closets. **Pros:** close to Metro and sights; access to on-site bikes; eco-friendly. **Cons:** expensive valet parking; hotel is spread out in two buildings, which can be inconvenient; extra fee to access certain amenities. [$] *Rooms from: $271* ✉ *200 C St. SE, Capitol Hill* ☎ *202/543–6000* 🌐 *www.capitolhillhotel-dc.com* 🛏 *153 suites* 🍴 *Free Breakfast* [M] *Capitol S.*

City House Hostel Washington DC
$ | HOTEL | It looks like a hole-in-the-wall, but the City House Hostel is a clean, comfortable oasis for backpackers and other cost-conscious travelers in the heart of the bustling H Street corridor near public transit. **Pros:** smack in the center of a lively strip of bars, restaurants, and grocery stores; good chance to meet fellow travelers; by far the cheapest option close to the Capitol. **Cons:** H Street can be noisy; cramped accommodations, with only a few private rooms. [$] *Rooms from: $25* ✉ *506 H St. NE, Capitol Hill* ☎ *202/370–6390* 🌐 *www.cityhousehostels.com* 🛏 *11 rooms, 3 private* 🍴 *No meals* [M] *Union Station.*

Hilton Garden Inn Washington DC/U.S. Capitol
$ | HOTEL | Just a block away from a Metro stop, this hotel, though a bit off the beaten path, is convenient for getting around the city. **Pros:** great views; indoor pool; business-friendly, including free Wi-Fi and printing. **Cons:** no pets allowed; not in the center of town; no self-parking, and valet parking is pricey. [$] *Rooms from: $138* ✉ *1225 1st St. NE, Capitol Hill* ☎ *202/408–4870* 🌐 *www.hiltongardeninn.com* 🛏 *204 rooms* 🍴 *No meals* [M] *NoMa–Gallaudet U.*

Hyatt Regency Washington on Capitol Hill
$ | HOTEL | A favorite for political events, fund-raising dinners, and networking meetings, this standard-issue business hotel is a solid choice if you're planning on spending a lot of time on the Hill. **Pros:** beautiful sky-lit, heated indoor pool and outdoor sundeck; quick walk to Union Station; Old Town Trolley Tours stops at hotel. **Cons:** always very busy; expensive parking; anonymous feel. [$] *Rooms from: $109* ✉ *400 New Jersey Ave. NW, Capitol Hill* ☎ *202/737–1234, 800/233–1234* 🌐 *www.hyatt.com* 🛏 *838 rooms* 🍴 *No meals* [M] *Union Station.*

★ **Kimpton George Hotel**
$$$ | HOTEL | We cannot tell a lie—D.C.'s first contemporary boutique hotel is still one of its best, and the public areas and stylishly soothing guest quarters still excel at providing a fun and funky alternative to cookie-cutter chains with a convenient location near Union Station. **Pros:** complimentary wine hour nightly; popular in-house restaurant; free access to bikes for touring. **Cons:** small closets; some reports of street noise; ultramodern feel not everyone's cup of tea. [$] *Rooms from: $328* ✉ *15 E St. NW, Capitol Hill* ☎ *202/347–4200, 800/576–8331* 🌐 *www.hotelgeorge.com* 🛏 *139 rooms* 🍴 *No meals* [M] *Union Station.*

The Liaison Capitol Hill
$$$ | HOTEL | If the city's most stately buildings weren't steps away, you could easily think you had checked into a sleek Manhattan hotel, with a trendy buzz and guest rooms defined by modern chic. **Pros:** fantastic rooftop pool and deck open seasonally; pet friendly; 24-hour fitness center. **Cons:** can be noisy; no

great room views; expensive parking. $ *Rooms from: $319* ✉ *415 New Jersey Ave. NW, Capitol Hill* ☎ *202/638–1616, 888/513–7445* 🌐 *www.jdvhotels.com* 🛏 *340 rooms* 🍴 *No meals* [M] *Union Station.*

Phoenix Park Hotel
$ | **HOTEL** | If you prefer to be near the Hill but not in a convention hotel, the small but beautifully appointed and comfortable guest rooms in this family-owned European-style inn across the street from Union Station may fit the bill. **Pros:** comfy beds with good linens; friendly service; free Wi-Fi. **Cons:** no swimming pool; small rooms; some rooms are noisy. $ *Rooms from: $129* ✉ *520 N. Capitol St. NW, Capitol Hill* ☎ *202/638–6900, 855/371–6824* 🌐 *www.phoenixparkhotel.com* 🛏 *149 rooms* 🍴 *No meals* [M] *Union Station.*

Washington Court Hotel
$ | **HOTEL** | If you're searching for the city's newest "It" hotel, keep looking, but these soothing guest rooms done in soft grays and browns fit the bill for a reliable, clean, comfortable place to stay that's convenient to the Metro and sights. **Pros:** Capitol views from many rooms; executive king rooms have sofa beds; 24-hour fitness and business centers. **Cons:** some reports of mixed service; complaints of hidden fees; expensive valet parking. $ *Rooms from: $202* ✉ *525 New Jersey Ave. NW, Capitol Hill* ☎ *202/628–2100* 🌐 *www.washingtoncourthotel.com* 🛏 *259 rooms, 6 suites* 🍴 *No meals* [M] *Union Station.*

Nightlife

BARS AND LOUNGES

Biergartenhaus
BREWPUBS/BEER GARDENS | Step off H Street and into a boisterous bit of Bavaria. There might be football on TV, but that's not enough to break the spell of a place so genuinely Germanic. With about a dozen German drafts on offer, along with other authentic specialties—apfel schnapps?—and a full bar, there's something for everyone, including a variety of spaces. Get cozy inside, or head for the courtyard, which is heated in winter. In pleasant weather, the second-story terrace also packs in visitors. ✉ *1355 H St. NE, Capitol Hill* ☎ *202/388–4085* 🌐 *www.biergartenhaus.com.*

Dubliner
BARS/PUBS | A short walk from Union Station and Capitol Hill, this Washington institution offers cozy paneled rooms, rich pints of Guinness, and other authentic fare. It's especially popular with Hill staffers and Georgetown law students. While offering live Irish music seven nights a week, this charming spot never charges a cover, save for St. Patrick's Day. ✉ *4 F St. NW, Capitol Hill* ☎ *202/737–3773* 🌐 *www.dublinerdc.com* [M] *Union Station.*

Granville Moore's
BARS/PUBS | Beer and mussels: the appeal is that simple, and they're that satisfying. But the narrow, rustic bars on two floors are as popular for drinkers as diners. The Belgian-themed gastropub has one of the largest selections of beer, from pilsners to Flemish reds, in D.C. If you are hungry, offerings in this cozy spot go beyond mussels, and include steak au poivre, Liège waffles, and a hearty brunch selection. ✉ *1238 H St. NE, Capitol Hill* ☎ *202/399–2546* 🌐 *www.granvillemoores.com* [M] *Union Station.*

H Street Country Club
BARS/PUBS | The only D.C. bar to offer indoor miniature golf, shuffleboard, and Skee-Ball has a friendly, laid-back vibe. Fish tacos and an impressive margarita list round out the fun mix at this popular nightspot. Big-screen sports line the walls downstairs, but you can usually catch a breath of fresh air on the roof deck. ✉ *1335 H St. NE, Capitol Hill* ☎ *202/399–4722* 🌐 *www.hstcountryclub.com* [M] *Union Station.*

Harold Black

BARS/PUBS | Step back in time at this hideaway speakeasy, a relative newcomer to D.C.'s hipster scene near Eastern Market. Be aware, there are rules here: phones are discouraged, reservations are required (book online), and your seats are secured for only two hours. But those willing to play along are rewarded with a unique taste of the Roaring Twenties, a wonderfully quiet space for catching up with friends, and a host of delicious signature cocktails. A limited menu features a handful of munchies, small plates, and desserts, including a light artichoke hummus, fish tacos, beef short ribs, and a rich chocolate-hazelnut cake. ⊠ *212 7th St. SE, Eastern Market* ⊕ *www.harold-blackdc.com.*

Little Miss Whiskey's

BARS/PUBS | A purple light at the door marks the spot of this eclectic, New Orleans–themed watering hole–dance club at the center of H Street. The dark interior, illuminated in black lights, features old concert posters from cult favorites like Pantera and Iggy Pop. The bar downstairs offers an enormous list of bottled beers and a signature adult slushee—the "Awesomeness"—that packs a real punch. The upstairs bar hosts DJs every Friday and Saturday night, when the space heaves with dancers packed wall-to-wall. The bar's cheeky slogan—"a lousy bar for lousy people"—isn't quite right. The service here is great. ⊠ *1104 H St. NE, Capitol Hill* ⊕ *www. littlemisswhiskeys.com* Ⓜ *Union Station.*

MUSIC CLUBS

Echostage

MUSIC CLUBS | This sprawling complex of more than 30,000 square feet in Northeast D.C. effectively re-creates the vibe of an otherwise bygone era in D.C. of mega-nightclubs in retrofitted warehouses in derelict neighborhoods. With unobstructed sight lines to the stage and a German-imported sound system, it's the place for club kids to dance to the biggest names in E.D.M., from Calvin Harris to David Guetta to Tiesto. Catch your breath at one of the two 60-foot bars lining either side of the dance floor. ■ **TIP→ With no Metro stops nearby, driving or taking a cab/Uber is required.** ⊠ *2135 Queens Chapel Rd. NE, Northeast* ☎ *202/503–2330* ⊕ *www. echostage.com.*

Mr. Henry's

MUSIC CLUBS | Opened in 1966, this laid-back club is the last holdout of a once-thriving live-music scene on Capitol Hill. Roberta Flack got her start in the upstairs performance space, where a dozen or so tables are scattered around the wood-paneled room. There's never a cover. Check the website for upcoming acts. ⊠ *601 Pennsylvania Ave. SE, Capitol Hill* ☎ *202/546–8412* ⊕ *www.mrhenrys-dc.com* Ⓜ *Eastern Market.*

★ Rock & Roll Hotel

MUSIC CLUBS | This former funeral home, turned music venue and nightclub in 2006, is dedicated to the discovery and recovery of live music. Located in the H Street corridor, the building has three distinct floors. The ground floor features a 400-capacity concert hall that has hosted the likes of Bon Iver, St. Vincent, and Dua Lipa, while the lounge makes its home on the second floor, a venue packed with dance parties and live DJs every weekend. Check out the festive rooftop bar, with a great happy hour until 8 pm from Wednesday through Saturday (the venue is closed Sunday–Tuesday). Rock & Roll Hotel is a 15-block walk (or quick free ride on the DC Streetcar) from the Union Station Metro, though it may be easier to grab a taxi or Uber. ⊠ *1353 H St. NE, Capitol Hill* ☎ *202/388–7625* ⊕ *www. rockandrollhoteldc.com* Ⓜ *Union Station.*

 Performing Arts

The arts scene in Capitol Hill and Northeast D.C. has blossomed in recent years with the opening of several performance venues and the explosion of restaurants, bars, and stages along the emerging H Street corridor. Leading the charge is the Atlas Performing Arts Center, at the cutting edge of dance, music, and drama. For classical drama, you will discover great performances and an intimate atmosphere at the Folger Theatre near the Capitol.

MAJOR VENUES

Atlas Performing Arts Center

ARTS CENTERS | Known as the "People's Kennedy Center," this performance venue occupies a restored historic movie theater in one of Washington's up-and-coming neighborhoods. The Atlas's four theaters and three dance studios house a diverse group of resident arts organizations, including the Mosaic Theater Company of D.C., the Joy of Motion Dance Center, Step Afrika!, and the Capital City Symphony. Street parking can be difficult, but you can now take the DC Streetcar here from the Metro stop at Union Station. ⊠ 1333 H St. NE, Capitol Hill ☎ 202/399–7993 ⊕ www.atlasarts. org Ⓜ Union Station.

DANCE

Dance Place

DANCE | This studio theater showcases an eclectic array of local, national, and international dance and performance art talent in an assortment of modern and ethnic shows; performances take place most weekends. It also conducts drop-in dance classes daily. The company is a bit of a trek from Capitol Hill (about 3 miles north of the Capitol), but it's quite close to the Brookland–CUA Metro stop on the Red Line, just three stops from Union Station. ⊠ 3225 8th St. NE, Northeast ☎ 202/269–1600 ⊕ www.danceplace.org Ⓜ Brookland-CUA.

Joy of Motion

DANCE | Resident companies include El Teatro de Danza Contemporanea El Salvador, Furia Flamenca, and Silk Road Dance Company (traditional Middle Eastern and Central Asian), among others. They offer drop-in classes in three locations: the Atlas Performing Arts Center; the studio's Jack Guidone Theatre in Upper Northwest; and in Bethesda, Maryland. There are weekly performances in the Atlas Performing Arts Center. ⊠ Capitol Hill ☎ 202/362–3042 ⊕ www.joyofmotion.org Ⓜ Friendship Heights.

MUSIC

CHAMBER MUSIC

Coolidge Auditorium at the Library of Congress

CONCERTS | Since its first concert, in 1925, the Coolidge has hosted most of the 20th and 21st centuries' greatest performers and composers, including Copland and Stravinsky. Today, the theater draws musicians from all genres, including classical, jazz, and gospel, and the hall continues to wow audiences with its near-perfect acoustics and sight lines. Concert tickets are free, but must be ordered in advance through Ticketmaster. ■ TIP➔ Because of the Library's security procedures, patrons are urged to arrive 30 minutes before the start of each event. ⊠ Library of Congress, Jefferson Building, 101 Independence Ave. SE, Capitol Hill ☎ 800/551–7328 ⊕ www.loc. gov Ⓜ Capitol S.

Folger Shakespeare Library

CONCERTS | The library's internationally acclaimed resident chamber music ensemble, the Folger Consort, regularly presents medieval, Renaissance, and baroque pieces performed on period instruments. The season runs from October to May. ⊠ 201 E. Capitol St. SE, Capitol Hill ☎ 202/544–7077 ⊕ www. folger.edu Ⓜ Union Station or Capitol S.

CHORAL MUSIC
Basilica of the National Shrine of the Immaculate Conception
CONCERTS | Choral and church groups occasionally perform at the largest Catholic church in the Americas, and every summer, recitals featuring the massive pipe organ are offered. While you are there, be sure to go down to the crypt to experience the mysteries of the world's many Madonnas. See the website for times and visiting performers. ⊠ *400 Michigan Ave. NE, Northeast* ☎ *202/526–8300* ⊕ *www.nationalshrine. com* Ⓜ *Brookland–CUA.*

THEATER AND PERFORMANCE ART
Capital Fringe Festival
ARTS FESTIVALS | Since its founding in 2005, the Capital Fringe Festival has grown each year, and currently offers no fewer than 125 productions over a three-week period in July. Local and national performers display the strange, the political, the surreal, and the avant-garde to eclectic crowds at all times of the day in venues throughout the city. With tickets around $17, this is an affordable theater experience. ■ TIP➔ **Don't forget your Fringe Button, a pin that grants the holder access to all festival events and benefits from local retailers.** Be ready to party at the Fringe Arts Bar, just north of H Street, where performers, musicians, and patrons rock into the wee hours. ⊠ *Capitol Hill* ☎ *866/811–4111* ⊕ *www. capfringe.org.*

★ Folger Theatre
THEATER | The theater at the Folger Shakespeare Library, an intimate 250-seat re-creation of the inn-yard theaters of Shakespeare's time, hosts three to four productions each year of Shakespearean or Shakespeare-influenced works. Although the stage is a throwback, the sharp acting and inspired direction consistently challenge and delight audiences. ⊠ *Folger Shakespeare Library, 201 E. Capitol St. SE, Capitol Hill* ☎ *202/544–7077* ⊕ *www.folger.edu* Ⓜ *Union Station or Capitol S.*

Rorschach Theatre
THEATER | This company's intimate and passionate performances on the stages of H Street's Atlas Performing Arts Center are some of the most offbeat plays in Washington. The company offers lesser-known works by such playwrights as Fengar Gael, Jennifer Maisel, and José Rivera, as well as imaginative revivals of classics like Thornton Wilder's *The Skin of our Teeth.* ⊠ *1333 H St. NE, Capitol Hill* ☎ *202/452–5538* ⊕ *www.rorschachtheatre.com* Ⓜ *Union Station.*

Shopping

Capitol Hill is surprisingly good territory for shopping. Eastern Market and the unique shops and boutiques clustered around the historic redbrick building are great for browsing. Inside Eastern Market are produce and meat counters, plus places to buy flowers and sweets. ■ TIP➔ **The flea market, held on weekends outdoors, presents nostalgia and local crafts by the crateful. There's also a farmers' market on Saturday.** Along 7th Street you can find a number of small shops selling such specialties as art books, handwoven rugs, and antiques. Cross Pennsylvania Avenue and head south on 8th Street for historic Barracks Row, where shops, bars, and restaurants inhabit the charming row houses leading toward the Anacostia River. The other shopping lures near the Hill are Union Market and Union Station, D.C.'s gorgeous train station, these days actually a shopping mall that happens to also accommodate Amtrak and commuter trains.

Keep in mind that Union Station and Union Market are north of the Capitol, while Eastern Market is to the south. You can certainly walk between these sights, but be aware that, from Eastern Market, Union Station is roughly a mile away, and

Union Market is another mile beyond that—trekking that might prove taxing after time already spent on your feet in the shops.

BOOKS

Capitol Hill Books

BOOKS/STATIONERY | Pop into this two-story maze of used books, where the volumes are piled floor to ceiling and no flat surface is left bare. (Even the bathroom is stacked high.) The knowledgeable staff will help you browse through a wonderful collection of out-of-print history titles, political and fiction writings, and mysteries. On the second Saturday of every month, this cozy bookstore hosts a free wine-and-cheese reception from 4 to 7 and all purchases are discounted 10%. ⊠ *657 C St. SE, Eastern Market* ☎ *202/544–1621* ⊕ *www.capitolhill-books-dc.com* Ⓜ *Eastern Market.*

★ East City Bookshop

BOOKS/STATIONERY | A gathering spot for residents and visitors alike, East City stocks a wide selection of books, as well as art supplies, gifts, and toys. Check out the calendar of events, too—there's everything from storytime for children to author-led book discussions to musical performances. ⊠ *645 Pennsylvania Ave. SE, Suite 100, Capitol Hill* ☎ *202/290–1636* ⊕ *www.eastcitybookshop.com* Ⓜ *Eastern Market.*

★ Fairy Godmother

BOOKS/STATIONERY | FAMILY | This specialty store, in business since 1984, features a delightful selection of books for children, from infants through teens, in English, Spanish, and French, including an extensive nonfiction selection. It also sells puppets, games, dolls, puzzles, and toys. ⊠ *319 7th St. SE, Eastern Market* ☎ *202/547–5474* Ⓜ *Eastern Market.*

Riverby Books

BOOKS/STATIONERY | The Capitol Hill and Eastern Market area loves its books, and Riverby is another great shop that sells everything from best sellers to out-of-print rarities. ⊠ *417 E. Capitol St. SE, Capitol Hill* ☎ *202/543–4342* ⊕ *www. riverbybooksdc.com* Ⓜ *Capitol S.*

Solid State Books

BOOKS/STATIONERY | Opened in 2017, this new addition to D.C.'s independent bookseller scene lies smack in the middle of the H Street corridor. The bright, spacious shop features a generous selection of fiction, history, and the latest political reads. An on-site coffee bar also offers beer and wine. ⊠ *600 H St. NE, Capitol Hill* ☎ *202/897–4201* ⊕ *www.solidstate-booksdc.com* Ⓜ *Union Station.*

CHILDREN'S CLOTHING

Dawn Price Baby

CLOTHING | FAMILY | The infant and toddler clothing at this friendly row-house boutique has been carefully selected with an eye for supercomfortable fabrics and distinctive designs. The shop also stocks toys, gifts, strollers, and bibs for baby Democrats and Republicans. There's a second location in Georgetown. ⊠ *325 7th St. SE, Eastern Market* ☎ *202/543–2920* ⊕ *www.dawnpricebaby. com* Ⓜ *Eastern Market.*

CRAFTS AND GIFTS

Woven History/Silk Road

CRAFTS | Landmarks in this bohemian neighborhood, these connected stores sell gorgeous, handmade treasures from the mountain communities in India, Nepal, Turkey, Iran, Pakistan, and Tibet. You'll find everything from colorful weavings, pillows, and embroidered quilts to exotic jewelry and bags, as well as antique furniture. Woven History's rugs are made the old-fashioned way, with vegetable dyes and hand-spun wool, and sizes range from 3-by-5 feet to 8-by-10 feet. ⊠ *311–315 7th St. SE, Eastern Market* ☎ *202/543–1705* ⊕ *www.wovenhisto-ry.com* Ⓜ *Eastern Market.*

FOOD

Hill's Kitchen

FOOD/CANDY | If you're a cook or looking for a gift for someone who is, pop into this small shop next to the Eastern Market. You'll find cookbooks, baking pans, aprons, towels and potholders, cookie cutters, barware, grilling tools, specialty foods, and much more. ✉ 713 D St. SE, Eastern Market ☎ 202/543–1997 ⊕ www. hillskitchen.com Ⓜ Eastern Market.

MARKETS

★ Eastern Market

OUTDOOR/FLEA/GREEN MARKETS | For nearly 145 years, this has been the hub of the Capitol Hill community. Vibrantly colored produce and flowers; freshly caught fish; fragrant cheeses; and tempting sweets are sold at the market by independent vendors. On weekends year-round, local farmers sell fresh fruits and vegetables, and artists and exhibitors sell hand-made arts and crafts, jewelry, antiques, collectibles, and furniture from around the world. The city's oldest continuously operating public market continues to be a vibrant and lively gathering place, complete with entertainment, art showings, and a pottery studio for residents and visitors alike. ✉ 7th St. and North Carolina Ave. SE, Eastern Market ☎ 202/698–5253 ⊕ www.easternmarket-dc.com Ⓜ Eastern Market.

Radici

FOOD/CANDY | The name means "roots" in Italian, and this little shop has quickly settled its roots into the Capitol Hill neighborhood. The charming owners have created a warm and inviting gathering spot and store with its brick walls, Venetian glass light fixtures, terra-cotta tiles, beautiful food, and handmade Italian gift displays and tables both inside and out. This is a lovely spot for an afternoon pick-me-up of espresso and cannoli or an end-of-day glass of wine and cicchetti Veneziani (small bites). You'll also find everything you need for an Italian-themed picnic. Wine tastings are held on Thursday evening. ✉ 303 7th St. SE, Eastern Market ☎ 202/758–0086 ⊕ www.radici-market.com Ⓜ Eastern Market.

Union Market

LOCAL SPECIALTIES | FAMILY | Arriving in 2012, this sprawling one-room market is a feast for the senses that's quickly made it a destination for locals and out-of-town visitors alike. The space offers a smorgasborg of food and drink options, from freshly shucked oysters and piping hot empanadas to Bloody Marys and fish-and-chips. There are butchers and bakers and candles (though not candlestick makers—yet), as well as cheese vendors, hand-made gelato, and a spice shop offering seasonings you've never heard of. Other features include Politics and Prose, a famed D.C. bookseller, and District Cutlery, which offers an incredible selection of German and Japanese knives (sharpening available). It's all made the market enormously popular, particularly on weekends, when parents descend to sip chic coffee while the youngsters bound around a generous outdoor seating area, which features a host of lawn games. Directly behind the market is a pop-up movie theater, the Angelika, which shows new releases and classic favorites alike. ✉ 1309 5th St. NE, Capitol Hill ⊕ www.unionmarketdc.com Ⓜ NoMA-Gallaudet U.

Union Station

SHOPPING CENTERS/MALLS | Resplendent with marble floors and vaulted ceilings, Union Station is a shopping mall as well as a train station. Tenants include such familiar names as Ann Taylor, H&M, Jos. A. Banks Clothiers, MAC Cosmetics, Neuhaus Chocolatier, Swarovski Crystal, and Victoria's Secret, as well as restaurants and a food court with everything from sushi and smoothies to scones. The east hall is filled with vendors of expensive domestic and international wares who sell from open stalls. From April through October an outdoor market is held Monday to Saturday with dozens of vendors selling fresh produce, baked goods and quick snacks, and arts and crafts. The Christmas season brings lights, a train display, and seasonal gift shops. ⊠ *50 Massachusetts Ave. NE, Capitol Hill* ☎ *202/289–1908* ⊕ *www. unionstationdc.com* Ⓜ *Union Station.*

TOYS

Labyrinth Games & Puzzles

TOYS | You won't find any video games in this gem, but instead you'll discover an outstanding selection of handmade wooden puzzles and mazes, collectible card and travel games, board games, and brainteasers. An added bonus to stopping in are the dozens of activities and games for all ages you can play. ⊠ *645 Pennsylvania Ave. SE, Eastern Market* ☎ *202/544–1059* ⊕ *www.labyrinth-gameshop.com* Ⓜ *Eastern Market.*

Chapter 6

FOGGY BOTTOM

6

Updated by Barbara
Noe Kennedy

⊙ Sights	🍴 Restaurants	🛏 Hotels	🛍 Shopping	🍸 Nightlife
★★★★★	★★★☆☆	★★★☆☆	★☆☆☆☆	★★☆☆☆

NEIGHBORHOOD SNAPSHOT

TOP EXPERIENCES

■ **Department of State Diplomatic Reception Rooms:** One of D.C.'s best-kept secrets, this suite of rooms is filled with museum-quality art and historical treasures inspired by the country's founding years. You must reserve well in advance.

■ **John F. Kennedy Center for the Performing Arts:** See a free performance by anyone from They Might Be Giants to Thomas Mapfumo and his band from Zimbabwe here on the Millennium Stage, daily at 6 pm.

■ **Thompson Boat Center:** Take in Washington's marble monuments, lush Roosevelt Island, and the Virginia coastline with a kayak ride down the Potomac.

■ **Touring the White House:** The White House website has up-to-date information on White House tours.

GETTING HERE

The White House can be reached by the Red Line's Farragut North stop or the Silver, Blue, and Orange lines' McPherson Square and Farragut West stops. Foggy Bottom has its own Metro stop, also on the Silver, Blue, and Orange lines. A free shuttle runs from the station to the Kennedy Center. Many of the other attractions are a considerable distance from the nearest subway stop. If you don't relish long walks or if time is limited, check the map to see if you need to make alternate travel arrangements to visit specific sights.

PLANNING YOUR TIME

Touring the area around the White House could easily take a day or even two. If you enjoy history, you may be most interested in the buildings in the Lafayette Square Historic District, **DAR Museum,** and **State Department.** Save the **Kennedy Center** for the evening. You'll find some notable restaurants here as well, including the West End's Michelin-starred Blue Duck Tavern.

QUICK BITES

■ **Breadline DC.** Healthy sandwiches, salads, soups, and amazing breads are specialties of this popular lunch spot; expect long lines at noon. ✉ *1751 Pennsylvania Ave. NW* ⊕ *breadline.com* Ⓜ *Foggy Bottom–GWU.*

■ **Burger Tap & Shake.** This GWU campus favorite serves burgers with house-made toppings, hand-cut fries, shakes, and craft beers on tap. ✉ *2200 Pennsylvania Ave. NW* ⊕ *www. burgertapshake.com* Ⓜ *Foggy Bottom–GWU.*

■ **G Street Food.** At this popular spot, now located on 15th Street near McPherson Square, choose from inexpensive breakfast and lunch options inspired by street food found across the globe. Grab and go, or eat in. ✉ *1030 15th St. NW* ⊕ *www.gstreetfood.com* Ⓜ *McPherson Sq.*

The neighborhood comprising Foggy Bottom, the West End, and the White House includes some of D.C.'s most iconic attractions, the biggest being the White House itself, the home of every U.S. president but George Washington. But there are some excellent smaller museums, including the Octagon House, Renwick Gallery, Decatur House, and the Department of Interior Museum. You will find the Kennedy Center along the Potomac River and George Washington University's campus. The area has a strong residential character as well, and is home to some of D.C.'s oldest houses.

 Sights

The White House is, of course, the primo sight in these parts. You'll need to reserve far in advance (weeks, if not months) if you want to take a tour. If you miss out, be sure to stop by the nearby White House Visitor Center, which provides a good overview of the Executive Mansion's life and times. That said, the neighborhood also boasts a selection of smaller sights that are definitely worth your while, including the Museum of the Americas at the Organization of American States, Smithsonian's Renwick Gallery, and Decatur House. There's not tons of nightlife, but you'll discover some

headline restaurants that have made waves in the foodie world.

American Red Cross
BUILDING | The national headquarters for the American Red Cross, a National Historic Landmark since 1965, is composed of three buildings. Guided tours show off the oldest, a neoclassical structure of blinding-white marble built in 1917 to commemorate women who cared for the wounded on both sides during the Civil War. Three stained-glass windows designed by Louis Comfort Tiffany illustrate the values of the Red Cross: faith, hope, love, and charity. Other holdings you'll see on the 60-minute tour include an original N.C. Wyeth painting,

sculptures, and artifacts that belonged to Clara Barton. Weather permitting, the tour includes a visit to the memorial garden. Reservations are required for the free tour; schedule via email at tours@redcross.org. ✉ *430 17th St. NW, Foggy Bottom* ☎ *202/303–4233* ⊕ *www.red-cross.org* ✉ *Free* ⊗ *No tours Thurs. and Sat.–Tues.* Ⓜ *Farragut W.*

Art Museum of the Americas

MUSEUM | Changing exhibits highlight modern and contemporary Latin American and Caribbean artists in this small gallery, part of the Organization of American States (OAS). The collection has 2,000 objects reflecting the diversity of expression found in the region. ✉ *201 18th St. NW, Foggy Bottom* ☎ *202/370–0147* ⊕ *www.amamuseum.org* ✉ *Free* ⊗ *Closed Mon.* Ⓜ *Farragut W.*

Corcoran School of the Arts + Design at GW

MUSEUM | The Corcoran School, a prestigious art school since 1878, is now in partnership with George Washington University. As part of that collaboration, the work of students and visiting artists is put on display in shows and performances throughout the year. The iconic, beautifully restored beaux arts Flagg Building started life as the historic Corcoran Gallery of Art in 1890, which shuttered its doors in 2014. Part of its collection, which was transferred to the National Gallery of Art, will be returning to the Flagg Building as the NGA becomes a tenant of the Corcoran School on its second floor. Don't miss the first-floor Luther W. Brady Art Gallery, which showcases temporary exhibits by renowned artists. ✉ *500 17th St. NW, Foggy Bottom* ☎ *202/994–1700* ⊕ *go.gwu.edu/atcorcoran* Ⓜ *Farragut W or Farragut N.*

Daughters of the American Revolution (DAR) Museum

MUSEUM | FAMILY | The beaux arts–style Memorial Continental Hall was the site of the DAR's annual congress until the larger Constitution Hall was built and now serves as its headquarters. Today it's also home to Washington, D.C.'s only decorative arts museum. An entrance on D Street leads to the museum, where the enormous collection encompasses furniture, textiles, quilts, silver, china, porcelain, stoneware, earthenware, glass, and other items made and used in the daily lives of Americans from the colonial era through the early 20th century. Thirty-one period rooms reflect more than two centuries of American interiors, including a 1690s New England hall, an 1860s Texas bedroom, and a 1920s Ohio parlor. Two galleries feature changing exhibitions of decorative arts, and a study gallery allows researchers close access to the collection. Docent tours of the period rooms are available weekdays 10–2:30 and Saturday 9–4:30, depending on docent availability. The museum also hosts special events for children and adults; check the website for details. ✉ *1776 D St. NW, Foggy Bottom* ☎ *202/628–1776* ⊕ *www.dar.org/museum* ✉ *Free* ⊗ *Closed Sun.* Ⓜ *Farragut W.*

Decatur House

HOUSE | Decatur House was built in 1819 on Lafayette Square, just across from the White House, for naval hero Stephen Decatur. Designed by Benjamin Henry Latrobe, the country's first professional architect, it's one of Washington's oldest surviving homes. Decatur didn't have long to enjoy it, however, since he died tragically 14 months later after a duel with Commodore James Barron. Wealthy hotel and tavern owner John Gadsby purchased the distinguished Federal-style house as a retirement home in 1836. The large two-story dependency was used as quarters for numerous enslaved individuals in his household—Washington's only extant slave quarters. Tours—offered Monday at 11 am, 12:30 pm, and 2 pm—take in the house's rooms, much of which represent the taste of a later owner, Marie Beale, beloved for her salons with ambassadors and politicians. The White House Historical

Society operates one of its two gift shops here, where you'll find a wonderful selection of White House history–themed products including the annual Christmas ornament. ⊠ *748 Jackson Pl. NW, Foggy Bottom* ☎ *202/218–4337* ⊕ *www.whha. org/programs/decatur-house-tours.html* 🎫 *Free* Ⓜ *Farragut W.*

Federal Reserve Building

GOVERNMENT BUILDING | This imposing marble edifice, its bronze entryway topped by a massive eagle, was designed by Folger Shakespeare Library architect Paul Cret. Its appearance seems to say, "Your money's safe with us." Even so, there's no money here, as the Fed's mission is to set interest rates and keep the economy on track. The stately facade belies a friendlier interior, with a varied collection of art and several special art exhibitions every year. Tours of the building are available for groups of 10 or more, all aged 18 years or older; they must be booked at least two weeks in advance via email. ⊠ *20th St. and Constitution Ave. NW, Foggy Bottom* ☎ *202/452–3324* ✉ *SECY-VisitorServices@frb.gov* ⊕ *www.federalreserve.gov* 🎫 *Free* ⊘ *Closed weekends* Ⓜ *Foggy Bottom–GWU.*

The George Washington University Museum and The Textile Museum

MUSEUM | Designed to foster the study and appreciation of art, history, and culture, this 46,000-square-foot LEED Gold–certified museum facility is located on the campus of George Washington University. Rotating exhibits are taken from the museum's collections of global textile art and artifacts that tell the story of the nation's capital, as well as loans from other institutions. Galleries dedicated to The Textile Museum collections showcase rugs, textiles, and related objects that date from 3000 BC to the present. The Albert H. Small Gallery presents more than 1,000 maps, photographs, books, newspapers, manuscripts, and other artifacts that document D.C.'s history

from the 17th to the mid-20th centuries. Also within this impressive building are the Arthur D. Jekins Library for the Textile Arts, the Albert H. Small Center for National Capital Area Studies, and a museum shop. The museum also offers a dynamic range of lectures, tours, and activities that explore art, history, and culture. ⊠ *701 21st St. NW, Foggy Bottom* ☎ *202/994–5200* ⊕ *www.museum.gwu. edu* 🎫 *$8 suggested donation* ⊘ *Closed Tues.* Ⓜ *Foggy Bottom–GWU.*

The Octagon Museum

HOUSE | FAMILY | Designed by Dr. William Thornton (original architect of the U.S. Capitol), the Octagon House was built for John Tayloe III, a wealthy plantation owner, and was completed in 1801. Thornton chose the unusual shape to conform to the acute angle formed by L'Enfant's intersection of New York Avenue and 18th Street. After the British burned the White House in 1814, Thornton convinced the Tayloes to allow James and Dolley Madison to stay in the Octagon. From September 1814 until March 1815, the Octagon thereby became the temporary White House. It was in the second-floor study that the Treaty of Ghent, which ended the War of 1812, was ratified. The American Institute of Architects (AIA) established in 1898 their new national headquarters in the by-then-dilapidated building; they stayed there for 70 years, before moving into new modern headquarters directly behind. Self-guided tours take in historically furnished rooms, including the parlor, dining room, treaty room, and basement kitchen. Second-floor gallery spaces hold temporary exhibits on history, architecture, and design. ⊠ *1799 New York Ave. NW, Foggy Bottom* ☎ *202/626–7439* ⊕ *www.octagonmuseum.org* 🎫 *Free* ⊘ *Closed Sun.–Wed.* Ⓜ *Farragut W or Farragut N.*

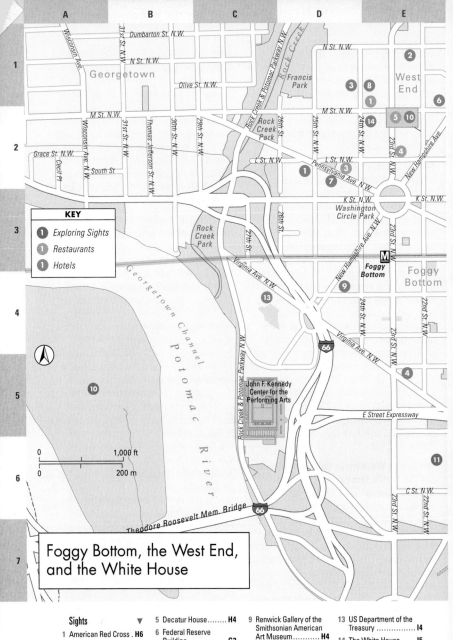

Foggy Bottom, the West End, and the White House

F   **G**   **H**   **I**   **J**

Duke Ellington Park

Scott Circle

Thomas Circle

Downtown

Farragut North

Farragut Square

Mcpherson Square

McPherson Square

Franklin Square

Farragut West

Lafayette Square

President's Park

Edward J. Kelly Park

Bolivar Park

Ellipse

National Aquarium

Department of Commerce

Freedom Plaza

Constitution Gardens Pond

The National Mall

★ **Renwick Gallery of the Smithsonian American Art Museum**

MUSEUM | This luscious French Second Empire–style building rises across the street from the White House and the Eisenhower Executive Office Building, and even with such lofty neighbors, it is still the most appealing architecture on the block. This was the country's first purpose-built art museum, and it was known then as "the American Louvre." Designed by James Renwick in 1859 to hold the art collection of Washington merchant and banker William Wilson Corcoran, the National Historic Landmark building has been a branch of the Smithsonian American Art Museum dedicated to American crafts since 1972. The Renwick's exhibits of American craft and decorative arts are showcased in a captivating, interactive environment designed to illustrate not only the history of craft in America, but also its future. Exhibits showcase exciting contemporary artists who are using materials in innovative ways, redefining what craft is, and taking contemporary craft in bold new directions. Recent shows, for example, have included "No Spectators: The Art of Burning Man" and "WONDER," featuring nine artists who created jaw-dropping site-specific installations in the museum's galleries. ⊠ *Pennsylvania Ave. at 17th St. NW, Foggy Bottom* ☎ *202/633-7970* ⊕ *www. renwick.americanart.si.edu* ⊠ *Free* Ⓜ *Farragut W.*

★ **Theodore Roosevelt Island**

NATIONAL/STATE PARK | Designed as a living memorial to the environmentally minded 26th U.S. President, this wildlife sanctuary is off the George Washington Parkway near the Virginia side of the Potomac—close to Foggy Bottom, Georgetown, East Potomac Park, and the Kennedy Center. Hikers and bicyclists can reach the island by crossing the Theodore Roosevelt Memorial Bridge or walking for 15 minutes from the Rosslyn Metro, but bikes are not allowed on the island and must be docked instead near the footbridge. Many birds and other animals live in the island's marsh and forests, and rangers are available for an Island Safari, where a statue of Teddy greets you with his arm raised. ⊠ *West Potomac Park* ☎ *703/289-2500* ⊕ *www. nps.gov/this* Ⓜ *Rosslyn.*

U.S. Department of State Diplomatic Reception Rooms

GOVERNMENT BUILDING | U.S. foreign policy is administered by battalions of brainy analysts in the huge Department of State building (often referred to as the State Department). All is presided over by the secretary of state, who is fourth in line for the presidency (after the vice president, speaker of the House, and president pro tempore of the Senate). On the top floor are the opulent Diplomatic Reception Rooms, decorated like the great halls of Europe and the rooms of wealthy colonial American plantations. Furnishings include a Philadelphia highboy (antique chest of drawers), a Paul Revere bowl, and the desk on which the Treaty of Paris, which ended the Revolutionary War, was signed in 1783. ■TIP→ **To visit the reception rooms, register online for a tour three months in advance.** ⊠ *2201 C St. NW, Foggy Bottom* ☎ *202/647-3241* ⊕ *receptiontours. state.gov* ⊠ *Free* ⊘ *No tours weekends* Ⓜ *Foggy Bottom–GWU.*

U.S. Department of the Interior Museum

MUSEUM | The outside of the building is plain, but inside a wealth of art, contained in two separate collections, reflects the department's work. The **Office of the Secretary Art Collection**, featuring heroic oil paintings of dam construction, gold panning, and cattle drives, is found throughout the building's hallways, offices, and meeting rooms. The **Department of the Interior Museum Collection** outlines the work of the Bureau of Land Management, the U.S. Geological Survey, the Bureau of Indian Affairs, the National Park Service, and other department branches. On Tuesday

A statue of Andrew Jackson during the battle of New Orleans presides over Lafayette Square.

and Thursday at 2 pm, you can view 26 photographic murals by Ansel Adams and many of the more than 40 dramatic murals painted by Maynard Dixon, John Steuart Curry, and other artists. Reservations are required for the Murals Tour; call at least two weeks in advance. The **Indian Craft Shop** across the hall from the museum sells Native American pottery, dolls, carvings, jewelry, baskets, and books. ⊠ *Stewart Lee Udall Department of the Interior Building, 1849 C St. NW, Foggy Bottom* ☎ *202/208–4743* ⊕ *www. doi.gov/interiormuseum* ⌦ *Free* ⊘ *Closed weekends* ☞ *Visitors 18 and older must show a government-issued ID to enter the Stewart Lee Udall Department of the Interior Building* Ⓜ *Farragut W.*

U.S. Department of the Treasury
GOVERNMENT BUILDING | Once used to store currency, this is the largest Greek Revival edifice in Washington. Robert Mills, the architect responsible for the Washington Monument and the Smithsonian American Art Museum, designed the colonnade on 15th Street. After the death of President Lincoln, the Andrew Johnson Suite was used as the executive office while Mrs. Lincoln moved out of the White House. Tours must be arranged through your Congressional representative or senator; participants must be U.S. citizens or legal residents. ⊠ *1500 Pennsylvania Ave. NW, Foggy Bottom* ☎ *202/622–2000 general info* ⊕ *home. treasury.gov/services/tours-and-library/ tours-of-the-historic-treasury-building* ⌦ *Free* Ⓜ *McPherson Sq. or Metro Center.*

The White House
GOVERNMENT BUILDING | America's most famous house was designed in 1792 by Irish architect James Hoban. It was known officially as the Executive Mansion until 1902, when President Theodore Roosevelt renamed it the White House, long its informal name. The house has undergone many structural changes: Andrew Jackson installed running water; James Garfield put in the first elevator; Harry Truman had the entire structure gutted and restored, adding a

second-story porch to the south portico; and Richard Nixon installed a one-lane bowling alley in 1969.

To see the White House you need to contact your U.S. representative or senator (or embassy if you aren't a U.S. citizen). Requests can be made up to three months in advance (especially for spring, summer, or December tour requests) and no less than 21 days in advance. You'll be asked for the names, birth dates, and Social Security numbers of everyone in your group. On the morning of your tour, call the White House Visitors Office information line for any updates; tours are subject to last-minute cancellations. Arrive 15 minutes early. Your group will be asked to line up in alphabetical order. Everyone 18 years and older must present government-issued photo ID, and no purses, backpacks, or bags are allowed on the tour (and no storage lockers are provided so leave them in your hotel room). There are no public restrooms, and you're allowed to take photos only with a smartphone or small compact camera. The security process will probably last as long as the tour itself, 20–25 minutes.

The self-guided tour includes rooms on the ground floor, but the State Floor has the highlights. The East Room is the largest room in the White House, the site of ceremonies and press conferences; this is also where Theodore Roosevelt's children roller-skated and one of Abraham Lincoln's sons harnessed a pet goat to a chair and went for a ride. The portrait of George Washington that Dolley Madison saved from torch-carrying British soldiers in 1814 hangs in the room, and the White House Christmas tree stands here every winter. The only president to get married in the White House, Grover Cleveland, was wed in the Blue Room. Esther, the second daughter of President Cleveland and First Lady Frances, holds the distinction of being the only child born in the White House. The Red Room, decorated

in early-19th-century American Empire style, has been a favorite of first ladies. Mary Todd Lincoln had her coffee and read the morning paper here. In 1961, First Lady Jacqueline Kennedy undertook an extensive restoration of the White House to preserve and showcase the historical and architectural significance of the home and its contents. The East Garden, which now bears her name, honors her contributions. Michelle Obama installed a vegetable and herb garden to promote healthy eating, as well as an apiary and pollinator garden for bees and other insects.

Your tour of the White House will be enhanced by visiting the White House Visitor Center at 1450 Pennsylvania Avenue NW, featuring displays, photos, and a 30-minute video about the White House. ⊠ *1600 Pennsylvania Ave. NW, Foggy Bottom* 🕾 *202/208–1631, 202/456–7041 24-hr info line* ⊕ *www.whitehouse. gov* 🖃 *Free* ⊗ *Closed Sun. and Mon.* Ⓜ *Federal Triangle, Metro Center, or McPherson Sq.*

White House Visitor Center
INFO CENTER | FAMILY | If you aren't able to obtain tickets to visit the White House (or even if you have), visiting the White House Visitor Center is an excellent Plan B. Displays, artifacts, photos, videos, and interactive exhibits recount the life and times of America's most famous house, providing behind-the-scenes insight into everything from the Oval Office's devotion to presidential food preferences to the integral ballet of moving day, when one president must be moved out and the next moved in, in a matter of hours. ⊠ *1450 Pennsylvania Ave. NW, Foggy Bottom* 🕾 *202/208–1631* ⊕ *www.nps.gov* Ⓜ *Metro Center or Federal Triangle.*

🍴 Restaurants

The history-steeped Foggy Bottom area boasts architectural landmarks like the Watergate Hotel. Around George

How to Visit the White House

To visit the White House, you'll need to contact your U.S. representative or senator (or embassy in Washington, D.C., if you aren't a U.S. citizen). Requests can be made up to three months in advance (recommended especially for spring, summer, and December) and no less than 21 days in advance. You'll be asked for the names, birth dates, and Social Security numbers of everyone in your group. Some members allow you to sign up for a tour online, some require you to call the office's tour coordinator.

On the morning of your tour, call the White House Visitors Office information line for any updates; tours are subject to last-minute cancellations. Arrive 15 minutes early. Everyone 18 years and older must present government-issued photo ID, and no purses, backpacks, bags, food, or beverages are allowed on the tour (and no storage lockers are provided, so leave them in your hotel room). We've scoured the immediate area, but there are also no places to check larger bags.

Photographs are allowed only from smartphones and compact cameras. There are no public restrooms. The security process will probably last as long as the tour itself, 20 to 25 minutes.

If you can't tour the White House itself, you can always visit the nearby White House Visitors Center at 1450 Pennsylvania Ave. NW. Unlike the White House, it's open every day.

Washington University there's cheaper, college-friendly fare like burrito joints and coffee shops. Nearby, the Kennedy Center draws a more mature crowd with tastes that have evolved past burgers and nachos. North of Foggy Bottom, the West End has become a popular dining destination.

★ Blue Duck Tavern

$$$$ | MODERN AMERICAN | With a kitchen firmly committed to artisanal and local ingredients, this high-end tavern, located in the Park Hyatt Washington D.C. hotel, wows with American-inspired dishes like moulard duck breast and oven-roasted bone marrow. Thanks to its much-deserved Michelin star, a visit here means being on the lookout for the city's biggest political names to claim their favorite tables. **Known for:** hand-cut steak fries doused in duck fat; stylish, rustic dining room; intimate chef's table with tasting menu. $ Average main: $38 ⊠ Park Hyatt Washington D.C., 1201 24th St. NW, West End ☎ 202/419–6755

⊕ www.blueducktavern.com Ⓜ Foggy Bottom–GWU.

Founding Farmers DC

$$ | MODERN AMERICAN | Inside this ultramodern take on the old-school farmhouse, affordable eco-chic is the mantra—though the sheer number of offerings can be a tad overwhelming (with 14 options for pastas and flatbreads alone). Farms from all over the country provide most of the fresh vegetables, beef, and poultry, and sustainable practices are used to catch every type of fish on the menu. **Known for:** kernal-speckled cornbread, served piping hot in a cast-iron skillet; throwback sodas, such as the daily rickey and lemon-lime ginger; the vegan-loving array of meat- and egg-free options. $ Average main: $18 ⊠ 1924 Pennsylvania Ave. NW, Foggy Bottom ☎ 202/822–8783 ⊕ www.wearefounding-farmers.com Ⓜ Foggy Bottom–GWU.

Marcel's by Robert Wiedmaier

$$$$ | **FRENCH** | Served in a warmly lit, elegant setting, the award-winning, Flemish-inspired French menu at Marcel's—the flagship restaurant of acclaimed chef Robert Wiedmaier—often includes multiple seafood choices (like perfectly seared diver scallops and Blue Bay mussels), succulent duck breast, and a selection of foie gras. In season, be sure to order the mixed-melon minestrone with yogurt sorbet and cream for dessert. **Known for:** very upscale multicourse menus that change daily; flavorful Blue Bay mussels; affordable pretheater menu. $ *Average main: $125* ✉ *2401 Pennsylvania Ave. NW, West End* ☎ *202/296–1166* ⊕ *www. marcelsdc.com* ☉ *No lunch* Ⓜ *Foggy Bottom–GWU.*

RIS

$$$ | **MODERN AMERICAN** | The brainchild of veteran chef Ris Lacoste (who knew Julia Child), RIS serves elevated but comforting seasonal new American fare in an earthy-chic, light-filled space, the sort of place you'll find locals, the after-work crowd, even a celebrity or two. You should definitely try the daily and seasonal specials, but you can always count on the mainstays, including onion soup, mussels, and RIS's "delicious meatlife." **Known for:** signature shrimp margaritas and Popsicle mimosas; a great "marquee menu" for pretheater diners, available 5 to 6:30 pm; daily specials featuring the chef's take on classic dishes. $ *Average main: $32* ✉ *2275 L St. NW, West End* ☎ *202/730–2500* ⊕ *risdc.com* Ⓜ *Foggy Bottom–GWU.*

Westend Bistro

$$$ | **MODERN AMERICAN** | Chef de cuisine Alvin Dela Cruz focuses on Americanized versions of bistro classics created from regional ingredients in this modern-style West End restaurant in the Ritz-Carlton Washington D.C. The patio is popular during warm weather among guests and locals alike, and innovative cocktails please the happy hour crowd. **Known for:**

a chef's table that guests can customize; Sunday brunch with bottomless mimosas; weekday happy hour featuring a special cocktail of the day. $ *Average main: $29* ✉ *The Ritz-Carlton Washington D.C., 1190 22nd St. NW, West End* ☎ *202/974–4900* ⊕ *www.westendbistrodc.com* ▭ *No credit cards* ☉ *No lunch weekends* Ⓜ *Foggy Bottom–GWU.*

Hotels

With the Kennedy Center for the Performing Arts anchoring its southwestern side and the George Washington University campus to the north, this D.C. community is hopping with youth, even though most of its residents are longtime Washingtonians and most of its homes hearken back to the 18th and 19th centuries. And nothing beats the early-morning views of the Potomac River, where sculls and shells skim along the surface as crews prepare for upcoming races.

Avenue Suites Georgetown

$$$ | **HOTEL** | **FAMILY** | Luxurious and practical at the same time, this is a great choice for families and groups because all the suites have separate bedrooms and full kitchens, and some have views of the city and the Potomac River. **Pros:** service oriented; complimentary Saturday-morning yoga; "Stock the Fridge" service with Trader Joe's. **Cons:** a long walk to the Mall (but close to Georgetown); expensive valet parking; there's a gym, but it's tiny. $ *Rooms from: $296* ✉ *2500 Pennsylvania Ave. NW, Foggy Bottom* ☎ *202/333–8060* ⊕ *www. avenuesuites.com* ↳ *124 rooms* ⦿ *No meals* Ⓜ *Foggy Bottom–GWU.*

Embassy Suites Washington, D.C. Georgetown

$$$ | **HOTEL** | **FAMILY** | All accommodations at this convenient hotel within walking distance of Georgetown and Dupont Circle have a living room and bedroom and surround an atrium filled with comfortable seating areas and the hotel's dining options. **Pros:** family-friendly; reception with complimentary drinks and apps every night; pool to keep the little ones—and sweaty tourists—happy. **Cons:** museums not in walking distance; four blocks from Metro; expensive parking (not valet). [$] *Rooms from: $319* ✉ *1250 22nd St. NW, Foggy Bottom* ☎ *202/857–3388, 800/362–2779* 🌐 *www.embassysuites.com* 🛏 *318 rooms* 🍴 *Free Breakfast* [M] *Foggy Bottom–GWU or Dupont Circle.*

★ The Fairmont, Washington, D.C., Georgetown

$$$ | **HOTEL** | Great for exploring Georgetown, this hotel centers on an elegant central courtyard and gardens, overlooked by the large glassed-in lobby and half of the bright, spacious rooms. **Pros:** fitness fanatics will love the gym and 50-foot indoor pool; great no-charge pet program includes homemade treats for dogs; tasty food options on-site. **Cons:** expensive parking; far from most major attractions; some rooms can be noisy. [$] *Rooms from: $309* ✉ *2401 M St. NW, Foggy Bottom* ☎ *202/429–2400, 866/540–4505* 🌐 *www.fairmont.com* 🛏 *413 rooms* 🍴 *No meals* [M] *Foggy Bottom–GWU.*

Hotel Hive

$$ | **HOTEL** | Hip and trendy, D.C.'s first microhotel is designed for travelers who care more about exploring and socializing than spending much time in their room. It features 83 "hives" ranging from 125 to 250 square feet with a choice of king, queen, twin, or bunk beds. **Pros:** great prices; on-site restaurant offers all-day dining; plenty of amenities including free Wi-Fi, Bluetooth music, and individual thermostats. **Cons:** occupancy limited to two people (usually with one bed); rooms on lower floors are noisy; very, very small rooms. [$] *Rooms from: $239* ✉ *2224 F St. NW, Foggy Bottom* ☎ *202/849–8499* 🌐 *www.hotelhive.com* 🛏 *83 rooms* 🍴 *No meals.*

Hotel Lombardy

$$$ | **HOTEL** | This romantic property near the White House is an idyllic urban retreat. **Pros:** homey rooms; beautiful lounge; complimentary Wi-Fi. **Cons:** old-fashioned decor; expensive valet parking; on busy street. [$] *Rooms from: $300* ✉ *2019 Pennsylvania Ave. NW, Foggy Bottom* ☎ *202/828–2600* 🌐 *www.hotellombardy.com* 🛏 *161 rooms* 🍴 *No meals* [M] *Foggy Bottom–GWU.*

Hyatt Place Washington DC/Georgetown/West End

$$$ | **HOTEL** | Families and business travelers will appreciate this modern hotel conveniently located in the West End neighborhood just a few blocks from the Foggy Bottom–GWU Metro. **Pros:** complimentary daily breakfast buffet; fitness center and heated indoor pool; free Wi-Fi. **Cons:** decor is not very distinctive; expensive valet parking; relatively far from major sights. [$] *Rooms from: $382* ✉ *2121 M St. NW, Foggy Bottom* ☎ *202/838–2222* 🌐 *www.hyatt.com* 🛏 *168 rooms* 🍴 *Free Breakfast* [M] *Foggy Bottom–GWU.*

Melrose Georgetown Hotel

$ | **HOTEL** | **FAMILY** | Gracious, traditional rooms done in a soothing palette of creams and grays with splashes of green, blue, and red all have oversize bathrooms and mini-refrigerators, and many have pullout sofa beds, making this boutique hotel a good choice for families and a good alternative to the District's many chain hotels. **Pros:** nice fitness center; closest Georgetown hotel to a metro (Foggy Bottom–GWU); walk to dining and shopping. **Cons:** street noise; no pool; fee for in-room Wi-Fi. [$] *Rooms from: $179* ✉ *2430 Pennsylvania Ave. NW, Georgetown* ☎ *202/955–6400, 800/635–7673* 🌐 *www.melrosehoteldc.com* 🛏 *240 rooms* 🍴 *No meals* [M] *Foggy Bottom–GWU.*

★ Park Hyatt Washington

$$$$ | **HOTEL** | **FAMILY** | Understated elegance and refined service can be found at this soothing city getaway, where the guest rooms—designer Tony Chi's minimalist tribute to the American experience—feature walnut floors, hard-covered books, and folk-art accents. **Pros:** spacious and luxurious rooms; in-house restaurant one of the best in the city; beautiful indoor saltwater pool. **Cons:** expensive valet parking; 10-minute walk to Foggy Bottom–GWU Metro; many rooms lack good views. [$] *Rooms from: $629* ✉ *1201 24th St. NW, Foggy Bottom* ☎ *202/789–1234* 🌐 *www.hyatt.com* 🛏 *220 rooms* 🍴 *No meals* [M] *Foggy Bottom–GWU.*

Residence Inn Washington, DC/Foggy Bottom

$$$ | **HOTEL** | This all-suites hotel is close to the Kennedy Center, George Washington University, and Georgetown. **Pros:** near Metro; rooftop pool overlooks the Watergate Hotel; friendly and helpful staff. **Cons:** far from the museums; too quiet for some; small fitness room. [$] *Rooms from: $379* ✉ *801 New Hampshire Ave. NW, Foggy Bottom* ☎ *202/785–2000* 🌐 *www.marriott.com* 🛏 *103 suites* 🍴 *Free Breakfast* [M] *Foggy Bottom–GWU.*

★ The Ritz-Carlton Washington, D.C

$$$$ | **HOTEL** | Luxury radiates from every polished marble surface at one of Washington's most upscale hostelries, and personalized service makes you feel pampered. **Pros:** attentive service; convenient to several parts of town; attached to fabulous health club, spa, and pool. **Cons:** pricey room rates, especially during peak times; expensive valet parking; sleepy neighborhood. [$] *Rooms from: $430* ✉ *1150 22nd St. NW, Foggy Bottom* ☎ *202/835–0500, 800/241–3333* 🌐 *www.ritzcarlton.com* 🛏 *300 rooms* 🍴 *No meals* [M] *Foggy Bottom–GWU.*

The St. Gregory Hotel Dupont Circle

$$ | **HOTEL** | This sophisticated and very chic boutique hotel offers the ideal accommodations for business and leisure travelers, thanks to the rooms that feature fully stocked kitchens and sofa beds. **Pros:** big rooms; central location near business district of K Street; 24-hour fitness center. **Cons:** far from museums; expensive valet parking; area is quiet at night. [$] *Rooms from: $269* ✉ *2033 M St. NW* ☎ *202/530–3600, 800/829–5034* 🌐 *www.stgregoryhotelwdc.com* 🛏 *156 rooms* 🍴 *No meals* [M] *Foggy Bottom–GWU or Farragut N.*

State Plaza Hotel

$$ | **HOTEL** | Just two blocks from the National Mall's west end and across the street from the State Department, this hotel is the perfect blend of comfort and elegance with its full-size kitchens and eating areas, large bathrooms with separate dressing areas and sleek furnishings in shades of gray, cream, and gold. **Pros:** all suites; free Internet access; walk to Metro; close to GWU; safe neighborhood at night. **Cons:** far from museums; expensive valet parking; small fitness center. [$] *Rooms from: $239* ✉ *2117 E St. NW, Foggy Bottom* ☎ *202/861–8200, 800/424–2859* 🌐 *www.stateplaza.com* 💳 *No credit cards* 🛏 *230 suites* 🍴 *No meals* [M] *Foggy Bottom–GWU.*

★ The Watergate Hotel

$$$$ | **HOTEL** | Beautifully situated along the Potomac River, the legendary Watergate radiates sophistication and glamour, both embracing its infamous past and celebrating its midcentury modernist style. **Pros:** beautiful mosaic-tiled saltwater pool; fun, cheeky historical touches; gorgeously designed bars and restaurant with excellent menus. **Cons:** some rooms are small; elevators are a bit complicated to use; 1960s style not for everyone. [$] *Rooms from: $450* ✉ *2650 Virginia Ave. NW, Foggy Bottom* ☎ *202/827–1600* 🌐 *www.thewatergatehotel.com* 🛏 *336 rooms* 🍴 *No meals* [M] *Foggy Bottom–GWU.*

Westin Georgetown, Washington D.C.
$$$ | **HOTEL** | **FAMILY** | Although not truly in Georgetown (but nearby), this Westin is in a busy West End location. **Pros:** quiet neighborhood; comfortable rooms; outdoor pool open seasonally. **Cons:** 10-minute walk to Metro; a bit out of the way for sightseeing; expensive parking. [$] *Rooms from: $400* ✉ *2350 M St. NW, Foggy Bottom* ☎ *202/429–0100* 🌐 *www.westingeorgetown.com* 🛏 *269 rooms* 🍴 *No meals* [M] *Foggy Bottom–GWU.*

Nightlife

The area near the White House and Foggy Bottom once offered a less frantic nightlife environment as the city center emptied out during the weekends. Today, some interesting clubs and restaurants have reenergized the area. Many are near—or in—major hotels, making the area more attractive to the going-out crowd.

DANCE CLUBS

Eden
DANCE CLUBS | This four-floor hot spot near the White House attracts Washington celebrities, foreign visitors, and the sophisticated elite. The club hosts a variety of local and big-name DJs and is famous for its rooftop deck, attracting big crowds in the summer. Bottle service is available. ✉ *1716 I St. NW, Foggy Bottom* ☎ *202/785–0270* 🌐 *www.edendc.com* [M] *Farragut W.*

Performing Arts

A wealth of venues offering concerts, films, music, and dance surround the president's home and the adjacent Foggy Bottom neighborhood. Here you'll find the John F. Kennedy Center for Performing Arts and George Washington University's Lisner Auditorium—two great venues for the performing arts. Both facilities present drama, dance, and music, offering a platform for some of the most famous American and international performers. Hungry and thirsty visitors to the Kennedy Center can dine and drink at the Roof Terrace Restaurant.

DANCE

The Washington Ballet
DANCE | The company's classical and contemporary dances are performed from September through April, with works by such choreographers as George Balanchine, Paul Taylor, Marius Petipa, Alexei Ratmansky, and more. The main shows are mounted at the Kennedy Center, Harman Center for the Arts, Warner Theatre, and THEARC in Southeast D.C. Each December the company also performs *The Nutcracker* at the Warner Theatre. ✉ *Washington* ☎ *202/362–3606* 🌐 *www.washingtonballet.org.*

MAJOR VENUES

DAR Constitution Hall
ARTS CENTERS | Acts ranging from the Bolshoi Ballet to U2 to B.B. King have performed at this 3,702-seat venue, one of Washington's grand old halls. It's well worth a visit for both the excellent performers it attracts as well as its awesome architecture and acoustics. ✉ *1776 D St. NW, Foggy Bottom* ☎ *202/628–4780* 🌐 *www.dar.org/constitution-hall* [M] *Farragut W.*

★ **John F. Kennedy Center for the Performing Arts**
ARTS CENTERS | Overlooking the Potomac River, the gem of the Washington, D.C., performing arts scene is home to the National Symphony Orchestra and the Washington National Opera. The best out-of-town acts perform at one of three performance spaces—the Concert Hall, the Opera House, or the Eisenhower Theater. An eclectic range of performances is staged at the center's smaller venues, which showcase chamber groups, experimental works, cabaret-style performances, and the KC Jazz Club. But that's not all. On the Millennium Stage in the center's Grand Foyer, you can catch free performances almost any day at 6 pm. A major expansion, designed by Steven

Holl and complete in 2019, provides a dynamic, open-air, collaborative space and a pedestrian bridge that connects with the other presidential memorials on the National Mall. ■TIP➜ On performance days, a free shuttle bus runs between the Kennedy Center and the Foggy Bottom–GWU Metro stop. ⊠ 2700 F St. NW, Foggy Bottom ☎ 202/467–4600, 800/444–1324 ⊕ www.kennedy-center.org Ⓜ Foggy Bottom–GWU.

Lisner Auditorium

ARTS CENTERS | A 1,500-seat theater on the campus of George Washington University hosts pop, classical, and choral music shows, modern dance performances, musical theater, and high profile political and celebrity speakers, attracting students and outsiders alike. ⊠ 730 21st St. NW, Foggy Bottom ☎ 202/994–6800 ⊕ lisner.gwu.edu Ⓜ Foggy Bottom–GWU.

MUSIC

Choral Arts Society of Washington

MUSIC | From fall to late spring, this 200-voice choir performs a musical array, ranging from classical to tango to Broadway hits, at the Kennedy Center Concert Hall and other venues. Three Christmas concerts are also scheduled each December, and in January or February there's a popular choral tribute to Martin Luther King Jr. ⊠ Washington ☎ 202/244–3669 ⊕ www.choralarts.org Ⓜ Friendship Heights.

Washington Performing Arts Society

MUSIC | One of the city's oldest arts organizations stages high-quality classical music, jazz, gospel, world music, modern dance, and performance art in major venues around the city. Past artists include the Alvin Ailey American Dance Theater, Yo-Yo Ma, the Chieftains, Herbie Hancock, and Savion Glover. ⊠ 1400 K St., Suite 500, Foggy Bottom ☎ 202/833–9800 ⊕ www.wpas.org.

OPERA

Washington National Opera

OPERA | Founded in 1956, the Washington National Opera presents a variety of classical works each year at the Kennedy Center Opera House. The operas are performed in their original languages with English supertitles. In 2012 the WNO created the American Opera Initiative, which produces three new 20-minute operas in the fall and an hour-long opera in the spring. The WNO also started the Domingo-Cafritz Young Artists Program in 2002 under the leadership of Plácido Domingo. These emerging international talents perform throughout the year. ⊠ John F. Kennedy Center for the Performing Arts, 2700 F St. NW, Foggy Bottom ☎ 202/467–4600, 800/444–1324 ⊕ www.kennedy-center.org/wno.

ORCHESTRA

National Symphony Orchestra

MUSIC | Under the leadership of music director Gianandrea Noseda, the orchestra performs classic works by composers such as Verdi, Handel, and Rossini in the Kennedy Center Concert Hall. In summer the orchestra performs at Wolf Trap National Park for the Performing Arts. On Memorial and Labor Day weekends and on July 4, the NSO performs on the West Lawn of the Capitol. ⊠ John F. Kennedy Center for the Performing Arts, 2700 F St. NW, Foggy Bottom ☎ 202/467–4600, 444–1324 ⊕ www.kennedy-center.org/nso Ⓜ Foggy Bottom–GWU.

🛍 Shopping

In the area best known for the nation's most famous house, you can also shop for official White House Christmas ornaments and Easter eggs, jewelry inspired by Jackie Kennedy, and crafts made by living Native American artists and artisans. If you're looking for a tasty treat, grab the fixings for a picnic lunch at the FRESHFARM market held every Thursday, April through mid-November,

Five Great Arts Experiences

■ **Arena Stage:** Housed in the audience-friendly Mead Center for American Theatre in the Southwest Waterfront, Arena Stage offers innovative new American plays as well as classic plays and musicals.

■ **John F. Kennedy Center for the Performing Arts:** The gem of the D.C. arts scene, this beautiful venue on the banks of the Potomac in Foggy Bottom is the one performance venue you might take with you if you were stranded on a desert island.

■ **Shakespeare Theatre Company:** Among the top Shakespeare companies in the world, this troupe, which performs in a couple of venues in Penn Quarter, excels at both classical and contemporary interpretations and doesn't limit itself to the works of the Bard.

■ **Studio Theatre:** With its four intimate theaters and its hip urban locale, this 14th Street landmark provides the best in contemporary dramas and comedies.

■ **Woolly Mammoth Theatre Company:** This remarkable theater company headquartered in the heart of the Penn Quarter stages some of the most creative and entertaining new plays from the nation's best playwrights.

---

on the corner of Lafayette Square—the produce that's sold here is said to be as fresh as food grown in the White House garden. Otherwise, it's a good spot for people-watching and fine dining, but alas there's very little shopping in this area.

CRAFTS AND GIFTS

★ Indian Craft Shop

CRAFTS | Jewelry, pottery, sand paintings, weavings, and baskets from more than 45 Native American tribes, including Navajo, Zuni, Cherokee, and Mohawk, are at your fingertips here—as long as you have a photo ID to enter the federal building. Items range from inexpensive jewelry costing as little as $5 on up to collector-quality art pieces selling for more than $10,000. This shop has been open since 1938. ⊠ *U.S. Department of the Interior, 1849 C St. NW, Room 1023, Foggy Bottom* ☎ *202/208–4056* ⊕ *www. indiancraftshop.com* ⊗ *Closed weekends and federal holidays, except 3rd Sat. of each month* Ⓜ *Farragut W or Farragut N.*

White House Historical Association Retail Shops

GIFTS/SOUVENIRS | The White House Historical Association operates two shops. The flagship store is in the White House Visitor Center, adjacent to the White House between 14th and 15th Streets, and the smaller shop is in the historic Decatur House on Lafayette Square just a block north of the White House (*1610 H Street NW, 202/218–4337, closed weekends*). Both shops sell the Association's official merchandise, which is all well made. You can find everything from the official White House Christmas ornament to jewelry, ties, T-shirts, books, and accessories. For $10 or less, you can get cocktail napkins, bookmarks, or a wooden Easter egg. The more expensive items include silk scarves, hand-painted enamel boxes, and jewelry with cameos of the White House. ⊠ *1450 Pennsylvania Ave. NW, Foggy Bottom* ☎ *202/208–7031* ⊕ *www. whitehousehistory.org* Ⓜ *Farragut W.*

MARKETS
FRESHFARM Foggy Bottom Market

OUTDOOR/FLEA/GREEN MARKETS | Pick up a crab cake, Belgian waffle, or small-batch craft spirit at this farmers' market on Wednesday from 3 to 7, in early April through November. Similar fare is available near Lafayette Park (810 Vermont Avenue NW) on Thursday 11–2, April–mid-November. Other FRESHFARM markets are in the Capitol Riverfront (Sunday 9–1, May–October), CityCenterDC (Tuesday 11–2, May–October), Dupont Circle (Sunday 8:30–1:30 year-round), Georgetown (Saturday 9–1, June–November), H Street NE (Saturday 9–12:30, April–mid-December), NoMa (Sunday 9–1, mid-May–October), at Penn Quarter (Thursday 3–7, April–mid-November), and Watkins SE (Wednesday 3–7, June–October). All locations sell local fruits and vegetables. ✉ 901 23rd St. NW, Foggy Bottom ☎ 202/362–8889 ⊕ www.freshfarmmarkets.org Ⓜ Foggy Bottom–GWU.

 # Activities

BOATING
Thompson Boat Center

BICYCLING | The center rents nonmotorized watercraft, including canoes, kayaks, and stand-up paddleboards (from $16 per hour, $64 per day), all on a first-come, first-served basis. Rowing sculls are also available (from $17 per hour), but you must be certified and validated for rental. Bikes are also available for rent ($11 per hour or $35 per day). The location provides a nice launching point into the Potomac, right in the center of the city, and close to the monuments. In addition to its access to the river, Thompson is conveniently sited for getting onto the Rock Creek Trail and the C&O Towpath. Note: Thompson closes from Halloween through mid-April, based on the water's temperature. ✉ 2900 Virginia Ave. NW, Foggy Bottom ☎ 202/333–9543 ⊕ www.thompsonboatcenter.com Ⓜ Foggy Bottom–GWU.

Chapter 7

GEORGETOWN

Updated by
Laura Rodini

⦿ Sights	🍴 Restaurants	🛏 Hotels	🛍 Shopping	🍸 Nightlife
★★★☆☆	★★★★☆	★★★★☆	★★★★★	★★★★☆

NEIGHBORHOOD SNAPSHOT

TOP EXPERIENCES

■ **C&O Canal:** Walk or bike along the path here, which offers bucolic scenery from the heart of Georgetown across Maryland.

■ **Dumbarton Oaks:** Stroll through the 10 acres of formal gardens—Washington's loveliest oasis.

■ **M Street:** Indulge in some serious designer retail therapy (or just window-shopping). Finish at Georgetown University by the base of the famously steep staircase that appeared in the film *The Exorcist*—and climb it, if you dare.

■ **Tudor Place:** Step into Georgetown's past with a visit to the grand home of the Custis-Peter family. On view are antiques from George and Martha Washington's home at Mount Vernon and a 1919 Pierce Arrow roadster.

■ **Washington Harbour and Waterfront Park:** Come on a warm evening to enjoy sunset drinks and fine dining while overlooking the Watergate, Kennedy Center, and Potomac River. Board a sightseeing cruise at the dock.

GETTING HERE

There's no Metro stop in Georgetown, so you have to take a bus or taxi or walk to this part of Washington. It's about a 20-minute walk from Dupont Circle and the Foggy Bottom Metro stations. Perhaps the best transportation deal in Georgetown is the Circulator (⊕ *www.dccirculator.com*). For a buck you can ride daily from Union Station, Dupont Circle, or the Rosslyn Metro to the heart of Georgetown.

PLANNING YOUR TIME

■ Georgetown is known for its shopping, but you can also spend a pleasant day here enjoying the sights. Main attractions (**C&O Canal, Georgetown University, Tudor Place, Dumbarton Oaks, Oak Hill Cemetery,** and **Dumbarton House**) are somewhat removed from the others, and the street scene, with its shops and people-watching, invites you to linger.

■ Georgetown is almost always crowded at night. At night take a bus or taxi.

QUICK BITES

■ **Chaia Tacos.** The artful creations here are locally sourced, vegetarian (think: kale and potatoes), and served on a grilled corn tortilla. ⊠ *3207 Grace St. NW* ⊕ *www.bluebottlecoffee.com.*

■ **Ching Ching Cha.** You'll feel like you've entered another world at this cozy tea shop with friendly service and artisanal brewed teas. ⊠ *1063 Wisconsin Ave. NW* ⊕ *www.bluebottlecoffee.com.*

■ **Georgetown Cupcake.** Satisfy a sweet tooth at the shop made famous on TLC's *DC Cupcakes.* The line is long but moves quickly. ⊠ *3301 M St. NW* ⊕ *www.georgetowncupcake.com.*

At first glance, Washington's oldest and wealthiest neighborhood may look genteel and staid, but don't be fooled: this is a lively part of town. Georgetown is D.C.'s top high-end shopping destination, with everything from eclectic antiques and housewares to shoes and upscale jeans. At night, particularly on weekends, revelers along M Street and Wisconsin Avenue eat, drink, and make merry. Although the coveted brick homes north of M Street are the province of Washington's high society, the rest of the neighborhood offers ample entertainment for everyone.

Sights

C&O Canal
NATIONAL/STATE PARK | FAMILY | George Washington was one of the first to advance the idea of a canal linking the Potomac with the Ohio River across the Appalachians. Work started on the Chesapeake & Ohio Canal in 1828, and when it opened in 1850, its 74 locks linked Georgetown with Cumberland, Maryland, 185 miles to the northwest (still short of its intended destination). Lumber, coal, iron, wheat, and flour moved up and down the canal, but it was never as successful as its planners had hoped due to damaging floods and competition from the Baltimore & Ohio Railroad. Today the canal is part of the National Parks system; walkers and cyclists follow the towpath once used by mules, while canoeists paddle the canal's calm waters. Ongoing construction to repair and restore locks can often result in towpath closures. The Georgetown Visitor Center is also closed until further notice. ☒ *1057 Thomas Jefferson St. NW, Georgetown* ☏ *301/739–4200 Great Falls Tavern* ⊕ *www.nps.gov/choh* ☒ *3-day pass from $5.*

Dumbarton House
HOUSE | Not to be confused with the Dumbarton Oaks museum, a beautiful garden and research center a few blocks away, this circa-1799 brick mansion

A History of Georgetown

The area that would come to be known as George (after George II), then George Towne, and finally Georgetown, was part of Maryland when it was settled in the early 1700s by Scottish immigrants, many of whom were attracted by the region's tolerant religious climate.

Georgetown's position—at the farthest point up the Potomac that's accessible by ship—made it an ideal transit and inspection point for farmers who grew tobacco in Maryland's interior. In 1789 the state granted the town a charter, but two years later Georgetown—along with Alexandria, its counterpart in Virginia—was included by George Washington in the Territory of Columbia, site of the new capital.

While Washington struggled, Georgetown thrived. Wealthy traders built their mansions on the hills overlooking the river; merchants and the working class lived in modest homes closer to the water's edge.

In 1810 a third of Georgetown's population was African American—both free people and slaves. The Mt. Zion United Methodist Church on 29th Street is the oldest organized black congregation in the city, and when the church stood at 27th and P Streets it was a stop on the Underground Railroad (the original building burned down in the mid-1800s).

Georgetown's rich history and success instilled in all its residents a feeling of pride that persists today. When Georgetowners thought the capital was dragging them down, they asked to be given back to Maryland, the way Alexandria was given back to Virginia in 1845.

Tobacco's star eventually fell, and Georgetown became a milling center, using waterpower from the Potomac. When the Chesapeake & Ohio (C&O) Canal was completed in 1850, the city intensified its milling operations and became the eastern end of a waterway that stretched 184 miles to the west.

The C&O took up some of the slack when Georgetown's harbor began to fill with silt and the port lost business to Alexandria and Baltimore, but the canal never became the success that George Washington had envisioned.

In the years that followed, Georgetown was a malodorous industrial district, a far cry from the fashionable spot it is today. Clustered near the water were a foundry, a fish market, paper and cotton mills, and a power station for the city's streetcar system.

Georgetown still had its Georgian, Federal, and Victorian homes, though, and when the New Deal and World War II brought a flood of newcomers to Washington, Georgetown's tree-shaded streets and handsome brick houses were rediscovered. Pushed out in the process were many of Georgetown's renters, including many of its black residents.

In modern times some of Washington's most famous residents have called Georgetown home, including former *Washington Post* executive editor Ben Bradlee; political pundit George Stephanopoulos; Congresswoman Nancy Pelosi; Secretaries of State John Kerry, Henry Kissinger, and Madeleine Albright; Senator John Warner and his wife at the time, Elizabeth Taylor; and *New York Times* op-ed doyenne Maureen Dowd.

once served as an urban farm. Today it's the headquarters for The Colonial Dames of America. Visitors can tour the antiques-filled Federalist home, which often hosts concerts, theatrical performances, and other community events. Docent-led tours are available on the weekend. ✉ 2715 Q St. NW, Georgetown 🕾 202/337–2288 ⊕ dumbartonhouse.org 🖃 $10 ⊘ Closed Mon. Ⓜ Dupont Circle.

★ Dumbarton Oaks Museum

HOUSE | Career diplomat Robert Woods Bliss and his wife, Mildred, bought the property in 1920 and tamed the sprawling grounds into 10 acres of splendid gardens designed by Beatrix Farrand. In 1940, the Blisses gave the estate to Harvard University as a study center, library, museum, and garden. The museum holds a small but world-renowned collection of Byzantine and pre-Columbian art, reflecting the enormous skill and creativity developed at roughly the same time in two very different parts of the world. The Byzantine collection includes beautiful examples of both religious and secular items executed in mosaic, metal, enamel, stone, textile, and ivory. Pre-Columbian works—artifacts and textiles from Mexico and Central and South America by peoples such as the Aztec, Maya, Inca, and Olmec—are arranged in an enclosed glass pavilion. Especially beautiful in the spring but worth visiting in any season, the gardens feature an orangery and a green terrace filled with iron furniture emblazoned with astrological motifs. ✉ 1703 32nd St. NW, Georgetown 🕾 202/339–6401, 202/339–6400 tours ⊕ www.doaks.org 🖃 Free; gardens $10 ⊘ Closed Mon. No tours in Aug. Ⓜ Dupont Circle.

Georgetown University

COLLEGE | The country's oldest Catholic university (founded in 1789) does not offer architectural tours, but visitors can download a self-guided campus tour from the university's website and explore on their own. The 100-acre campus features a mix of architectural styles with the most striking building being Healy Hall, a Victorian Gothic masterpiece whose construction nearly bankrupted the institution. Architects oriented its front toward the city, and not the Potomac River, as a way to signal its educational stature. Old North, which was modeled after Princeton's main hall, has played host to more than a dozen U.S. presidents. Also worth a peek is the turn-of-the-century Riggs Library, which boasts impressive cast-iron railings. At the southern end of campus, between M and Prospect Streets, a set of 75 super-steep steps were immortalized in the 1973 film *The Exorcist*. When the sun rises, less sinister beings can be seen racing up and down them—Georgetown's many joggers. ✉ 3700 O St. NW, Georgetown 🕾 202/687–0100 ⊕ www. georgetown.edu Ⓜ Foggy Bottom–GWU.

The Oak Hill Cemetery

CEMETERY | Fans of George Saunders's bestselling novel *Lincoln in the Bardo* trek to this hillside corner of Georgetown near Rock Creek. Notable sights include a Gothic Revival chapel designed by James Renwick and the Carroll Family mausoleum, which, during the Civil War, briefly interred Abraham Lincoln's son, Willie, who died in childhood from typhoid fever. Stop by the office for a free self-guided map. ✉ 3001 R St. NW, Georgetown 🕾 202/337–2835 ⊕ www. oakhillcemeterydc.org Ⓜ Dupont Circle.

Old Stone House

HOUSE | Washington's oldest surviving building, this fieldstone house in the heart of Georgetown was built in 1765 by a cabinetmaker named Christopher Layman. It was used as both a residence and place of business by a succession of occupants until 1953 when it was purchased by the National Park Service. Over the next seven years, the park service conducted an extensive restoration that has preserved the building's Revolutionary War–era architecture and design.

Georgetown

KEY
- ● Exploring Sights
- ● Restaurants
- ● Hotels

District of Columbia
↓
Virginia

Sights ▼
1 C&O Canal.............. **E7**
2 Dumbarton House....... **E3**
3 Dumbarton Oaks
  Museum.............. **C2**
4 Georgetown University **A4**
5 The Oak Hill Cemetery .. **E2**
6 Old Stone House........ **D5**
7 Tudor Place............. **C3**

Restaurants ▼
1 Bistrot Lepic........... **B1**
2 Bourbon Steak.......... **E5**
3 Cafe Milano............ **C5**
4 Chez Billy Sud.......... **D6**
5 Das Ethiopian Cuisine... **E5**
6 Farmers Fishers Bakers **D6**
7 Fiola Mare.............. **D6**

8 Kafe Leopold............ **B5**
9 La Chaumiere........... **E5**
10 Rocklands Barbeque and
   Grilling Company **B1**
11 1789 Restaurant......... **A5**

Hotels ▼
1 Four Seasons Hotel
  Washington, DC **E5**
2 Georgetown Suites...... **E5**

3 The Graham Washington
  DC Georgetown, Tapestry
  Collection by Hilton..... **D5**
4 The Ritz-Carlton
  Georgetown,
  Washington, D.C......... **D6**
5 Rosewood
  Washington DC **D6**

Five of the house's rooms are furnished with the simple, sturdy artifacts—plain tables, spinning wheels, and so forth—of 18th-century middle-class life. You can take a self-guided tour of the house and its lovely English-style gardens. ✉ *3051 M St. NW, Georgetown* ☎ *202/895–6070* 🌐 *www.nps.gov/olst* 🎫 *Free* [M] *Foggy Bottom–GWU.*

Tudor Place

HOUSE | Stop at Q Street between 31st and 32nd Streets; look through the trees to the north, to the top of a sloping lawn, and you can see the neoclassical Tudor Place, designed by Capitol architect Dr. William Thornton for one of Martha Washington's granddaughters. Completed in 1816, the house remained in the family for six generations, playing host to countless politicians, dignitaries, and military leaders. On the house tour you can see the largest collection of George and Martha Washington items on public display outside Mount Vernon, Francis Scott Key's law desk, and spurs belonging to soldiers who were executed as spies in the Civil War. You can only visit the house by guided tour (given hourly; last tour at 3), but before and afterward, until 4 pm, you can wander freely, with a map, through the formal garden full of roses and boxwoods, many of which are more than a century old. ✉ *1644 31st St. NW, Georgetown* ☎ *202/965–0400* 🌐 *www.tudorplace.org* 🎫 *$10; garden only $3 ($1 in Feb.)* 🕒 *Closed Mon. and Jan.* [M] *Dupont Circle.*

🍴 Restaurants

Georgetown's picturesque Victorian streetscapes make it D.C.'s most famous neighborhood, with five-star restaurants in historic row houses and casual cafés sandwiched between large national chain stores.

At its beginnings in the mid-1700s, Georgetown was a Maryland tobacco port. Today the neighborhood is one of D.C.'s premier shopping districts, as well as a tourist and architectural attraction. And while recent additions to the neighborhood seem more apt to be chains, there are some standout local restaurants that cater to the budgets of college students, middle-income travelers, and D.C.'s well-heeled elite.

Bistrot Lepic & Wine Bar

$$$ | **FRENCH** | Relaxed and upbeat, this neighborhood bistro is French in every regard—starting with the flirty servers. Traditional bistro fare has been replaced with more interesting variations, such as potato-crusted salmon served with cherry and Pernod sauce, but some standards, including braised veal cheeks, remain. **Known for:** busy neighborhood bistro; all-French wine list; upstairs wine bar with small plates. [$] *Average main: $29* ✉ *1736 Wisconsin Ave. NW, Georgetown* ☎ *202/333–0111* 🌐 *www.bistrotlepic.com* [M] *Foggy Bottom–GWU.*

Bourbon Steak

$$$$ | **STEAKHOUSE** | In a city full of steak houses catering to business travelers on expense accounts, it'd be easy to write off this restaurant in the Four Seasons. But expertly prepared all-natural meats, sides like truffle mac and cheese, and service that's attentive but not pretentious, makes this the prime choice for steaks in the District. **Known for:** one of the top steak houses in town; lively bar scene full of locals; more affordable menu in the lounge. [$] *Average main: $55* ✉ *Four Seasons Washington, DC, 2800 Pennsylvania Ave. NW, Georgetown* ☎ *202/944–2026* 🌐 *www.bourbonsteakdc.com* 🕒 *No lunch weekends* [M] *Foggy Bottom–GWU.*

Cafe Milano

$$$$ | **ITALIAN** | Expect authentic, sophisticated Italian cooking and a pricey wine list at this upscale Georgetown hot spot. Specialties are butter lettuce salad with lemon vinaigrette and crostini, thin-crust pizzas anchored by Naples-controlled San Marzano tomato sauce, and sumptuous

pasta dishes in pesto or fresh vegetable sauces. **Known for:** regulars that include local socialites, lobbyists, and diplomats; a patio that's great for people-watching; the front wall of windows opening onto the street in nice weather. $ *Average main: $42* ⊠ *3251 Prospect St. NW, Georgetown* ☎ *202/333–6183* ⊕ *www. cafemilano.net.*

Chez Billy Sud

$$ | FRENCH | This cozy gem spotlights southern French cooking and serves lunch, dinner, and weekend brunch. If it's a nice day, request a table on the brick patio. **Known for:** chicken liver mousse appetizer; elegant atmosphere; fine selection of French wines. $ *Average main: $26* ⊠ *1039 31st St. NW, Georgetown* ☎ *202/965–2606* ⊕ *www.chezbillysud.com* ⊘ *No lunch Mon.*

Das Ethiopian Cuisine

$$ | ETHIOPIAN | If Das marks your first foray into upscale Ethiopian dining, the delightful chicken and beef combination sampler and harvest vegetable specialty provide a taste of the genre at its best. And don't worry about running out of the pancakelike injera bread used in place of utensils—your server will keep bringing it. **Known for:** rare Ethiopian fine dining; spicy sauces; patio dining in nice weather. $ *Average main: $18* ⊠ *1201 28th St. NW, Georgetown* ☎ *202/333–4710* ⊕ *www.dasethiopian.com* ⊘ *No lunch Mon. and Tues.* Ⓜ *Foggy Bottom–GWU.*

★ Farmers Fishers Bakers

$$ | AMERICAN | FAMILY | This restaurant near the waterfront is owned by a collective of farmers and places an emphasis on sustainability for all the ingredients served. The menu runs the gamut from sea to shining sea: fresh-baked bread to sushi rolls, burgers to pizza, wild-caught salmon to locally raised chicken and beef, including many vegetarian options. **Known for:** weekend brunch buffet; fried chicken jambalaya; extensive menu that satisfies even picky eaters. $ *Average main: $26* ⊠ *3000 K St. NW, Georgetown*

☎ *202/298–8783* ⊕ *www.farmersfishersbakers.com* Ⓜ *Foggy Bottom–GWU.*

Fiola Mare

$$$$ | ITALIAN | The harborside setting for Fabio Trabocchi's ode to Italian-style seafood makes perfect sense. Dine alfresco and watch the water taxis float by, or sip an Aperol spritz on a banquette by the open kitchen and raw bar: you may think you've traded D.C. for Venice. **Known for:** lobster ravioli; well-priced three-course lunch prix fixe; mouthwatering Italian desserts. $ *Average main: $60* ⊠ *3050 K St. NW, Georgetown* ☎ *202/525–1402* ⊕ *www.fiolamaredc.com* Ⓜ *Foggy Bottom–GWU.*

Kafe Leopold

$$ | AUSTRIAN | As Euro-trendy as it gets, Leopold has an all-day coffee and drinks bar, menu items including olive-and-onion tarts, crisp schnitzel paired with arugula, and a to-die for assortment of pastries. The setting is an architecturally hip dining space, with roll-up window walls and a chic patio complete with a fountain. **Known for:** hearty Austrian fare; arty crowd great for people-watching; great weekend brunch and daily breakfast served until 4. $ *Average main: $18* ⊠ *3315 Cady's Alley NW, Georgetown* ☎ *202/965–6005* ⊕ *www.kafeleopolds.com.*

La Chaumière

$$ | FRENCH | A rustic and unpretentious atmosphere meets traditional French cuisine at this Georgetown stalwart with many devoted local fans. Dishes like the boudin blanc and pike dumplings baked in lobster sauce will warm you on the inside just like the large central stone fireplace does on the outside. **Known for:** French country-style dishes and ambience; cassoulet with duck confit, lamb stew, and sausage; great wine list with lots of French options. $ *Average main: $23* ⊠ *2813 M St. NW, Georgetown* ☎ *202/338–1784* ⊕ *www.lachaumieredc.com* ⊘ *Closed Sun.* Ⓜ *Foggy Bottom–GWU.*

Rocklands Barbeque and Grilling Company

$ | BARBECUE | FAMILY | The original branch of the popular local barbecue chain now has a dining room, so you can sit and enjoy the baby back ribs and tender smoked chicken. Additional locations can be found in Arlington and Alexandria, and inside the Capital One Arena. **Known for:** beef and pork ribs; delicious sides like cornbread, mac and cheese, and baked beans; hardwood grill. $ *Average main: $14 ⊠ 2418 Wisconsin Ave. NW, Georgetown ☎ 202/333–2558 ⊕ www. rocklands.com.*

1789 Restaurant

$$$$ | AMERICAN | This dining room with Early American paintings and a fireplace could easily be a room in the White House. But all the gentility of this 19th-century town-house restaurant is offset by the down-to-earth food dressed up in effervescent presentations, with a daily changing menu. **Known for:** rack of lamb; historic upscale setting; several prix-fixe options. $ *Average main: $49 ⊠ 1226 36th St. NW, Georgetown ☎ 202/965–1789 ⊕ www.1789restaurant. com ⛨ Jacket required.*

Hotels

Even to other native Washingtonians, this high-end neighborhood—home to Washington's elite—is a tourist destination in itself. Historic homes on quiet streets with plenty of trees and a canal make this area ideal for strolling. M Street and Wisconsin Avenue restaurants and shops also make it the hottest spot in town for those with money to burn. Georgetown University students keep this area bustling into the early hours.

Four Seasons Hotel, Washington, D.C

$$$$ | HOTEL | FAMILY | This favorite with celebrities, hotel connoisseurs, and families is on the edge of Georgetown and offers luxurious, ultramodern rooms outfitted in calming neutrals featuring heavenly beds and French limestone or marble baths with separate showers and sunken tubs. **Pros:** impeccable service; excellent fitness center and spa; gorgeous saltwater lap pool. **Cons:** astronomically expensive; challenging street parking; far from Metro. $ *Rooms from: $795 ⊠ 2800 Pennsylvania Ave. NW, Georgetown ☎ 202/342–0444, 800/332–3442 ⊕ www.fourseasons.com/ washington ⇱ 222 rooms ¡O¡ No meals Ⓜ Foggy Bottom–GWU.*

Georgetown Suites

$ | HOTEL | FAMILY | If you're looking for plenty of space in a top location, these suites vary in size, but all come with fully equipped kitchens and separate sitting rooms, and offer a welcome break from standard hotel rooms. **Pros:** spacious suites; good choice for a family that wants to spread out; laundry facilities. **Cons:** limited underground garage parking is expensive; no pool; street noise. $ *Rooms from: $155 ⊠ 1111 30th St. NW, Georgetown ☎ 202/298–7800, 800/348–7203 ⊕ www.georgetownsuites.com ⇱ 221 suites ¡O¡ Free Breakfast Ⓜ Foggy Bottom–GWU.*

The Graham Washington DC Georgetown, Tapestry Collection by Hilton

$$$ | HOTEL | Named after Alexander Graham Bell, the inventor who once lived in Georgetown, this upscale boutique hotel is on a residential street just steps from M Street's shops and eateries. **Pros:** quiet and spacious accommodations; nice water and city views; free Wi-Fi. **Cons:** expensive parking; no pool; small fitness room. $ *Rooms from: $309 ⊠ 1075 Thomas Jefferson St. NW, Georgetown ☎ 202/337–0900 ⊕ www. thegrahamgeorgetown.com ⇱ 57 rooms ¡O¡ No meals Ⓜ Foggy Bottom–GWU.*

The Ritz-Carlton Georgetown, Washington, D.C.

$$$ | HOTEL | FAMILY | Once an incinerator dating from the 1920s, this building still topped with a smokestack might seem the most unlikely of places for a luxury hotel, but settle into one of the large and

Hot Hotel Bars and Lounges

Some of the most iconic examples of power bars, where inside-the-Beltway decision makers talk shop and rub elbows, are housed in many of this town's historic hotels. So grab a snifter of single malt and begin your people-watching at these classic D.C. hotel bars.

Quill at **The Jefferson** is a hidden gem in Downtown with live piano music, an outdoor terrace, and cocktail menus that change monthly. Ask for a basic drink and the bartenders will add their creative touches to your handcrafted cocktail, all while providing great service. Plus the nibbles of olives and nuts are simply divine.

The **Off the Record** bar at Downtown's **Hay-Adams Hotel** advertises itself as the place to be seen and not heard. And while it's just steps from the White House, that couldn't be more true. It's tucked away in the historic hotel's basement, and you really never know who you might run into here.

Although they don't boast the same old-world dark wood and red-leather charm of the bars at the historic hotels, the **Dirty Habit** at the decidedly more modern **Hotel Monaco** and **P.O.V.** on the roof of the **W Washington, D.C.** (both Downtown) hold their own as stops on the see-and-be-seen hotel bar scene.

chicly designed guest rooms (upper-level suites overlook the river) and you'll agree the concept works. **Pros:** excellent new spa and fitness center; soaking tubs in all room categories; personalized service. **Cons:** far from the Metro; expensive; expensive parking. $ *Rooms from: $325* ✉ *3100 South St. NW, Georgetown* ☎ *202/912–4200* ⊕ *www.ritzcarlton. com* ⤴ *86 rooms* |◎| *No meals* Ⓜ *Foggy Bottom–GWU.*

★ **Rosewood Washington D.C.**
$$$ | HOTEL | Superlative in every way, from the rooftop infinity pool that affords views of the Washington Monument, Kennedy Center, and Potomac River, to the personalized attention each guest receives—even before check-in. **Pros:** easy walking distance to both M Street shops and Washington Harbour; showstopping onyx bar in the Rye Bar; D.C.'s only luxury hotel with a rooftop pool. **Cons:** expensive; far from Metro and Mall; expensive valet parking. $ *Rooms from: $398* ✉ *1050 31st St. NW, Georgetown* ☎ *202/617–2400* ⊕ *www.*

rosewoodhotels.com/en/washington-dc ⤴ *61 rooms* |◎| *No meals* Ⓜ *Foggy Bottom–GWU.*

 Nightlife

Due to its proximity to the university, weekends (and even weeknights) are a happening affair in Georgetown. A number of bars serve as restaurants by day, until the college and intern crowds take over at night. Although most venues here tend to attract a younger set, the neighborhood still offers many options for patrons over thirty, such as the legendary Blues Alley. There's little parking here, and no easy Metro access, so if you're not staying nearby your best bet is a taxi. In late spring and summer, head to the Washington Harbour for drinks and a riverside stroll.

BARS AND LOUNGES
Degrees
BARS/PUBS | Hidden away inside the Ritz-Carlton hotel, in what was once the Georgetown Incinerator, this modern bar

is a breath of fresh air in the neighborhood's rather monotone scene. There's an extensive wine and cocktail selection behind the black granite bar and a hip, well-dressed set of patrons in front of it. When the weather's nice, head out to the multilevel brick patio and sit by the fireplace. ✉ *The Ritz-Carlton Georgetown, 3100 South St. NW, Georgetown* ☎ *202/912–4146* 🌐 *www.ritzcarlton.com.*

Eno

$ | WINE BAR | Start your night at this casual, cozy Georgetown hot spot—or even make it an evening in and of itself; while Eno offers wine by the bottle and glass, it's the wine-tasting flights of three 2.5-ounce pours where it really excels. You can also munch on cheese, charcuterie, and chocolate boards—many of the ingredients are locally sourced. [$] *Average main: $14* ✉ *Four Seasons Hotel, 2810 Pennsylvania Ave. NW, Georgetown* ☎ *202/342–0444* 🌐 *www.fourseasons.com* 🕒 *Closed Mon.* [M] *Foggy Bottom–GWU.*

J Paul's

BARS/PUBS | Located in a historic building that's more than 100 years old, this neighborhood saloon is a festive place to go for a beer and a game. The menu is extensive, but stick to the great hamburgers and seafood dishes. J Paul's attracts a diverse crowd from students to lobbyists to politicians. ✉ *3218 M St. NW, Georgetown* ☎ *202/333–3450* 🌐 *www.jpaulsdc.com.*

Nick's Riverside Grille

BARS/PUBS | This perch on the Georgetown waterfront affords a great view of the Potomac and, in winter, the ice-skating rink. When the weather's nice, crowds of college students flock to the outdoor tables. The food is fine but the draw is location, location, location. ✉ *3050 K St. NW, Georgetown* ☎ *202/342–3535* 🌐 *www.nicksriversidegrill.com.*

The Sovereign

$$ | | BARS/PUBS | With two bars serving 50 beers on tap and another 350 in bottles, the Sovereign's devotion to suds is not in doubt. Ask your bartender or waiter for help to try a new brew without the risk of drinking a dud. If you're hungry, too, the menu focuses on tasty Belgian fare like mussels with herbed mayonnaise. ✉ *1206 Wisconsin Ave. NW, Georgetown* ✣ *Entrance is off alley next to Abercrombie & Fitch* ☎ *202/774–5875* 🌐 *www.thesovereigndc.com* [M] *Foggy Bottom–GWU.*

The Tombs

BARS/PUBS | Visitors to Georgetown University looking for a pint or some pub grub head down the stairs below 1789 restaurant to this traditional, half-century-old collegiate watering hole adorned with rowing paraphernalia and steeped in charming Georgetown boosterism. One block from the main gate, it's the closest bar to campus so it gets crowded with students at night. ✉ *1226 36th St. NW, Georgetown* ☎ *202/337–6668* 🌐 *www.tombs.com.*

Tony and Joe's

BARS/PUBS | Right on Georgetown's waterfront, this seafood restaurant has a large outdoor patio where you can enjoy a drink alfresco on a spring or summer evening. The cocktails are a little pricey, but you can't beat the view of the Potomac River and Kennedy Center at night. ✉ *3000 K St. NW, Georgetown* ☎ *202/944–4545* 🌐 *www.tonyandjoes.com.*

MUSIC CLUBS

★ Blues Alley

MUSIC CLUBS | Head here for a classy evening in an intimate setting, complete with great blues, jazz, and R&B music from well-known performers such as Mose Allison and Wynton Marsalis and outstanding New Orleans–style grub. Expect to pay a cover charge as well as a food or drink minimum. **TIP→ You can come for just the show, but those who enjoy**

a meal get better seats. ✉ *1073 Wisconsin Ave. NW, near M St., Georgetown* ☎ *202/337–4141* ⊕ *www.bluesalley.com* Ⓜ *Foggy Bottom–GWU.*

 Performing Arts

Georgetown entertainment goes far beyond barhopping on a Saturday night. Smaller drama groups stage productions in several of Georgetown's larger churches; check local publications for the latest offerings.

MUSIC
CHAMBER MUSIC
Dumbarton Concerts

CONCERTS | A fixture in Georgetown since 1772 (in its current location since 1850), Dumbarton United Methodist Church sponsors a concert series that has been host to such musicians as the Harlem Quartet, the Smithsonian Jazz Masterworks, and the St. Petersburg String Quartet. ■TIP→ **Before or after a performance, take a stroll through the nearby Dumbarton Oaks estate and park.** ✉ *Dumbarton United Methodist Church, 3133 Dumbarton Ave. NW, Georgetown* ☎ *202/965–2000* ⊕ *dumbartonconcerts.org* Ⓜ *Foggy Bottom–GWU.*

Shopping

Although Georgetown, the capital's center for famous residents, is not on a Metro line and street parking is tough to find, people still flock here to shop. It's also a hot spot for restaurants, bars, and nightclubs.

National chains and designer shops now stand side by side with the specialty shops that first gave the district its allure, but the historic neighborhood is still charming and its street scene lively. Most stores lie east and west on M Street and to the north on Wisconsin Avenue. The intersection of M and Wisconsin is the nexus for chain stores and big-name designer shops. The

farther you venture in any direction from this intersection, the more eclectic and interesting the shops become. Some of the big-name stores are worth a look for their architecture alone; several shops blend traditional Georgetown town-house exteriors with airy modern showroom interiors.

Shopping in Georgetown can be expensive, but you don't have to add expensive parking lot fees. ■TIP→ **The DC Circulator is your best bet for getting into and out of Georgetown, especially if it's hot or if you are laden down with many purchases. This $1 bus runs along M Street and up Wisconsin Avenue, the major shopping strips.** The nearest Metro station, Foggy Bottom–GWU, is a 10- to 15-minute walk from the shops.

ANTIQUES AND COLLECTIBLES
Cherub Antiques Gallery

ANTIQUES/COLLECTIBLES | Operating in the same Victorian row house since 1983, Cherub specializes in antiques from the art nouveau and art deco periods. A glass case by the door holds a collection of more than 100 cocktail shakers, including Prohibition-era pieces disguised as penguins, roosters, and dumbbells. ✉ *2918 M St. NW, Georgetown* ☎ *202/337–2224* ⊕ *www.trocadero.com/cherubgallery* Ⓜ *Foggy Bottom–GWU.*

Jean Pierre Antiques

ANTIQUES/COLLECTIBLES | Very Georgetown, but fairly close to Dupont Circle, this gorgeous shop sells antique 18th- to 20th-century European furniture, paintings, ornaments, and home accessories from France, Germany, Sweden, and Italy. The charming owner's vintage bar carts and American Lucite tables are simply sublime. ✉ *2601 P St. NW, Georgetown* ☎ *202/337–1731* Ⓜ *Dupont Circle.*

Marston Luce

ANTIQUES/COLLECTIBLES | House and garden accessories are in the mix here, but the emphasis is on 18th- and 19th-century French and Swedish painted furniture, discovered by the owner on yearly buying trips in Europe. ✉ *1651 Wisconsin Ave. NW, Georgetown* ☎ *202/333–6800* ⊕ *www.marstonluce.com* Ⓜ *Foggy Bottom–GWU.*

★ **Opportunity Shop of the Christ Child Society**

ANTIQUES/COLLECTIBLES | This gem of a consignment–thrift store has been a Georgetown landmark since 1954. You'll find gorgeous fine jewelry, antiques, crystal, silver, and porcelain. Prices are moderate, and profits go to a good cause—the Christ Child Society provides for the needs of local children. It's closed Sunday. ✉ *1427 Wisconsin Ave. NW, Georgetown* ☎ *202/333–6635* ⊕ *www. christchilddc.org* Ⓜ *Foggy Bottom–GWU.*

ART GALLERIES

Addison Ripley

ART GALLERIES | Stunning, large-scale contemporary work by national and local artists, including painters Manon Cleary and Wolf Kahn and photographer Frank Hallam Day, is exhibited at this well-respected gallery, which is closed both Sunday and Monday. ✉ *1670 Wisconsin Ave. NW, Georgetown* ☎ *202/338–5180* ⊕ *www.addisonripleyfineart.com* Ⓜ *Foggy Bottom–GWU.*

★ **Cross MacKenzie Gallery**

ART GALLERIES | Vibrant and unusual contemporary ceramic pieces are shown here, plus paintings and photography. There's a new exhibit almost every month, which makes this a stunning showcase of art from D.C.-based and international artists. It's closed Sunday through Tuesday. ✉ *1675 Wisconsin Ave. NW, Georgetown* ☎ *202/333–7970* ⊕ *www.crossmackenzie.com* Ⓜ *Foggy Bottom–GWU.*

Maurine Littleton Gallery

ART GALLERIES | Even if the prices are as untouchable as the art in this gallery devoted to glass, metal, and ceramics, it's worth a look to see work by some of the world's finest contemporary artists.

The intimate, bright space is owned and managed by the daughter of Harvey K. Littleton, founder of the American Studio Glass movement, but open by appointment only. ✉ *1667 Wisconsin Ave. NW, Georgetown* ☎ *202/494–2666* ⊕ *www.littletongallery.com* Ⓜ *Foggy Bottom–GWU.*

Susan Calloway Fine Arts

ART GALLERIES | Stunning art draws people into this two-floor gallery where a mix of vintage, contemporary, and classical paintings are hung salon-style. You'll find large abstract oils and a lovely selection of landscapes, but don't miss the box full of small original paintings in the back, most priced under $100. The gallery is closed Monday. ✉ *1643 Wisconsin Ave., Georgetown* ☎ *202/965–4601* ⊕ *www. callowayart.com* Ⓜ *Foggy Bottom–GWU or Dupont Circle.*

BOOKS

Bridge Street Books

BOOKS/STATIONERY | This charming independent store focuses on politics, history, philosophy, poetry, literature, music, film, and Judaica. ✉ *2814 Pennsylvania Ave., NW, Georgetown* ☎ *202/965–5200* ⊕ *www.bridgestreetbooks.com* Ⓜ *Foggy Bottom–GWU.*

CHILDREN'S CLOTHING AND TOYS

Egg by Susan Lazar

CLOTHING | Adorable is the world that instantly comes to mind when you step into this boutique from designer Susan Lazar. There are clothes for newborns to size 8 in organic and environmentally friendly material with simple and colorful eye-catching patterns and designs. ✉ *1661 Wisconsin Ave. NW, Georgetown* ☎ *202/338–9500* ⊕ *www.egg-baby.com* Ⓜ *Foggy Bottom–GWU.*

Tugooh Toys

TOYS | FAMILY | You might have a difficult time getting your children to leave this fun toy store filled with educational and eco-friendly toys. From puzzles, games, and building toys to dolls, puppets, and dress-up clothes, you are bound to find the perfect gift for youngsters. ✉ *1355 Wisconsin Ave. NW, Georgetown* ☎ *202/338–9476* ⊕ *www.tugoohtoys. com* Ⓜ *Foggy Bottom–GWU.*

HOME FURNISHINGS

★ A Mano

HOUSEHOLD ITEMS/FURNITURE | The name is Italian for "by hand," and it lives up to its name, stocking colorful hand-painted ceramics, hand-dyed tablecloths, blown-glass stemware, hand-embroidered bed linens, and other home and garden accessories by American, English, Italian, and French artisans. Some of the jewelry pieces are simply stunning, and the kids' gifts are adorable. ✉ *1677 Wisconsin Ave. NW, Georgetown* ☎ *202/298–7200* ⊕ *www.amano.bz.*

Random Harvest

ANTIQUES/COLLECTIBLES | Whether you're looking for something that's decorative or functional (or a combination of both), you'll find it here. Random Harvest sells new and antique treasures for the home, including pillows, mirrors, glassware, barware, and lamps. There's also a nice selection of American and European vintage furniture. ✉ *1313 Wisconsin Ave. NW, Georgetown* ☎ *202/333–5569* ⊕ *www.randomharvesthome.com* Ⓜ *Foggy Bottom–GWU.*

JEWELRY

Ann Hand

JEWELRY/ACCESSORIES | Catering to Washington's powerful and prestigious, this jewelry and gift shop specializing in patriotic pins may seem intimidating, but prices begin at $35. Hand's signature pin, the Liberty Eagle, is $200. Photos on the walls above brightly lit display cases show who's who in Washington wearing you-know-who's designs, making this a worthwhile visit while shopping in Georgetown, though it's closed on weekends. ✉ *3236 Prospect St. NW, Georgetown* ☎ *202/333–2979* ⊕ *www. annhand.com.*

Brilliant Earth

JEWELRY/ACCESSORIES | This Cady's Alley jeweler uses ethically sourced diamonds and gemstones in unique new and vintage settings. Create your own design, or choose from a selection by master craftsmen. By appointment only. ✉ *3332 Cady's Alley, NW, Georgetown* ☎ *202/448–9055* ⊕ *www.brilliantearth. com* Ⓜ *Foggy Bottom–GWU.*

Lou Lou

JEWELRY/ACCESSORIES | A rainbow array of statement necklaces, scarves, and earrings can be found here (most under $30). Vegan leather handbags, hats, and a small selection of clothing from designers like Free People are also on offer from this family-owned, Virginia-based boutique. ✉ *1304 Wisconsin Ave. NW, Georgetown* ☎ *202/333–3574* ⊕ *www.loulouboutiques.com* Ⓜ *Foggy Bottom–GWU.*

MUSIC

Hill & Dale Records

MUSIC STORES | Georgetown's only vinyl record store carries a wonderful collection of new vinyl LPs—yes, it's true, they are new; there's nothing used at this store. Genres include jazz, country, pop, folk, blues, rock, and electronica. From Billie Holiday's "Body and Soul" to beloved D.C. groups like Fugazi and Thievery Corporation, the selection is bound to delight any music lover. Also on display in this bright and airy spot are photos and posters that celebrate music. It's closed Monday. ✉ *1054 31st St. NW, Georgetown* ✛ *Canal Sq.* ☎ *202/333–5012* ⊕ *www.hillanddalerecords.com.*

SHOES

Hu's Shoes

SHOES/LUGGAGE/LEATHER GOODS | This cutting-edge selection would shine in Paris, Tokyo, or New York. Luckily for Washingtonians, Hu's brings ballet flats, heels, and boots from designers like Chloé, Fendi, Manolo Blahnik, Proenza Schouler, and Valentino right to Georgetown. ✉ *3005 M St. NW, Georgetown*

☎ 202/342–0202 ⊕ www.husonline.com
Ⓜ Foggy Bottom–GWU.

SHOPPING MALLS
Georgetown Park
SHOPPING CENTERS/MALLS | There's a good
mix of retailers at this mall in the center
of Georgetown, including a new Anthropologie & Co. (which has floors devoted
to housewares and bridal), Dean &
DeLuca, DSW, Forever 21, H&M, Home-
Goods, J. Crew, and T.J. Maxx. Stop at
the Georgetown Visitor Center inside
the main entrance to learn about what's
happening in the neighborhood. You can
even try your hand at bocce or bowling
at Pinstripes, a bistro and entertainment
spot with a wonderful patio. ✉ 3222 M
St. NW, Georgetown ☎ 202/965–1280
⊕ www.georgetownpark.com Ⓜ Foggy
Bottom–GWU.

SPAS AND BEAUTY SALONS
Bluemercury
SPA/BEAUTY | Hard-to-find skin-care lines—
La Mer and Trish McEvoy, among others—are what set this homegrown, now
national, chain apart. The retail space
up front sells soaps, lotions, perfumes,
cosmetics, and skin- and hair-care products. Behind the glass door is the "skin
gym," where you can treat yourself to
facials, waxing, and oxygen treatments.
You'll also find branches in Dupont Circle,
Downtown, and Union Station. ✉ 3059
M St. NW, Georgetown ☎ 202/965–1300
⊕ www.bluemercury.com Ⓜ Foggy
Bottom–GWU.

WOMEN'S CLOTHING
Ella-Rue
CLOTHING | Although it's a small shop,
you'll find a wonderful selection of high-
end consignment clothing, shoes, and
handbags here. On any given day, you
might discover pieces by designers like
Carolina Herrera, Gucci, Stella McCartney, or Zac Posen. The staff is especially
helpful and works hard to help you find
the perfect ensemble for your next special event or important meeting. ✉ 3231

P St. NW, Georgetown ☎ 202/333–1598
⊕ www.ella-rue.com.

Hu's Wear
CLOTHING | Ladies looking for just-off-
the-runway looks to go with their Hu's
Shoes just need to cross the street to
find designs by The Row, Isabel Marant,
and Stella McCartney. ✉ 2906 M St. NW,
Georgetown ☎ 202/342–2020 ⊕ www.
husonline.com Ⓜ Foggy Bottom–GWU.

★ The Phoenix
CLOTHING | All under one roof (with 30
solar panels) in a delightful shop owned
and operated by the Hays family since
1955, you can find contemporary clothing
in natural fibers by designers such as
Eileen Fisher, OSKA, White+Warren,
Michael Stars, and Lilla P. There's also a
stunning selection of jewelry from Germany, Turkey, Israel, and Italy; gorgeous
leather handbags by Annabel Ingall;
floral arrangements from a sustainable
farm in Virginia; and fine- and folk-art
pieces from Mexico. ✉ 1514 Wisconsin
Ave. NW, Georgetown ☎ 202/338–4404
⊕ www.thephoenixdc.com Ⓜ Foggy
Bottom–GWU.

★ Reddz Trading
CLOTHING | You can't miss the bright red
storefront of this consignment shop
which sells clothing, accessories, jewelry, and shoes. Unlike traditional consignment stores, Reddz buys its merchandise
for cash or trade so inventory is added
regularly. It's not uncommon to find
pieces with the price tags still attached.
✉ 1413 Wisconsin Ave. NW, Georgetown
☎ 202/506–2789 ⊕ www.reddztrading.
com.

relish
CLOTHING | In fashionable Cady's Alley,
this dramatic space holds a women's
collection handpicked seasonally by the
owner. Modern, elegant, and practical
selections include European classics and
well-tailored modern designers, such
as Marc Jacobs, Pierre Hardy, Thom
Browne, Uma Wang, and Dries Van

Noten. It's closed Sunday. ✉ *3312 Cady's Alley NW, Georgetown* ☎ *202/333–5343* ⊕ *www.relishdc.com* Ⓜ *Foggy Bottom–GWU.*

 ## Activities

BIKING

The numerous trails in the District and its surrounding areas are well maintained and clearly marked, including those along the C&O Canal segment in Georgetown. Washington's large parks are also popular with cyclists. Plus, with new bike lanes on all major roads and the Capital Bikeshare scheme (and other rental outlets), it's also a great way to get around town.

Big Wheel Bikes

BICYCLING | This 45-year-old company near the C&O Canal Towpath rents multispeed and other types of bikes hourly or for the day. Rates begin at $35 per day for an adult bike. Tandem bikes, kids' bikes, and bikes with baby carriers are also available. Other locations are in Bethesda, near the Capital Crescent Trail, and Alexandria, if you want to ride the Mount Vernon Trail. ✉ *1034 33rd St. NW, Georgetown* ☎ *202/337–0254* ⊕ *www.bigwheelbikes.com.*

Capital Crescent Trail

BICYCLING | Suited for bicyclists, walkers, rollerbladers, and strollers, this paved trail stretches along the old Georgetown Branch, a B&O Railroad line that was completed in 1910 and was in operation until 1985. The 7.5-mile route's first leg runs from Georgetown near Key Bridge to central Bethesda at Bethesda and Woodmont Avenues. At Bethesda and Woodmont the trail heads through a well-lighted tunnel near the heart of Bethesda's lively business area and continues into Silver Spring. The 3.5-mile stretch from Bethesda to Silver Spring is gravel, though the all-volunteer Coalition for the Capital Crescent Trail is spearheading efforts to pave it. The Georgetown Branch Trail, as this section is officially named, connects with the Rock Creek Trail, which goes to Rockville in the north and Memorial Bridge past the Washington Monument in the south. On weekends when the weather's nice, all sections of the trails are crowded. ✉ *Washington* ☎ *202/234–4874 Coalition for the Capital Crescent Trail* ⊕ *www.cctrail.org.*

Chapter 8

DUPONT CIRCLE AND KALORAMA

Updated by
Celia Wexler

8

◉ Sights	🍴 Restaurants	🛏 Hotels	💼 Shopping	🍸 Nightlife
★★★☆☆	★★★★★	★★★★☆	★★★★☆	★★★★☆

NEIGHBORHOOD SNAPSHOT

TOP EXPERIENCES

■ **Dupont Circle:** Grab a cup of coffee and a *CityPaper* and soak up the always-buzzing scene around the fountain.

■ **National Geographic Society:** See *National Geographic* magazine come to life in rotating exhibits at the society's Explorers Hall.

■ **Phillips Collection:** Admire masterpieces such as Renoir's *Luncheon of the Boating Party* and Degas's *Dancers at the Barre* at the country's first museum of modern art.

■ **Woodrow Wilson House:** Glimpse the life of the 28th American president, who lived here during his retirement, surrounded by all the modern luxuries of the early 1900s.

GETTING HERE

Dupont Circle has its own stop on the Metro's Red Line. Exit on Q Street for the Phillips Collection, Anderson House, and Kalorama attractions. On-street parking in residential areas is becoming increasingly difficult to find, especially on weekend evenings.

PLANNING YOUR TIME

The Dupont Circle neighborhood charms whatever the time or season. By day, there is the Phillips Collection's impressive collection of impressionist art, the historic Woodrow Wilson House, and Kramerbooks & Afterwords for browsing. Evenings, the neighborhood's restaurants, bars, nightclubs, and its own adult game room keep things hopping. Locals prize the FRESHFARM market, open Sunday mornings year-round.

SAFETY

Dupont Circle is one of the safer areas in Washington, but muggings still occur here from time to time. Avoid dark, empty areas between bars late at night; stay sober; and avoid crowds on sidewalks, where you might encounter pickpockets.

QUICK BITES

■ **Greek Deli.** South of Dupont Circle, owner Kostas Fostieris has been wowing office workers for nearly 30 years with his meatballs, spinach pie, and rack of lamb, as well as baklava and yogurt to die for. There may be a line around lunchtime, but it moves quickly. The deli is closed on weekends. ⊠ *1120 19th St. NW* ⊕ *greekdelidc.com* Ⓜ *Farragut W.*

■ **Teaism Dupont Circle.** A few blocks northeast of Dupont Circle and closer to the neighborhood's galleries, your break can be enhanced in the tranquil surroundings of D.C.'s favorite tea salon, which offers a variety of teas, intriguing sweets, and Asian-inspired comfort food. ⊠ *2009 R St. NW* ⊕ *www.teaism.com* Ⓜ *Dupont Circle.*

■ **Un Je Ne Sais Quoi Patisserie Française.** This French bakery specializes in "les merveilleux" (towers of meringue, cream, and ganache), which are from the owners' native region of northern France. The bakery also serves more conventional French sweets. Its small space is charming, with framed prints, an elegant antique loveseat, and bistro-sized chairs and tables. ⊠ *1361 Connecticut Ave. NW* ⊕ *unjenesaisquoipastry.com* Ⓜ *Dupont Circle.*

Dupont Circle, named for Civil War hero Admiral Samuel F. Dupont, is the grand hub of D.C., literally. This traffic circle is essentially the intersection of the main thoroughfares of Connecticut, New Hampshire, and Massachusetts Avenues. More important though, the area around the circle is a vibrant center for urban and cultural life in the District.

Along with wealthy tenants and basement-dwelling young adults, several museums and art galleries also call this upscale neighborhood home. Offbeat shops, bookstores, coffeehouses, and varied restaurants help the area stay funky and diverse. Nearby, the Kalorama neighborhood's mansions welcome powerful movers and shakers from both political parties. Embassies enhance the elegance.

Add to the mix stores and clubs catering to the neighborhood's gay community and this area becomes a big draw for nearly everyone. Perhaps that's why the fountain at the center of the Dupont traffic island is such a great spot for people-watching.

 ## Sights

When you think of sightseeing in Washington, D.C., the Dupont Circle neighborhood does not leap to mind immediately. This is an area made for strolling, people-watching, drinking, dancing, eating, and shopping. Nevertheless, there are definitely a few Dupont landmarks worth visiting. Unlike D.C.'s major museums and monuments, which are operated by

the Federal government, some of these sites charge an admission fee.

Anderson House
LIBRARY | The palatial Gilded Age Anderson House is the headquarters of the Society of the Cincinnati, the nation's oldest historical organization promoting knowledge and appreciation of America's independence. The Society was founded by Revolutionary War veterans in 1783—George Washington was its first president general—and this has been its home since 1938. Guided tours of the first and second floors reveal the history of the Society, the significance of the American Revolution, and the lives and collections of the home's first owners, Larz and Isabel Anderson. Built in 1905, the home was the Andersons' winter residence and retains much of its original contents—an eclectic mix of furniture, tapestries, paintings, sculpture, and Asian art. Larz, a U.S. diplomat from 1891 to 1913, and his wife, Isabel, an author and benefactress, assembled their collection as they traveled the world during diplomatic postings. Today, the house also features an exhibition gallery and research library, and hosts concerts and lectures. ✉ 2118 Massachusetts

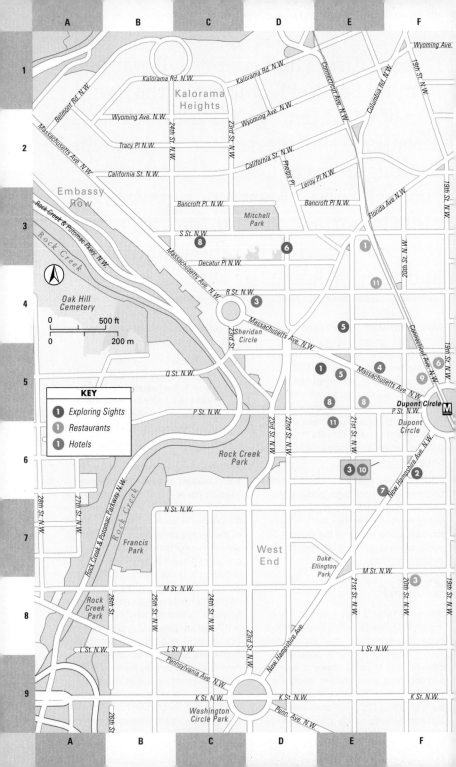

Sights ▼

1. Anderson House E5
2. Heurich House Museum F6
3. The Mansion on O Street Museum E6
4. National Geographic Museum I8
5. The Phillips Collection E4
6. Spanish Steps D3
7. The Whittemore House G5
8. Woodrow Wilson House C3

Restaurants ▼

1. Bistrot Du Coin E3
2. Hank's Oyster Bar Dupont Circle .. I5
3. Honeysuckle F8
4. Iron Gate H7
5. Komi I5
6. Kramerbooks & Afterwords F5
7. Little Serow I5
8. Obelisk E5
9. Sweetgreen F5
10. Tabard Inn Restaurant H7
11. Teaism Dupont Circle E4

Hotels ▼

1. Akwaaba DC I4
2. The Dupont Circle Hotel G5
3. Embassy Circle Guest House D4
4. The Embassy Row Hotel E5
5. The Fairfax at Embassy Row E5
6. Kimpton Carlyle Hotel Dupont Circle H4
7. Kimpton Hotel Madera E6
8. Kimpton Hotel Palomar Washington DC E5
9. Kimpton Rouge Hotel J6
10. The Mansion on O Street E6
11. Residence Inn Washington, DC/Dupont Circle E6
12. Swann House H3

8

Dupont Circle and Kalorama

Ave. NW, Dupont Circle ☎ *202/785–2040* ⊕ *www.societyofthecincinnati.org* ✉ *Free* ◷ *Closed Mon.* Ⓜ *Dupont Circle.*

Heurich House Museum

HOUSE | This opulent Romanesque Revival mansion, also known as the Brewmaster's Castle, was the home of Christian Heurich, a German immigrant who made his fortune in the beer business. Heurich's brewery was in Foggy Bottom, where the Kennedy Center stands today. The building, a National Register of Historic Places landmark, is considered one of the most intact Victorian houses in the country, and all the furnishings were owned and used by the Heurichs. The interior is an eclectic gathering of plaster detailing, carved wooden doors, and painted ceilings. The downstairs Breakfast Room, which also served as Heurich's *bierstube* (or beer hall), is decorated like a Rathskeller with the German motto "A good drink makes old people young." Heurich must have taken proverb seriously. He drank beer daily, had three wives, and lived to be 102. The museum hosts twice-monthly Brewmeister Tours that include a tour and a beer tasting. Hour-long guided tours are offered at 11:30, 1, and 2:30; reservations (suggested) can be made online. ✉ *1307 New Hampshire Ave. NW, Dupont Circle* ☎ *202/429–1894* ⊕ *www.heurichhouse.org* ✉ *$10* ◷ *Closed Sun.–Wed.* Ⓜ *Dupont Circle.*

The Mansion on O Street Museum

HOUSE | FAMILY | This is D.C.'s funkiest museum, a reimagining of your grandma's attic by surreal filmmaker Federico Fellini, full of dozens of secret doors and passageways, rooms overflowing with antiques, pictures and figures of medieval angels, and memorabilia including 60 signed Gibson guitars, stuffed animals, chandeliers, and books everywhere. The museum, housed in five interconnecting town houses, also doubles as an inn, but visitors can get a peek of themed rooms when not occupied by rock stars or CEOs, who value the mansion's privacy and security. Rooms pay homage to notables including John Lennon, Winston Churchill, and Rosa Parks, once a frequent visitor. ✉ *2020 O St. NW, Dupont Circle* ☎ *202 /496–2020* ⊕ *www.omuseum.org* ✉ *Tours $15 (reservations required).*

National Geographic Museum

MUSEUM | FAMILY | Founded in 1888, the National Geographic Society is best known for its magazine, and entering this welcoming 13,000-square-foot exhibition space feels like stepping into its pages. The compact museum offers family-friendly, if pricey, interactive exhibitions delving into the historical, cultural and scientific research that distinguishes *National Geographic Magazine*. There are items from the permanent collections—cultural, historical, and scientific—as well as traveling exhibitions. It also has a new virtual-reality theater experience introduced in 2018. Nat Geo Nights—presentations by explorers with interactive activities, music, and food and drink specials—are held the third Thursday of every month. The M Street Lobby photography exhibit, as well as the outdoor photo display around the perimeter of the museum, are free. ✉ *17th and M Sts. NW, Dupont Circle* ✛ *A few blocks from Farragut N Metro stop* ☎ *202/857–7700, 202/857–7689* ⊕ *www.nationalgeographic.org/dc* ✉ *From $15* Ⓜ *Farragut N.*

★ The Phillips Collection

MUSEUM | With its setting on a quiet residential street, and its low-key elegance, the Phillips Collection offers visitors unhurried access to its first-rate collection of masterpieces from the 19th century and later. At the heart of the collection are works by distinguished impressionist and modern artists, including Pierre-Auguste Renoir, Vincent van Gogh, Paul Cézanne, Edgar Degas, Pablo Picasso, Paul Klee, and Henri Matisse. A stunning quartet of Mark Rothko works merits its own room. The museum opened in 1921 in the Georgian Revival mansion of collector Duncan Phillips, who wanted to showcase his art in a museum that would stand as a memorial to his father and brother. In the intervening years, the museum expanded, and now includes much more gallery space, a café, gift shop, and an auditorium. On Thursday, the Phillips is open until 8:30 pm and, on the first Thursday of the month, Phillips After 5 combines live music, gallery talks, food, and a cash bar. A Sunday concert series is held from October through May in the mansion's elegant music room. ⊠ *1600 21st St. NW, Dupont Circle* ☎ *202/387-2151* ⊕ *www.phillipscollection.org* 🖾 *Free weekdays; from $10* ⊗ *Closed Mon.* Ⓜ *Dupont Circle.*

Spanish Steps

NEIGHBORHOOD | Named for the Spanish Steps in Rome, D.C.'s Spanish Steps aren't quite as grand as their European counterpart, but they do provide a tranquil reprieve from the hustle and bustle of the city. Located next to Embassy Row, the steps offer a view of D.C.'s Dupont Circle neighborhood. A lion-head fountain at the top is a good place to relax with a book or make a wish in the fountain with pennies. The steps are near the Woodrow Wilson House. ⊠ *1725 22nd St. NW, Dupont Circle* Ⓜ *Dupont Circle.*

The Whittemore House

HOUSE | You don't have to be a Democrat to enjoy this historic building, which became the headquarters for the Women's National Democratic Club in 1927. The exquisitely decorated mansion, built in the 1890s and designed by D.C. architect Harvey Page for opera singer Sarah Adams Whittemore, has housed senators and cabinet members over the years. Now it's best known for its library, where Eleanor Roosevelt did her radio broadcasts, and its full-length portraits of first ladies, painted in a whimsical style by folk artist April Newhouse. ⊠ *1526*

New Hampshire Ave. NW, Dupont Circle ☎ *202/232-7363* ⊕ *democraticwoman. org/art-exhibitsmuseum/* ⊗ *Closed Fri.– Mon. in Aug.* Ⓜ *Dupont Circle (Q St. exit).*

Woodrow Wilson House

HOUSE | President Wilson and his second wife, Edith Bolling Wilson, retired in 1921 to this Georgian Revival house designed by Washington architect Waddy B. Wood. It was on this quiet street that Wilson lived out the last few years of his life. It is the only presidential museum in the nation's capital. Wilson died in 1924—Edith survived him by 37 years—and bequeathed the house and its contents to the National Trust for Historic Preservation. Tours of the home provide a wonderful glimpse into the lives of this couple and the dignitaries who visited them here. Items on display include his cane collection, a Gobelins tapestry, a mosaic from Pope Benedict XV, the pen used by Wilson to sign the declaration of war that launched the United States into World War I, and the shell casing from the first shot fired by U.S. forces in the war. The house also contains memorabilia related to the history of the short-lived but influential League of Nations, including the colorful flag Wilson hoped would be adopted by that organization. ⊠ *2340 S St. NW, Dupont Circle* ☎ *202/387-4062* ⊕ *www.woodrowwilsonhouse.org* 🖾 *$10* ⊗ *Closed Mon., also Tues.–Thurs. in Jan. and Feb.* Ⓜ *Dupont Circle.*

🍴 Restaurants

Diners who want to spend $200 per person for an exquisite meal as well as those looking for something memorable yet more affordable will be happy in this neighborhood. Connecticut Avenue alone offers blocks and blocks of interesting restaurants. Throught the neighborhood, happy hours—often with creative small bites—abound, even at many upscale venues. Greek, Italian, French, Asian, Russian, Latin American, and Middle

The many fountains in Dupont Circle make it a nice place for a walk.

Eastern cuisines are represented, as is distinctive American regional cooking.

Bistrot du Coin

$$ | **FRENCH** | An instant hit in its Dupont Circle neighborhood, this moderately priced French bistro with a monumental zinc bar offers a traditional menu of French favorites, including onion soup, duck breast, cassoulet, and steaks garnished with a pile of crisp fries. Wash it down with house Beaujolais, Côtes du Rhône, or an Alsatian white. **Known for:** many varieties of mussels; a big party every July 14, Bastille Day; fun local hangout. [$] *Average main: $26* ✉ *1738 Connecticut Ave. NW, Dupont Circle* ☎ *202/234–6969* 🌐 *www.bistrotducoin.com* [M] *Dupont Circle.*

★ **Hank's Oyster Bar**

$$ | **SEAFOOD** | The watchword is simplicity at this chic take on the shellfish shacks of New England. A half-dozen oyster varieties are available daily on the half shell, both from the West Coast and local Virginia waters, plus daily fish specials, and a "meat-and-two" daily special for those who prefer turf to surf. **Known for:** a bittersweet chocolate chunk at the end of the meal; half-price oyster bar happy hours; no desserts. [$] *Average main: $26* ✉ *1624 Q St. NW, Dupont Circle* ☎ *202/462–4265* 🌐 *www.hanksdc.com* [M] *Dupont Circle.*

Honeysuckle

$$$ | **AMERICAN** | After climbing down an unpromising flight of stairs, you will find an attractive dining room where a decorous chandelier shares a ceiling with a wildly colorful mural depicting the chef's tattoos. Likewise, the food, which often includes generous infusions of butter and cream, reflects chef and owner Hamilton Johnson's South Carolina roots, but also flirts with the cuisine of Iceland. **Known for:** elegant but lighthearted ambience; daily happy hour from 5 to closing; great breads. [$] *Average main: $35* ✉ *1990 M St. NW, Dupont Circle* ☎ *202/659–1990* 🌐 *honeysuckledc.com* 🕒 *No lunch weekends.*

Iron Gate

$$ | MEDITERRANEAN | In the former carriageway and stable house of a Dupont Circle town house, Iron Gate's romantic setting compliments its upscale Mediterranean fare, served either à la carte or via a tasting menu with optional wine pairings. The menu changes but always includes a seasonal variation on the house foccacia, buratta and feta dip, and staples like the mixed grill and whole fish for two. **Known for:** five-course menu and multicourse "family" table tasting menus; patio adorned with fairy lights and wisteria vines; eclectic cocktails. $ *Average main: $25* ⊠ *1734 N St. NW, Dupont Circle* ☎ *202/524–5202* ⊕ *www. irongaterestaurantdc.com* ⊗ *No lunch Mon.* Ⓜ *Dupont Circle.*

★ Komi

$$$$ | MEDITERRANEAN | Johnny Monis, the young, energetic chef-owner offers one of the most adventurous dining experiences in the city in a tiny space. The prix-fixe menu includes multiple courses and showcases contemporary fare with a distinct Mediterranean influence. **Known for:** intimate ambience; impressive wine list (but no cocktails); reservations that book up very quickly. $ *Average main: $165* ⊠ *1509 17th St. NW, Dupont Circle* ☎ *202/332–9200* ⊕ *www.komirestaurant. com* ⊗ *Closed Sun. and Mon. No lunch* Ⓜ *Dupont Circle.*

Kramerbooks & Afterwords

$$ | CAFÉ | FAMILY | You'll find chatty diners at this bookstore-café almost any time during its long hours, which stretch from early-morning breakfast until after midnight, and even later on weekends. Morning fare is popular, as are many crab-inflected dishes and spicy pastas. **Known for:** crave-worthy desserts; full bar; late-night brunch. $ *Average main: $21* ⊠ *1517 Connecticut Ave. NW, Dupont Circle* ☎ *202/387–3825* ⊕ *kramers.com* Ⓜ *Dupont Circle.*

★ Little Serow

$$$$ | THAI | This basement hideout next door to chef Johnny Monis's world-beating Komi gives the wunderkind chef a chance to cook Thai *his* way⎯which happens to be the northern Thai way. The ingredients are spicy, the presentations sometimes off-putting (what is a snakehead fish?), and the waiters can be sullen, but for sheer moxie and skill, the food is among the best in the city. **Known for:** walk-in only, no reservations; strict no-substitutions or special-requests policy; Mekhong whiskey-marinated pork ribs. $ *Average main: $49* ⊠ *1511 17th St. NW, Dupont Circle* ⊕ *www.little-serow.com* ⊗ *Closed Sun., Mon., and (usually) late Aug.–early Sept. No lunch* Ⓜ *Dupont Circle.*

Obelisk

$$$$ | ITALIAN | Despite its tiny dining room, this Italian stalwart, under the helm of veteran chef Esther Lee, has maintained a pull on special-occasion diners since the late 1980s, offering a pricey five-course prix-fixe dinner that changes nightly. A sample menu—with its mouthwatering delicacies—is posted on the website to give diners an idea of what to expect. **Known for:** standout burrata; attentive service; accommodating many dietary restrictions with advance notice, but not vegans. $ *Average main: $80* ⊠ *2029 P St. NW, Dupont Circle* ☎ *202/872–1180* ⊕ *www.obeliskdc. com* ⊗ *Closed Sun. and Mon. No lunch* ☞ *Doesn't take American Express* Ⓜ *Dupont Circle.*

Sweetgreen

$ | ECLECTIC | The brainchild of three Georgetown University graduates, Sweetgreen now includes 20 D.C.-area locations and many more throughout the United States. At lunchtime, many millennials can be found in the small but attractive dining space, savoring the locally sourced menu that changes seasonally and offers build-your-own salads, as well as "warm bowls" featuring a medley of meat, rice or quinoa, and vegetables. **Known for:** low-key, casual vibe; enough space for on-site dining; house-made beverages with fresh fruit and herbs. *$ Average main: $10 ⊠ 1512 Connecticut Ave. NW, Dupont Circle ☎ 202/387–9338 ⊕ www.sweetgreen. com* Ⓜ *Dupont Circle.*

Tabard Inn Restaurant

$$$ | AMERICAN | The inn is historic, with its fireplaces and antique furnishings, but the restaurant's culinary sensibilities are thoroughly modern. The menu consistently offers interesting seafood and vegetarian options and changes seasonally. **Known for:** D.C. landmark where movers and shakers sometimes breakfast; great brunch (complete with homemade doughnuts); attractive patio. *$ Average main: $30 ⊠ Hotel Tabard Inn, 1739 N St. NW, Dupont Circle ☎ 202/331–8528 ⊕ www.tabardinn.com* Ⓜ *Dupont Circle.*

Teaism Dupont Circle

$ | ASIAN FUSION | The imposing exterior belies the spare yet serene two-story space offering breakfast specialties, healthy Japanese and Thai-style entrées, and desserts. There's a lovely street view from the second level. **Known for:** large variety of teas; Japanese bento boxes; salty oat cookies. *$ Average main: $12 ⊠ 2009 R St. NW, Dupont Circle ✛ 2 blocks north of Dupont Circle Metro ☎ 202/667–3827 ⊕ www.teaism.com* Ⓜ *Dupont Circle.*

Hotels

Akwaaba DC

$$ | B&B/INN | The brainchild of former *Essence* editor Monique Greenwood, this 1890s town house turned guesthouse—one of three inns Greenwood has opened—celebrates the richness of African American literature. **Pros:** lovely neighborhood location; applause-worthy breakfast; afternoon refreshments. **Cons:** $50 nonrefundable deposit to reserve a room; two-night minimum stay required

for advance reservations; no elevator. *$ Rooms from: $225 ⊠ 1708 16th St. NW, Dupont Circle ☎ 877/893–3233 ⊕ www.dcakwaaba.com ⇆ 8 rooms* ⦿❘ *Free Breakfast* Ⓜ *Dupont Circle.*

★ The Dupont Circle Hotel

$$$$ | HOTEL | In 2018, the hotel transformed its lobby into a cozy club with midcentury furnishings designed to make it look like an upscale city apartment, complete with fireplace. **Pros:** right on Dupont Circle; free Wi-Fi; fitness center. **Cons:** traffic and noise on Dupont Circle; hallways on some guest floors are a bit narrow and dimly lit; limited storage space in some rooms. *$ Rooms from: $509 ⊠ 1500 New Hampshire Ave. NW, Dupont Circle ☎ 202/483–6000 ⊕ www. doylecollection.com/dupont ⇆ 327 rooms* ⦿❘ *No meals* Ⓜ *Dupont Circle.*

★ Embassy Circle Guest House

$$ | B&B/INN | Owners Laura and Raymond Saba have lovingly restored the former Taiwan embassy, transforming the 1902 mansion into a warm and friendly home away from home. **Pros:** all rooms have a work area and relaxation area and very modern tile baths; elevator on-site; free Wi-Fi. **Cons:** no bathtubs; two-night minimum and nonrefundable $35 reservation deposit; no TV on premises. *$ Rooms from: $265 ⊠ 2224 R St. NW, Dupont Circle ☎ 202/232–7744 ⊕ www. dcinns.com ⇆ 11 rooms* ⦿❘ *Free Breakfast* Ⓜ *Dupont Circle.*

The Embassy Row Hotel

$$$ | HOTEL | Just steps from Dupont Circle, this modern boutique hotel has a stylish, playful lobby in subdued colors and rooms designed for a young, hip crowd. **Pros:** yoga classes offered on the rooftop in good weather; Keurig coffeemakers in each room; business center. **Cons:** hotel amenity fee and pricey valet parking; smallish baths and closets; rooftop pool area can get crowded. *$ Rooms from: $379 ⊠ 2015 Massachusetts Ave. NW, Dupont Circle ☎ 202/265–1600 ⊕ www.destinationhotels.com/*

embassy-row-hotel ⤳ 255 rooms ⫯○⫯ No meals Ⓜ Dupont Circle.

The Fairfax at Embassy Row

$$$ | HOTEL | Rooms at this grande dame, a longtime favorite for many travelers, are spacious and elegant, albeit a tad old-fashioned, but the lobby, bar, and restaurant area were extensively renovated in 2018. **Pros:** historic hotel and boyhood home of Al Gore; imposing building complete with chandeliers and a sweeping staircase; great location. **Cons:** expensive valet parking; no full restaurant on-site. Ⓢ *Rooms from: $339* ✉ *2100 Massachusetts Ave. NW, Dupont Circle* ☎ *202/293–2100, 888/625–5144* ⊕ *www. fairfaxwashingtondc.com* ⤳ *279 rooms* ⫯○⫯ *No meals* Ⓜ *Dupont Circle.*

Kimpton Carlyle Hotel Dupont Circle

$$$$ | HOTEL | FAMILY | Tucked away on a quiet tree-lined street, this stylish Kimpton property makes for a comfortable and convenient base for exploring the city. **Pros:** very pet friendly with dog park close by; rooms have either walk-in closets or kitchenettes; Kimpton benefits, including coffee and tea in lobby and free wine in the evening. **Cons:** rooms can be noisy; no business center; an added amenity fee. Ⓢ *Rooms from: $439* ✉ *1731 New Hampshire Ave. NW, Dupont Circle* ☎ *202/234–3200* ⊕ *www.carlylehoteldc. com* ⤳ *198 rooms* ⫯○⫯ *No meals* Ⓜ *Dupont Circle.*

Kimpton Hotel Madera

$$$$ | HOTEL | FAMILY | Despite its tiny lobby, this sophisticated and art-focused Kimpton hotel, just south of vibrant Dupont Circle, provides the perfect respite after an evening restaurant and club hopping along P Street and Connecticut Avenue. **Pros:** coffee and tea in lobby, and nightly wine hour; nice residential neighborhood convenient to Metro; spacious rooms. **Cons:** no pool or gym on-site; small bathrooms; amenity fee. Ⓢ *Rooms from: $419* ✉ *1310 New Hampshire Ave. NW, Dupont Circle* ☎ *202/296–7600, 800/430–1202* ⊕ *www.hotelmadera.*

com ⤳ 82 rooms ⫯○⫯ No meals Ⓜ Dupont Circle.

★ Kimpton Hotel Palomar Washington DC

$$$$ | HOTEL | Aside from the hard-to-beat location, these modern rooms are some of the largest in town and are decorated with cool abstract art, accessories in rich jewel tones, and plush purple-and-fuchsia furnishings. **Pros:** complimentary coffee and tea and free wine during nightly happy hour; free bikes on loan; heated outdoor pool. **Cons:** even in suites, baths are smallish; expensive valet parking and amenity fee; shampoos and soaps in large dispensers rather than hotel size. Ⓢ *Rooms from: $449* ✉ *2121 P St. NW, Dupont Circle* ☎ *202/448–1800* ⊕ *www. hotelpalomar-dc.com* ⤳ *335 rooms* ⫯○⫯ *No meals* Ⓜ *Dupont Circle.*

Kimpton Rouge Hotel

$$$$ | HOTEL | FAMILY | This upscale hotel certainly lives up to its name with bright "in-your-face" red walls and sparkly red floors in the small but comfortable lobby, and rooms with platform beds, red velvet curtains, and plenty of red accents. **Pros:** gay-friendly vibe; good location near two Metro stations; Kimpton amenities of free coffee and tea and nightly free wine happy hours. **Cons:** small fitness center; decor may be overwhelming to some; amenity fee. Ⓢ *Rooms from: $459* ✉ *1315 16th St. NW, Dupont Circle* ☎ *202/232–8000, 800/738–1202* ⊕ *www. rougehotel.com* ⤳ *137 rooms* ⫯○⫯ *No meals* Ⓜ *Dupont Circle.*

The Mansion on O Street

$$$ | HOTEL | FAMILY | Rock 'n' roll palace meets thrift shop in this guesthouse, a funky D.C. landmark that nevertheless draws celebrities and notables. **Pros:** also doubles as a museum that can be toured; fun ambience; nearly all the items are on sale. **Cons:** claustrophobic for those who like uncluttered decor; a few rooms are close to the catering kitchen; nonrefundable reservation deposit of one-night's lodging. Ⓢ *Rooms from: $350* ✉ *2020 O St. NW, Dupont Circle* ☎ *202/496–2020*

⊕ *www.omansion.com* ⤺ *23 rooms* ⊙| *No meals* Ⓜ *Dupont Circle.*

Residence Inn Washington, D.C./Dupont Circle

$$$ | **HOTEL** | **FAMILY** | This hotel is not posh, but it is ideal for families or business travelers staying for a few days, and all rooms have kitchen facilities, including a full-size refrigerator. **Pros:** free hot breakfast daily in very attractive dining area; two blocks from Metro; clean and comfortable. **Cons:** small gym and business center; no pool; corporate, uninspiring decor. Ⓢ *Rooms from: $329* ⊠ *2120 P St. NW, Dupont Circle* ☎ *202/466–6800, 800/331–3131* ⊕ *www.marriott.com/wasri* ⤺ *107 suites* ⊙| *Free Breakfast* Ⓜ *Dupont Circle.*

★ Swann House

$$$ | **B&B/INN** | Whether you are eating breakfast in the formal dining room or unwinding with a glass of sherry in the parlor, everything is lovely at this elegant urban retreat. **Pros:** guest computer and free Wi-Fi; fireplaces in some rooms; most rooms have tubs, and a few have whirlpool baths. **Cons:** have to carry your own luggage; no elevator; many rooms have two-night minimums in spring and fall. Ⓢ *Rooms from: $369* ⊠ *1808 New Hampshire Ave. NW, Dupont Circle* ☎ *202/265–4414* ⊕ *www.swannhouse.com* ⤺ *12 rooms* ⊙| *Free Breakfast* Ⓜ *Dupont Circle.*

▼ Nightlife

Bars and nightclubs dot Connecticut Ave, where the Eighteenth Street Lounge is a go-to spot for Dupont's hip denizens any day of the week, and after 10 most nights, Café Citron brings out the bongos and pulses to a Latin rhythm. Close by, you'll find Dupont's gay scene (or what's left of it), concentrated mainly on 17th Street. A variety of gay-friendly, lively, and offbeat bars and restaurants stretch between P and R Streets, many with outdoor seating. JR's Bar & Grill and Cobalt are favorites. D.I.K. Bar is the place to be on Tuesday, Friday, and Saturday for the always-popular karaoke nights. On the Tuesday before Halloween, the annual High Heel Drag Race proceeds down 17th Street; elaborately costumed drag queens and other revelers strut their stuff along the route from Church to R Streets and then race to the finish line.

BARS AND LOUNGES

Board Room

BARS/PUBS | "Put down your smart phone and interact!" is the motto at this pub with 20-plus beers on tap, a full bar, and many board games to rent, from tried-and-true classics to vintage oddities. To enhance the fun, you can bring in your own food or have it delivered. Just don't bring in booze or other beverages; you are expected to buy them on the premises. Kids welcome on occasion, but the rule is 21 and older. Reservations are accepted. ⊠ *1737 Connecticut Ave. NW, Dupont Circle* ☎ *202/518–7666* ⊕ *www.boardroomdc.com* Ⓜ *Dupont Circle.*

★ Eighteenth Street Lounge

BARS/PUBS | This multilevel space's division into an array of sofa-filled rooms makes an evening at this home away from home for Washington's hipper globalists seem like a chill house party. Live bands perform Tuesday through Saturday. Jazz musicians often entertain on the top floor of the former mansion, and the luxe back deck, complete with hanging chandeliers, provides summer visitors with two extra bars and a fresh-air dance floor. Fans of ambient house music flock here as it's the home of the ESL record label and the renowned musical duo Thievery Corporation. ∎**TIP→ Dress up a little, especially on Fridays and Saturdays, because the club frowns on baseball caps and athletic wear like tank tops and jerseys; men should also avoid shorts and open-toe shoes.** ⊠ *1212 18th St. NW, Dupont Circle* ☎ *202/466–3922* ⊕ *www.18thstlounge.com* Ⓜ *Dupont Circle.*

Hank's Oyster Bar

BARS/PUBS | A small, sleek, and unpretentious nautical-themed bar offers a half-price raw bar after 10 pm every night of the week, here and at its locations on Capitol Hill, the Wharf, and Old Town Alexandria. The bartenders are friendly, giving you tastes of different wines or drinks to try, along with recommendations on the daily catch and other food options, including one of the best lobster rolls around. ✉ *1624 Q St. NW, Dupont Circle* ☎ *202/462–4265* ⊕ *www.hanksoysterbar.com* Ⓜ *Dupont Circle.*

JR's Bar & Grill

BARS/PUBS | This narrow, window-lined space is a popular institution on the 17th Street strip that packs in a mostly male, mostly professional, gay crowd. Various nights offer show-tunes singalongs, trivia contests, and a "Sunday Funday" daylong happy hour. ✉ *1519 17th St. NW, Dupont Circle* ☎ *202/328–0090* ⊕ *www.jrsbar-dc.com* Ⓜ *Dupont Circle.*

Russia House Restaurant and Lounge

BARS/PUBS | The Russia House has an old-world feel to it. Mount the steep stone steps, and you'll find yourself in a cozy bar and lounge with red damask wallpaper, comfortable leather chairs, and understated chandeliers. You may be listening to Russian rappers as you drink a wide assortment of vodkas and indulge in happy hour plates of Russian favorites. Dinner menu also offers traditional Russian dishes. ✉ *1800 Connecticut Ave. NW, Dupont Circle* ☎ *202/234–9433* ⊕ *www.russiahouselounge.com* Ⓜ *Dupont Circle.*

St. Arnold's Mussel Bar on Jefferson

BARS/PUBS | This unassuming space in the basement of a Dupont town house is named after the patron saint of brewing, and it's certainly blessed with its choice of hard-to-find Belgian beers. The Belgian theme continues in the menu, and mussels (available in essentially half-price pots during happy hour) are prepared in numerous ways. There's an additional location in Cleveland Park. ✉ *1827 Jefferson Pl. NW, Dupont Circle* ☎ *202/833–1321* ⊕ *www.starnoldsmusselbar.com* Ⓜ *Dupont Circle.*

DANCE CLUBS

Cafe Citron

BARS/PUBS | Mojitos are the specialty at this Latin bar and dance club, with six varieties available, from the standard to a mojito mule made with fresh ginger and ginger beer. From Monday through Saturday, the café becomes a nightclub after 10, featuring DJs who play primarily Latin music, spiced with Euro dance and techno. The café offers daily happy hours until 8, with a late-night happy hour after 9 on Friday and Saturday. (It's closed Sunday.) Free salsa and bachata lessons are offered nightly. ✉ *1343 Connecticut Ave. NW, Dupont Circle* ☎ *202/530–8844* ⊕ *www.cafecitrondc.com* Ⓜ *Dupont Circle.*

Cobalt

DANCE CLUBS | Popular among the gay and lesbian crowd, this venue anchors the 17th Street strip with three distinct floors: the bottom floor is the Level One restaurant, the chic 30 Degrees lounge occupies the second level, and above that is the booming dance club Cobalt. Karaoke, DJs, "gaymer," and drag nights all add to the fun. ✉ *1639 R St. NW, Dupont Circle* ☎ *202/232–4416* ⊕ *www.cobaltdc.com* Ⓜ *Dupont Circle.*

🎭 Performing Arts

Talented troupes in unique venues are sprinkled throughout the Dupont Circle neighborhood, among them the Keegan Theatre on Church Street, which aims to present classic and modern plays and musicals at affordable ticket prices. Sunday chamber concerts also are performed at the Phillips Collection, providing an exquisite venue for both eyes and ears.

FILM

National Geographic Society

FILM | Documentary films with a scientific, geographic, or anthropological focus are shown regularly at National Geographic's Grosvenor Auditorium. An easy walk from Dupont Circle, "NatGeo" also hosts speakers, concerts, and photography exhibits year-round. Be sure to check out the new virtual-reality films. ⊠ *1145 17th St. NW, Dupont Circle* ☎ *202/857–7700* ⊕ *www.nationalgeographic.org/dc* Ⓜ *Farragut N.*

MUSIC

Phillips Collection

MUSIC | Duncan Phillips's mansion is more than an art museum. On Sunday afternoon from October through May, chamber groups from around the world perform in the elegant Music Room. Plus, on the first Thursday of the month, from 5 to 8:30 pm, the museum offers Phillips After 5, treating visitors to musical performances, food and drink, gallery talks, films, and more. The Sunday concerts begin at 4 pm. ⊠ *1600 21st St. NW, Dupont Circle* ☎ *202/387–2151* ⊕ *www. phillipscollection.org* Ⓜ *Dupont Circle.*

THEATER

The Keegan Theatre

THEATER | Renovated in 2013, this 120-seat theater offers a rich variety of classic and modern plays and musicals, with a focus on powerful storytelling in an intimate setting. ⊠ *1742 Church St. NW, Dupont Circle* ☎ *703/892–0202* ⊕ *keegantheatre.com* Ⓜ *Dupont Circle.*

Theater J

THEATER | One of the country's most distinguished Jewish performance venues offers an ambitious range of programming that includes work by noted playwrights, directors, designers, and actors. Past performances have included one-person shows featuring Sandra Bernhard and Judy Gold as well as more edgy political pieces. Theater J is under renovation, and performances are being held in a variety of venues until the work is complete. Renovated theater will reopen by September 2019. ⊠ *1529 16th St. NW, Dupont Circle* ☎ *202/518–9400* ⊕ *www.theaterj.org* Ⓜ *Dupont Circle.*

Shopping

You might call Dupont Circle a younger, less staid version of Georgetown—almost as pricey, but with more apartment buildings than houses. Its many restaurants, offbeat shops, and specialty stores give it a cosmopolitan air. The street scene here is more urban than Georgetown's, with bike messengers and chess aficionados filling up the park. The Sunday farmers' market attracts shoppers with organic food, artisanal cheeses, homemade soap, and hand-spun wool. Browsing is an adventure in this neighborhood. Several boutiques offer designer clothing for women, and Dupont shops also include exquisite jewelry from Turkey as well as inexpensive bling and well-designed products for home and baby.

ART GALLERIES

I A & A at Hillyer

ART GALLERIES | Around the corner from the Phillips Collection, this art space features works from local, regional, and international contemporary artists, and also regularly hosts artist talks and other events. With a mission to support emerging artists and to encourage artistic collaboration across the globe, Hillyer offers intellectually stimulating exhibits that provoke and intrigue. Every third Thursday, the gallery partners with local groups and embassies to offer a Culture-Blast event, which can feature anything from an Iranian-American rapper to an interactive quilting project that includes a discussion of gender and personal history. The gallery also attracts a big crowd during Dupont Circle's gallery crawl every first Friday, but it's typically closed the week before the crawl. ⊠ *9 Hillyer Ct. NW, Dupont Circle* ☎ *202/338–0325* ⊕ *athillyer.org* Ⓜ *Dupont Circle.*

Marsha Mateyka Gallery

ART GALLERIES | Just around the corner from the Phillips Collection sits this gallery that showcases the work of nearly 20 contemporary artists. You'll find paintings, sculptures, photography, drawings, and prints by international artists including Athena Tacha, Jae Ko, William T. Wiley, Nathan Oliveira, and the estate of Gene Davis. It's open only on Thursday, and otherwise by appointment only. ⊠ 2012 R St. NW, Dupont Circle ☎ 202/328–0088 ⊕ www.marshamateyk-agallery.com Ⓜ Dupont Circle.

★ Studio Gallery

ART GALLERIES | Founded in 1956 by Jennie Lea Knight (whose work is in the collections of many D.C. museums), Studio exhibits contemporary work by local artists, some of whom have also received international acclaim. The spacious gallery occupies two floors in an elegant town house and exhibitions change frequently. Don't miss the sculpture garden in the back of the house. It's typically open only Wednesday–Saturday. ⊠ 2108 R St. NW, Dupont Circle ☎ 202/232–8734 ⊕ www.studiogallerydc.com Ⓜ Dupont Circle.

BOOKS

★ Kramerbooks & Afterwords Café

BOOKS/STATIONERY | One of Washington's best-loved independent bookstores has a choice selection of fiction and nonfiction. Open until 3 am on Friday and Saturday, it's a convenient meeting place. It also hosts many author book talks throughout the year. Kramerbooks shares space with Afterwords Café, which is open from early morning until late at night. ⊠ 1517 Connecticut Ave. NW, Dupont Circle ☎ 202/387–1400 ⊕ www.kramers.com Ⓜ Dupont Circle.

Second Story Books

BOOKS/STATIONERY | One of the largest used and rare book stores in the country, Second Story Books has gentrified along with its neighborhood, and its orderly and classy space houses rare books, signed first editions, maps, posters, manuscripts, CDs, prints, and DVDs. (There are often bargain books for sale, usually outside the store.) A knowledgeable staff is always on hand to help you shop. ⊠ 2000 P St. NW, Dupont Circle ☎ 202/659–8884 ⊕ www.secondstory-books.com Ⓜ Dupont Circle.

CLOTHING

★ Betsy Fisher

CLOTHING | Catering to women of all ages and sizes in search of contemporary and trendy styles, this elegant shop offers one-of-a-kind accessories, clothes, shoes, and jewelry by American, Canadian, and European designers, including popular Montreal designers Marie Saint Pierre, Iris Setlakwe, and Judith & Charles. ⊠ 1224 Connecticut Ave. NW, Dupont Circle ☎ 202/785–1975 ⊕ www.betsyfisher.com Ⓜ Dupont Circle.

★ Proper Topper

CLOTHING | As its name suggests, this gem of a boutique carries a delightful collection of hats for women, men, and children for any occasion or season. But upon entering, you'll find so much more: unusual gifts for the home, delightful clothes and shoes for the young ones in your life, funky jewelry, clothing from Virginia designer Kim Schalk and fair-trade line Mata Traders. The store now has its own in-house designed T-shirts with D.C. themes. ⊠ 1350 Connecticut Ave. NW, Dupont Circle ☎ 202/842–3055 ⊕ proper-topper.com.

★ Secondi

CLOTHING | One of the city's finest consignment stores carries a well-chosen selection of women's designer and casual clothing, accessories, and shoes. Its airy and well curated second-story space offers Isabel Marant, Louis Vuitton, Donna Karan, Prada, Chanel, and Marchesa labels. ⊠ 1702 Connecticut Ave. NW, 2nd fl., Dupont Circle ☎ 202/667–1122 ⊕ www.secondi.com Ⓜ Dupont Circle.

8

Dupont Circle and Kalorama

CRAFTS AND GIFTS

The Chocolate Moose

CRAFTS | This store is simple, sheer fun for adults and kids alike. Looking for clacking, windup teeth? You can find them here, along with unusual greeting cards, whimsical and colorful socks, and unique housewares and handicrafts. If playing with all those fun toys makes you hungry, you can pick up a select line of premium European chocolates. It's closed on Sunday. ⊠ *1743 L St., NW, Dupont Circle* ☎ *202/463–0992* ⊕ *www. chocolatemoosedc.com* Ⓜ *Farragut N.*

Shop Made in DC

GIFTS/SOUVENIRS | If you're looking to buy something that was actually made in the District and not in a far-off land, this Dupont Circle shop offering a rotating selection of strictly locally made goods should be your first stop. Whether it's food (8Myles gourmet sauces and seasonings or Harper Macaw chocolates) or something else (candles by JSquared Candle Co., T-shirts from Bailiwick Clothing Co. or District of Clothing), you'll be able to buy it here. An on-site café sells local coffees and teas (and local beers and spirits) to accompany a rotating selection of local fast-casual food. The gift boxes are highly prized. ⊠ *1330 19th St. NW, Dupont Circle* ⊕ *www.shopmadeindc.com.*

HOME FURNISHINGS

★ Tabletop

HOUSEHOLD ITEMS/FURNITURE | This is a delightful place to find distinctive gold earrings by Daphne Olive, the designer and store owner, as well as wooden bookends, bento boxes, and game sets from Wolfum of California. Orla Kiely bags and kitchenware offer bold floral designs. A baby and children's section displays adorable clothing as well as books for the smallest feminist. Walls are adorned by Chive ceramic flowers. ⊠ *1608 20th St. NW, Dupont Circle* ☎ *202/387–7117* ⊕ *www.tabletopdc.com* Ⓜ *Dupont Circle.*

JEWELRY

Bloom

JEWELRY/ACCESSORIES | Whether you're looking for a simple pair of earrings for a job interview or a stunning statement piece for a New Year's Eve party, you'll find it here, along with exquisite sterling silver jewelry with precious and semiprecious stones from Turkey. There's also a small collection of handmade makeup pouches, wall hangings, colorful plates, linens, and purses. ⊠ *1719 Connecticut Ave. NW, Dupont Circle* ☎ *202/621–9049* Ⓜ *Dupont Circle.*

lou lou

JEWELRY/ACCESSORIES | A "blingful" boutique, jam-packed with costume jewelry and bags at price points that please the purse, draws lots of ladies looking for the latest trendy item. You'll also find lou lou boutiques in Georgetown, the U Street Corridor, and two Downtown locations. ⊠ *1601 Connecticut Ave. NW, Dupont Circle* ☎ *202/588–0027* ⊕ *www. loulouboutiques.com* Ⓜ *Dupont Circle.*

Chapter 9

ADAMS MORGAN

Updated by
Sabrina Medora

● Sights	🍴 Restaurants	🛏 Hotels	🛍 Shopping	🍸 Nightlife
★☆☆☆☆	★★★★★	★★☆☆☆	★★★☆☆	★★★★★

NEIGHBORHOOD SNAPSHOT

TOP EXPERIENCES

■ **Eat ethnic food:** Adams Morgan rivals U Street with its plentiful and delicious Ethiopian restaurants. If you'd rather dine using utensils, you can choose among Japanese, Brazilian, Salvadorian, Mexican, Indian, and other cuisines.

■ **Hang out like a local:** The residents of Adams Morgan make an art of relaxing. Follow their lead and settle into one of Tryst's overstuffed armchairs with a laptop or a copy of the *New Republic* and a coffee, or kill hours browsing the "rare and medium-rare" selections at Idle Time Books.

■ **Move to the beat:** Every evening from 3 to 9 pm and on Sunday afternoon, drummers from all walks of life form the Drum Circle in Meridian Hill Park, bashing out the beats while some dance and others simply sit back and watch.

■ **Stay out all night:** If you want to party on until the break of dawn, this is the place to do it. Don't miss the live blues music at Madam's Organ, the salsa dancing at Habana Village, and the cool kids making the scene at the Black Squirrel or Bourbon.

GETTING HERE

Adams Morgan has two Metro stops that are a pleasant 10-minute walk away. From the Woodley Park–Zoo/Adams Morgan Metro station take a short walk south on Connecticut, then turn left on Calvert Street, and cross over Rock Creek Park on the Duke Ellington Bridge. If you get off at the Dupont Circle Metro stop walk east, turning left on 18th Street.

The heart of Adams Morgan is at the intersection of Columbia Road and 18th Street. Don't even dream about finding parking here on weekend evenings.

If you take the Metro, remember that stations close at midnight, or 3 am on Friday and Saturday nights. If you're not ready to turn in by then, you'll need to hail a cab.

PLANNING YOUR TIME

■ Start your day walking around the neighborhood's few tourist attractions, slowly making your way to the restaurant-centric area. Stop in at the Line Hotel for a coffee at The Cup We All Race For or settle in for high tea at Brothers and Sisters. Keep moving on to 18th Street for some window-shopping, cocktails, small plates, and live music. Dance the night away at the various clubs and bars, then grab some late-night pizza or empanadas.

QUICK BITES

■ **Brothers and Sisters.** The restaurant in the Line Hotel takes a quirky and award-winning approach to multicultural cuisines. ✉ *1770 Euclid St. NW* ⊕ *www.thelinehotel.com* Ⓜ *Woodley Park–Zoo/Adams Morgan.*

■ **Julia's Empanadas.** Freshly baked, handmade empanadas hit the spot any time of day (or late at night). ✉ *2452 18th St. NW* ⊕ *www. juliasempanadas.com* Ⓜ *Columbia Heights.*

■ **Tryst.** This popular, dog-friendly community hangout serves up brunch, salads, pies, and the neighborhood's favorite coffee. ✉ *2459 18th St. NW* ⊕ *www. trystdc.com* Ⓜ *Woodley Park–Zoo/Adams Morgan.*

To the urban and hip, Adams Morgan is like a beacon in an otherwise stuffy landscape. D.C. may have a reputation for being staid and traditional, but drab suits, classical tastes, and bland food make no appearance here. Adams Morgan takes its name from two elementary schools that came together in 1958 after desegregation. It remains an ethnically diverse neighborhood with a blend of cuisines, offbeat shops, and funky bars and clubs.

Adams Morgan and its neighboring Columbia Heights comprise the city's Latin Quarter. The area wakes up as the sun goes down, and young Washingtonians in their weekend best congregate along the sidewalks, crowding the doors of this week's hot bar or nightclub. Typical tourist attractions are sparse, but the scene on a Saturday night has its own appeal. If you're here on the second Saturday in September, sample the vibrant neighborhood culture at the Adams Morgan Day Festival, which happens to be D.C.'s largest neighborhood festival.

◉ Sights

Less touristy and more community-based, Adams Morgan is great for a day of light sightseeing followed by window-shopping and heavy eating. Known for its bustling food and live music scene, there's always a place to pop into and lose track of time.

Meridian Hill Park

CITY PARK | Landscape architect Horace Peaslee created Meridian Hill Park, a noncontiguous section of Rock Creek Park, after a 1917 study of the parks of Europe. As a result, the garden contains elements of gardens in France, Italy, and Switzerland. John Quincy Adams lived in a mansion here after his presidency, and the park later served as an encampment for Union soldiers during the Civil War. All 50 states are represented by a state tree or flower. Meridian Hill is unofficially known as **Malcolm X Park** in honor of the civil rights leader. Weekends bring a mix of pickup soccer games, joggers running the stairs, and a weekly (weather permitting) drum circle. A statue of **Joan of Arc** poised for battle on horseback stands above the terrace, and a statue of **Dante** is on a pedestal below. A ranger-led tour and cell-phone tours illuminate the history of the landmarks inside the park. ⊠ *16th and Euclid Sts., Adams Morgan*

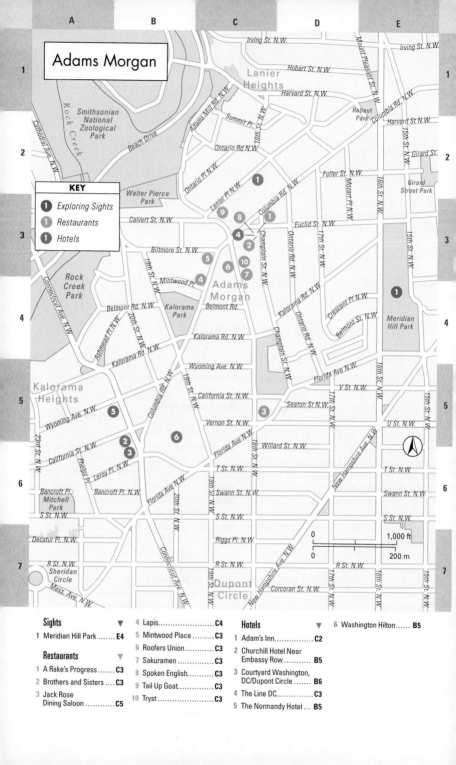

Adams Morgan

KEY

① *Exploring Sights*

① *Restaurants*

① *Hotels*

🌐 *www.nps.gov/mehi* [M] *U St./African-Amer Civil War Memorial/Cardozo or Columbia Heights.*

🍴 Restaurants

In Adams Morgan, find everything from greasy spoons and jumboslice pizza joints to exquisite fine-dining options. The next culinary frontier lies just east along Columbia Road, where immigrant communities dine while young families flock to increasingly upscale bistros for refined takes on comfort-food favorites.

A Rake's Progress
$$ | **AMERICAN** | Dedicated to using ingredients only found within the local food system, James Beard award-winning chef Spike Gjerde puts on a hearth show and feast every evening. From pork to trout to rabbit, each dish proves to be complex and impressive. **Known for:** using local ingredients; popular brunch; great cocktail menu. [$] *Average main: $25* ✉ *The Line DC, 1770 Euclid St. NW, Adams Morgan* ☎ *202/864–4190* 🌐 *www.thelinehotel.com* 🕑 *No lunch weekdays* [M] *Woodley Park–Zoo/Adams Morgan.*

Brothers and Sisters
$ | **AMERICAN** | The lobby of the Line Hotel in D.C. provides a vibrance unlike any other, entirely on account of this restaurant, which celebrates the multicultural nature of the city. Enjoy twists on American classics with Asian flavors (duck consommé with wontons, mussels fried in a wok with chili oil), a simple but compelling cocktail menu, and an extensive selection of cakes and pastries. **Known for:** afternoon or high tea; late-night bar menu; fresh baked goods. [$] *Average main: $13* ✉ *The Line DC, 1770 Euclid St. NW, Adams Morgan* ☎ *202/588–0525* 🌐 *www.brothersandsistersdc.com* [M] *Woodley Park–Zoo/Adams Morgan.*

★ **Jack Rose Dining Saloon**
$$$ | **AMERICAN** | With 2,687 bottles of whiskey currently on the wall (your experience may vary), the food sometimes gets overshadowed here. But Southern-inspired dishes like smoked whiskey wings, crispy chicken skin bites, pickled corn hush puppies, and mushroom risotto make the menu much more than just something to accompany all the booze. **Known for:** small plates of modern Southern cuisine; fun rooftop tiki bar; immense selection of whiskeys. [$] *Average main: $27* ✉ *2007 18th St. NW, U Street* ☎ *202/588–7388* 🌐 *www.jackrosediningsaloon.com* [M] *U St./African-Amer Civil War Memorial/Cardozo.*

★ **Lapis**
$ | **AFGHAN** | The modern Afghan cuisine shines at this chic yet comfortable—and well-priced—Adams Morgan spot. Eight different varieties of kebabs (prepared via a secret recipe "known only to our mom and the NSA") are the stars of the menu, but you'll also want to try the dumplings. **Known for:** different types of kebabs prepared with top-secret family recipe; carefully crafted cocktails; excellent bottomless brunch. [$] *Average main: $15* ✉ *1847 Columbia Rd. NW, Adams Morgan* ☎ *202/299–9630* 🌐 *www.lapisdc.com* 🕑 *No lunch* [M] *Dupont Circle.*

Mintwood Place
$$$ | **FRENCH** | At this saloon-inspired venue, you're invited to dive into French-influenced takes on American dishes, like an escargot hush puppy. The happy hour menu excels both in terms of value and flavor. **Known for:** French meets American cuisine; great happy hour deals; brunch menu that includes a creative flammekueche tart. [$] *Average main: $29* ✉ *1813 Columbia Rd. NW, Adams Morgan* ☎ *202/234–6732* 🌐 *www.mintwoodplace.com* 🕑 *Closed Mon. No lunch weekdays.*

Roofers Union
$$ | **CONTEMPORARY** | The cavernous space that once hosted one of the capital's most notoriously crazy bars is now a symbol of the area's maturation, thanks to a slick makeover and classy comfort-food lineup. The hearty but

The stairs in Meridian Hill Park are popular with joggers: run up and down ten times, and you've covered almost one mile.

well-designed fare includes four types of house-made sausage and a fried-chicken sandwich redolent of sriracha sauce that will rock a spice-lover's world. **Known for:** comfort food with great sausage options; hip, youthful vibe; excellent rooftop deck and bar. [$] *Average main: $23* ✉ *2446 18th St. NW, Adams Morgan* ☎ *202/232–7663* 🌐 *www.roofersuniondc.com* 🕑 *No lunch* [M] *Woodley Park–Zoo/Adams Morgan.*

Sakuramen

$ | **RAMEN** | Gourmet versions of Japanese ramen soup have become the latest trend to storm the city, and this hole-in-the-wall gem strikes the perfect balance between keep-it-simple affordability and adventurous flair. Embodying both of those traits in one bowl is the D.C. Miso, which pairs traditional fish cake and seaweed with a shot of Monterey Jack cheese. **Known for:** innovative ramen; casual basement vibe; beef buns and crispy dumplings. [$] *Average main: $14* ✉ *2441 18th St. NW, Adams Morgan* ☎ *202/656–5285* 🌐 *www.sakuramen.net* 🕑 *Closed Mon. No lunch Tues.–Thurs.*

★ **Spoken English**

$ | **ASIAN** | A restaurant unlike any other in D.C., Spoken English is tucked away within the kitchen of Brothers and Sisters. The *tachinomiya*-style (standing only) setup encourages adventurous eating and conversation among friends and strangers. **Known for:** small plates of Asian street food; standing room only; exclusive sake selections. [$] *Average main: $13* ✉ *The Line DC, 1770 Euclid St. NW, Adams Morgan* ✣ *Ask hostess at Brothers and Sisters to direct you* ☎ *202/588–0525* 🌐 *www.thelinehotel.com/dc* 🕑 *Closed Sun. and Mon. No lunch* [M] *Woodley Park–Zoo/Adams Morgan.*

★ **Tail Up Goat**

$$ | **CONTEMPORARY** | This instant favorite features cuisine influenced by the island of St. John, where one of the three founders was raised. Standouts on the carb-heavy menu—bread gets its own section—include cavatelli with a spicy

pork-belly ragù and seaweed sourdough bread. **Known for:** lots and lots of carbs; constantly changing menu; small groups only (five people or less). $ *Average main: $23* ⊠ *1827 Adams Mill Rd. NW, Adams Morgan* ✛ *Entrance on Lanier Pl. side of building* ☎ *202/986–9600* ⊕ *www. tailupgoat.com* ⊘ *No lunch* Ⓜ *Woodley Park–Zoo/Adams Morgan.*

Tryst

$ | **AMERICAN** | **FAMILY** | Bohemian and unpretentious, this coffeehouse bar serves fancy sandwiches and exotic coffee creations. Comfy chairs and couches fill the big open space, where you can sit for hours sipping a cup of tea—or a martini—while chatting or clacking away at your laptop. **Known for:** excellent coffee; all-day brunch menu; premium sandwiches and design-your-own salads. $ *Average main: $11* ⊠ *2459 18th St. NW, Adams Morgan* ☎ *202/232–5500* ⊕ *www.trystdc.com* Ⓜ *Woodley Park–Zoo/Adams Morgan.*

 Hotels

This thriving multiethnic community is the place to be for a fabulous assortment of aromas, languages, tastes, and late-night entertainments. A short walk from a nearby hotel or Metro stop gives you salsa, hip-hop, jazz, or the latest in experimental performance art. Its neighborhoods of 19th- and early-20th-century homes and row houses and its proximity to Rock Creek Park provide this bustling area with a tranquil shell.

Adam's Inn

$ | **B&B/INN** | Live like a local at this cozy and affordable, Victorian-style bed-and-breakfast spreading through three residential town houses near Adams Morgan, the zoo, and Dupont Circle. **Pros:** near Metro; lively neighborhood; backyard garden is a Certified Wildlife Habitat by the National Wildlife Federation. **Cons:** some shared baths; steps to climb; some guests complain of noise between

rooms. $ *Rooms from: $174* ⊠ *1746 Lanier Pl. NW, Woodley Park, Adams Morgan* ☎ *202/745–3600, 800/578–6807* ⊕ *www.adamsinn.com* ➶ *27 rooms* ⦿ *Free Breakfast* Ⓜ *Woodley Park–Zoo/Adams Morgan.*

Churchill Hotel Near Embassy Row

$$ | **HOTEL** | One of the Historic Hotels of America, this beaux arts landmark built in 1906 has spacious guest rooms that are comfortable and elegant, include small work and sitting areas, and many have excellent views. **Pros:** good-sized rooms; relaxed and quiet; comfortable walking distance to Adams Morgan and northern Dupont Circle. **Cons:** older building; some rooms very small; limited room service hours. $ *Rooms from: $289* ⊠ *1914 Connecticut Ave. NW, Adams Morgan* ☎ *202/797–2000, 800/424–2464* ⊕ *www. thechurchillhotel.com* ➶ *173 rooms* ⦿ *No meals* Ⓜ *Dupont Circle.*

Courtyard Washington, D.C./Dupont Circle

$$$ | **HOTEL** | The standard Courtyard amenities come with a big plus here; some of the south-facing rooms on higher floors enjoy fantastic panoramic views of the city that take in the Washington Monument and other historic landmarks through the floor-to-ceiling windows. **Pros:** amazing views from some rooms; good location for restaurants and shopping; friendly, helpful staff. **Cons:** a busy location on Connecticut Avenue; chain-hotel feel with few unique touches; expensive valet parking. $ *Rooms from: $300* ⊠ *1900 Connecticut Ave. NW, Adams Morgan* ☎ *202/332–9300* ⊕ *www.marriott.com* ➶ *148 rooms* ⦿ *No meals* Ⓜ *Dupont Circle.*

★ The Line DC

$$ | **HOTEL** | A stay in this converted neoclassical-style church allows you to experience culinary and cocktail mastery, an art gallery, and historical architecture all at once. **Pros:** extremely well-equipped 24-hour fitness room; excellent restaurants with 24-hour room service; pets (dogs, cats, large, small) stay free. **Cons:**

can be loud; lots of stairs to climb; rooms are on the small side. $ *Rooms from: $268* ✉ *1770 Euclid St. NW, Adams Morgan* ☎ *202/588–0525* ⊕ *www.thelinehotel.com/dc* ⮐ *220 rooms* ⦿ *No meals.*

The Normandy Hotel

$$$ | **HOTEL** | On a quiet street in the embassy area of Connecticut Avenue stands this small Irish chain hotel. **Pros:** quiet location; coffee and tea served in garden room every afternoon; complimentary access to nearby fitness center and spa. **Cons:** smallish rooms; no room service; no restaurant. $ *Rooms from: $309* ✉ *2118 Wyoming Ave. NW, Adams Morgan* ☎ *202/483–1350, 800/424–3729* ⊕ *www.thenormandydc.com* ⮐ *75 rooms* ⦿ *No meals* Ⓜ *Dupont Circle.*

Washington Hilton

$$$ | **HOTEL** | Yes, it's a fairly large hotel and can be busy at times, but this historic 1965 hotel, at the intersection of Dupont Circle, Adams Morgan, and U and 14th Streets, has a great location and is a perfect spot to unwind after a day of business or seeing the sights. **Pros:** great lobby; plenty of services; lots of restaurants and shops within walking distance. **Cons:** corporate feel; busy, noisy location; fee for Wi-Fi. $ *Rooms from: $348* ✉ *1919 Connecticut Ave. NW, Adams Morgan* ☎ *202/328–2080* ⊕ *www.washington.hilton.com* ⮐ *1,117 rooms* ⦿ *No meals* Ⓜ *Dupont Circle.*

Nightlife

Adams Morgan is Washington's version (albeit much smaller) of New Orleans's French Quarter. The streets are jammed on the weekends with people of all ages and descriptions. Bars and restaurants of all types line the streets, making it easy to find one that will suit your tastes. Be prepared for crowds on the weekends and a much tamer vibe on weeknights. Getting here is easy, with four nearby Metro stops: Woodley Park–Zoo/Adams Morgan (Red Line), Dupont Circle (Red Line), Columbia Heights (Green and Yellow lines), and U Street/African-Amer Civil War Memorial/Cardozo (Green and Yellow lines). Taxis also are easy to find, except after last call when the crowds pour out of bars.

BARS AND LOUNGES

Bourbon

BARS/PUBS | A more mature Southern-tinged drinking and dining experience diverges from the typical Adams Morgan scene. Though you can dance on the second floor into the wee hours Friday and Saturday, earlier in the evening you'll find interesting whiskey, scotch, and bourbon options coupled with Southern goodies like barbecue chicken salads, grits, and mac and cheese. It's casual, sometimes crowded, and the outdoor porch in summer is a welcome respite from the 18th Street crowd. ✉ *2321 18th St. NW, Adams Morgan* ☎ *202/332–0800* ⊕ *www.bourbondc.com* Ⓜ *Woodley Park–Zoo/Adams Morgan.*

L'Enfant Cafe

BARS/PUBS | This French-flavored café boasts the most sidewalk seating in Adams Morgan, superb for watching the world go by at the intersection where Adams Morgan meets Dupont Circle. Inside, things get very intimate with a corner transformed on occasion to offer cabaret. The mood is downright bacchanalian, however, during Saturday's "La Boum" brunch that gets the nightlife started long before the sun goes down and has D.C.'s bohemian set clamoring to get in, making reservations mandatory. Dancing on the bar during La Boum with a sparkler in one hand and a tambourine in the other is optional—but hardly discouraged. The event is so popular, it spawned a weekly Saturday night offshoot, La Boum Boum Room, "A Pansexual Paradise" where reservations are also required. ✉ *2000 18th St. NW, Adams Morgan* ☎ *202/319–1800* ⊕ *www.lenfantcafe.com* Ⓜ *Dupont Circle.*

Madam's Organ

BARS/PUBS | Neon lights behind the bar, walls covered in kitsch, and works from local artists add to the gritty feel of three levels that play host to an eclectic clientele that listens to live music performed every night (open-mike night is Tuesday) and soaks up rays on the roof deck by day. This is a place that's hard to miss and hard not to like. ⊠ 2461 18th St. NW, Adams Morgan ☎ 202/667–5370 ⊕ www.madamsorgan.com Ⓜ Woodley Park–Zoo/Adams Morgan.

MUSIC CLUBS

Columbia Station

MUSIC CLUBS | An unpretentious retreat on the 18th Street strip attracts a diverse crowd, many of whom were pulled in off the street by the good vibes emanating from this place. Amber lights and morphed musical instruments adorn the walls, and high-quality live local jazz and blues fills the air. The large, open windows up front keep the place cool—much like the music—in summer months. Reservations are available, though the tunes, and not the mediocre food, are the real draw. ⊠ 2325 18th St. NW, Adams Morgan ☎ 202/462–6040 ⊕ www.columbiastationdc.com Ⓜ Woodley Park–Zoo/Adams Morgan.

🎭 Performing Arts

Adams Morgan has long been the hub of the city's best avant-garde performances, primarily offered by the District of Columbia Arts Center. You can enjoy an incredible meal at one of many nearby ethnic restaurants, see a performance at the Gala Hispanic Theatre, and then head to one of the neighborhood's colorful bars after the show.

THEATER AND PERFORMANCE ART

District of Columbia Arts Center

ARTS CENTERS | Known by area artists as DCAC, this cross-genre space shows changing exhibits in its gallery and presents avant-garde performance art, improv, and experimental plays in its tiny, funky black-box theater. DCAC is the home of Washington's oldest experimental theater group, Theatre Du Jour. ⊠ 2438 18th St. NW, Adams Morgan ☎ 202/462–7833 ⊕ www.dcartscenter. org Ⓜ Woodley Park–Zoo/Adams Morgan.

Gala Hispanic Theatre

THEATER | This company attracts outstanding Hispanic actors from around the world, performing works by such leading dramatists as Federico García Lorca and Mario Vargas Llosa. Plays are presented in English or in Spanish with projected subtitles. The company performs in the Tivoli Theatre in Columbia Heights, a hot spot for Latino culture and cuisine. ⊠ Tivoli Sq., 3333 14th St. NW and Park Rd., Columbia Heights, Adams Morgan ☎ 202/234–7174 ⊕ www.galatheatre.org Ⓜ Columbia Heights.

🛍 Shopping

Scattered among the dozens of Latin, Ethiopian, and international restaurants in this most bohemian of Washington neighborhoods is a score of eccentric shops. If quality is what you seek, Adams Morgan and nearby Woodley Park can be a minefield; tread cautiously. Still, this is good turf for the bargain hunter. ■ TIP→ If bound for a specific shop, you may wish to call ahead to verify hours. The evening hours bring scores of revelers to the row, so plan to go before dark unless you want to couple your shopping with a party pit stop.

How to get there is another question. Though the Woodley Park–Zoo/Adams Morgan Metro stop is relatively close to the 18th Street strip (where the interesting shops are), getting off here means that you will have to walk over the bridge on Calvert Street. Five minutes longer, the walk from the Dupont Circle Metro stop is more scenic; you cruise north on 18th Street through tree-lined streets of row houses and embassies. You can also easily catch Metrobus No. 42 or a cab from Dupont to Adams Morgan.

BOOKS

Idle Time Books

BOOKS/STATIONERY | FAMILY | Since 1981, this multilevel used-book store has been selling "rare to medium rare" books with plenty of meaty titles in all genres, especially out-of-print literature. ⊠ *2467 18th St. NW, Adams Morgan* ☎ *202/232–4774* Ⓜ *Woodley Park–Zoo/Adams Morgan.*

CHOCOLATE

The Chocolate House

FOOD/CANDY | FAMILY | For chocoholics with a gourmet palate, this is one-stop shopping. Offerings are both foreign (Michel Cluizel from France and Amedei from Italy) and domestic (Askinosie from Missouri and Amano from Utah). Selections from D.C.-area chocolatiers make for tasty souvenirs. If you can, attend one of their classes. ⊠ *1904 18th St. NW, Adams Morgan* ☎ *202/903–0346* ⊕ *www.thechocolatehousedc.com* Ⓜ *Dupont Circle.*

CLOTHING

Meeps

CLOTHING | Catering to fans of retro glamour and low prices, this shop near the bottom of the Adams Morgan strip stocks vintage clothes and costumes for women and men from the '60s through the '90s. ⊠ *2104 18th St. NW, Adams Morgan* ☎ *202/265–6546* ⊕ *www.meepsdc.com* Ⓜ *Dupont Circle.*

Mercedes Bien Vintage

CLOTHING | Carefully selected vintage clothing and shoes include everything from cocktail dresses to cowboy boots. You will also find jewelry and belts, all handpicked by the owner, Mercedes. This small shop offers exceptional, personal service and is only open on weekends. ⊠ *2423 18th St. NW, Adams Morgan* ☎ *202/360–8481* Ⓜ *Woodley Park–Zoo/ Adams Morgan.*

SHOES

Fleet Feet Sports Shop

SPECIALTY STORES | The expert staff at this friendly shop will assess your feet and your training schedule before recommending the perfect pair of new running shoes. Shoes, along with apparel and accessories for running, swimming, soccer, and cycling, crowd the small space. ⊠ *1841 Columbia Rd. NW, Adams Morgan* ☎ *202/387–3888* ⊕ *www.fleetfeetdc.com* Ⓜ *Woodley Park–Zoo/Adams Morgan.*

Chapter 10

U STREET CORRIDOR AND SHAW

Updated by
Alison Thoet

⊙ Sights	🍴 Restaurants	🛏 Hotels	🛍 Shopping	🍸 Nightlife
★★☆☆☆	★★★★★	★☆☆☆☆	★★★★☆	★★★★★

NEIGHBORHOOD SNAPSHOT

TOP EXPERIENCES

■ **African American Civil War Memorial and Museum:** Learn about the lives of slaves and freedmen, and discover whether your ancestors fought in black Civil War regiments.

■ **Ben's Chili Bowl:** This D.C. institution has perfected its recipe over the last 50 years.

■ **Boutiques:** Whether you're after funky footwear or flashy housewares, hit the shops on U and 14th Streets.

■ **Ethiopian food:** Nothing brings you closer to your meal than eating with your hands.

■ **Live music:** Music greats like Duke Ellington made this neighborhood famous back in the 1920s. Dance at the U Street Music Hall, or rock out at the 9:30 Club or Black Cat.

GETTING HERE

The Green Line Metro stops at 13th and U. To get to the African American Civil War Memorial, exit onto 10th Street. There's limited street parking, but you are better off taking a cab or other car service since the area is popular.

The area is walkable, with U Street, Logan Circle, and Shaw all near each other or a short cab ride away. Buses 90 and 92 travel from Woodley Park through Adams Morgan to 14th and U, while Buses 52, 53, and 54 travel north from several downtown Metro stops up 14th Street (check ⊕ *www.wmata. com* for information).

PLANNING YOUR TIME

You'll need half a day at most to see U Street's attractions and visit its boutiques. You can fill an evening with a traditional theater experience or a live music show. U Street has become the nightlife destination for the city, while Shaw is a resource of craft cocktail bars and unique dining. Take a cab to save time or be prepared to walk from the Shaw–Howard University metro station.

QUICK BITES

■ **Ben's Chili Bowl.** This U Street institution still serves its original chili half-smoke, plus burgers, sandwiches, and breakfast platters. ✉ *1213 U St. NW* ⊕ *www.benschilibowl.com* Ⓜ *Shaw–Howard U.*

■ **Busboys and Poets.** For a more intellectual snack, step into this multipurpose bookstore, restaurant, and performance space that serves up omelets, sandwiches, pizzas, and poems. Named in honor of Langston Hughes, this gathering place holds readings and musical performances. ✉ *2021 14th St. NW* ⊕ *www. busboysandpoets.com* Ⓜ *Shaw-Howard U.*

■ **Seylou Bakery and Mill.** Forego the chains and and head to Seylou for phenomenal coffees and teas, as well as whole-grain and naturally sourced baked goods, snacks, and even bread to go. ✉ *926 N St. NW, Suite A* ⊕ *www.seylou.com* Ⓜ *Mt. Vernon Sq. 7th St.– Convention Center.*

Home-style Ethiopian food, offbeat boutiques, and live music are fueling the revival of the U Street, Logan Circle, and Shaw areas. This part of the District once survived on memories of its heyday as a center of black culture and jazz music in the first half of the 20th century; now it's a vibrant, food-savvy restaurant and nightlife destination.

The area was especially vibrant from the 1920s to the 1950s, when it was home to jazz genius Duke Ellington, social activist Mary McLeod Bethune, and poets Langston Hughes and Georgia Douglas Johnson. In the 1950s Supreme Court Justice Thurgood Marshall, then still a lawyer, organized the landmark *Brown v. Board of Education* case at the 12th Street YMCA. Now, murals and artwork speckled across the Shaw neighborhood reflect the art and artists that added to the town's vibrancy, among a lively resurgence of culture, cuisine, and nightlife.

U Street has become a nightlife destination with music venues and theaters, but Shaw and Logan Circle have emerged as the new restaurants strips for fantastic and niche culinary experiences.

 Sights

This area of the District is not one for sightseers, but there's one noteworthy museum you may wish to visit.

African American Civil War Memorial and Museum

MUSEUM | This museum highlights and commemorates the contributions of the 209,145 members of the United States Colored Troops, who have long been ignored in the history of the Civil War. It also sets out to serve the educational needs of the local, national, and international community through learning and experiences within the interpretation on the history of the USCT. The museum is free to visitors. Give yourself an hour to explore the main exhibit, "Glorious March to Liberty, Civil War to Civil Rights." ☒ *1925 Vermont Ave. NW, Logan Circle* ☎ *202/667–2667* ⊕ *www.afroam-civilwar.org* ☚ *Free* Ⓜ *Shaw–Howard U.*

Mary McCloud Bethune Council House National Historic Site

HOUSE | The site of the first headquarters for the National Council of Negro Women, the Mary McLeod Bethune Council House celebrates the life and legacy of Bethune, who founded the Council and also served as president of the National Association of Colored Women. It was the Council's headquarters from 1943 to 1966, and Bethune herself lived there from 1943 to 1949. The archives of the history of African American women in the United States and Bethune's legacy are housed here as well. It's been under construction for nearly four years to

update the archival research areas and to stabilize the physical foundations, but it opened once again to the public in December 2018. ⊠ *1318 Vermont Ave. NW, Shaw* ☎ *202/426–5961* ⊕ *www.nps. gov/mamc* Ⓜ *Dupont Circle.*

🍴 Restaurants

U Street links Shaw, centered near Howard University's campus, to Adams Morgan, and is known for indie rock clubs, edgy bars, and trendy restaurants. Although the urban hipster vibe is being threatened by skyrocketing rents and the intrusion of chain stores, you'll still find more tattoos and sneakers than pinstripes and pearls here. Logan Circle is southwest from both of Shaw's Metro stations: U Street/African-American Civil War Memorial/Cardozo and Shaw–Howard University (both on the Green and Yellow lines).

All Purpose Pizzeria

$ | ITALIAN | You can get nearly any pizza you might want, from a classic Margherita style with the Standard (mozzarella and tomato with oregano) to more elaborate pizzas like Enzo the Baker (smoked bacon, Calabrian chilies, and red onion). For lighter fare, try some of the hand-selected meats off of the salumi menu, or one of the *spuntini* ("little snacks") that include braised octopus and squash "hummus." There is no shortage of antipasti and salad offerings, either. **Known for:** seasonally inspired pizzas; delicious antipasti; pickup and delivery. Ⓢ *Average main: $16* ⊠ *1250 9th St. NW, Shaw* ☎ *202/849–6174* ⊕ *allpurposedc.com* Ⓜ *Mt. Vernon Sq. 7th St.–Convention Center.*

★ Ben's Chili Bowl

$ | AMERICAN | FAMILY | Long before U Street became hip, Ben's was serving chili: chili on hot dogs, chili on Polish-style sausages, chili on burgers, and just plain chili. The shiny red-vinyl stools give the impression that little has changed since the 1950s (the original location still doesn't accept credit cards), but don't be fooled—this favorite of former president Barack Obama has rocketed into the 21st century with an iPhone app and an upscale Southern cuisine restaurant next door. **Known for:** legendary half-smoke chili bowls; Southern-style breakfast; cheese fries and milk shakes. Ⓢ *Average main: $7* ⊠ *1213 U St. NW, U Street* ☎ *202/667–0058* ⊕ *www. benschilibowl.com* 🖃 *No credit cards* Ⓜ *U St./African-Amer Civil War Memorial/ Cardozo.*

The Bird

$$ | AMERICAN | From the same minds that brought you The Pig, enjoy this fowl-themed restaurant and its menu of poultry of every variety, all from responsible sources. The menu draws from a variety of cuisines and from every part of the bird. **Known for:** fowl-themed menu; excellent craft cocktails (and mixology classes); small and large plates. Ⓢ *Average main: $20* ⊠ *1337 11th St. NW, Logan Circle* ☎ *202/518–3609* ⊕ *www. thebirddc.com* Ⓜ *Mt. Vernon Sq. 7th St.– Convention Center.*

Chaplin's

$ | ASIAN | Inspired by the 1930s star Charlie Chaplin, this is the first ramen house–cocktail bar in Shaw. Burmese chef Myo Htun transports you with his take on traditional gyoza, shumai, and any number of ramen combinations, while Ari and Micah Wilder offer carefully curated cocktails. **Known for:** delicious ramen and gyoza; house-made cocktails; 1930s film theme. Ⓢ *Average main: $14* ⊠ *1501 9th St. NW, Shaw* ☎ *202/644–8806* ⊕ *www. chaplinsdc.com* Ⓜ *Mt. Vernon Sq. 7th St.–Convention Center.*

Chercher Ethiopian Restaurant

$ | ETHIOPIAN | For the traditional Ethiopian food that has made its home in Shaw, this celebrated name offers both authentic tastes and great prices. Named for the West Hararghe zone of Ethiopia, this restaurant celebrates the traditional

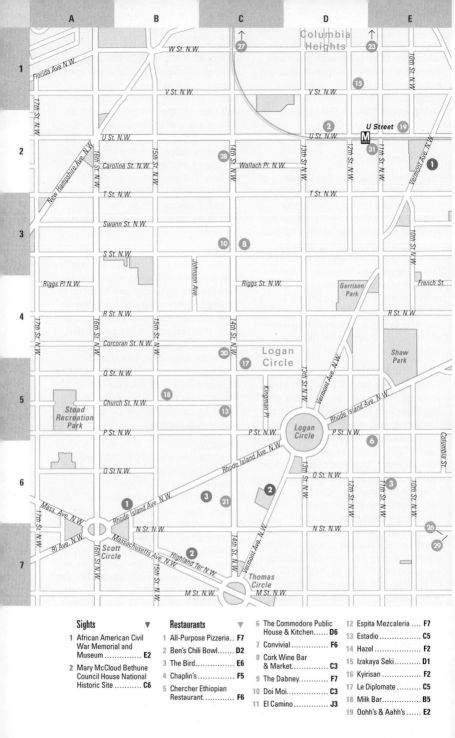

Sights ▼

1 African American Civil War Memorial and Museum **E2**
2 Mary McCloud Bethune Council House National Historic Site **C6**

Restaurants ▼

1 All-Purpose Pizzeria.. **F7**
2 Ben's Chili Bowl....... **D2**
3 The Bird................ **E6**
4 Chaplin's **F5**
5 Chercher Ethiopian Restaurant............. **F6**
6 The Commodore Public House & Kitchen...... **D6**
7 Convivial **F6**
8 Cork Wine Bar & Market.............. **C3**
9 The Dabney............ **F7**
10 Doi Moi................. **C3**
11 El Camino **J3**
12 Espita Mezcaleria **F7**
13 Estadio **C5**
14 Hazel **F2**
15 Izakaya Seki........... **D1**
16 Kyirisan **F2**
17 Le Diplomate **C5**
18 Milk Bar................ **B5**
19 Oohh's & Aahh's **E2**

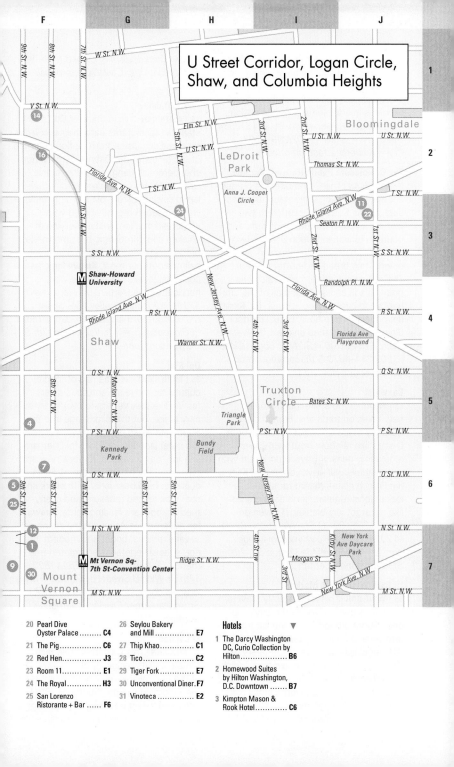

9th St. N.W.
8th St. N.W.
7th St. N.W.
W St. N.W.

V St. N.W.
(14)

(16)
Florida Ave. N.W.
Elm St. N.W.
5th St. N.W.
U St. N.W.
3rd St. N.W.
2nd St. N.W.
U St. N.W.   U St. N.W.
Bloomingdale

2

LeDroit
Park
Thomas St. N.W.

7th St. N.W.
T St. N.W.
Anna J. Cooper
Circle
T St. N.W.

(24)
Rhode Island Ave. N.W.
(11)
(22)
Seaton Pl. N.W.

3

S St. N.W.
2nd St. N.W.
Randolph Pl. N.W.
S St. N.W.
1st St. N.W.

M Shaw-Howard
University

Rhode Island Ave. N.W.
R St. N.W.
New Jersey Ave. N.W.
R St. N.W.
Florida Ave. N.W.

Shaw
Warner St. N.W.
4th St. N.W.
3rd St. N.W.
Florida Ave
Playground

4

8th St. N.W.
Marion St. N.W.
Q St. N.W.
Q St. N.W.

7th St. N.W.
Truxton
Circle
Bates St. N.W.

5

Triangle
Park
P St. N.W.
P St. N.W.
P St. N.W.

(4)
Kennedy
Park
Bundy
Field
New Jersey Ave. N.W.

(7)
O St. N.W.
O St. N.W.
O St. N.W.

6

(5)
(25)
9th St. N.W.
8th St. N.W.
7th St. N.W.
6th St. N.W.
5th St. N.W.
N St. N.W.
N St. N.W.

(12)
(1)
4th St. nw
New York
Ave Daycare
Park
N St. N.W.

(9)
M Mt Vernon Sq-
7th St-Convention Center
Ridge St. N.W.
Morgan St
Kirby St. N.W.
3rd St

7

(30)
Mount
Vernon
Square
M St. N.W.
New York Ave. N.W.
M St. N.W.

cuisine that is eaten mostly utensil-free, using a special spongy bread, injera, to scoop up the stews that are laid out on a large platter. **Known for:** authentic and delicious injera; plenty of vegan options; great value. [$] *Average main: $14* ✉ *1334 9th St. NW, Shaw* ☎ *202/299–9703* 🌐 *www.chercherrestaurant.com.*

The Commodore Public House & Kitchen
$ | **AMERICAN** | The Commodore is burger central, offering custom-made favorites such as the Squirrel Kicker (with two patties, smoked Gouda, onion jam, and bourbon mayo) and Neon Smash (two patties with cheddar, bacon, pickled onions, and bread-and-butter pickles). The casual pub-style kitchen also has great salads and sides and all of the draft beers and cans you could wish for. **Known for:** popular happy hour; casual outdoor dining; delicious fried chicken. [$] *Average main: $15* ✉ *1100 P St. NW, Logan Circle* ☎ *202/234–6870* 🌐 *thecommodoredc. com* [M] *Shaw–Howard U.*

Convivial
$$ | **FRENCH** | The shareable plates of new takes on traditional French dishes instantly made Convivial a local favorite. Dishes like rainbow trout with caviar atop snow peas or braised pork butt with papparadelle will leave you raving. **Known for:** French plates meant for sharing; lots of local regulars; ambitious dishes like escargot in a blanket. [$] *Average main: $25* ✉ *801 O St. NW, Logan Circle* ☎ *202/525–2870* 🌐 *www.convivialdc. com* 🕓 *No lunch* [M] *Mt. Vernon Sq. 7th St.–Convention Center.*

★ **Cork Wine Bar & Market**
$$ | **WINE BAR** | This rustic, dimly lit wine bar brings chic cuisine to the city's hippest neighborhood. The wine list features rare varietals—with a dozen still under $11 per glass—but even teetotalers will be enchanted by the menu's classic dishes. **Known for:** more than 50 wines by the glass; relaxing patio; favorite small plates to share. [$] *Average main: $24* ✉ *1805 14th St. NW, U Street* ☎ *202/265–2675* 🌐 *www.corkdc.com* 🕓 *Closed Mon.* [M] *U St./African-Amer Civil War Memorial/ Cardozo.*

★ **The Dabney**
$$ | **AMERICAN** | While many of D.C.'s standout restaurants earn their accolades for takes on cuisine from far-flung corners of the globe, at the Dabney, Virginia-born chef Jeremiah Langhorne draws rave reviews for his commitment to mid-Atlantic cuisine. Larger plates might include whole lacquered quail stuffed with cornbread or a family-style serving of chicken and dumplings, but small plates predominate, and waiters will help you balance out your meal. **Known for:** creative cocktails; low-key farmhouse vibe; handcrafted desserts. [$] *Average main: $21* ✉ *122 Blagden Alley NW, Shaw* ☎ *202/450–1015* 🌐 *www.thedabney.com* 🕓 *Closed Mon.* [M] *Mt. Vernon Sq. 7th St.–Convention Center.*

Doi Moi
$$ | **MODERN ASIAN** | The rise of foodie culture can leave adventurous diners feeling like they've turned over every culinary stone, but this pilgrimage into the Southeast Asian unknown will wow even the most jaded eater. Doi Moi (Vietnamese for "new changes") puts a new spin on several traditional Southeast Asian cuisines: fried beef jerky with shark sriracha, wok-tossed mussels, and crispy-fried snapper are leading lights. **Known for:** adventurous Asian cuisine spanning several regions; bright and modern interior; special vegetarian and gluten-free menus. [$] *Average main: $25* ✉ *1800 14th St. NW, U Street* ☎ *202/733–5131* 🌐 *www.doimoidc.com* 🕓 *No lunch* [M] *U St./African-Amer Civil War Memorial/ Cardozo.*

El Camino
$ | **MEXICAN** | This California-style taco temple and its rockabilly charm was one of the first reliable, quality restaurants in the Bloomingdale neighborhood. Slide into a red velvet booth and try the organic local chicken braised in Oaxacan-style

mole or the ever-popular burrito. **Known for:** cheap à la carte tacos; chilaquiles for brunch; mezcal cocktails. $ *Average main: $15* ⊠ *108 Rhode Island Ave. NW, U Street* ☎ *202/847–0419* ⊕ *elcaminodc. com* ⊗ *No lunch Mon.–Thurs.* ▭ *No credit cards* Ⓜ *Shaw–Howard U.*

Espita Mezcaleria
$$$ | MEXICAN | Espita runs on *maíz* (corn) and agave, the two cornerstones of the restaurant's food and drink menus. Serving authentic Mexican food small plates, mains, and desserts, this is a place to order a few things to try for the table to gain the full experience of the menu offerings. **Known for:** popular weekend happy hour; extensive mezcal list and themed cocktails; authentic Mexican flavor. $ *Average main: $28* ⊠ *1250 9th St. NW, Logan Circle* ☎ *202/621–9695* ⊕ *espitadc.com* ⊗ *No lunch weekdays* Ⓜ *Shaw–Howard U.*

★ Estadio
$$$ | SPANISH | The name of this polished palace means "stadium," and its gorgeously baroque interior, which surrounds a high-wire open kitchen, makes a perfect stage for energetic and flavorful uses of top-notch ingredients. The menu, developed during research jaunts throughout Spain, is a master class in tapas, with smoky grilled scallions punched up by garlicky romesco sauce and *tortilla española* smoother than any served in Barcelona. **Known for:** classic Spanish tapas with new flavors; boozy slushies. $ *Average main: $28* ⊠ *1520 14th St. NW, Logan Circle* ☎ *202/319–1404* ⊕ *www.estadio-dc.com* ⊗ *No lunch Mon.–Thurs.* Ⓜ *U St./African-Amer Civil War Memorial/Cardozo.*

★ Hazel
$$ | CHIU CHOW | Asian-influenced medium-size plates like fava bean falafal and sourdough potato bread with miso butter have made this U Street spot one of the hottest openings in recent years. The zucchini bread (with foie-gras mousse) is a recipe from the chef's grandmother,

the restaurant's namesake. **Known for:** family-recipe zucchini bread; steak tartare with egg yolk and tater tots; dim-sum brunch. $ *Average main: $25* ⊠ *808 V St. NW, U Street* ☎ *202/847–4980* ⊕ *www.hazelrestaurant.com* ⊗ *No lunch Mon.–Sat.* Ⓜ *U St./African-Amer Civil War Memorial/Cardozo.*

Izakaya Seki
$$ | JAPANESE | If the District's other Japanese restaurants are as Chipotle is to Mexican cuisine, this is an actual authentic taste of Tokyo. The only crowd-pleasing flourishes here are the freshness of the scallop carpaccio and the perfect sear on the grilled yellowtail jaw, and that's all adventurous foodies will need to make the most of a quiet evening at this family-owned, off-the-beaten-path spot marked by little more than a red Japanese lantern outside the door. **Known for:** authentic, non-Americanized Japanese cuisine; timed reservations for large groups; small, adventurous plates like beef tongue. $ *Average main: $22* ⊠ *1117 V St. NW, U Street* ☎ *202/588–5841* ⊕ *www.sekidc.com* ⊗ *Closed Mon. No lunch* Ⓜ *U St./African-Amer Civil War Memorial/Cardozo.*

Kyirisan
$ | ASIAN FUSION | A unique fusion of French and Chinese cuisines sweeps you away with delightful takes on dishes reminiscient of a French bistro but always with some Asian-inspired twist. The French-style seared scallops sit in a bed of coconut rice topped with basil ice cream, while Asian-style chicken wings are doused in a crème fraîche sauce. **Known for:** French-Chinese fusion; house-made cocktails and sake list; modern, lively interior. $ *Average main: $16* ⊠ *1924 8th St. NW, Shaw* ☎ *202/525–2383* ⊕ *www. kyirisandc.com* ⊗ *Closed Mon. No lunch weekdays* Ⓜ *Shaw–Howard U.*

★ Le Diplomate
$$$ | BRASSERIE | In this faithful re-creation of a convivial Parisian bistro, the attention to detail makes a night here into more

than just a meal. This excellent spot prizes quality above all, from graceful martinis and hand-stuffed ricotta ravioli to succulent, textbook-worthy steak frites and roasted chicken. **Known for:** Parisian-bistro vibe; juicy steak frites; popular brunch menu. $ *Average main: $30* ⊠ *1610 14th St. NW, U Street* ☎ *202/332–3333* ⊕ *www.lediplomatedc. com* ⊘ *No lunch weekdays.*

Milk Bar Flagship @ Logan Circle

$ | AMERICAN | If you're a fan of sprinkles, pie, ice cream, and birthday cake, then this is the place for you to eat in or grab something to go. But don't expect run-of-the-mill pastries at Milk Bar, where founder Christina Tosi has created an empire of modernized American pastries and cakes. **Known for:** American desserts with a modern twist; signature birthday layer cake and cereal milk soft serve; baking classes. $ *Average main: $6* ⊠ *1525 15th St. NW, Logan Circle* ⊹ *Corner of 15th St. and Church St. NW* ☎ *202/506–1357* ⊕ *milkbarstore.com* Ⓜ *Dupont Circle or Mt. Vernon Sq. 7th St.–Convention Center.*

Oohhs & Aahhs

$ | SOUTHERN | No-frills soul food is what you can find at this friendly eat-in or take-out place where the price is right and the food is delicious. Ultrarich macaroni and cheese, succulent chicken and waffles, and teriyaki salmon just beg to be devoured. **Known for:** home-style soul cooking; mac and cheese, collard greens, and hummingbird cake; late-night weekend hours. $ *Average main: $15* ⊠ *1005 U St. NW, U Street* ☎ *202/667–7142* ⊕ *www.oohhsnaahhs.com* Ⓜ *U St./African-Amer Civil War Memorial/Cardozo.*

Pearl Dive Oyster Palace

$$ | SEAFOOD | Chef Jeff Black does serve three kinds of po'boys, but that's about as working-class as it gets at this dazzlingly decorated homage to the bivalve. East and West Coast oysters come raw, with perfect dipping sauces—at half-price all day on Monday and during happy hour every other day—or warm in five irresistible guises, from bacon wrapped to crusted in cornmeal and sprinkled with sweet potato hash. **Known for:** upscale oysters (both raw and warm); steak options for nonoyster lovers; classy cocktails. $ *Average main: $24* ⊠ *1612 14th St. NW, U Street* ☎ *202/319–1612* ⊕ *www.pearldivedc.com* ⊘ *No lunch Mon.–Thurs.* Ⓜ *U St./African-Amer Civil War Memorial/Cardozo.*

The Pig

$$ | AMERICAN | From the same owners as The Bird, this rustic restaurant has a pork-centric menu that includes fried pork-belly buns, Moroccan-spiced ribs, a confit pork shank, and a delicious pan-seared pork chop. Enjoy the signature cocktails always on draft, the Three Little Pigs—8 Weeks 'til the Slaughter (a Manhattan), the Pegroni (negroni), and the Swine Boulevard (boulevardier). **Known for:** pork-themed menu; craft cocktails; both small and large plates. $ *Average main: $20* ⊠ *1320 14th St. NW, Logan Circle* ☎ *202/290–2821* ⊕ *www.thepigdc. com* Ⓜ *Mt. Vernon Sq. 7th St.–Convention Center.*

★ The Red Hen

$$$ | AMERICAN | The cozy farmhouselike setting helped make the Red Hen a must-try for Italian-influenced takes on American dishes. If the name and giant hen on the facade have you thinking poultry, you'd be right to follow your instincts and order the pan-roasted half chicken. **Known for:** savvy wine list; pan-roasted half chicken; delicious pasta options. $ *Average main: $28* ⊠ *1822 1st St. NW, U Street* ☎ *202/525–3021* ⊕ *www. theredhendc.com* ⊘ *No lunch* Ⓜ *Shaw–Howard U.*

★ Room 11

$ | WINE BAR | You're invited to the coolest house party in the city, where deft hands in a tiny kitchen turn out urbane plates that go down like a designer outfit hidden on the sale rack. From the roasted mushroom risotto at dinner to the perfectly assembled breakfast sandwich on a bis-cuit for brunch, this small wonder has a dish for every mood. **Known for:** intimate (read: tiny) hip space; brunch-time biscuit sandwich; outdoor patio with heating lamps in winter. $ *Average main: $15* ✉ *3234 11th St. NW, U Street* ☎ *202/332–3234* ⊕ *www.room11dc.com* ⊙ *No lunch weekdays* Ⓜ *Columbia Heights.*

The Royal

$ | **LATIN AMERICAN** | The Royal is both a Michelin-honored restaurant and a well-priced, local favorite for breakfast, lunch, dinner, or just for a matcha latte while working on your laptop at the bar. The second concept by Vinoteca owner Paul Carlson, it's a celebration of his family's international roots, with a strong emphasis on vegetarian and gluten-free options. **Known for:** Colombian-inspired food; small plates and house-made cock-tails; neighborhood favorite. $ *Average main: $15* ✉ *501 Florida Ave. NW, Shaw* ☎ *202/332–7777* ⊕ *www.theroyaldc.com* Ⓜ *Shaw–Howard U.*

San Lorenzo Ristorante + Bar

$$ | **ITALIAN** | Chef and owner Massimo Fabbri, previously of Tosca and Posto, has opened the first restaurant of his own in the heart of Shaw to highlight the tastes of Tuscany and to pay homage to his own roots in the region. Named for the patron saint of chefs, this soothing restaurant reminds you of Italy itself with a cream and golden palette, wooden beams, distressed plaster, and Italian art. **Known for:** sophisticated yet casual style; classic Tuscan dishes like rosticciana and pappardelle with rabbit ragù; homemade pastas. $ *Average main: $25* ✉ *1316 9th St. NW, Shaw* ☎ *202/588–8954* ⊕ *www.sanlorenzodc.com* Ⓜ *Mt. Vernon Sq. 7th St.–Convention Center.*

★ Seylou Bakery and Mill

$ | **AMERICAN** | Skip the Starbucks and Compass coffee, and and head to Sey-lou, a phenomenal coffee and whole-grain bakeshop. Offering classic, fresh sourdough and favorites like the whole wheat almond croissant and seasonal veggie frittata, Seylou has become a beloved local Shaw bakery. **Known for:** freshly made breads and whole wheat pastries; specialty coffees and teas; locally sourced ingredients. $ *Average main: $7* ✉ *926 N St. NW, Suite A, Shaw* ☎ *202/842–1122* ⊕ *www.seylou. com* ⊙ *Closed Mon. and Tues. No dinner* Ⓜ *Mt. Vernon Sq. 7th St.–Convention Center.*

Thip Khao

$ | **LAO** | **FAMILY** | Chef Seng Luangrath's legendary Thai destination in suburban Virginia, Bangkok Golden, drew so many curious diners to its Laotian menu that she was inspired to find a home for it in D.C. proper. Now its quirky yet delicious offerings, from yellow curry puffs (*khanom mun falang*) to grilled pork with lemongrass and ginger (*piing*), fill up diners on U Street. **Known for:** deep menu of authentic Laotian cuisine; minced-meat salads known as laab; bourbon and ginger cider drinks. $ *Average main: $16* ✉ *3462 14th St. NW, Logan Circle* ☎ *202/387–5426* ⊕ *thipkhao.com* ⊙ *No lunch Mon.–Thurs.* Ⓜ *Columbia Heights.*

Tico

$$ | **LATIN AMERICAN** | One of Boston's celebrity chefs, Michael Schlow, scored prime real estate for this fast-paced parade of small Latin and South Amer-ican plates with big personalities. The half-dozen seviches add witty touches like pressed watermelon and crispy rice, while the tacos thrill with inventive ingredients from shrimp to duck-skin "cracklings." **Known for:** exciting (and tasty) vegetarian options; very small plates (so ordering several is a must); all-night happy hour on Monday. $ *Average main: $25* ✉ *1926 14th St. NW, U Street* ☎ *202/319–1400* ⊕ *www.ticodc.com* ⊙ *No lunch* Ⓜ *U St./African-Amer Civil War Memorial/Cardozo.*

Tiger Fork

$ | **CHINESE FUSION** | Come here if you're looking for something from the cooler, gritty side of Hong Kong cuisine among the more traditional tastes. Try pork ribs slathered in soy and ginger sauce, a tofu claypot, *cheung fun* with shrimp and flowering chives, or chili wontons. **Known for:** Asian street-style food; late-night menu; bubble waffles. $ *Average main: $16* ⊠ *922 N St. NW, Shaw* ⊕ *Enter in rear, off Blagden Alley* ☎ *202/733–1152* ⊕ *www.tigerforkdc.com* Ⓜ *Mt. Vernon Sq. 7th St.–Convention Center.*

Unconventional Diner

$$ | **AMERICAN** | All of the typical diner and Southern favorites on the menu here have an unusual twist, befitting the name of this restaurant. Start with the kale nachos or potpie poppers, then, if you're really hungry, dive into a plate of fried chicken or the "French Dip" pappardelle next. **Known for:** modernized American diner food; potpie poppers (bite-size chicken potpies); good daily breakfast and weekend brunch. $ *Average main: $20* ⊠ *1207 9th St. NW, Shaw* ☎ *202/847–0122* ⊕ *unconventionaldiner. com* Ⓜ *Mt. Vernon Sq. 7th St.–Convention Center.*

Vinoteca

$$ | **WINE BAR** | This Euro-chic wine bar has one of the best patios in D.C. With a Tuscan vibe and a bocce court to match, the inviting outdoor plaza allows happy-hour revelers and casual diners to nosh on an abbreviated menu of smaller plates from the increasingly impressive kitchen, which turns out delicate house-made ricotta over seasonal salad to go with a stellar manchego and skirt steak flatbread. **Known for:** awesome outdoor dining with a bocce court; kimchi burger; steak and eggs poutine at brunch; extensive wine list. $ *Average main: $23* ⊠ *1940 11th St. NW, U Street* ☎ *202/332–9463* ⊕ *www.vinotecadc. com* ☾ *No lunch weekdays* Ⓜ *U St./African-Amer Civil War Memorial/Cardozo.*

Hotels

Staying in this hip neighborhood gives a cooler, local feel to your stay where you will experience the District like the locals do. These hotels put you right in the mix of some of the most unique restaurants and bars in the area, while still only a Metro or car ride away from the city's major sites and museums.

The Darcy Washington DC, Curio Collection by Hilton

$$$ | **HOTEL | FAMILY** | One of the city's latest hotel triumphs, this stylish treasure just around the corner from the buzzy 14th Street Corridor aims to bring a sophisticated European touch to the cosmopolitan capital city. **Pros:** sophisticated style and lobby; chef-inspired restaurant and coffee shop; warm welcome for both kids and pets. **Cons:** no spa or pool; only expensive valet parking available; extra fee for Wi-Fi unless you are a Hilton Honors member. $ *Rooms from: $300* ⊠ *1515 Rhode Island Ave. NW, Logan Circle* ☎ *202/232–7000* ⊕ *www.thedarcyhotel.com* ⇩ *226 rooms* ⊚ *No meals* Ⓜ *Dupont Circle.*

Homewood Suites by Hilton, Washington, D.C. Downtown

$$$$ | **HOTEL | FAMILY** | Suites with kitchens, a free grocery-shopping service, and complimentary hot breakfast buffet daily make this a popular choice for tourists, but the large family-room-style lobby may well also be abuzz with people in suits preparing presentations. **Pros:** roomy suites; evening social Monday through Thursday; great for cooking in your room. **Cons:** difficult street parking; 10 minutes to Metro; chain-hotel feel. $ *Rooms from: $429* ⊠ *1475 Massachusetts Ave. NW, Logan Circle* ☎ *202/265–8000* ⊕ *www.homewoodsuites.com* ⇩ *175 suites* ⊚ *Free Breakfast* Ⓜ *McPherson Sq.*

Kimpton Mason & Rook Hotel

$$$ | **HOTEL** | A nod to the country's forefathers and the game of chess,

this stylish Kimpton hotel has spacious rooms designed in rich shades of browns and grays, featuring large flat-screen TVs, plush bedding, and Bluetooth speakers. **Pros:** chic rooftop pool and lounge open seasonally; excellent service; complimentary bikes and nightly wine hour. **Cons:** long walk to the Metro; low ceilings; nightly amenity fee on top of room cost. [$] *Rooms from: $399* ✉ *1430 Rhode Island Ave. NW, Logan Circle* ☎ *202/462–9001, 866/508–0658* 🌐 *www.masonandrookhotel.com* 🛏 *178 rooms* 🍴 *No meals* [M] *McPherson Sq.*

Nightlife

Decades ago, the U Street Corridor was famous as D.C.'s Black Broadway. After many dormant years, today the neighborhood has come roaring back with a lively bar, club, and music scene that's expanding both north and south along 14th Street. The U Street Corridor is easily accessible from the U Street/African-American Civil War Memorial/Cardozo Metro stop, on the Green and Yellow lines. Taxis also are easy to find.

In the last couple of years nearby Shaw has become the most revitalized downtown neighborhood in the capital. But any night out in Shaw almost by default includes spending time in the U Street Corridor to the north and west—especially because some destinations, like the Howard Theatre and the 9:30 Club, straddle both increasingly diverse urban neighborhoods. Shaw is centered on 7th Street, with Howard University and Hospital to the north and the Washington Convention Center at the very southern edge.

BARS AND LOUNGES

A&D Neighborhood Bar

BARS/PUBS | From the street, A&D is camouflaged with a front window brimming with houseplants. Don't be fooled. Inside, you'll find a friendly bar serving a young, fashionably relaxed crowd some of the best cocktails in town. (Be sure to try the namesake cocktail, a tangy and tart twist on a dirty martini.) Happy hour starts off mellow, but the place is often jumping in the later hours. And while other trendy spots are still offering the game on TV, A&D's only sports action is the foosball table in the back room. If you're hungry, and want more than the few variations on bar staples and snacks, bring in something from the bar's sister gourmet sandwich shop, Sundevich, in the adjacent alley. A&D is closed Sunday, but has late-night happy hours on Wednesday and Thursday. ✉ *1314 9th St. NW, Shaw* ☎ *202/290–1804* 🌐 *www.andbardc.com* [M] *Mt. Vernon Sq. 7th St.–Convention Center.*

All Souls

BARS/PUBS | All Souls feels like the perfect dive to meet up with friends and chat away in a booth, fresh cocktail or craft beer in hand. The cocktails are simple, yet refined, and described in loving detail alongside interesting wines and craft brews on signs at the bar. You can order some small snacks, but customers may also bring food in or have it delivered, making it feel even more like a friendly, neighborhood hangout. ✉ *725 T St. NW, Shaw* ☎ *202/733–5929* 🌐 *allsoulsbar.com* [M] *Shaw–Howard U.*

Anxo Cidery

BREWPUBS/BEER GARDENS | Take a trip to Spain at Anxo (an-cho) Cidery. Here you can try a multitude of ciders, a drink tied to the culture of the Basque country, and explore the unusual combinations produced from apples: from bright or fruit-forward to structured or rustic. Try one of the many flights, some dessert ice cider, and even some obscure, rare ciders as well. There are also beer, wine, and cocktails for those who want something more familiar, but remember that the cider at Anxo is far beyond the typical grocery-store ciders. There's also a menu of small bar bites, or "pintxos." ✉ *300*

Florida Ave. NW, Shaw 🖀 *202/986–3795*
⊕ *www.anxodc.com* Ⓜ *Shaw–Howard U.*

Black Jack

BARS/PUBS | A red-velvet, almost vaude-
ville-like interior around the bar offers a
saucy experience upstairs from the highly rated Pearl Dive Oyster Palace. In the
back, you'll find a bocce court surrounded
by stadium-style seats so onlookers can
recline, imbibe, and cheer simultaneously. Though the most exquisite cocktail
confections can be pricey, there's also an
impressive beer lineup and a worthwhile
menu ranging from mussels to pizza.
Happy hour is every day, including weekends, and all day on Sunday. ⊠ *1612 14th
St. NW, Logan Circle* 🖀 *202/319–1612*
⊕ *www.blackjackdc.com* Ⓜ *U St./Afri-
can-Amer Civil War Memorial/Cardozo.*

★ The Brixton

BARS/PUBS | An English pub with an
upscale D.C. twist offers three levels of
fun in the heart of the U Street bustle. The
menu is inspired by the Commonwealth's
reach, including Indian, some Caribbean
spice, and outstanding English, right down
to the fish-and-chips. The sprawling roof
deck offers a change of pace with two
bars (enclosed in the winter), great views,
and DJs on Thursday, Friday, and Saturday
nights. In between, the second-floor
Lodge Bar is wide open. Brixton also
offers trivia contests and comedians.
⊠ *901 U St. NW, U Street* 🖀 *202/560–
5045* ⊕ *www.brixtondc.com* Ⓜ *U St./
African-Amer Civil War Memorial/Cardozo.*

Busboys and Poets

BARS/PUBS | Part eatery, part bookstore,
and part event space, this popular local
hangout draws a diverse crowd and
hosts a wide range of entertainment,
from poetry open mics to music to guest
authors and activist speakers. The name
is an homage to Langston Hughes,
who worked as a busboy in D.C. before
becoming a famous poet. This original
location is open until 1 am on Friday and
Saturday—there's another downtown
(at 1025 5th Street NW), as well as

outposts in upper D.C., Maryland, and
Virginia. ⊠ *2021 14th St. NW, U Street*
🖀 *202/387–7638* ⊕ *www.busboysandpo-
ets.com* Ⓜ *U St./African-Amer Civil War
Memorial/Cardozo.*

Café Saint-Ex

BARS/PUBS | Named for Antoine de
Saint-Exupéry, French pilot and author
of *The Little Prince,* this bi-level bar has
a split personality. The upstairs brasserie
has pressed-tin ceilings and a propeller
hanging over the polished wooden bar.
Downstairs is the Gate 54 nightclub,
designed to resemble an airplane hangar,
with dropped corrugated-metal ceilings
and backlit aerial photographs. The downstairs DJs draw a fairly young crowd,
while the upstairs menu attracts a more
subdued clientele for dinner. ⊠ *1847
14th St. NW, U Street* 🖀 *202/265–7839*
⊕ *www.saint-ex.com* Ⓜ *U St./African-Am-
er Civil War Memorial/Cardozo.*

Calico

BARS/PUBS | Tucked away in Blagden Alley
in the heart of Shaw, this hipster's dream
offers kitschy decor made modern and an
ethereal garden backyard. Take a boozy
adult juice box to the urban backyard,
featuring a 3,000-square-foot patio with
farmhouse tables, string lights, plants,
and a vintage greenhouse. Formerly a
boxing gym and art studio, the restaurant
offers a menu with elevated takes on
cookout classics like crab cakes, short
ribs, and hoagies. To respect sound
ordinances, the patio closes at 10:30
on weeknights, 12:30 am on weekends. ⊠ *50 Blagden Alley NW, Shaw*
🖀 *202/791–0134* Ⓜ *Mt. Vernon Sq. 7th
St.–Convention Center.*

Chi-Cha Lounge

BARS/PUBS | Groups of young profession-
als relax on sofas and armchairs in this
hip hangout modeled after an Ecuado-
rian hacienda, while Latin jazz mingles
with pop music in the background and
old movies run silently behind the bar.
The place gets packed on weekends, so
come early to get a coveted sofa along

the back wall. Down the tasty tapas as you enjoy the namesake drink—think sangria with a bigger kick. Or try a hookah filled with a range of flavored tobaccos, from apple to watermelon. A dress-to-impress dress code is strictly enforced. ⊠ *1624 U St. NW, U Street* ☎ *202/234–8400* ⊕ *www.chicha-loungedc.com* Ⓜ *U St./African-Amer Civil War Memorial/Cardozo.*

ChurchKey

BARS/PUBS | There's an astounding selection of beers at ChurchKey—555 varieties from more than 30 countries, including 50 beers on tap, and exclusive draft and cask ales. If you have trouble making a choice, bartenders will offer you 4-ounce tasters. The urban-vintage vibe balances unassuming and pretentious in pretty much equal measure, reflected in a menu that ranges from tater tots, a Caesar salad, and rotating flatbread options. ⊠ *1337 14th St. NW, Logan Circle* ☎ *202/567–2576* ⊕ *www.churchkey-dc.com* Ⓜ *McPherson Sq.*

★ Columbia Room

BARS/PUBS | Derek Brown's two-time James Beard–nominated ode to the American cocktail is located in downtown D.C.'s hippest neighborhood for gourmands. Perhaps the coolest and chicest cocktail bar in Shaw, the Columbia Room features a curated drinks list that changes seasonally and includes combinations that dazzle and surprise. Tucked away in Blagden Alley, you can find the Punch Garden up flight of steps offering a special seasonal menu outside, or step into the Spirits Library for one of the many featured cocktails, or even no-proof cocktails. An even grander experience awaits in the Tasting Room, where you can get an elaborate cocktail tasting accompanied by bites to enhance the flavors. ⊠ *124 Blagden Alley NW, Shaw* ☎ *202/316–9396* ⊕ *www.columbiaroom-dc.com* Ⓜ *Mt. Vernon Sq. 7th St.–Convention Center.*

★ Cork Wine Bar

WINE BARS—NIGHTLIFE | On weekends, the crowds can spill onto 14th Street—but one of the best wine bars in D.C. is worth the wait. An outstanding wine list (mainly French and Italian) is matched with delectable small plates, perfect for sharing. ⊠ *1805 14th St. NW, U Street* ☎ *202/265–2675* ⊕ *www.corkdc.com* Ⓜ *U St./African-Amer Civil War Memorial/Cardozo.*

The Dabney Cellar

BARS/PUBS | A separate concept from The Dabney restaurant, the Cellar is hidden down a set of stone steps in the restaurant's basement. The dim lighting and small size make you feel as if you stumbled on a D.C. speakeasy, but the bar itself shares a lot of the same open, earthy tones of the larger restaurant. The Cellar riffs off classic cocktails for its specialty list and has a large selection of wines, cider, and beer. If you feel peckish, try some of the night's specialty bar snacks, written on the blackboard nightly. You can't go wrong with the raw bar or the carefully selected cheeses and charcuterie. ⊠ *The Dabney, 1222 9th St. NW, Shaw* ⊹ *Basement entrance* ☎ *202/450–1015* ⊕ *thedabney.com* Ⓜ *Mt. Vernon Sq. 7th St.–Convention Center.*

Dacha Beer Garden

BREWPUBS/BEER GARDENS | Set off by a three-story mural of Elizabeth Taylor, Dacha has become the go-to outdoor drinking venue in midtown D.C., with lines of people (and their dogs) waiting to get in most evenings anytime of year whenever the weather isn't bitterly cold or inclement. (A windscreen wall and heaters further help keep patrons toasty during the winter.) The beer garden serves drafts of craft beers from Germany, Belgium, and the United States as well as Bavarian-inspired nosh, while the adjoining café serves hot coffee and bagels and sandwiches during the day. ⊠ *1600 7th St. NW, Shaw* ☎ *202/350–9888* ⊕ *www.dachadc.com* Ⓜ *Shaw–Howard U.*

El Centro D.F.

BARS/PUBS | A sunny spot—whatever the weather—on D.C.'s 14th Street, this Richard Sandoval outpost celebrates tequila with a ridiculously expansive selection and an expert staff to guide you, particularly in crafting a personalized flight. The real draw, however, is the roof deck, where the young and boisterous keep the fiesta going. Great nightly happy hour on weekdays from 3 to 7. ☒ *1819 14th St. NW, Logan Circle* ☎ *202/328–3131* ⊕ *www.eatelcentro.com* Ⓜ *U St./African-Amer Civil War Memorial/Cardozo.*

La Jambe

WINE BARS—NIGHTLIFE | Named both for the legs of a wine and a leg of ham, this is the place to fill your metaphorical hollow leg with wine, cheese, and charcuterie. Choose from a variety of reds, whites, and everything in between, and even a few French cider styles, or go for a flight of brandy and whisky. All of the cocktails and spirits here are either from France or the District. Happy hour is offered from 5 to 7 Tuesday through Friday, and brunch is served from 11 to 3 on weekends. ☒ *1550 7th St. NW, Shaw* ☎ *202/627–2988* ⊕ *www.lajambedc.com* Ⓜ *Shaw–Howard U.*

Maxwell Park

WINE BARS—NIGHTLIFE | At Maxwell Park, dinner and dessert are both a glass of wine. The menu changes monthly and by theme, offering more than 50 wines by the glass in a wide variety of types. Try a sweet wine or aperitif for dessert, or a cocktail to mix it up, like house-made tonics for seasonal gin and tonics. If you don't know what you want, ask one of the trained sommeliers about the 500 labels on the bottle list or have a 2.5-ounce tasting glass (just watch the prices because there are some rare wines here). Enjoy the outdoor patio, heated in the winter, or cozy into the bar, open nightly at 5. ☒ *1336 9th St. NW, Shaw* ☎ *202/792–9522* ⊕ *maxwelldcwine.com* Ⓜ *Mt. Vernon Sq. 7th St.–Convention Center.*

★ The Morris

BARS/PUBS | The brainchild of David Strauss, previously of Le Diplomate and the original Founding Farmers, this Shaw nightlife standout offers cool-blue color-blocked walls, a 1950s feel, and spectacular cocktails. You'll feel like you're simultaneously at a 1950s-era diner, sitting on a backyard patio, and in a Wes Anderson film. The happy-hour menu features slightly cheaper cocktail options, wine, and beer, while the full menu offers cleverly crafted cocktails that stand out on their own. Both menus change monthly, so make sure you return to see what's new, and if you're unsure, just ask a bartender. ☒ *1020 7th St. NW, Shaw* ☎ *833/366–7747* ⊕ *morrisbardc.com* Ⓜ *Mt. Vernon Sq. 7th St.–Convention Center.*

Nellie's Sports Bar

BARS/PUBS | This popular sports bar with a gay following makes everyone feel welcome. Catch the games on multiple screens, or try your luck with "drag bingo" or trivia games. Spaces in this eclectic two-story venue range from roof deck to cozy pub room to a dining area serving all-American pub grub meets Venezuelan specialties—from empanadas to arepas. And every weekend brings a reservations-required brunch buffet with drag queens as servers and, of course, performers. ☒ *900 U St. NW, U Street* ☎ *202/332–6355* ⊕ *www.nelliessportsbar.com* Ⓜ *U St./African-Amer Civil War Memorial/Cardozo.*

Number Nine

BARS/PUBS | The heart of Logan Circle nightlife is a predominantly male gay bar attracting guests of all ages. The downstairs lounge offers plush banquettes and street views, while big-screen viewing is offered upstairs at the 9½ video bar. The daily happy hour (5–9 pm) offers two-for-one drinks. At any time this is a great place for a cocktail and some good conversation in a bustling neighborhood that includes, a block away on 14th Street,

Trade, which is another popular, no-frills gay bar from the same owners as Number Nine. ✉ *1435 P St. NW, Logan Circle* ☎ *202/986–0999* ⊕ *www.numberninedc. com* Ⓜ *Dupont Circle.*

The Passenger

BARS/PUBS | If you're looking for Chartreuse on tap, a handwritten crafted cocktail list, and a laid-back vibe, this is the place for you. It has the feeling of a local dive bar but with the cocktail menu and bar bites of a funky D.C. bar. Feel dazed by the seemingly hundreds of bottles lining the bar and enjoy the occasional band upstairs on weekends. ✉ *1539 7th St. NW, Shaw* ☎ *202/853–3588* ⊕ *www.passengerdc.com* Ⓜ *Mt. Vernon Sq. 7th St.–Convention Center.*

The Saloon

BARS/PUBS | A classic watering hole has no TVs, no light beer, and no martinis. What you can find are locals engaged in conversation—a stated goal of the owner—and some of the world's best beers, including the rare Urbock 23, an Austrian brew that is rated one of the tastiest and strongest in the world, with 9.6% alcohol content (limit one per customer). The Saloon also offers a broader bar menu, too. ✉ *1205 U St. NW, U Street* ☎ *202/462–2640* Ⓜ *U St./African-Amer Civil War Memorial/Cardozo.*

Satellite Room

BARS/PUBS | Pre- and postconcert patrons of the adjacent 9:30 Club can enjoy boozy milk shakes like the Frank Costello (chocolate, mint, and bourbon) or Count Creamy (Bailey's Irish Cream, vanilla ice cream, and Count Chocula cereal). Delicious, albeit greasy, American-inspired fare is also on offer, including snacks, wings, and pizzas. A walled-off patio and dark, hip vibe can provide the perfect complement to a musical night out. ✉ *2047 9th St. NW, U Street* ☎ *202/506–2496* ⊕ *www.satellitedc.com* Ⓜ *U St./African-Amer Civil War Memorial/Cardozo.*

U Street Music Hall

DANCE CLUBS | This basement dance hall boasts one of the best sound systems in the city and features both DJs and live acts playing indie rock, dance, and electro music. The diverse crowd can feature young hipsters here for the bands early evening followed by club kids when DJs take over. Check the website to plan your visit accordingly. ✉ *1115 U St. NW, Suite A, U Street* ☎ *202/588–1889* ⊕ *www. ustreetmusichall.com* Ⓜ *U St./African-Amer Civil War Memorial/Cardozo.*

Vinoteca

WINE BARS—NIGHTLIFE | The sophisticated set flocks here for a solid list of around 100 wines, a menu of delicious small bites, and weekend brunches. There's a daily happy hour (5–7 pm), and the flights of wine to sample are attractively priced. On Thursday nights there are live flamenco performances. In good weather you can dine on the front patio, and out back there's a large bar and a bocce court. Vinoteca also offers wine classes for small groups in the private rooms upstairs. ✉ *1940 11th St. NW, U Street* ☎ *202/332–9463* ⊕ *www.vinotecadc.com* Ⓜ *U St./African-Amer Civil War Memorial/Cardozo.*

DANCE CLUBS

★ Flash

DANCE CLUBS | The decline of megaclubs in D.C. has coincided with a rise in more intimate and inviting venues for those serious about dancing. This photography-themed jewel is near the Howard Theatre that replaced a pawnshop—a telling sign of this changing neighborhood. An operational photo booth is an entry point to the main upstairs dance floor, which envelops you in walls lined with 10,000 LED lights and a best-in-the-business Funktion One sound system. Pioneering underground DJs—Carl Craig, Chus & Ceballos—move their flocks of a couple hundred fans while intermittently flashing them from the rigged 24 parabolic reflectors behind them. ✉ *645 Florida*

Ave. NW, Atlas District ☎ *202/827–8791* ⊕ *www.flashdc.com* Ⓜ *Shaw–Howard U.*

Local 16
BARS/PUBS | When they have to remove all the chairs in the joint to make more room for dancing, you know you've picked a good spot. Locals and out-of-towners alike pack in on weekends to enjoy the joyful pop music, multiple dance rooms, and the outdoor-deck bar perched one story above 16th Street. Luxe couches, chandeliers, vintage pieces, and winding staircases enhance the atmosphere of a Victorian house party with a modern twist. Outstanding happy hour and brunch on weekends. ✉ *1602 U St. NW, U Street* ☎ *202/265–2828* ⊕ *www.local-sixteen.com* Ⓜ *U St./African-Amer Civil War Memorial/Cardozo.*

JAZZ AND BLUES
New Vegas Lounge
MUSIC CLUBS | The New Vegas Lounge may be a vestige from a grittier, less affluent era, but the Logan Circle club is in its nearly fifth decade of offering live blues every weekend. Vegas Lounge is run by the wife and sons of its late founder, known as Dr. Blues. Friday- and Saturday-night performances by the house ensemble the Out of Town Blues Band attract an eclectic crowd, from veteran blues fans to newer residents who don't know from Muddy Waters— drawn to the club out of sheer curiosity, or because it's a refreshing cultural and historical diversion in the neighborhood. After all, even in a now-tony neighborhood such as Logan Circle, people still get the blues. ✉ *1415 P St. NW, Logan Circle* ☎ *202/483–3971* ⊕ *www.newvegasloungedc.com* Ⓜ *Dupont Circle.*

Twins Jazz
MUSIC CLUBS | For nearly three decades, twin sisters Kelly and Maze Tesfaye have been offering great jazz, featuring some of D.C.'s strongest straight-ahead jazz players, as well as groups from as far away as New York. The food is nothing to write home about, but it's easy to

meet the nightly minimum with drinks. Connections with local universities bring in new and experimental talent. ✉ *1344 U St. NW, U Street* ☎ *202/234–0072* ⊕ *www.twinsjazz.com* Ⓜ *U St./African-Amer Civil War Memorial/Cardozo.*

ROCK AND POP
★ Black Cat
MUSIC CLUBS | Way before its stretch of 14th Street became the trendiest few blocks in town, the Black Cat was a destination for alternative music and quirky nostalgic dance parties. The venue is a host for midsize rock concerts and smaller, local acts focused on indie, alternative, and underground music, with favorites such as the Dandy Warhols, the Ravonettes, and Ex Hex. The Black Cat also regularly hosts artistic events, including comedy, edgy burlesque, and independent film nights. The postpunk crowd whiles away the time in the ground floor's Red Room, a side bar with pool tables, an eclectic jukebox, and no cover charge. The club is also home to Food for Thought, a legendary vegetarian café. ✉ *1811 14th St. NW, U Street* ☎ *202/667–4490* ⊕ *www.blackcatdc.com* Ⓜ *U St./African-Amer Civil War Memorial/Cardozo.*

DC9
MUSIC CLUBS | With live music most days of the week, this small two-story rock club with an upper deck hosts fledgling indie bands and the occasional nationally known act. There's a narrow bar on the ground floor, a sizable concert space on the second floor, and an enclosed roof deck on top. DJs take the controls for weekend-night dance parties. Concertgoers can enjoy snacks, sandwiches, and burgers every night and until 1 am on weekends. ✉ *1940 9th St. NW, U Street* ☎ *202/483–5000* ⊕ *www.dcnine.com* Ⓜ *U St./African-Amer Civil War Memorial/Cardozo.*

★ 9:30 Club
MUSIC CLUBS | Consistently ranked as one of the best concert venues in the country, the 9:30 Club is the intimitable place bands aspire to play and music fans love

to attend. The best indie and up-and-coming performers are the main attraction, though every now and then a bigger act such as Adele, Drake, Ed Sheeran, and Leon Bridges stop by to soak up the vibe of this large but cozy space wrapped by balconies on three sides. Once graced by legends such as Nirvana, Bob Dylan, and Johnny Cash, the venue is now a great spot for big labels looking for an intimate vibe. Recent acts have included critical darlings like Jack White, Pink, Justin Timberlake, and the Foo Fighters. For its various music genres from country to pop, this venue has become one of the most attended clubs of its size. ■TIP→ **There are no bad views here and the excellent sound system means you can stand anywhere for a great show experience.** ⊠ *815 V St. NW, U Street* ☎ *202/265–0930* ⊕ *www.930.com* Ⓜ *U St./African-Amer Civil War Memorial/Cardozo.*

Velvet Lounge

MUSIC CLUBS | Squeeze up the narrow stairway and check out the eclectic local and national bands that play at this unassuming, tiny neighborhood joint. In addition to performers ranging from indie mainstays to critically touted up-and-comers, the venue regularly hosts comedy and variety shows. ⊠ *915 U St. NW, U Street* ☎ *202/462–3213* ⊕ *www.velvet-loungedc.com* Ⓜ *U St./African-Amer Civil War Memorial/Cardozo.*

⚫ Performing Arts

The U Street Corridor is enjoying a renaissance and is starting to reclaim its former title of Washington's "Black Broadway." The Howard Theatre offers great productions from diverse sources while the Lincoln Theatre offers music from the best in country, reggae, pop, and more. Try some of the smaller venues in this neighborhood for original and compelling performances.

MAJOR VENUES

★ The Howard Theatre

MUSIC | What was once was "the largest colored theatre in the world" at its opening in 1920, the Howard Theatre has been operating again in the heart of Washington since 2012. The Howard now hosts a regular array of musical acts from Kid Creole & The Coconuts, to Ginger Baker's Jazz Confusion and the Harlem Gospel Choir. ⊠ *620 T St. NW, U Street* ☎ *202/803–2899* ⊕ *thehowardtheatre. com* Ⓜ *Shaw–Howard U.*

Lincoln Theatre

MUSIC | The Lincoln Theatre is a historical venue from 1922, back when Washington natives Duke Ellington and Pearl Baily were joined by the likes of Ella Fitzgerald, Billie Holiday, Nat King Cole, and Louis Armstrong. Today, the 1,200-seat theater is part of the lively U Street Corridor and presents modern musical artists, including Kendrick Lamar, Hozier, and Billy Idol, as well as comedic performers like Demetri Martin, Tig Notaro, and Ilana Glazer. ⊠ *1215 U St. NW, U Street* ☎ *202/328–6000* ⊕ *www.thelincolndc. com* Ⓜ *U St./African-Amer Civil War Memorial/Cardozo.*

THEATER

★ Studio Theatre

THEATER | One of the busiest groups in the city, this multifaceted theater company produces an eclectic season of contemporary European and offbeat American plays in four spaces: the original Mead and Milton theaters, the newer 200-seat Metheny Theatre, and the experimental Stage 4. The theater is part of Washington's energetic 14th Street Corridor. ⊠ *1501 14th St. NW, Dupont Circle* ☎ *202/332–3300* ⊕ *www. studiotheatre.org* Ⓜ *Dupont Circle.*

The In Series

MUSIC | Trademark cabaret, experimental chamber opera, and Spanish musical theater (also known as zarzuela) are among the hallmarks of this company founded in 1982, which performs at

Source, GALA Hispanic Theater, and the Atlas Performing Arts Center. ✉ *1835 14th St. NW, U Street* ☎ *202/204–7763* ⊕ *www.inseries.org.*

Washington Stage Guild

THEATER | This company performs neglected classics as well as contemporary literary plays in the Undercroft Theatre of Mount Vernon Place United Methodist Church. In recent years they have offered lesser-known works by Oscar Wilde and George Bernard Shaw. Contemporary plays such as *Tryst* by Karoline Leach and David Marshall Grant's *Pen* are also offered. ✉ *900 Massachusetts Ave. NW, Logan Circle* ☎ *240/582–0050* ⊕ *www. stageguild.org* Ⓜ *Dupont Circle.*

🛍 Shopping

In the 1930s and 1940s U Street was known for its classy theaters and jazz clubs. After decades of decline following the 1968 riots, the neighborhood has been revitalized. The area has gentrified at lightning speed, but has retained a diverse mix of multiethnic young professionals and older, working-class African Americans. U Street resident and associate justice of the Supreme Court Sonia Sotomayor says, "U Street is the East Village." At night the neighborhood's club, bar, and restaurant scene comes alive. During the day the street scene is more laid-back, with more locals than tourists occupying the distinctive shops.

ANTIQUES AND COLLECTIBLES

★ GoodWood

ANTIQUES/COLLECTIBLES | It's described by its owners as an American mercantile and dry goods store, but when you open the door, you'll feel as if you've been invited into a friend's warm and inviting loft. Displays throughout the store beautifully showcase 19th-century antique furniture. You'll also discover leather goods; vintage mirrors and other decorative home items; men's and women's grooming products and perfumes from around the

world; Peruvian alpaca and wool scarves; Swedish clogs; and comfortable dresses, sweaters, and tops from American and international designers. ✉ *1428 U St. NW, U Street* ☎ *202/986–3640* ⊕ *www. goodwooddc.com* Ⓜ *U St./African-Amer Civil War Memorial/Cardozo.*

ART GALLERIES

★ Hemphill Fine Arts

ART GALLERIES | This spacious showcase for contemporary art shows mid-career and established artists such as William Christenberry, John Dreyfuss, Linling Lu, and Julie Wolfe, with works in all media. ✉ *1515 14th St. NW, 3rd fl., Logan Circle* ☎ *202/234–5601* ⊕ *www.hemphillfine-arts.com* Ⓜ *Dupont Circle.*

BEAUTY/COSMETICS

Aesop Skincare

PERFUME/COSMETICS | With its first signature store in the District, this Australian skin-care company brings its finest-quality plant-based and laboratory-made ingredients. Stop in for effective, unique skin, hair, and fragrance products. ✉ *1924 8th St. NW, Space 110, Shaw* ☎ *202/299–9435* ⊕ *www.aesop.com* Ⓜ *Shaw–Howard U.*

Le Labo

PERFUME/COSMETICS | The French-influenced New York perfumerie has landed in its first D.C. brick-and-mortar location that reflects the cool, indie vibe of the Shaw neighborhood in both its design and products. Preferring "soulful fragrance" to everyday perfumes, Le Labo's manifesto is to create luxuriously handcrafted, non-animal-tested fragrance for "passionate souls." Visit this unique shop and take a whiff of some of the best-selling fragrances, like Santal 33, Rose 31, Bergemote 22, and Thé Noir 29. ✉ *1924 8th St. NW, No. 120, Shaw* ☎ *202/986–0600* ⊕ *www.lelabofragranc-es.com* Ⓜ *Shaw–Howard U.*

CLOTHING

Bonobos

CLOTHING | This signature men's shop achieved its fame with comfortable, stylish pants. Shopping and shipping are made easy here: simply go into the guideshop, find your style and fitting, and then have your finds shipped directly to you. You can make a one-hour appointment (with a complimentary beer), walk out without bags, and enjoy free shipping and returns. ✉ *1924 8th St. NW, No. 123, Shaw* ☎ *202/868–1210* ⊕ *bonobos.com/guideshop* Ⓜ *Shaw–Howard U.*

Current Boutique

CLOTHING | Don't be fooled by the new dresses in the front—this shop is a consignment shopper's dream. "Current" styles from brands such as Tory Burch, BCBG, Marc Jacobs, and Diane Von Furstenberg just might fit better when you buy them at a third of their original price. ✉ *1809 14th St. NW, U Street* ☎ *202/588–7311* ⊕ *www.currentboutique.com* Ⓜ *U St./African-Amer Civil War Memorial/Cardozo.*

★ Lettie Gooch Boutique

CLOTHING | Named after the owner's grandmother, this hip boutique attracts many of D.C.'s fashionistas with its wonderful collection of cutting-edge designers, including Prairie Underground, Collective Concepts, The Odells, Curator, Bridge and Burn, and Amodi, among others. Many of the lines are created with environmentally sustainable materials. After you've selected that perfect party dress, check out the bold, colorful jewelry and purses for an outfit that is uniquely yours. And if you need a souvenir for friends back home, the shop carries a selection of handmade soaps and candles from emerging artisans. ✉ *1921 8th St. NW, Suite 110, U Street* ☎ *202/332–4242* ⊕ *www.lettiegooch.com.*

Marine Layer

CLOTHING | This San Francisco–based retailer is known for its soft, eco-friendly, and durable T-shirts. The company's signature fabric, MicroModal, is made from beech-wood pulp and woven into the product line for men and women. In addition to T-shirts, you'll find equally comfortable dresses, pants, outerwear, loungewear, sweaters, and hats. ✉ *1627 14th St. NW, Logan Circle* ☎ *202/864–6686* ⊕ *www.marinelayer.com* Ⓜ *U St./African-Amer Civil War Memorial/Cardozo.*

ModCloth DC

CLOTHING | The only other shop in the District is by Bonobos and is similar in its mission. This is a brick-and-mortar version of ModCloth, the Web company that strives to make vintage clothing modern. While you can buy real, one-of-a-kind vintage clothing, you can also shop the floor for ModCloth originals. All of the sizes are kept in the back for you to try on, and if you purchase, your order will ship to you in a matter of days with free express shipping. Head in for personalized styling assistance and fittings as well. ✉ *1924 8th St. NW, No. 130, Shaw* ☎ *202/804–5589* ⊕ *www.modcloth.com* Ⓜ *Shaw–Howard U.*

Read Wall

CLOTHING | Well-tailored, American-made men's sportswear is the speciality at Read Wall. You'll find sport coats, chinos, dress pants, cashmere sweaters, bright waxed-cotton jackets, shorts, and lambswool scarves. The company also offers custom tailoring. ✉ *1921 8th St. NW, Suite 105, Shaw* ☎ *202/733–1913* ⊕ *www.readwall.com* Ⓜ *Shaw–Howard U.*

Redeem

CLOTHING | With street-smart clothes and accessories from all over the globe, women and men who are stuck in a fashion rut can find redemption here with brands like Bad Form, Oak, and Won Hundred. There's also a nice selection of chic jewelry, candles, and perfumes. ✉ *1810 14th St. NW, U Street* ☎ *202/332–7447* ⊕ *www.redeemus.com* Ⓜ *U St./African-Amer Civil War Memorial/Cardozo.*

HOME FURNISHINGS

Home Rule

HOUSEHOLD ITEMS/FURNITURE | Here you can find some of the latest design elements for the bathroom, kitchen, and dining room. There are also playful tissue holders and other fun and affordable household items in cheerful colors. ✉ 1807 14th St. NW, U Street ☎ 202/797–5544 ⊕ www.homerule.com Ⓜ U St./African-Amer Civil War Memorial/Cardozo.

★ Miss Pixie's

HOUSEHOLD ITEMS/FURNITURE | The well-chosen collectibles—handpicked by Miss Pixie herself—include gorgeous textiles, antique home furnishings, lamps, mirrors, glass- and silverware, and artwork. The reasonable prices will grab your attention, as will the location, in an old car-dealer showroom. ✉ 1626 14th St. NW, U Street ☎ 202/232–8171 ⊕ www.misspixies.com Ⓜ U St./African-Amer Civil War Memorial/Cardozo or Dupont Circle.

Zawadi

HOUSEHOLD ITEMS/FURNITURE | The name means "gifts" in Swahili, but you may want to buy the beautiful African art, textiles, home accessories, and jewelry for yourself. ✉ 1524 U St. NW, Suite 1, U Street ☎ 202/232–2214 ⊕ www.zawadi-arts.com Ⓜ U St./African Civil War Memorial/Cardozo.

SPECIALTY STORES

Cherry Blossom Creative

BOOKS/STATIONERY | While you can find modern, upscale stationery brands and office products here, what you should come in for are the unique neighborhood maps the company has produced. Colorful and creative, they are decorative and beautiful—and certainly suitable for framing. Many District and other trendy neighborhoods are represented in the series, including Brooklyn, Manhattan, San Francisco, Chicago, and Baltimore. The store is closed on Monday and Tuesday. ✉ 2128 8th St. NW, Shaw ☎ 202/319–2979 ⊕ www.cherryblossom-workshop.com Ⓜ Shaw–Howard U.

Shinola

SPECIALTY STORES | Once a Studebaker showroom in the 1920s, this gorgeous shop is now one of Michigan-based Shinola's nationwide flagship stores. You'll find leather-band watches; supple leather bags, coats, and journals; elegant and classic silver, gold, and rose gold jewelry designed by Pamela Love; home accessories; and yes, even bicycles. ✉ 1631 14th St. NW, U Street ☎ 202/470–0200 ⊕ www.shinola.com Ⓜ U St./African-Amer Civil War Memorial/Cardozo.

Chapter 11

UPPER NORTHWEST

Updated by
Bob Carden

⊙ Sights	🍴 Restaurants	🛏 Hotels	🛍 Shopping	🍸 Nightlife
★★★★☆	★★☆☆☆	★★☆☆☆	★★★★☆	★☆☆☆☆

NEIGHBORHOOD SNAPSHOT

TOP EXPERIENCES

■ **House museums:** The Hillwood Estate, Museum and Gardens showcase cereal heiress Marjorie Merriweather Post's collection of Imperial Russian art and Fabergé eggs, and 25 gorgeous acres of formal French and Japanese gardens. Chagalls, Picassos, and Monets inside contrast with the architecture at the modernist Kreeger Museum.

■ **National Zoo:** Visit the giant pandas, elephants, lions, and other members of the animal kingdom while you enjoy a stroll outdoors.

■ **Shopping in Friendship Heights:** Once the closest thing D.C. had to Rodeo Drive, this area is still a great shopping destination but isn't as high-end anymore; sure, there are still loads of big names, including Cartier, Tiffany, and Saks Fifth Avenue, but now those upscale retailers are sharing equal billing with T.J. Maxx and H&M.

■ **U.S. Naval Observatory:** View the heavens through one of the world's most powerful telescopes (on Monday evening with a reservation).

■ **Washington National Cathedral:** Look for the Darth Vader gargoyle on the soaring towers of this landmark, then relax among the rosebushes in the Bishop's Garden. Concerts are held here, too.

GETTING HERE

Connecticut Avenue attractions, such as the zoo, are accessible from the Red Line Metro stops between Woodley Park–Zoo/Adams Morgan and Van Ness–UDC. The Friendship Heights bus travels north from Georgetown along Wisconsin Avenue and takes you to the National Cathedral.

Parking can be tricky along Massachusetts Avenue. It is more practical for good walkers to hoof it up the street or take Bus N2, N3, N4, or N6 between Dupont Circle and Friendship Heights. For more-outlying sights, driving or cabbing it may be the best way to visit.

PLANNING YOUR TIME

■ The area has plenty of restaurants and some sights but limited nightlife compared to other parts of the city.

■ You may want to plan your zoo trip around daily programs, such as the elephant-training session or the small-mammal feeding. Animals are most active in the early morning and late afternoon.

■ Sights can be far apart, so leave time for travel and parking, if necessary.

QUICK BITES

■ **Cava.** This fast-casual restaurant offers a variety of Greek and Mediterranean bowls and is open until 10. ✉ *4237 Wisconsin Ave. NW* ⊕ *www.cava.com* Ⓜ *Tenleytown–AU.*

■ **Rocklands Barbeque.** Stop in here for great barbecue that's tasty, fast, and reasonably priced (though not near a Metro station). ✉ *2418 Wisconsin Ave. NW* ⊕ *www.rocklands.com* Ⓜ *Woodley Park–Zoo/Adams Morgan.*

■ **Vace Italian Deli.** Great pizza (whole or by the slice) and subs are all fast and good. It's open most nights until 9. ✉ *3433 Connecticut Ave. NW* ⊕ *www.vaceitaliandeli.com* Ⓜ *Cleveland Park.*

The Upper Northwest corner of D.C. is predominantly residential and in many places practically suburban. There are several good reasons, however, to visit the leafy streets, including the National Zoo and National Cathedral. If the weather is fine, spend an afternoon strolling through Hillwood Gardens or tromping through Rock Creek Park's many acres. You'll have to travel some distance to see multiple attractions in one day, but many sights are accessible on foot from local Metro stops.

Sights

Fort Reno Park

CITY PARK | At 429 feet above sea level, this highest point in Washington has been used in different eras as a Civil War fort, the site of telegraph and radio towers, and a reservoir. In 1864 Abraham Lincoln watched nearby as outnumbered Union troops defended the capital from a formidable Confederate advance led by General Early, in the only battle to take place in the capital. Today, the park is enjoyed by soccer players, dog-park regulars, and picnickers. Most of the Civil War–era earthworks are gone, and two curious faux-medieval towers, built in 1929, mark the reservoir site, which is not accessible to the public. Nonetheless, the park has an appealing city view and plenty of room to run around. A popular, free outdoor concert series takes place every summer featuring many of the area's most esteemed indie-rock acts, from Fugazi to Dismemberment Plan to Priests. ⊠ *Chesapeake St. NW at Nebraska Ave. NW, Upper Northwest* ☎ *202/895–6070 visitor information, 202/521–1493 summer concert info only* ⊕ *www.fortreno.com* Ⓜ *Tenleytown–AU.*

Glover-Archbold Park

NATIONAL/STATE PARK | Groves of beeches, elms, and oaks flourish at this 183-acre park, part of the Rock Creek system, which begins just west of Georgetown and ends, 3½ miles later, near Van Ness Street. Along the way you'll experience a stream valley with ancient trees and possible bird sightings. And chances are you'll have the trail mostly to yourself. ⊠ *Wisconsin Ave. at Van Ness St. NW, Upper Northwest* ⊕ *www.nps.gov/pohe/index.htm* Ⓜ *Tenleytown–AU.*

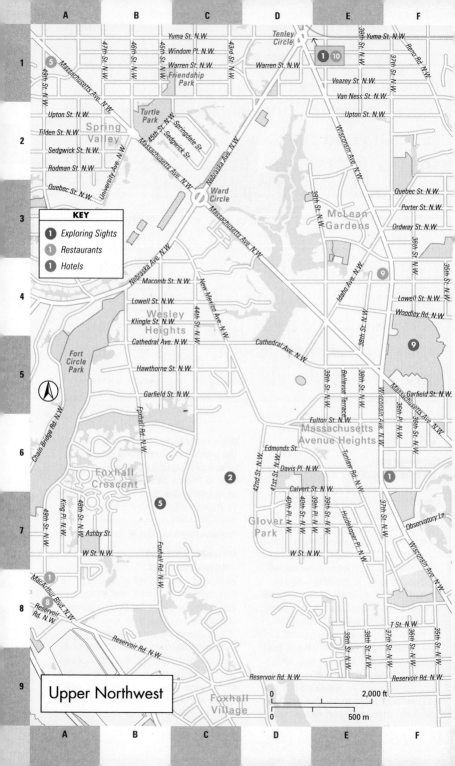

Upper Northwest

Sights ▼

1 Fort Reno Park **E1**
2 Glover-Archbold Park **C6**
3 Hillwood Estate, Museum
  and Gardens........................ **J1**
4 Khalil Gibran
  Memorial Garden **H7**
5 The Kreeger Museum **B7**
6 President Lincoln's Cottage **J7**
7 Rock Creek Park **J7**
8 Smithsonian National
  Zoological Park **J5**
9 Washington National Cathedral .. **F5**

Restaurants ▼

1 BlackSalt Fish Market &
  Restaurant......................... **A8**
2 Comet Ping Pong **G1**
3 District Kitchen **J6**
4 Duke's Counter..................... **I5**
5 Millie's.............................. **A1**
6 Parthenon Restaurant
  & Chevy Chase Lounge **G1**
7 St. Arnold's Mussel Bar........... **I3**
8 Sakedokoro Makoto............... **A8**
9 2 Amys **F4**
10 Sushiko Chevy Chase **E1**

Hotels ▼

1 Kimpton Glover Park Hotel **F6**
2 Omni Shoreham Hotel.............. **I6**
3 Washington Marriott
  Wardman Park **I6**
4 Woodley Park Guest House **I6**

11

Upper Northwest

Hillwood Estate, Museum and Gardens

HOUSE | Long before the age of Paris Hilton, cereal heiress Marjorie Merriweather Post was the most celebrated socialite of the 20th century, famous for her fabulous wealth and beauty, as well as her passion for collecting art and creating some of the world's most lavish homes. Of these, the 25-acre Hillwood Estate, which Merriweather Post bought in 1955, is the only one now open to the public. The 36-room Georgian mansion, where she regularly hosted presidents, diplomats, and royalty, is sumptuously appointed, with a formal Louis XVI drawing room, private movie theater and ballroom, and magnificent libraries filled with portraits of the glamorous hostess and her family and acquaintances, as well as works from her rich art collection. She was especially fascinated with Russian art, and her collection of Russian icons, tapestries, gold and silver work, and Fabergé eggs is considered to be the largest and most significant outside Russia. She devoted equal attention to her gardens; you can wander through 13 acres of them. Allow two to three hours to tour. ⊠ *4155 Linnean Ave. NW, Upper Northwest* ☎ *202/686–5807, 202/686–8500* ⊕ *www.hillwoodmuseum. org* ⊠ *$18 ($15 weekdays if purchased online)* ⊗ *Closed Mon.* Ⓜ *Van Ness–UDC.*

Kahlil Gibran Memorial Garden

CITY PARK | In a town known for political combat, this tiny urban park is a wonderful place to find some peace. The shady park combines Western and Arab symbols and is perfect for contemplation. From the Massachusetts Avenue entrance, a stone walk bridges a grassy swale. Farther on are limestone benches, engraved with sayings from Gibran that curve around a fountain and a bust of the namesake Lebanese-born poet, who emigrated to the United States at the turn of the 20th century and remains one of the best-selling poets of all time. The garden is near the grounds of the United States Naval Observatory and across from the British Embassy. ⊠ *3100 block of Massachusetts Ave. NW, Upper Northwest* ☎ *202/895–6000* ⊠ *Free* Ⓜ *Woodley Park–Zoo/Adams Morgan or Dupont Circle.*

The Kreeger Museum

MUSEUM | The cool white domes and elegant lines of this postmodern landmark stand in stark contrast to the traditional feel of the rest of the Foxhall Road neighborhood. Designed in 1963 by iconic architect Philip Johnson, the building was once the home of GEICO insurance executive David Lloyd Kreeger and his wife, Carmen. Music is a central theme of the art and the space: the Kreegers wanted a showpiece residence that would also function as a gallery and recital hall. The art collection includes works by Renoir, Degas, Cézanne, and Munch, African artifacts, and outstanding examples of Asian art. Especially stunning are the outdoor sculptures, including works by Henry Moore and Leonardo Nierman, among others, and six large-scale John L. Dreyfuss pieces that surround the museum's reflecting pool. The domed rooms also have wonderful acoustics, and serve as an excellent performance venue for the classical concerts that are regularly performed here. The museum is not reachable by Metro; you need to take a car or taxi to get here. ⊠ *2401 Foxhall Rd. NW, Upper Northwest* ☎ *202/338–3552* ⊕ *www.kreegermuseum.org* ⊠ *$10, Sculpture Garden free* ⊗ *Closed Sun. and Mon.*

President Lincoln's Cottage

HOUSE | In June 1862 President Lincoln moved from the White House to this Gothic Revival cottage on the grounds of the Soldiers' Home to escape the oppressive heat of Washington and to grieve for the loss of his son Willie. Lincoln and his wife, Mary, lived in the cottage until November of that year, and because they found it to be a welcome respite from wartime tensions, they returned again during the summers of 1863 and 1864. Lincoln ultimately spent a quarter of his presidency at this quiet retreat; he was here just one day before he was assassinated. Considered the most significant historic site of President Lincoln's presidency outside the White House, it was here that the president developed the Emancipation Proclamation. Visitors may picnic on the cottage grounds, which have been landscaped to look as they did when Lincoln lived here. ■ TIP→ As you go up the hill toward the Cottage, there's a panoramic view of the city, including the Capitol dome. The 251-acre Soldier's Home sits atop the third-tallest point in D.C. ⊠ Armed Forces Retirement Home, 140 Rock Creek Church Rd. and Upshur St. NW, Petworth ☎ 202/829–0436 ⊕ www.lincolncottage.org ⊠ $15 Ⓜ Georgia Ave.–Petworth.

★ Rock Creek Park

NATIONAL/STATE PARK | FAMILY | The 1,800 acres surrounding Rock Creek have provided a cool oasis for visitors and D.C. residents ever since Congress set them aside for recreational use in 1890. The bubbling, rocky stream draws nature lovers to the miles of paved walkways. Bicycle routes, jogging and hiking paths, and equestrian trails wind through the groves of dogwoods, beeches, oaks, and cedars, and 30 picnic areas are scattered about. An asphalt bike path running through the park has a few challenging hills but is mostly flat, and it's possible to bike several miles without having to stop for cars (the roadway is closed entirely to cars on weekends). The most popular run in Rock Creek Park is along a trail that follows the creek from Georgetown to the National Zoo, about 4 miles round-trip. Rangers at the Nature Center and Planetarium introduce visitors to the park and keep track of daily events; guided nature walks leave from the center on weekends at 2. The park is open only during daylight hours. ⊠ 5200 Glover Rd. NW, Nature Center and Planetarium, Upper Northwest ☎ 202/895–6070 ⊕ www.nps.gov/rocr.

★ Smithsonian National Zoological Park

ZOO | FAMILY | The Smithsonian's National Zoo features 1,800 animals, representing 300 species, in as close as you can get to their native surroundings. Get there between 11 and 2 (weather permitting), and you can catch organgutans traversing the "O" line, a series of cables and towers near the Great Ape House that allow the primates to swing hand over hand about 35 feet above your head. The giant pandas, Tian Tian and Mei Xiang, have been the zoo's most famous residents since 2000; one of their cubs also resides here and delights visitors of all ages. The zoo was designed by famed landscape architect Frederick Law Olmsted, who also designed New York's Central Park. Try visiting early morning or late afternoon since many animals sleep midday. Nighttime visits are especially fun during the Thanksgiving and Christmas holidays as the zoo sparkles with the annual ZooLights event. ⊠ 3001 Connecticut Ave. NW, Upper Northwest ☎ 202/673–4800, 202/673–4717 ⊕ nationalzoo.si.edu ⊠ Free Ⓜ Cleveland Park or Woodley Park–Zoo/Adams Morgan.

★ Washington National Cathedral

RELIGIOUS SITE | Construction of the sixth-largest cathedral in the world began in 1907 with a rock from the village of Bethlehem and has been the spiritual symbol of Washington ever since. Like its 14th-century Gothic counterparts, the stunning structure has a nave, flying buttresses, transepts, and vaults, all built stone by stone. The cathedral is Episcopalian, but it's the site of frequent interfaith services. State funerals for presidents Eisenhower, Reagan, and Ford as well as Senator John McCain were held here, and the tomb of Woodrow Wilson is on the south side of the grounds. The Pilgrim Observation Gallery provides a wonderful view of the city, and the cathedral is blessed with the lovely Bishop's Garden, with boxwoods, ivy, yew trees and stone work from European ruins. In 2011, the cathedral sustained earthquake damage; restoration work is expected to continue for several years, but the cathedral remains open during the process. ✉ *Wisconsin and Massachusetts Aves. NW, Upper Northwest* ☎ *202/537–6200, 202/537–6207 tour information* ⊕ *www. nationalcathedral.org* ⚑ *From $12* Ⓜ *Cleveland Park or Tenleytown–AU, then take any 30 series bus.*

🍴 Restaurants

After the requisite cooing over the pandas and other cuddly creatures at the National Zoo, consider wandering around this popular neighborhood, where you'll see plenty of locals eating, drinking, and playing. Many Hill staffers, journalists, and other inside-the-Beltway types live along this hilly stretch of Connecticut Avenue. Eateries and shops line the few blocks near each of the Red Line Metro stops. Restaurants in Cleveland Park range from tiny takeout spots to upscale restaurants where you stand a good chance of spying your favorite Sunday-morning talk-show guests at a nearby table. International cuisines are abundant here, especially in Cleveland Park. Lined up along the stately stretch of modern row houses are diverse dining options ranging from Afghan to Thai.

BlackSalt Fish Market & Restaurant

$$$ | SEAFOOD | Just beyond Georgetown in the residential neighborhood of Palisades, BlackSalt is part fish market, part gossipy neighborhood hangout, part swanky restaurant. Fish offerings dominate, and vary from classics like oysters Rockefeller and fried Ipswich clams to more-offbeat fixings like cocoa-spiced big-eye tuna and a butterscotch *pot de crème* for dessert. **Known for:** fresh fish dishes; one of the best brunches in D.C.; brioche French toast. Ⓢ *Average main: $33* ✉ *4883 MacArthur Blvd., Upper Northwest* ☎ *202/342–9101* ⊕ *www. blacksaltrestaurant.com* ⊘ *No lunch Mon.–Sat.*

Comet Ping Pong

$ | PIZZA | FAMILY | Pizza (and beer) in the front, Ping-Pong (and foosball) in the back make this pizza joint a neighborhood favorite for folks of all ages. While you can make your own pizza (including one with a gluten-free crust) from almost three dozen toppings, you'll be well served opting for one of the kitchen's specialty pizzas. **Known for:** make-your-own pizzas with dozens of toppings; Ping-Pong and foosball tables; sunrise pizza for brunch. Ⓢ *Average main: $12* ✉ *5037 Connecticut Ave. NW, Upper Northwest* ☎ *202/364–0404* ⊕ *www. cometpingpong.com* ⊘ *No lunch Mon.–Thurs.* Ⓜ *Cleveland Park.*

District Kitchen

$$ | AMERICAN | FAMILY | The exposed brick and warm woods may signal upscale saloon, but District Kitchen is much more, offering an eclectic, farm-to-table menu featuring the restaurant's signature dish, a large and tasty bowl of paella. Sure, there are burgers, steaks, and the like, but also charcuterie, cheese plates, mussel plates, seared shrimp, and a load of fish dishes. **Known for:** monster signature paella dish; good seafood; nice beer selection. Ⓢ *Average main: $20* ✉ *2606 Wisconsin Ave. NW, Woodley Park* ☎ *202/238–9408* ⊕ *www.districtkitchen. com* ⊘ *No lunch Mon.–Thurs.* Ⓜ *Woodley Park–Adams Morgan/Zoo.*

Duke's Counter

$ | BRITISH | FAMILY | A shabby-chic bar-restaurant directly across the street from the National Zoo has been deemed by one local paper to have the best burger in D.C. If it's not the best, it's close: a big, tasty patty made from charbroiled Angus beef that's on a pub menu with other Continental options, including British breakfasts offered all day. **Known for:** excellent burgers; wide-ranging menu of sandwiches and small plates; small and busy (so get there early or wait). Ⓢ *Average main: $14* ✉ *3000 Connecticut Ave., Northwest* ☎ *202/733–4808* ⊕ *www.*

dukescounter.com Ⓜ *Woodley Park–Zoo/ Adams Morgan.*

Millie's

$$ | AMERICAN | FAMILY | This classic neighborhood bar and restaurant has a menu that concentrates on seafood, with both Cape Cod and Baja influences, bringing a coastal dining experience to the city with a winning formula. The menu includes cod, lobster rolls, fish tacos, and even panfried trout. **Known for:** inventive seafood; casual coastal atmosphere; takeout ice cream counter. Ⓢ *Average main: $21* ✉ *4866 Massachusetts Ave. NW, Northwest* ☎ *202/733–5789* ⊕ *www. milliesdc.com* Ⓜ *Tenleytown–AU.*

★ Parthenon Restaurant & Chevy Chase Lounge

$$ | GREEK | You can never have enough Greek restaurants, and Parthenon is among the best in town. This is traditional Greek food, including great moussaka, pastitsio, salads, and grilled fish. **Known for:** traditional Greek cooking in a blue and white taverna setting; large portions; attached to Chevy Chase Lounge. Ⓢ *Average main: $25* ✉ *5510 Connecticut Ave. NW, Upper Northwest* ☎ *202/966–7600* ⊕ *www.parthenon-restaurant.com* Ⓜ *Friendship Heights.*

Sakedokoro Makoto

$$$$ | JAPANESE | Leave your shoes at the door upon entering this Japanese *omakase* restaurant, where the chef's ever-changing menu showcases modern Japanese cooking. In the past, dishes in these multicourse meals have included tempura soft shell crabs, a pan-seared sea urchin with crispy rice cake, and pork in a cabbage roll. **Known for:** traditional omakase restaurant; strict reservation policy; always changing, multicourse menus. Ⓢ *Average main: $70* ✉ *4822 MacArthur Blvd. NW, Upper Northwest* ☎ *202/298–8866* ⊕ *sakedokoromakoto. com* ☾ *Closed Sun. and Mon. No lunch.*

St. Arnold's Mussel Bar

$$ | BELGIAN | FAMILY | A casual spot near the zoo, this Belgian restaurant offers loads of Belgian beers on tap, large plates of mussels and fries, and Belgian waffles for dessert. The restaurant has two levels, but the street level is much more inviting. **Known for:** great mussels and beer; outdoor dining in the summer; fun happy hour. Ⓢ *Average main: $18* ✉ *3433 Connecticut Ave. NW, Cleveland Park* ☎ *202/621–6719* ⊕ *starnoldsmusselbar.com* Ⓜ *Cleveland Park.*

Sushiko Chevy Chase

$$ | JAPANESE | At the city's self-touted first raw-fish restaurant, the cuts are always ocean fresh, the cocktails fruity, and the presentations classic. Think blue crab topped with avocado and tuna crowned by jalapeño, while hot delicacies like melt-on-the-tongue fried tempura are always reliable. **Known for:** pioneer of the D.C. sushi scene; classic sushi presentations; bread pudding with green tea mousse for dessert. Ⓢ *Average main: $24* ✉ *5455 Wisconsin Ave. NW, Chevy Chase* ☎ *301/961–1644* ⊕ *www.sushiko-restaurants.com* Ⓜ *Friendship Heights.*

★ 2 Amys

$$ | PIZZA | FAMILY | Call it the Brando of D.C. pizzerias, because this Neapolitan sensation has played godfather to a number of throne-stealing wood ovens elsewhere in town since it opened more than a decade ago. Simple recipes allow the ingredients to shine through and make the "wine bar" menu of small Italian plates as exemplary as the pies. **Known for:** authentic Neapolitan wood-fired pizza with a chewy crust; pancetta happy hour on Saturday; family-friendly (read: noisy) atmosphere. Ⓢ *Average main: $20* ✉ *3715 Macomb St. NW, Upper Northwest* ☎ *202/885–5700* ⊕ *2amyspizza. com* ▭ *No credit cards* ☾ *No lunch Mon.*

Hotels

Whether you travel north through Rock Creek Park on a scenic jaunt, or head up Connecticut Avenue past the National Zoo, or take Wisconsin Avenue starting at the Washington National Cathedral, you see a diverse collection of prosperous neighborhoods with single-family homes, apartment high-rises, and shopping districts. These Upper Northwest communities won't have as many museums or as much history as the other parts of D.C., but they still have plenty of sights, movie theaters, and minimalls.

Kimpton Glover Park Hotel
$$ | **HOTEL** | In the heart of Embassy Row (and near Washington Cathedral and Dumbarton Oaks) is this Kimpton hotel and its beautifully decorated rooms with lovely views of the city. **Pros:** classic Kimpton service, charm, and extras; spacious rooms; great Italian restaurant. **Cons:** distance from Metro and Downtown; valet parking is $35 per day; hefty daily amenity fee. [$] *Rooms from: $289* ✉ *2505 Wisconsin Ave. NW, Upper Northwest* ☎ *202/337–9700* 🌐 *www.gloverparkhotel.com* 🛏 *150 rooms* 🍴 *No meals* [M] *Woodley Park–Zoo/Adams Morgan.*

★ **Omni Shoreham Hotel**
$$$$ | **HOTEL** | **FAMILY** | Since its opening in 1930, this elegant landmark overlooking Rock Creek Park, a Historic Hotel of America, has welcomed heads of state, U.S. politicians, and celebs like the Beatles, Judy Garland, and Bob Hope. **Pros:** historic property with gorgeous grounds; great pool and sundeck; good views from many rooms; walking/jogging trails through Rock Creek Park. **Cons:** not near major sights; noisy at times; extremely large. [$] *Rooms from: $409* ✉ *2500 Calvert St. NW, Woodley Park, Upper Northwest* ☎ *202/234–0700, 800/834–6664* 🌐 *www.omnihotels.com* 🛏 *834 rooms* 🍴 *No meals* [M] *Woodley Park–Zoo/Adams Morgan.*

Washington Marriott Wardman Park
$$$ | **HOTEL** | **FAMILY** | In a pleasant neighborhood, this is a good choice for families—kids will love the outdoor pool and the proximity to the pandas at the zoo—and is popular with groups. **Pros:** right next to Metro stop; light-filled sundeck and pool; pretty residential neighborhood with lots of restaurants. **Cons:** busy and hectic public areas; massive size; fee for in-room Wi-Fi. [$] *Rooms from: $379* ✉ *2660 Woodley Rd. NW, Woodley Park, Upper Northwest* ☎ *202/328–2000, 800/228–9290* 🌐 *www.marriott.com* 🛏 *1152 rooms* 🍴 *No meals* [M] *Woodley Park–Zoo/Adams Morgan.*

★ **Woodley Park Guest House**
$$ | **B&B/INN** | Experience the height of hospitality at this charming bed-and-breakfast on a quiet residential street near the zoo. **Pros:** close to Metro; excellent breakfast; friendly and welcoming hosts. **Cons:** some shared baths; limited privacy; no television. [$] *Rooms from: $260* ✉ *2647 Woodley Rd. NW, Woodley Park, Upper Northwest* ☎ *202/667–0218, 866/667–0218* 🌐 *www.dcinns.com* 🛏 *15 rooms* 🍴 *Free Breakfast* [M] *Woodley Park–Zoo/Adams Morgan.*

Performing Arts

Summer is when the performing arts come alive in Upper Northwest D.C. One of the city's gems is Carter Barron, an outdoor amphitheater in Rock Creek Park that offers a variety of musical and cinema events during August. Other venues include the refurbished Avalon Theatre, which features outstanding documentaries and hard-to-find independent films. Some of the biggest blockbuster films are presented at the historic Loews Cineplex Uptown, which has the largest film screen in town.

FILM

AMC Loews Uptown 1
FILM | This is a true movie palace, with art deco flourishes; a wonderful balcony;

and—in two happy concessions to modernity—crystal clear Dolby sound and a Christie Dual-Projector 3-D system. The theater boasts the town's largest movie screen, almost three times the size of a standard screen with triple the effect. ✉ *3426 Connecticut Ave. NW, Cleveland Park, Upper Northwest* ☎ *202/966–5400* ⊕ *www.amctheatres. com/uptown1* Ⓜ *Cleveland Park.*

Avalon Theatre

FILM | FAMILY | This classic movie house from 1923 is D.C.'s only nonprofit film center. The theater offers a wide array of studio films and independent and foreign films, plus monthly showcases of the best in French, Israeli, Czech, and Greek cinema. The theater also offers programming for families and children. ✉ *5612 Connecticut Ave. NW, Upper Northwest* ☎ *202/966–6000 info line, 202/966– 3464 box office* ⊕ *www.theavalon.org* Ⓜ *Friendship Heights.*

MUSIC

Washington National Cathedral

MUSIC | Concerts and recitals by visiting musicians augment the choral and church groups that frequently perform in this breathtaking cathedral. Organ recitals on the massive pipe organ are offered every Sunday afternoon and the choir sings Evensong most weekdays around 5:30. Admission is frequently free. ✉ *Massachusetts and Wisconsin Aves. NW, Cathedral Heights, Upper Northwest* ⊹ *From Tenleytown–AU Metro station, take any 30 series bus south* ☎ *202/537–6207* ⊕ *www.nationalcathe-dral.org* Ⓜ *Tenleytown–AU.*

🛍 Shopping

The major thoroughfare, Wisconsin Avenue, runs northwest through the city from Georgetown toward Maryland. It crosses the border in the midst of the Friendship Heights shopping district, which is also near Chevy Chase. It's at this border where you'll find the Chevy

Chase Pavilion with retailers, including H&M, J.Crew, Marshalls, Nordstrom Rack, Old Navy, and World Market. Other chains like Anthropologie, Saks Fifth Avenue, and Bloomingdale's can be found at The Shops at Wisconsin Avenue and at Mazza Gallerie. This neighborhood also boasts stand-alone designer stores like Christian Dior, Jimmy Choo, Ralph Lauren, and Tiffany and Co. There are a few local gems in the surrounding area. Other neighborhoods in the District yield more interesting finds and offer more enjoyable shopping and sightseeing, but it's hard to beat Friendship Heights/Upper Northwest for sheer convenience and selection.

BOOKS

★ Politics and Prose

BOOKS/STATIONERY | After being bought by two former *Washington Post* reporters in 2011, this legendary independent continues the tradition of jam-packed author events and signings. In the coffee shop and wine bar downstairs, The Den, you can debate the issues of the day or read a book while enjoying a casual meal or snack. ✉ *5015 Connecticut Ave. NW, Upper Northwest* ☎ *202/364–1919* ⊕ *www.politics-prose.com* Ⓜ *Van Ness–UDC.*

CLOTHING

★ Catch Can

CLOTHING | Bright and breezy clothes made of mostly natural fibers, plus comfortable but playful shoes and funky rain boots, make casual wear as fun as it is practical. The owners' love of color continues with a sizeable collection of jewelry, greeting cards, housewares, and soaps. ✉ *5516 Connecticut Ave. NW, Upper Northwest* ☎ *202/686–5316* ⊕ *www.catchcan.com* Ⓜ *Friendship Heights.*

Everett Hall

CLOTHING | D.C.'s own Everett Hall designs men's suits that are richly classic in their material and cutting-edge in their design, color, and sensibility. Starting at around

$1,500, the suits appeal to professionals who want something unique. ⊠ *Chevy Chase Pavillion, 5301 Wisconsin Ave. NW, Friendship Heights* ☏ *202/362–0191* ⊕ *www.everetthallboutique.com* Ⓜ *Friendship Heights.*

Julia Farr

CLOTHING | Women who lobby on Capitol Hill and lunch at the country club look to Julia for a professional and polished look. Decorated in soothing sea shades, her boutique carries classic styles from emerging and established designers. Farr also has her own fashion line of classic and elegant wardrobe staples including skirts, blouses, jackets, and dresses inspired by D.C.'s historical and cultural landmarks. And, since they're named after these landmarks, any item would make a beautifully practical souvenir. Appointments are welcomed. ⊠ *5232 44th St. NW, Upper Northwest* ☏ *202/364–3277* ⊕ *www.juliafarrdc.com* Ⓜ *Friendship Heights.*

Tabandeh

CLOTHING | Located in the Mazza Gallerie, this avant-garde women's collection includes an expertly selected cache of Rick Owens tops and Ann Demeulemeester clothing, along with accessories including stunning leather belts and handbags. The jewelry pieces in the store are dazzling—rings, necklaces, earrings, and pendants made with precious and semiprecious stones from designers like Samiar 13 and Erickson Beamon—and are sure to add panache to your wardrobe. ⊠ *5300 Wisconsin Ave. NW, Upper Northwest* ☏ *202/966–5080* ⊕ *www. tabandehjewelry.com* Ⓜ *Friendship Heights.*

FOOD AND WINE

Calvert Woodley Fine Wines and Spirits

FOOD/CANDY | In addition to the excellent selection of wine and hard liquor, 200 kinds of cheese and other picnic and cocktail-party fare is on hand. The international offerings have made this a favorite pantry for embassy parties. ⊠ *4339 Connecticut Ave. NW, Upper Northwest* ☏ *202/966–4400* ⊕ *www.calvertwoodley. com* Ⓜ *Van Ness–UDC.*

Rodman's Discount Foods and Drugstore

FOOD/CANDY | The rare store that carries wine, cheese, and space heaters, Rodman's is a fascinating hybrid of Target and Dean & DeLuca. The appliances are downstairs, the imported peppers and chocolates upstairs. ⊠ *5100 Wisconsin Ave. NW, Upper Northwest* ☏ *202/363–3466* ⊕ *www.rodmans.com* Ⓜ *Friendship Heights.*

GIFTS

Periwinkle Gifts

FOOD/CANDY | A panoply of gift options are available in these warm and welcoming surroundings: boutique chocolates, cases of nutty and gummy treats, handmade jewelry, Stonewall Kitchen snacks, hand-designed wrapping paper, scented bath products, and printed note cards. ⊠ *3815 Livingston St. NW, Upper Northwest* ☏ *202/364–3076* ⊕ *www.periwinklegiftsdc.com* Ⓜ *Friendship Heights.*

Chapter 12

D.C. WATERFRONT

Updated by
Alison Thoet

◉ Sights	🍴 Restaurants	🛏 Hotels	🛍 Shopping	🍸 Nightlife
★★★★☆	★★★★★	★★★★★	★★★★☆	★★★★★

NEIGHBORHOOD SNAPSHOT

TOP EXPERIENCES

■ **The Wharf:** The newest spot on the District's waterfront offers many dining options at all price points, live music offerings, seasonal events, and waterfront recreation.

■ **Pier at The Wharf:** From bench swings and boardwalks to paddleboards and a kids' park, the piers at The Wharf are the best place to experience the waterfront in D.C.

■ **The Yards:** The Yards offer miles of walking track along D.C.'s waterfront, a grassy area for picnics and concerts, first-class restaurants, D.C.'s first winery, and a wading pool for the kids.

■ **Music Venues:** The Anthem is the District's newest music venue and great for a night out, with its 6,000-person-capacity industrial space packed with the newest performers. Also, check out Union Stage and Pearl Street Warehouse at The Wharf.

■ **Dining:** Waterfront restaurants are among the best and newest in the District, with tons of different cuisine, style, and price options. Be sure to reserve: they're also popular.

GETTING HERE

By road, Metro, or via the Potomac River, the Waterfront has many options for transportation. Take the Green Line directly to the Navy Yard–Ballpark station to put you right by The Yards and Nationals Stadium. The Waterfront station will put you a 10- to 15-minute walk from The Wharf. The round-trip SW Neighborhood Shuttle also runs daily between The Wharf and L'Enfant Plaza/VRE station, the National Mall, and L'Enfant Retail on 10th Street SW. The Wharf also has water-taxi service from Transit Pier, connecting to stops in Georgetown, Maryland's National Harbor, and Old Town Alexandria in Virginia. Check out The Wharf's website for hours of operation. Parking at the Waterfront can be limited and expensive, so keep that in mind before going, and expect heavy traffic on weekends. The Green Line continues on to Anacostia, but you can also reach the area by bicycle, bus, or even boat.

PLANNING YOUR TIME

■ Allow extra time if exploring any of the museums. If you are in the mood for a concert, check out the many venues. All the restaurants here are popular and busy, so make reservations. Most of the shops in the Waterfront are open daily and great if you have time to kill before a meal. If you want a sportier day, pack accordingly for getting in the Potomac or pool.

QUICK BITES

■ **Dolcezza.** When in need of coffee on The Wharf, pick up an Italian espresso and perhaps a gelato or pastry as well. ⊠ *99 District Sq. SW* ⊕ *dolcezzagelato.com* Ⓜ *Waterfront.*

■ **Milk Bar.** Stop in for delicious and unique desserts like "crack pie," Cereal Milk soft serve, or birthday cake like you've never seen. ⊠ *49 District Sq. SW* ⊕ *milkbarstore.com* Ⓜ *Waterfront.*

■ **Shake Shack.** The famous one-stop shop for all things burgers, fries, and shakes. ⊠ *975 Wharf St. SW* ⊕ *www.shakeshack.com* Ⓜ *Waterfront.*

The District has finally expanded the Waterfront area with the Navy Yard and The Wharf, the two newest areas along the water. World-class parks, waterfront recreation, convenient shopping, one-of-a-kind dining, two sports stadiums, and premier events are all part of Capitol Riverfront, a 500-acre neighborhood along the Anacostia River in Southeast D.C. that encompasses the Navy's oldest outpost on shore. The Naval Yard is where you'll find the National Museum of the U.S. Navy; its west side is flanked by a waterfront boardwalk that is part of the Anacostia Riverwalk Trail, which is popular for cyclists, runners, and walkers. Waterfront recreation is abundant along the boardwalk with its 52-slip marina, where you can rent kayaks, canoes, and paddleboards.

👁 Sights

Some of the sights in this area are actually in the Navy Yard. To gain entrance, you'll need a government-issued photo ID (driver's license, passport card, or passport) if you are over 18.

Audi Field

SPORTS VENUE | Soccer is incredibly popular in the nation's capital, finding a major following among the international residents who miss the big matches of home, as well as families whose kids play the sport. In 2018, fans of

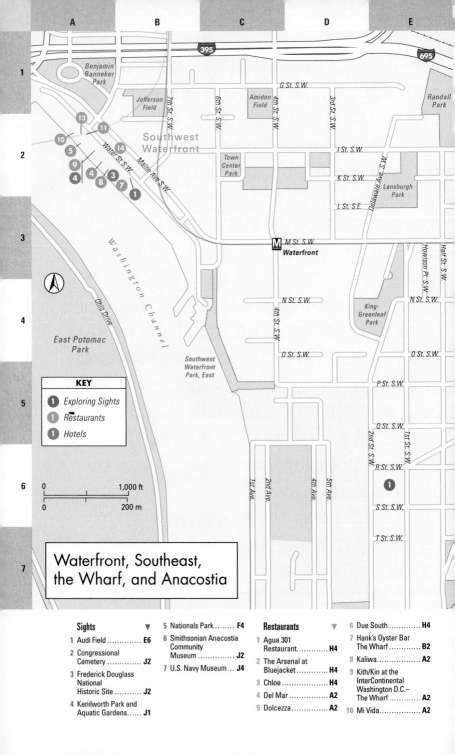

Waterfront, Southeast, the Wharf, and Anacostia

KEY
- ① Exploring Sights
- ① Restaurants
- ① Hotels

| 0 | 1,000 ft |
| 0 | 200 m |

Washington's Major League Soccer team, D.C. United, were wowed with the opening of Audi Field, an innovative 20,000-seat stadium near the revitalized Southwest waterfront and just a few blocks from Nationals Park. Aside from the 31 luxury suites, the facility boasts 500,000 square feet of on-site retail, office, and residential space. The team's 2018 acquisition of the international superstar Wayne Rooney has only fueled the excitement. ⊠ *100 Potomac Ave. SW, Southwest* ☎ *202/587–5000* ⊕ *www.dcunited.com/audi-field* Ⓜ *Navy Yard–Ballpark.*

Congressional Cemetery

CEMETERY | Established in 1807 "for all denomination of people," this cemetery is the final resting place for such notables as U.S. Capitol architect William Thornton, Marine Corps march composer John Philip Sousa, Civil War photographer Mathew Brady, FBI director J. Edgar Hoover, and many members of Congress. Air Force veteran and gay rights activist Leonard Matlovich is also buried here under a tombstone that reads "When I was in the military, they gave me a medal for killing two men and a discharge for loving one." The cemetery is about a 20-minute walk from the Capitol. You can take your own self-guided tour year-round during daylight hours; pick up a map at the gatehouse or download one from the cemetery website. On Saturday from April through October, you can join one of the free, one-hour docent-led tours at 11 am; no reservations are required. Additionally, on the third Saturday of the month at 1 pm, there are often Civil War–themed tours. ⊠ *1801 E St. SE, Capitol Hill* ☎ *202/543–0539* ⊕ *www.congressionalcemetery.org* Ⓜ *Stadium–Armory or Potomac Ave.*

Frederick Douglass National Historic Site

GARDEN | Cedar Hill, the Anacostia home of abolitionist Frederick Douglass, was one of the first Black National Historic Sites that Congress designated.

Douglass, a former slave born in 1818 who escaped to freedom and delivered rousing abolitionist speeches at home and abroad, resided here from 1877 until his death in 1895. The house has a wonderful view of Washington across the Anacostia River and contains many of Douglass's personal belongings. The home has been meticulously restored to its original grandeur; you can view Douglass's hundreds of books displayed on his custom-built bookshelves, and Limoges china on the family dining table. A short film on Douglass's life is shown at a nearby visitor center. Entry to the home requires participation in a 30-minute ranger-led tour, for which you must arrive 30 minutes in advance; reserve by phone or online (⊕ *www.recreation.gov*). ⊠ *1411 W St. SE, Anacostia* ☎ *202/426–5961, 202/444–6777 museum tours* ⊕ *www. nps.gov/frdo* 🎟 *House $2; garden and visitor center free* Ⓜ *Anacostia.*

Kenilworth Park and Aquatic Gardens

GARDEN | Exotic water lilies, lotuses, hyacinths, and other water-loving plants thrive in this 8-acre sanctuary of quiet ponds, protected wetlands, and marshy flats, listed on the National Register of Historic Places. The gardens' wetland animals include turtles, frogs, beavers, spring azure butterflies, and dozens of species of birds, which may be seen along the 1.5-mile walking trails. ■ TIP → **Visit in July for the peak lily bloom; 9 am is the best time to see early morning blossoms.** There's a tiny, child-friendly museum in the visitor center. The nearest Metro stop is a 10-minute walk away, but there is ample free parking. Exit gates are locked promptly at 4. ⊠ *1550 Anacostia Ave., Anacostia* ✛ *At Douglas St. NE* ☎ *202/692–6080* ⊕ *www.nps.gov/keaq* 🎟 *Free* Ⓜ *Deanwood.*

Nationals Park

SPORTS VENUE | Just over a decade ago, Nationals Park opened and brought new life to the Navy Yard area, where new bars and restaurants are constantly springing to life. The ballpark hosts 81 games per season, and while Nats fans come out in droves, the park isn't just for lovers of the game. Nationals Park was created to bring high-quality entertainment to the District and now has a reputation for some of the best outdoor concerts in the area, with past performances by Billy Joel, Bruce Springsteen, Elton John, Taylor Swift, the Eagles, and James Taylor. Whether you come for a game or concert, there are plenty of retail spaces and food-service venues like the Budweiser Terrace with its happy hour, a Ben's Chili Bowl, and the Chesapeake Crab Cake Company. There are also activities and areas for children and families with the brand-new Kids Play Area, Virtual Reality Home Run Derby, and a state-of-the-art Nursing Mothers Lounge. ⊠ *1500 S. Capitol St. SE, Navy Yard* ☎ *202/675–6287* ⊕ *www.mlb.com/was/ ballpark/information* 🖃 *Tours $15* Ⓜ *Navy Yard–Ballpark.*

Smithsonian Anacostia Community Museum
MUSEUM | FAMILY | A pioneer in the community museum movement, in a historically black neighborhood in Southeast Washington, this museum examines the impact of contemporary social issues on urban communities, including environment, urban life, and encounters with other cultures. The engaging exhibitions employ video, art, crafts, and photography, along with dynamic public programs including musical performances, crafts workshops, and storytellers. The museum's striking facade features traditional African design elements: brickwork patterns evoke West African kente cloth, the concrete cylinders reference the stone towers of Zimbabwe, and diamond patterned adornments resemble those found on the adobe houses of Mali. The museum is near the Frederick Douglass National Historic Site and Kenilworth Aquatic Gardens. There's free on-site parking if you drive. ⊠ *1901 Fort Pl. SE, Anacostia* ☎ *202/633–4820,*

202/633–4844 group tours ⊕ *anacostia. si.edu* 🖃 *Free* Ⓜ *Anacostia, then bBus W2/W3.*

U.S. Navy Museum
MUSEUM | The history of the U.S. Navy, from the Revolution to the present, is chronicled here, with exhibits ranging from the fully rigged foremast of the USS *Constitution* (better known as *Old Ironsides*) to a U.S. Navy Corsair fighter plane hanging from the ceiling. All around are models of fighting ships, a real Vietnam-era Swift boat, working periscopes, and displays on famous naval battles along with portraits of the sailors who fought in them. In front of the museum is a collection of guns, cannons, and missiles. The **Navy Art Collection,** including many works by Navy artists, is also housed in the museum. Explore the **Cold War Gallery** in Building 70 with exhibits that explore the Navy's response to the threat of Soviet military power and communist ideology. ⚠ **All visitors to the museum must have a valid photo ID and report to the Visitor Control Center (VCC) at the Washington Navy Yard's primary access gate at 11th and O Streets. The VCC is only open weekdays until 3:30 pm. If you're planning to visit the museum on the weekend, you must be prevetted. A Base Access Pass Registration must be submitted at least seven days before your visit. Call 202/433–3018 for access-related questions.** ⊠ *Navy Yard, 805 Kidder Breese St. SE, Building 76, Southeast* ⊹ *Enter through visitor gate at 11th and O Sts. SE and show a valid photo ID; you'll receive a pass and map of surroundings* ☎ *202/685–0589 museum, 202/433–4882 USS Barry* ⊕ *www.history. navy.mil* 🖃 *Free* Ⓜ *Eastern Market or Navy Yard–Ballpark.*

 Restaurants

Some great new restaurants have opened in The Wharf to supplement the area's other dining spots. Many of these restaurants are particularly popular on game days.

Agua 301 Restaurant

$$ | **MEXICAN** | If you are looking to get your Mexican food fix, you'll be impressed with the modern approaches to traditional Mexican food on this sophisticated menu. More traditional tacos and empanadas stand beside innovative Mexican-inflected takes on paella and chicken Milanese. **Known for:** modern Mexican cuisine; great empanadas and tacos; extensive mezcal and tequila list. [$] *Average main: $20* ✉ *Yards Park, 301 Water St. SE, Navy Yard* ☎ *202/484–0301* 🌐 *www.agua301.com* [M] *Navy Yard–Ballpark.*

The Arsenal at Bluejacket

$$ | **CONTEMPORARY** | Most restaurants pair beers with food, but here you'll find the opposite: refined but hearty new American fare designed to complement the 20 brews on tap. If you're not sure whether an herbal saison or the spicy fruit of a Scotch ale would go best with a bone-in beef short rib in a Kansas City rub, don't be afraid to ask the gracious cast of servers. **Known for:** in-house brewery that produces excellent speciality beer; industrial vibe; fantastic Sunday brunch. [$] *Average main: $22* ✉ *300 Tingey St. SE, Navy Yard* ☎ *202/524–2862* 🌐 *www.bluejacketdc.com* 🕒 *No lunch Sat.*

Chloe

$$ | **INTERNATIONAL** | Perfectly positioned between casual and sophisticated, local and upscale, this is the perfect neighborhood restaurant in Navy Yard. Chef Haidar Karoum, previously at Proof, Estadio, and Doi Moi, traces a delicious personal culinary journey at Chloe with influences from all over the globe, all served with noteworthy flair. **Known for:** seasonal, internationally inspired small plates; superb desserts; sophisticated yet casual dining experience. [$] *Average main: $25* ✉ *1331 4th St. SE, Navy Yard* ☎ *202/313–7007* 🌐 *restaurantchloe.com* 🕒 *No lunch weekdays* [M] *Navy Yard–Ballpark.*

Del Mar

$$$$ | **SPANISH** | The newest concept by celebrated chef Fabio Trabocchi celebrates coastal Spain with authentic seafood fare, tapas, paella, aged charcuterie, and fresh fish and meats. Start your meal in this elegant yet fun restaurant with a seasonal gin and tonic made with house-mixed tonics and additions. **Known for:** traditional Spanish cuisine emphasizing seafood; large menu of mostly shareable plates; elegant dining experience. [$] *Average main: $36* ✉ *791 Wharf St. SW, D.C. Waterfront* ☎ *202/525–1402* 🌐 *www.delmardc.com* [M] *Waterfront.*

Dolcezza

$ | **ITALIAN** | This local chain has become a District favorite for gelato, offering nearly 10 locations plus the original factory near Gallaudet University. The Wharf has the newest branch, which is one of the largest with fully fledged breakfast offerings in addition to gelato. **Known for:** Italian gelato; great coffee; Southern-style breakfast. [$] *Average main: $10* ✉ *99 District Sq. SW, D.C. Waterfront* ☎ *202/414–7595* 🌐 *dolcezzagelato.com/locations/wharf/* [M] *Waterfront.*

Due South

$$ | **AMERICAN** | If you are looking for good renditions of Southern cuisine in the District, with the addition of flavorful, modernist twists, you'll feel at home here. You can't go wrong with the blackened catfish sandwich and a side of mac and cheese, and definitely don't skip out on dessert, often served with handmade ice cream from the shop next door. **Known for:** buttermilk fried chicken; shrimp and grits; frosé. [$] *Average main: $25* ✉ *301 Water St. SE, Navy Yard* ☎ *202/479–4616* 🌐 *duesouthdc.com* [M] *Navy Yard–Ballpark.*

Hank's Oyster Bar The Wharf

$$ | **AMERICAN** | The "urban beach food" you'll find here, not to mention the decor, will transport you to New England with such classics as fried oysters and delicious crab cakes, though those who don't like fish aren't left out given

the restaurant's popular fried chicken and four-cheese mac and cheese. One of several locations in the metro area created by chef Jamie Leeds, The Wharf location is the biggest Hank's yet and offers both indoor and outdoor seating for the full waterfront effect. **Known for:** New England seafood and decor; waterfront views for happy hour; seasonal seafood and cocktails. [$] *Average main: $21* ✉ *701 Wharf St. SW, D.C. Waterfront* ☎ *202/817–3055* 🌐 *hanksoysterbar.com* [M] *Waterfront.*

Kaliwa

$$ | **ASIAN FUSION** | One of the more unique culinary experiences at The Wharf, Kaliwa offers an Asian-fusion style incorporating tastes from the Philippines, Korea, and Thailand, all cooked in an open kitchen that may make you feel like you're in an Asian street market. The menu includes everything from cold, sushi-type small plates to full-on spicy Thai-style curries. **Known for:** Asian-style street food; dishes drawing from three distinct Asian cuisines; fun drinks. [$] *Average main: $22* ✉ *751 Wharf St. SW, D.C. Waterfront* ☎ *202/516–4739* 🌐 *www.kaliwadc.com* [M] *Waterfront.*

Kith/Kin at the InterContinental Washington D.C. - The Wharf

$$ | **CARIBBEAN** | The only restaurant of its kind in the District, this Afro-Caribbean hot spot could be the next big thing in town. Within the upscale InterContinental Washington D.C.–The Wharf, executive chef Kwame Onwuachi has crafted a menu of unique flavors and unusual dishes from his own culture that surprise beyond measure. **Known for:** Afro-Caribbean food; authentic cuisine and unusual dishes; handcrafted cocktails. [$] *Average main: $24* ✉ *801 Wharf St. SW, D.C. Waterfront* ☎ *202/878–8600* 🌐 *kithandkindc.com* [M] *Waterfront.*

Mi Vida

$$$ | **MEXICAN** | Spanning two floors and with waterfront patio seating, Mi Vida is good whether you are looking for a popular happy hour or a full meal in the heart of The Wharf. The menu is Mexican, focusing on home cooking and street food, prepared in a more modern style and served alongside an expansive list of mezcals and tequilas, as well as the signature mango margarita with ginger, agave, lime, and passion fruit. **Known for:** frozen mango margarita; great happy hour; fantastic views. [$] *Average main: $29* ✉ *98 District Sq. SW, D.C. Waterfront* ☎ *202/516–4656* 🌐 *mividamexico.com* [M] *Waterfront.*

Milk Bar @ The Wharf

$ | **AMERICAN** | The Wharf branch of this modernized American bakery offers the same eye-catching confetti cookies and cakes, including the signature "crack pie" and "compost cookie." Milk Bar's second location in the District also serves up cereal milk soft serve, cake truffles, and famous birthday cake. You can grab the cakes to go here, or enjoy a shake while exploring The Wharf. **Known for:** modernized traditional desserts; cereal milk soft serve; birthday cake and compost cookies. [$] *Average main: $10* ✉ *49 District Sq. SW, D.C. Waterfront* ☎ *202/849–8710* 🌐 *milkbarstore.com* [M] *Waterfront.*

Osteria Morini

$$$ | **ITALIAN** | The stylish design and superlative pastas of this take on cuisine from northern Italy's Emilia-Romagna region might seem like an unexpected match for the sports fans flocking to Nationals Park. But you can't ask for a better way to cap off a day at the ballpark than the wood-grilled meats here. **Known for:** prosciutto, mortadella, and wood-grilled meats; fantastic brunch burger; proximity to the baseball stadium. [$] *Average main: $32* ✉ *301 Water St. SE, Navy Yard* ☎ *202/484–0660* 🌐 *osteriamorini.com* [M] *Navy Yard–Ballpark.*

Requin

$$$ | **FRENCH** | With its waterfront views and central location, one of the newest restaurants on The Wharf may be one of the best. The cuisine is a contemporary

style of classic French food, with influences from French colonies like Morocco and Vietnam, all with modern takes on tradition, new flavor profiles, and unique presentation. **Known for:** lobster thermidor; escargot croissants; fantastic views. $ *Average main: $30* ⊠ *100 District Sq. SW, D.C. Waterfront* ☎ *202/827–8380* ⊕ *requinbymic.com* ⊘ *Closed Mon.* Ⓜ *Waterfront.*

Toastique
$ | **AMERICAN** | Aptly named, this little spot serves all things on toast, including the "Avocado Smash" (with marinated tomatoes and radishes, the hands-down favorite), the "PB Crunch" (with bananas, strawberries, and granola), and "Tomato Burrata" (also with herbed ricotta, basil, and a basalmic glaze). But the restaurant is not created from bread alone; you'll also find a variety of juices, smoothies, and fruit bowls. **Known for:** gourmet toasts; cold-pressed juices; refreshing smoothies. $ *Average main: $10* ⊠ *764 Main Ave. SW, D.C. Waterfront* ☎ *202/484–5200* ⊕ *www.toastique.com* Ⓜ *Waterfront.*

Whaley's
$$$ | **AMERICAN** | Nothing makes you want seafood more than being on the District Waterfront, and this restaurant certainly fulfills that craving with its mountainous seafood platters and seasonal bites. Stepping inside, you're greeted with an open, airy spot that looks straight out of Nantucket. **Known for:** raw bar and seafood tower; menu of small plates or shareable dishes; cocktails in the Rosé Garden. $ *Average main: $30* ⊠ *301 Water St. SE, Suite 115, Navy Yard* ☎ *202/484–8800* ⊕ *whaleysdc.com* Ⓜ *Navy Yard–Ballpark.*

🛏 Hotels

The Waterfront is by far one of the most interesting areas in which to stay right now, with spectacular views, unique and sophisticated dining, and plenty of water and outdoor activities to keep busy. There is also a great nightlife here with lots of bars and hip music venues. All of the hotels are very new and chic, as well as conveniently located for the Waterfront and National Mall.

Canopy by Hilton Washington DC The Wharf
$$$ | **HOTEL** | **FAMILY** | This new concept hotel by Hilton is at the forefront of the new Wharf hospitality, offering stylish rooms with rustic barn doors, a cool tan-and-beige palette, and waterfront views in the majority of rooms, plus plenty of extras. **Pros:** most rooms have water views; fun rooftop bar; convenient location. **Cons:** no pool; shared space with Hyatt House; can be loud at night. $ *Rooms from: $370* ⊠ *975 7th St. SW, D.C. Waterfront* ☎ *202/488–2500* ⊕ *canopy3.hilton.com* ⤳ *175 rooms* ⦿ *Free Breakfast* Ⓜ *Waterfront.*

Courtyard Washington Capitol Hill/Navy Yard
$ | **HOTEL** | Just a block from a Metro station and within walking distance to Nationals Park, this is a smart choice for budget-savvy travelers. **Pros:** good value; popular bar; fitness center and heated indoor pool. **Cons:** popular with groups, so some nights may be noisy; parking in nearby garage is expensive; restaurants in area can be busy. $ *Rooms from: $200* ⊠ *140 L St. SE, Navy Yard, Navy Yard* ☎ *202/479–0027* ⊕ *www.marriott.com* ⤳ *204 rooms* ⦿ *No meals* Ⓜ *Navy Yard–Ballpark.*

Hyatt House Washington DC/The Wharf
$$$ | **HOTEL** | Just above the hubbub of The Wharf waterfront, the Hyatt House offers a new hotel in a convenient location with some welcome amenities, including a pool and even family-sized suites with kitchenettes. **Pros:** family-friendly setup; convenient location; outdoor pool. **Cons:** the area can be noisy; shared spaces with Canopy Hotel; restaurants can be very busy. $ *Rooms from: $400* ⊠ *725 Wharf St. SW, D.C. Waterfront*

☎ 202/554–1234 🌐 hyatt.com 🛏 237 rooms 🍴 Free Breakfast [M] Waterfront.

InterContinental Washington D.C.–The Wharf

$$$ | **HOTEL** | Styling itself as an urban resort, D.C.'s new InterContinental offers spacious, modern rooms and a dazzling, soaring, wood-and-stone open atrium lobby with floor-to-ceiling windows looking out over the river. Rooms, nearly 70% of which have some waterfront views, are comfortable and spacious, with fast Wi-Fi, Nespresso coffeemakers, and digital controls for everything. **Pros:** fantastic rooms with great views; central location; unique spa and pool. **Cons:** area can be loud at night; restaurants in area can be very busy; no meals included. *[$] Rooms from: $400 ✉ 801 Wharf St. SW, D.C. Waterfront ☎ 202/800–0844 🌐 www.intercontinental.com 🛏 278 rooms 🍴 No meals [M] Waterfront.*

🍸 Nightlife

This increasingly busy area is starting to become a place to go after dark.

BARS AND LOUNGES

The Brighton SW1

BARS/PUBS | The Brighton is like your local neighborhood pub if it were bigger, more modern, and with carafe-sized cocktails. Offering a massive British footprint on The Wharf, this sprawling space has huge bar, outside seating, and even a second floor called the Lookout Lounge. Next door to the Anthem, it's particularly popular on weekends or after a show. Grab a craft British-themed cocktail, like the shareable (for four or five drinkers!) Pimm's Cup renamed here for Queen's Freddie Mercury, or sip on any of the dozen beers on draft, from sours to darks. Upstairs you can have a glass of frozé. The pub-themed food menu can be enjoyed everywhere. Happy hour is daily from 4 to 6, and there's also a late-night menu of smaller snacks. *✉ 949 Wharf St. SW, D.C. Waterfront ☎ 202/735–5398 🌐 www.brighton-dc.com [M] Waterfront.*

Cantina Bambina

BARS/PUBS | Above the Anthem's box office and Water Taxi's ticket office—and just across from the music venue—this ultracasual bar and snack bar has become a favorite of concertgoers in The Wharf area, and of those just looking for a drink and some spectacular views. Feast your eyes on the long margarita and cocktail list and grab some small bites at the bar stand downstairs. It gets busy here, so expect to stand during your visit, but that just makes it easier to take in the waterfront views. *✉ 960 Wharf St. SW, D.C. Waterfront 🌐 www.cantinabambina.com [M] Waterfront.*

District Winery

WINE BARS—NIGHTLIFE | D.C.'s first-ever winery is a unique in the heart of The Yards, serving all locally made small-batch wines, which can also be paired with a meal in its new full-service restaurant, Ana. You can tour the winery and learn how head winemaker Conor McCormack produces his vintages and enjoy a tasting, then indulge in a dinner overlooking the Anacostia River. The menu at Ana changes seasonally, and there's lunch, dinner, a happy hour on weekdays, and brunch on the weekends. The winery also hosts weddings and offers a date-night package for the romantically inclined. *✉ The Yards, 385 Water St. SE, Southeast ☎ 202/484–9210 🌐 districtwinery.com [M] Navy Yard–Ballpark.*

Kirwan's Irish Pub

BARS/PUBS | With genuinely Irish decor, music, and booze, this pub is about as Irish as it gets in the District. Started by a former Guinness employee, Kirwan's is the place to bask in live Irish music with a good pint on real Irish furniture, or at the authentic carved bar. There is plenty of space here with two floors and a full restaurant if you want a good Irish meal before the nightlife takes over. *✉ Canopy* by Hilton Washington DC The Wharf, 749 Wharf St. SW, D.C. Waterfront ✛ On hotel's roof ☏ 202/554–3818 ⊕ www. kirwansonthewharf.com Ⓜ Waterfront.

Mission

BARS/PUBS | One of the largest bars in the city, with two floors, a gigantic 150-foot bar, and 600 feet of outdoor balconies, Mission is easily the roomiest spot for pregame or postwork get togethers. There's both a daily happy hour as well as a late-night happy hour from 10 to close Thursday through Sunday. Stop in for a glass of wine, beer, Tito's, or even a house margarita, all on tap, and some traditional Mexican mixed with Tex-Mex food. Weekends include bottomless margaritas and guacamole. ✉ 1221 Van St. SE, Southeast ☏ 202/810–7010 ⊕ missionnavyyard.com Ⓜ Navy Yard–Ballpark.

Whiskey Charlie

BARS/PUBS | You may have to search a bit to find this bar, but walk through the lobby of the Canopy by Hilton and go up the special elevator to the roof. You'll find yourself with views of the waterfront like no other in the city and will quickly forget the journey. Munch on some light bites and choose from the well-curated menu of craft cocktails (go for the Mermaid margarita), all while enjoying a view of the Capitol building to the Pentagon, or sit inside with floor-to-ceiling windows and sophisticated decor. ✉ 975 7th St. SW, D.C. Waterfront ☏ 202/488–2500 ⊕ whiskeycharliewharf. com Ⓜ Waterfront.

MUSIC CLUBS

The Anthem

MUSIC CLUBS | The coolest new music venue in D.C. has made its home at the helm of The Wharf and has made a splash with the music world's biggest indie and alternative rock labels, even presenting Foo Fighters on opening night. The venue itself feels vast and industrial but with some elegant design touches. The first midsize venue of its kind in the District (there's a max of

6,000) and with specially angled seats for optimal viewing, you'll find no bad seats or standing spots in this venue. Enjoy beer on tap or in the can, cocktails and homemade Belgian waffles ("Wharfles") before or during the show in the open-air Marquee Bar upstairs (it's also open when there's no performer). ✉ 901 Wharf St. SW, D.C. Waterfront ☏ 202/888–0020 ⊕ www.theanthemdc.com Ⓜ Waterfront.

Pearl Street Warehouse

MUSIC CLUBS | The 1950s diner-inspired space may make you feel as if you were in New Orleans or Nashville, but walk through a garage door, and you'll find an intimate, modern (there are plugs under the bar to recharge your phone), and lively entertainment space for small bands. The diner serves breakfast on weekends and stays open even if shows are going on. A bar links the performance space to the outside alleyway. You don't have to buy a ticket to enjoy the music and drinks offered here; just sit at the bar and bask in the musical glory. All seating is first-come, first-served, and some shows sell out. The restaurant is open Monday through Wednesday from 3 to midnight, and from 8:30 to midnight Thursday through Sunday. ✉ 33 Pearl St. SW, D.C. Waterfront ☏ 202/380–9620 ⊕ www. pearlstreetwarehouse.com Ⓜ Waterfront.

Union Stage

MUSIC CLUBS | This unique live music venue is also a popular spot in the neighborhood for pizza, beer, and seasonal cocktails. The Tap Room bar serves 16 beers on tap and 16 in cans, as well as good cocktails, wine, and soft drinks. Downstairs is the music and another bar. Performances here may be by emerging or established talent, but it's an intimate space with exceptional sound and lighting. Even when there's no show, people come in to grab a now-famous Jersey-style bar pie pizza with a variety of toppings. Another pizza take-out window is across from the Anthem on Wharf Street. ✉ 740 Water St. SW, D.C.

Waterfront ☎ *877/987–6487* ⊕ *www. unionstage.com* Ⓜ *Waterfront.*

 Performing Arts

★ Arena Stage

THEATER | The first regional theater company to win a Tony Award performs innovative American theater, reviving such classic plays as *Oklahoma* and also showcasing the country's best new playwrights. The architecturally magnificent Mead Center for American Theatre houses three stages and, after the Kennedy Center, is the second-largest performing arts complex in Washington. Near the Waterfront neighborhood in Southwest D.C., the Mead Center features the Fichandler Stage, a theater-in-the-round seating 680; the Kreeger Theater, a modified thrust seating 514; and the Kogod Cradle, a 200-seat black-box theater for new or experimental productions. ■TIP→ **Inside the Mead, the Richard's Place Café serves meals inspired by the shows playing that evening.** ✉ *1101 6th St. SW, Southwest* ☎ *202/554–9066* ⊕ *www.arenastage.org* Ⓜ *Waterfront.*

Shopping

BOOKS

Politics and Prose

BOOKS/STATIONERY | The second of now three locations of this well-loved local institution is a welcome go-to spot for a book for travelers at nearby hotels, or for visitors who want a good book to sit with on one of the many piers at The Wharf. This location has all of the books, stationery, and gifts you need, as well as ample room to amble around the store or listen to a speaker at an event. Author events are most weeknights from 7 to 8; the store is open until 10 nightly. ✉ *70 District Sq. SW, D.C. Waterfront* ☎ *202/488–3867* ⊕ *www.politics-prose. com/wharf* Ⓜ *Waterfront.*

CLOTHING

A Beautiful Closet

CLOTHING | Step into A Beautiful Closet for fair trade international goods with a selection of jewelry, clothing, home decor, and accessories. All items here are curated by former World Bank staff member Pamela Sofola. When in a rush or if you just can't decide, you can get a personalized styling consultation. ✉ *20 District Sq. SW, D.C. Waterfront* ☎ *202/488–1809* ⊕ *abeautifulclosetdc. com* Ⓜ *Waterfront.*

d/eleven

CLOTHING | Brought to you by the designer of Gigi Hadid's famed leather jackets, the new boutique d/eleven evokes a contemporary vibe with brands like Michelle Mason, Pamela Love, and Frame Denim. You can pick up a dress to go out in, some great shoes and accessories, or gifts to bring home. ✉ *11 District Sq. SW, D.C. Waterfront* ☎ *202/554–0915* ⊕ *d11concept.com* Ⓜ *Waterfront.*

COSMETICS/PERFUME

Blush

PERFUME/COSMETICS | A premier skin-care destination in the District, Blush offers results-oriented facial treatments uniquely designed to restore and hydrate skin. Each month, founder and skin-care expert Dr. Arleen Lambda develops new treatments using all-natural ingredients. Blush also offers a curated selection of clean beauty products, beauty tools, and fragrances. ✉ *40 District Sq. SW, D.C. Waterfront* ☎ *202/632–5874* ⊕ *www. blushskinfit.com* Ⓜ *Waterfront.*

GIFTS

Anchor

GIFTS/SOUVENIRS | Drop into Anchor for that bathing suit you forgot at home, a life vest for your kid, or just some sunscreen. This is the all-stop shop for marine wear and also has daily deliveries of sandwiches and fare from local restaurants that you can grab and go for a picnic on The Wharf. You can also choose from a selection of beer, wine, and nonalcoholic drinks for your day on the pier by delivery or pick up. There are also great charter options here for guided fishing tours with an Anchor staff member. ✉ *709 Wharf St. SW, D.C. Waterfront* ☎ *202/484–8000* ⊕ *www.anchormarinashipstore.com* Ⓜ *Waterfront.*

Willow
JEWELRY/ACCESSORIES | Willow is just across the waterfront and a perfect spot to shop before a meal or ballgame with its boutique clothing, jewelry, and gifts. Willow designs its own glassware and a few other small items in-house, while other cards, gifts, and plants are sourced through local companies. There's a great collection of baby items here, too. ✉ *1331 4th St. SE, Southeast* ☎ *202/643–2323* ⊕ *www.willowstores. com* Ⓜ *Navy Yard–Ballpark.*

HOME FURNISHINGS
Ligne Roset
HOUSEHOLD ITEMS/FURNITURE | Whether you're really planning to return home with more than simply travel memories, Ligne Roset is a store worth seeing with its modern furniture, accessories, and lighting that inspire you to redecorate your whole home. You can receive expert assistance here for interior design and space planning to fit that new couch or lamp. Explore the showroom for more bold collection items as well. It's closed on Monday. ✉ *10 District Sq. SW, D.C. Waterfront* ☎ *202/758–2624* ⊕ *www. ligneroset-dc.com* Ⓜ *Waterfront.*

Patrick's Fine Linens & Home Décor
HOUSEHOLD ITEMS/FURNITURE | Patrick's is a well-known source in Alexandria for upscale furniture, home decor, dishes, and perfumes; its first branch is now open at The Wharf. Complement your home with top-notch designer goods, like those from Hermès China, Juliska, Vista Alegre, Ralph Lauren, and more dinnerware companies. Pick up a bottle of perfume or cologne by Carthusia, C.O. Bigelow, or Santa Maria Novella, or take home a luxury candle from Lafco, Nest, or Thymes. ✉ *771 Wharf St. SW, D.C. Waterfront* ⊕ *www.patricksdesigns.com* Ⓜ *Waterfront.*

JEWELRY
Diament Jewelry
JEWELRY/ACCESSORIES | Diament Jewelry is a unique treasure trove of vintage and handmade jewelry, along with gifts and accessories from local makers. The neatly displayed clothing, candles, paper goods, and accessories lend a high-class feel to this neat, floral-inspired boutique, while the piles of vintage rings, bracelets, and necklaces laid out make you want to dig for your next favorite treasure. Prices range here from inexpensive bracelets, to one-of-a-kind vintage diamond rings. Follow the shop on social media for the owner's latest finds. ✉ *33 District Sq. SW, D.C. Waterfront* ⊕ *www.diamentjewelry.com* Ⓜ *Waterfront.*

SPORTING GOODS
Pacers Running
SPORTING GOODS | Pacers Running is a perfect fit for the Navy Yard, selling sports and running gear to the Yard's ever-active, outdoorsy clientele. You can get specialty footware, running shoes and clothing, and lifestyle gear, as well as active and injury-prevention accessories. ✉ *300 Tingey St. SE, No. 160, Southeast* ☎ *202/554–1216* ⊕ *www.runpacers.com* Ⓜ *Navy Yard–Ballpark.*

Chapter 13

ARLINGTON

Updated by
Sabrina Medora

⊙ Sights	🍴 Restaurants	🛏 Hotels	🛍 Shopping	🍸 Nightlife
★★★★☆	★★☆☆☆	★★☆☆☆	★★★★☆	★☆☆☆☆

NEIGHBORHOOD SNAPSHOT

TOP EXPERIENCES

■ **Arlington National Cemetery:** The most visited cemetery in the country is the final resting place for more than 400,000 Americans, from unknown soldiers to John F. Kennedy and his wife, Jacqueline Kennedy Onassis.

■ **Udvar-Hazy Center (National Air and Space Museum):** See the Boeing B-29 *Enola Gay,* space shuttle *Discovery,* and hundreds of other aviation and space artifacts in these immense hangars near Dulles International Airport.

■ **United States Air Force Memorial:** Just south of Arlington Cemetery, this memorial honors members of the Air Force who've given their lives in service to the country.

■ **United States Marine Corps War Memorial:** Commonly called the *Iwo Jima Memorial,* it's located just north of Arlington cemetery and is a powerful tribute to all of the marines who have lost their lives in battle since 1775.

GETTING HERE

You can reach Arlington Cemetery and the U.S. Air Force and Marine Corps Memorials by Metro (Arlington Cemetery on the Blue Line, Pentagon City on the Blue or Yellow lines, Rosslyn on the Orange, Blue, or Silver lines) or Metrobus, although there will be some walking involved. You can also get to these sites with a car or via Big Bus Tours or Old Town Trolley Tours. Your best bet is to use Metro to visit the Pentagon and 9/11 Memorial (Pentagon stop via Blue or Yellow line). You'll need a car to visit the Udvar-Hazy Center.

PLANNING YOUR TIME

You can easily combine a visit to Arlington Cemetery with visits to the DEA Museum, the Pentagon and 9/11 Memorial, and U.S. Air Force and Marine Corps memorials; it will be a full day and require advance planning for the Pentagon tour.

VISITING THE UDVAR-HAZY CENTER

■ A visit to the Udvar-Hazy Center (National Air and Space Museum) will require a good part of a day due to its location; a car is needed and you'll probably encounter some traffic. If you're flying out of nearby Dulles Airport, you can combine a morning visit to the center with a late afternoon or evening departure.

QUICK BITES

■ **Cheesetique.** This cheese and wine store is also a full-service restaurant. The menu is entirely focused on cheesy delights like mac 'n' cheese, sandwiches, fondues, and more. ⊠ *800 N. Glebe Rd., Arlington* ⊕ *www.cheesetique.com* Ⓜ *Ballston–MU.*

■ **Good Stuff Eatery.** Top Chef Spike Mendelsohn's burger joint is perfect for a quick, hearty bite. This location is in Arlington's busiest area—Crystal City. ⊠ *2110 Crystal Dr., Arlington* ⊕ *www.goodstuffeatery.com* Ⓜ *\Crystal City.*

■ **Kabob Palace.** Widely known to have Arlington's best kabobs. ⊠ *2315 S. Eads St., Arlington* ⊕ *www. kabobpalaceusa.com* Ⓜ *Crystal City.*

Discover American treasures, historical attractions, diverse dining, first-class shopping, and eclectic arts and entertainment in the northern Virginia city of Arlington. Just across the Potomac River from D.C. (complete with easy Metro access), this area offers a great blend of history and urban excitement. Some other noteworthy spots are further out in northern Virginia, without the Metro access, including some good restaurants in Falls Church.

Spend a day or two visiting Arlington National Cemetery, the Marine Corps War Memorial, the Air Force Memorial, and the National 9/11 Pentagon Memorial. If you're traveling with kids or just want to ooh and aah over very cool planes and rockets, don't miss the Udvar-Hazy Center in Chantilly near Dulles International Airport. This companion facility to the National Air and Space Museum on the National Mall displays thousands of aviation and space artifacts in huge hangars; you can even watch restoration projects in progress.

◉ Sights

★ Arlington National Cemetery
CEMETERY | Nearly 400,000 American war dead, as well as many notable Americans (among them Presidents William Howard Taft and John F. Kennedy, General John Pershing, and Admiral Robert E. Peary), are interred in these 624 acres across the Potomac River from Washington, established as the nation's cemetery in 1864. Prior to 1857, George Washington Parke Custis built Arlington House on plantation land as a memorial to his step-grandfather, George Washington. The land was set aside for military burials by the third year of the Civil War to accommodate the rising death toll. Today, it's the most famous national cemetery in the country, with an average of 30 funerals held every weekday and another six to eight funerals on Saturday for people who did not require or request military honors. Visit dozens of notable grave sites, monuments, and even an arboretum. Tour bus services are provided for a fee every 15 to 25 minutes (buy tickets in the Welcome Center). Wheelchairs and strollers are not allowed. For a map of the cemetery or help finding a grave, download the cemetery's app, ANC Explorer, or use the computers at the Welcome Center. ⊠ *West end of*

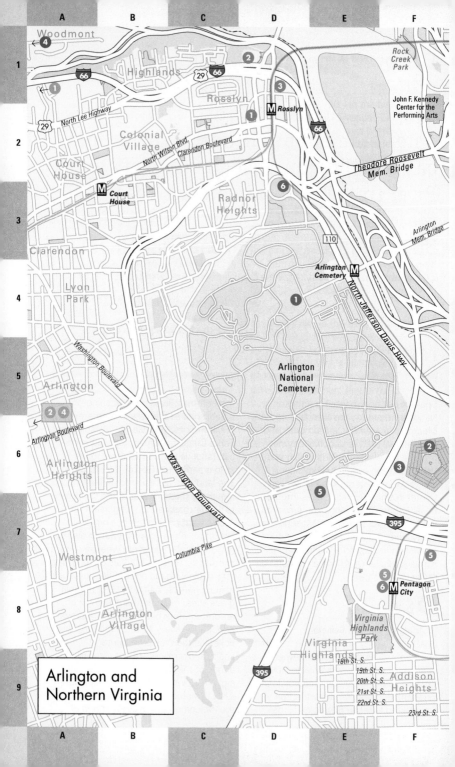

Arlington and Northern Virginia

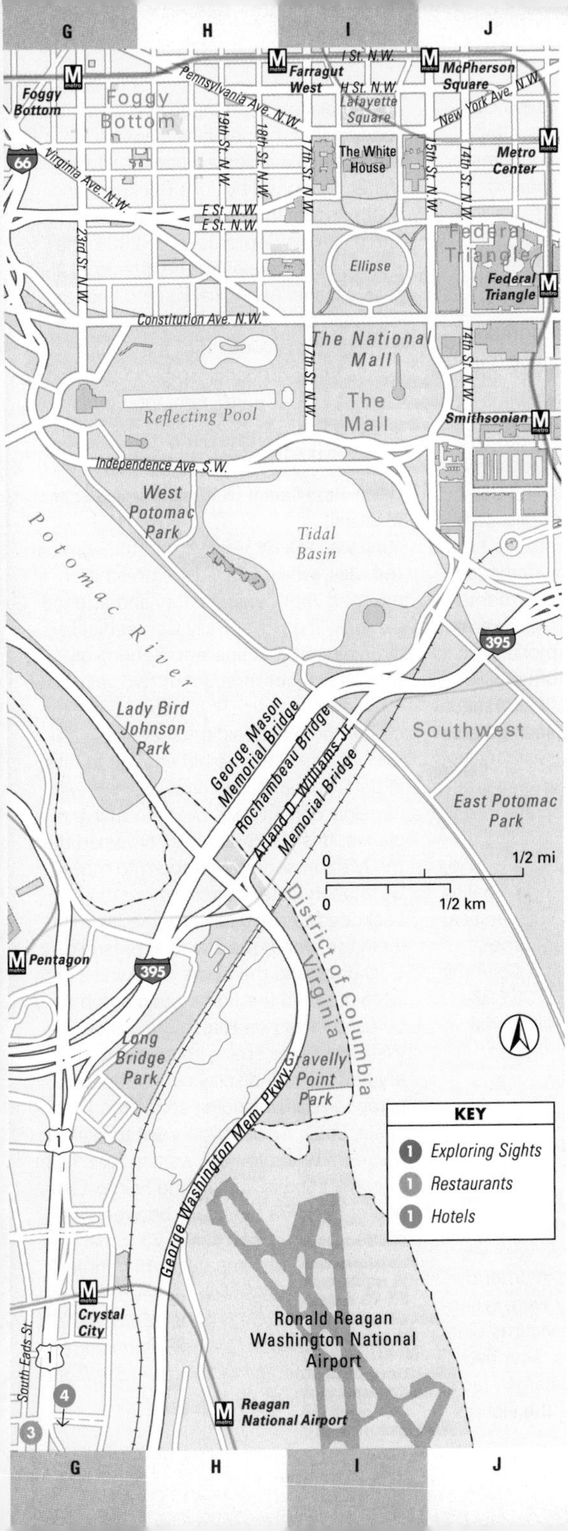

Sights ▼

1 Arlington National Cemetery..... **D4**
2 Pentagon **F6**
3 Pentagon Memorial **F6**
4 Udvar-Hazy Center (National Air and Space Museum) **A1**
5 United States
  Air Force Memorial............... **D6**
6 United States Marine Corps
  War Memorial..................... **D3**

Restaurants ▼

1 Ashby Inn.......................... **A1**
2 Inn at Little Washington........... **A6**
3 Kabob Palace **G9**
4 2941 Restaurant................... **A6**
5 Yong Kang Street **F8**

Hotels ▼

1 Hyatt Centric Arlington........... **D2**
2 Key Bridge Marriott **D1**
3 Le Méridien Arlington............. **D1**
4 Renaissance Arlington
  Capital View Hotel................ **G9**
5 Residence Inn Arlington
  Pentagon City **F7**
6 The Ritz-Carlton Pentagon City.... **F8**

KEY

- 1 *Exploring Sights*
- 1 *Restaurants*
- 1 *Hotels*

Memorial Bridge, Arlington ☎ *877/907–8585 for general information and to locate a grave* ⊕ *www.arlingtoncemetery. mil* ✉ *Free; parking from $2 per hr; Arlington National Cemetery tours $14* Ⓜ *Arlington Cemetery.*

Pentagon

GOVERNMENT BUILDING | The headquarters of the United States Department of Defense is the largest low-rise office building in the world. Approximately 24,000 military and civilian workers arrive daily. Astonishingly, the mammoth structure, completed in 1943, took less than two years to construct. Following the September 11, 2001, crash of hijacked American Airlines Flight 77 into the northwest side of the building, the damaged area was removed in just over a month and repaired in a year. In this same area is the America's Heroes Memorial and Chapel, which pays tribute to the civilians and military members killed in the attack. South of the building is the 2-acre outdoor Pentagon Memorial, with its 184 benches commemorating the lives lost on 9/11. Tours of the Pentagon are free and last about 60 minutes, including a presentation and approximately 1½ miles of walking. They must be reserved online through the Pentagon Tour Office at least two weeks, but no more than three months, in advance. ✉ *I–395 at Columbia Pike and Rte. 27, Arlington* ☎ *703/697–1776* ⊕ *pentagontours.osd.mil* ✉ *Free* ⊙ *No tours weekends* Ⓜ *Pentagon.*

Pentagon Memorial

MEMORIAL | Washington's own "9/11 memorial" honors the 184 people who perished when the hijacked American Airlines Flight 77 crashed into the northwest side of the Pentagon. Stainless-steel-and-granite benches engraved with the victims' names are arranged in order by date of birth and where they were when they died. The names of the victims who were inside the Pentagon are arranged so that visitors reading their names face the Pentagon, and names of the victims

on the plane are arranged so that visitors reading their names face skyward. At each bench is a lighted pool of flowing water. Designed by Julie Beckman and Keith Kaseman, the memorial opened to the public on September 11, 2008, the seventh anniversary of the attacks. Volunteer docents periodically stand near the entrance and answer questions. There is no public parking, with the exception of five stalls for handicap-permitted vehicles. ✉ *1 Rotary Rd., Pentagon, Arlington* ☎ *301/740–3388* ⊕ *www.pentagonmemorial.org* ✉ *Free* Ⓜ *Pentagon.*

Udvar-Hazy Center (National Air and Space Museum)

MUSEUM | **FAMILY** | Unlike the museum on the Mall, which is divided into smaller galleries with dense history and science exhibits, the Udvar-Hazy Center displays large aircraft and spacecraft, hung as though in flight throughout two vast, multilevel hangars. This focus makes the center more appealing for families with kids who may not be old enough to take in detailed historical narratives, but will certainly ooh and aah over the marvelous planes. It is also much less crowded than the Mall museum, with room to move. Gaze upon historic aircrafts like the Lockheed SR-71 Blackbird, the fastest jet in the world; the sleek, supersonic Concorde; and the *Enola Gay,* which in 1945 dropped the first atomic bomb to be used in war on Hiroshima, Japan. Walk alongside space shuttle Discovery and browse displays of astronaut paraphernalia, including space food and space underwear! If you want to visit the museum while you are waiting for a flight or connection at Dulles, the Fairfax Connector Bus 983 runs daily between the museum and airport for $1.75 (SmarTrip card or cash); the trip takes 15 minutes. ✉ *14390 Air and Space Museum Pkwy., Chantilly* ☎ *703/572–4118, 866/868–7774 IMAX information* ⊕ *www.airandspace. si.edu* ✉ *Free; IMAX film from $9; flight simulators from $8.*

Continued on page 274

ARLINGTON, THE NATION'S CEMETERY

The most famous, most visited cemetery in the country is the final resting place for close to 400,000 Americans, from unknown soldiers to John F. Kennedy. With its tombs, monuments, and "sea of stones," Arlington is a place of ritual and remembrance, where even the most cynical observer of Washington politics may find a lump in his throat or a tear in his eye.

EXPERIENCING THE SEA OF STONES

In 1864, a 200-acre plot directly across the Potomac from Washington, part of the former plantation home of Robert E. Lee, was designated America's national cemetery. Today, the cemetery covers 624 acres.

Today, Arlington's major monuments and memorials are impressive, but the most striking experience is simply looking out over the thousands upon thousands of headstones aligned across the cemetery's hills.

Most of those buried here served in the military—from reinterred Revolutionary War soldiers to troops killed in Iraq and Afghanistan. As you walk through the cemetery, you're likely to hear a trumpet playing taps or the report of a gun salute. An average of 27 funerals a day are held here, Monday through Friday. There currently are nearly 400,000 graves in Arlington; it's projected that the cemetery will be filled by 2060.

FINDING A GRAVE
At the Welcome Center, staff members and computers can help you find the location of a specific grave. You need to provide the deceased's full name and, if possible, the branch of service and year of death.

WHO GETS BURIED WHERE

With few exceptions, interment at Arlington is limited to active-duty members of the armed forces, veterans, and their spouses and minor children. In Arlington's early years as a cemetery, burial location was determined by rank (as well as, initially, by race), with separate sections for enlisted soldiers and officers. Beginning in 1947, this distinction was abandoned. Grave sites are assigned on the day before burial; when possible, requests are honored to be buried near the graves of family members.

ABOUT THE HEADSTONES

Following the Civil War, Arlington's first graves were marked by simple white-washed boards. When these decayed, they were replaced by cast-iron markers covered with zinc to prevent rusting. Only one iron marker remains, for the grave of Captain Daniel Keys (Section 13, Lot 13615, Grid G-29/30).

In 1873, Congress voted in the use of marble headstones, which continues to be the practice today. The government provides the standard-issue stones free of charge. Next of kin may supply their own headstones, though these can only be used if space is available in one of the sections where individualized stones already exist.

THE SAME, BUT DIFFERENT

Regulation headstones can be engraved with one of 54 symbols indicating religious affiliation. In section 60, the headstones of soldiers killed in Afghanistan and Iraq reflect the multicultural makeup of 21st-century America. Along with a variety of crosses and the Star of David, you see the nine-pointed star of the Baha'i; a tepee and three feathers representing the Native American faiths; the Muslim crescent and star; and other signs of faith. (Or lack of it. Atheism is represented by a stylized atom.)

Opposite: Sea of Stones; Upper left: Burial ceremony; Bottom left: A soldier placing flags for Memorial Day. Right: Coast Guard headstone.

PLANNING YOUR VISIT TO ARLINGTON

ARLINGTON BASICS

Getting Here: You can reach Arlington on the Metro, by foot over Arlington Memorial Bridge (southwest of the Lincoln Memorial), or by car—there's a large parking lot by the Visitors Center on Memorial Drive. Also, the Big Bus Tours (☎ 877/332–8689 ⊕ www.bigbustours.com) and Old Town Trolley (☎ 202/832–9800 ⊕ www.oldtowntrolley.com) both have Arlington National Cemetery stops in their loops. But only Old Town Trolley offers 7 stops within the cemetary (☎ $13.50).

⊘ Apr.–Sept., daily 8–7; Oct.–Mar., daily 8–5.

☎ Cemetery free, parking $2 per hr.

☎ 877/907–8585 for general information and to locate a grave.

⊕ www.arlingtoncemetery.mil

✕ No food or drink is allowed at the cemetery. There are water fountains in the Welcome Center, and from fall through spring a water fountain operates near the amphitheater at the Tomb of the Unknowns. You can also purchase bottled water at the Women's Memorial.

TOURING OPTIONS

Your first stop at the cemetery should be the Welcome Center, where you can pick up a free brochure with a detailed map. Once there you have a choice: tour by bus or walk.

Arlington by Bus. Arlington National Cemetery Tours leave every 15 to 25 minutes from just outside the Welcome Center April through September, daily 8:30–6, and October through March, daily 8:30–4. The 45 to 60-minute tour includes stops at the Kennedy grave sites, The Tomb of the Unknown Soldier, and Arlington House. Your bus driver will provide basic facts about the cemetery.

Arlington on Foot. Walking the cemetery requires some stamina, but it allows you to take in the thousands of graves at your own pace. On the facing page is a walking tour that includes the major points of interest. Audio tours are available in the Welcome Center.

Above: 3rd Infantry Honor Guard

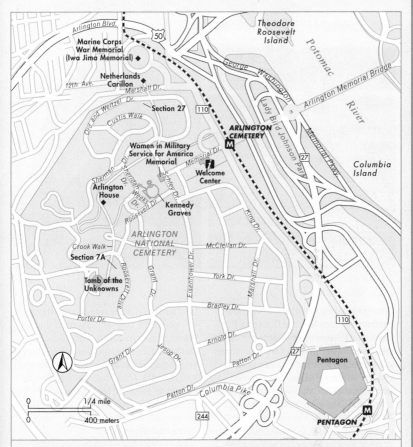

A WALKING TOUR

■ Head west from the Welcome Center on Roosevelt Drive and turn right on Weeks Drive to reach the **Kennedy graves;** just to the west is **Arlington House.** (1/4 mile)

■ Take Crook Walk south, following the signs, to the **Tomb of the Unknowns**; a few steps from the tomb is **Section 7A**, where many distinguished veterans are buried. (3/10 mile)

■ To visit the graves of soldiers killed in Afghanistan and Iraq, take Roosevelt Drive past Section 7 and turn right on McClellan Drive, turn right when you get to Eisenhower Drive, then go left onto York Drive. The graves will be on your right. (6/10 mile)

■ Walk north along Eisenhower Drive, which becomes Schley Drive; turn right onto Custis Walk, which brings you to **Section 27,** where 3,800 former slaves are buried. (3/4 mile)

■ Leave the cemetery through the Ord and Weitzel Gate, cross Marshall Drive carefully, and walk to the 50-bell **Netherlands Carillon**, where there's a good vista of Washington. To the north is the **United States Marine Corps War Memorial**, better known as the **Iwo Jima Memorial**. (1/4 mile)

ARLINGTON'S MAIN ATTRACTIONS

The Kennedy Graves

Once while taking in the view of Washington from Arlington National Cemetery, President John F. Kennedy commented, "I could stay here forever." Seeing Kennedy's grave is a top priority for most visitors. He's buried beneath an eternal flame, next to graves of two of his children who died in infancy, and of his wife, Jacqueline Kennedy Onassis. Across from them is a low wall engraved with quotations from Kennedy's inaugural address. Nearby, marked by simple white crosses, are the graves of Robert F. Kennedy and Ted Kennedy.

The gas-fueled flame at the head of John F. Kennedy's grave was lit by Jacqueline Kennedy during his funeral. A continuously flashing electric spark reignites the gas if the flame is extinguished by rain, wind, or any other cause.

Many visitors ask where Kennedy's son John F. Kennedy Jr. is buried. His ashes were scattered in the Atlantic Ocean, near the location where his plane went down in 1999.

Arlington House

Long before Arlington was a cemetery, it was part of the 1,100-acre estate of George Washington Parke Custis, a grandchild of Martha and (by marriage) George Washington. Custis built Arlington House between 1802 and 1818. After his death, the property went to his daughter, Mary Anna Randolph Custis, who wed Robert E. Lee in 1831. The couple made Arlington House their home for the next 30 years.

In 1861 Lee turned down the position of commander of the Union forces and left Arlington House, never to return. Union troops turned the house into an Army headquarters, and 200 acres were set aside as a national cemetery. By the end of the Civil War headstones dotted the estate's hills.

The house looks much as it did in the 19th century and a quick tour takes you past objects once owned by the Custises, the Lees, and the Washingtons. The views from Arlington House remain spectacular. ☎ 703/235–1530 ⊕ www.nps.gov/arho ✉ Free ⊙ Daily 9:30–4:30.

Robert E. Lee

The Tomb of the Unknown Soldier

The first burial at the Tomb of the Unknowns, one of the cemetery's most imposing monuments, took place on November 11, 1921. In what was part of a world-wide trend to honor the dead after the unparalleled devastation of World War I, an unidentified soldier was interred under the large white-marble sarcophagus. Unknown servicemen killed in World War II and Korea joined him in 1958.

The Memorial Amphitheater west of the tomb is used for ceremonies on Veterans Day, Memorial Day, and Easter. Decorations awarded to the unknowns are displayed in an indoor trophy room.

One of the most striking activities at Arlington is the precision and pageantry of the changing of the guard at the Tomb of the Unknowns. From April through September, soldiers from the Army's U.S. Third Infantry (known as the Old Guard) change guard every half hour during the day. For the rest of the year, and at night all year long, the guard changes every hour.

The Iwo Jima Memorial

Ask the tour bus driver at Arlington where the Iwo Jima is, and you might get back the quip "very far away." The memorial commonly called the Iwo Jima is officially named the United States Marine Corps War Memorial, and it's actually located just north of the cemetery. Its bronze sculpture is based on one of the most famous photos in American military history, Joe Rosenthal's February 23, 1945, shot of five marines and a navy corpsman raising a flag atop Mt. Suribachi on the Japanese island of Iwo Jima. By executive order, a real flag flies 24 hours a day from the 78-foot-high memorial. ☎ 703/289–2500

On Tuesday evening at 7 PM from early June to mid-August there's a Marine Corps sunset parade on the grounds of the Iwo Jima Memorial. On parade nights a free shuttle bus runs from the Arlington Cemetery visitors' parking lot.

The Old Guard are not making a fashion statement in their sunglasses—they're protecting their eyes from the sun's glare off the white marble of the tomb.

United States Air Force Memorial

MEMORIAL | On a beautiful hillside in Arlington, the Air Force Memorial honors the service and sacrifice of America's airmen. Three stainless-steel, asymmetrical spires slice through the skyline up to 270 feet, representing flight, the precision of the "bomb burst" maneuver performed by the Air Force Thunderbirds, and the three core values of the Air Force: Integrity first, Service before self, and Excellence in all we do. The spires are adjacent to the southern portion of Arlington National Cemetery and visible from the Tidal Basin and Interstate 395 near Washington. At the base of the spires is an 8-foot statue of the honor guard, a glass wall engraved with the missing man formation, and granite walls inscribed with Air Force values and accomplishments. On Friday evenings throughout the summer, the United States Air Force Band performs concerts on the memorial lawn. ✉ *1 Air Force Memorial Dr., off Columbia Pike, Arlington* ☎ *703/979–0674* ⊕ *www. airforcememorial.org* ✆ *Free* Ⓜ *Pentagon City or Pentagon.*

United States Marine Corps War Memorial

MEMORIAL | FAMILY | Also known as the Iwo Jima memorial, it is inspired by the iconic photograph taken during the Battle of Iwo Jima in World War II. The memorial depicts six Marines raising the current U.S. flag and honors all U.S. Marine Corps personnel whose lives were lost since 1775. It's a 15-minute walk from the Metro station at Arlington National Cemetery, much of it uphill. ✉ *U.S. Marine Corps War Memorial, U.S. Marine Memorial Cir., Arlington* ⊕ *www.nps.gov/ gwmp/learn/historyculture/usmcwarmemorial.htm* Ⓜ *Arlington Cemetery.*

🍴 Restaurants

Ashby Inn

$$$$ | AMERICAN | If there's a recipe for a perfect country inn restaurant, chef Tom

Whitaker and sommelier Stuart Brennen have it. Head an hour or so west of D.C., and your reward is extraordinary comfort food. **Known for:** intimate country inn dining; views of the Blue Ridge Mountains; prix-fixe menus with local ingredients. 🅢 *Average main: $65* ✉ *692 Federal St., Paris* ☎ *540/592–3900* ⊕ *www.ashbyinn. com* ☾ *Closed Mon. and Tues.*

★ Inn at Little Washington

$$$$ | FRENCH | This particularly well-regarded hotel restaurant is a 90-minute drive from the District that takes you past hills and farms to an English-style country manor, where the service matches the setting. You can choose from one of three different menus: Enduring Classics (four decades of stellar dishes), Gastronauts (contemporary endeavors), and Good Earth (vegetarian). **Known for:** themed (and pricey) tasting menus; special-occasion dining destination; old English manor vibe. 🅢 *Average main: $218* ✉ *309 Middle St., Washington* ⊹ *At Main St.* ☎ *540/675–3800* ⊕ *www.theinnatlittlewashington.com* ☾ *No lunch.*

★ Kabob Palace

$ | AFGHAN | FAMILY | The sign out front says parking is reserved for taxis, but it's not so they can pick up passengers—it's so the drivers can duck into this fast-casual restaurant for the area's top kebabs. Open 24 hours a day, seven days a week, its chicken, lamb, and spicy beef kebabs are cooked to perfection and best dipped in chutney sauce and chased with a bite of naan. **Known for:** authentic kebabs; crispy, chewy naan; open 24/7. 🅢 *Average main: $15* ✉ *2315 S. Eads St., Arlington* ☎ *703/486–3535* ⊕ *www. kabobpalaceusa.com* Ⓜ *Crystal City.*

★ 2941 Restaurant

$$$ | MODERN AMERICAN | Soaring ceilings, a woodsy lakeside location, and a koi pond make this one of the most striking dining rooms in the area. The playful cooking continually surprises, with plates

Did You Know?

On September 11, 2001, 184 people were killed when American Airlines Flight 77 crashed into the Pentagon. The outdoor Memorial was dedicated by President George W. Bush in 2008. It's the only place on Pentagon grounds where photography is permitted.

like wild boar cannelloni and shiitake mushrooms, seafood matelote in a mussel broth, and a rich peanut butter baked Alaska. **Known for:** romantic date-night dining; peanut butter baked Alaska; gorgeous decor. $ *Average main: $35* ✉ *2941 Fairview Park Dr., Falls Church* ☎ *703/270–1500* ⊕ *www.2941.com* ⊙ *No lunch Sat. Closed Sun.*

Yong Kang Street

$ | CANTONESE | FAMILY | Inspired by an actual street in Taipei, this dumpling house is located within Pentagon City's famous Fashion Centre Mall. Aside from the signature dumplings, it's also known for noodles and shrimp fried rice. **Known for:** great dumplings; fast service; cheap prices. $ *Average main: $6* ✉ *Fashion Centre at Pentagon City, 1100 S. Hayes St., Arlington* ☎ *571/982–4718* Ⓜ *Pentagon City.*

 # Hotels

Across the Potomac, with excellent Metro access and views of D.C., you'll find Arlington County, one of the largest areas in the Washington metro area. Its neighborhoods include Pentagon City with its three popular malls: Pentagon Row, Fashion Centre, and Pentagon Centre; Crystal City with its underground network of corridors linking offices and shops to high-rise apartments; Ballston, home to the Washington Capitals National Hockey League training facility; and Rosslyn, a former ferry landing turned transportation hub for rail, car, and bike. These thriving communities might not offer as much as D.C. proper, but they have everything the weary traveler might need in terms of accommodations, cuisine, and entertainment, sometimes at a more affordable price point.

Hyatt Centric Arlington

$$ | HOTEL | If you're feeling energetic, it's just a five-minute walk to Georgetown over Key Bridge from this solid over-the-Potomac choice, but if energy is lacking, the hotel is just across from the Rosslyn Metro station. **Pros:** across from a Metro station; runners and walkers can receive trail maps and GPS watches; nice-sized rooms. **Cons:** dull neighborhood; not great for kids; not close to any major sights. $ *Rooms from: $279* ✉ *1325 Wilson Blvd., Arlington* ☎ *703/525–1234* ⊕ *www.hyatt.com* ⊅ *318 rooms* ⋈ *No meals* Ⓜ *Rosslyn.*

Key Bridge Marriott

$$ | HOTEL | Camera-ready views and proximity to Georgetown, which is just across Key Bridge, may help you overlook the 1960s style and small rooms here. **Pros:** near the Metro; nice indoor-outdoor pool; Georgetown and monument views. **Cons:** area is dull at night; chain-hotel ambience; fee for in-room Wi-Fi. $ *Rooms from: $279* ✉ *1401 Lee Hwy., Arlington* ☎ *703/524–6400* ⊕ *www.marriott.com* ⊅ *571 rooms* ⋈ *No meals* Ⓜ *Rosslyn.*

Le Méridien Arlington

$$ | HOTEL | This modern gem, just over the bridge from Georgetown and steps from the Metro, offers stylish and comfortable rooms, many with great views of the Potomac River. **Pros:** convenient to Metro and Arlington Cemetery; nice artwork throughout; great views of the skyline. **Cons:** unhip location; fee for in-room Wi-Fi unless you're an SPG member; some rooms are small. $ *Rooms from: $293* ✉ *1121 N. 19th St., Arlington* ☎ *703/351–9170* ⊕ *www.lemeridienarlingtonhotel.com* ⊅ *154 rooms* ⋈ *No meals* Ⓜ *Rosslyn.*

Renaissance Arlington Capital View Hotel

$$$ | HOTEL | Spacious rooms, excellent service, and a good on-site contemporary Italian restaurant all add up to an excellent hotel choice outside the city. **Pros:** nice-sized fitness center and heated indoor pool; stunning lobby with dramatic artwork; delightful coffee shop. **Cons:** fee for in-room Wi-Fi; noise from trains on one side of hotel; a bit of a walk to restaurants. $ *Rooms from: $379* ✉ *2800 Potomac Ave., Arlington*

☎ 703/413–1300, 888/236–2427 🌐 www.marriott.com/hotels/travel/waspy-renaissance-arlington-capital-view-hotel 🛏 300 rooms 🍴 No meals [M] Crystal City or Ronald Reagan Washington National Airport.

★ Residence Inn Arlington Pentagon City

$$$ | **HOTEL** | **FAMILY** | The view across the Potomac of the D.C. skyline and the monuments is magnificent from these suites in a high-rise adjacent to the Pentagon and two blocks from the Fashion Centre at Pentagon City. **Pros:** indoor pool and fitness center; lovely public areas; airport shuttle to/from Ronald Reagan Washington National. **Cons:** parking fee of $29 per day; neighborhood dead at night. *[$] Rooms from: $349 ✉ 550 Army Navy Dr., Arlington ☎ 703/413–6630, 800/331–3131 🌐 residenceinn.marriott.com 🛏 299 suites 🍴 Free Breakfast [M] Pentagon City.*

The Ritz-Carlton Pentagon City

$$$$ | **HOTEL** | **FAMILY** | The feel is more contemporary and casually chic than generally associated with this luxury chain, and it's convenient for both downtown D.C. and Ronald Reagan Washington National Airport, with direct access to the Metro. **Pros:** connected to shops and restaurants; welcome amenity kit for children; 24-hour fitness center including sauna and steam facilities. **Cons:** daily fee for Wi-Fi; less luxurious than other Ritz properties; expensive, given the location. *[$] Rooms from: $419 ✉ 1250 S. Hayes St., Arlington ☎ 703/415–5000, 800/241–3333 🌐 www.ritzcarlton.com/PentagonCity 🛏 366 rooms 🍴 No meals [M] Pentagon City.*

Nightlife

Just across the Potomac, Arlington and Alexandria boast some top-notch bars and lounges—with considerably more parking and less hectic traffic than D.C. Also accessible by the Metro, revitalized Ballston and Clarendon are interesting and enjoyable places, though more laid-back, even quiet, to visit at night.

MUSIC CLUBS

State Theatre

MUSIC CLUBS | This is the place to go to see concerts by aging hit makers from the past such as the Smithereens or tribute bands to the likes of Led Zeppelin, Pink Floyd, and Bon Jovi. You have the choice of sitting or standing in this renovated movie theater, which is about 10 miles south of D.C. The popular 1980s retro dance parties, featuring the Legwarmers tribute band, draw locals who like to dress the part. *✉ 220 N. Washington St., Falls Church ☎ 703/237–0300 🌐 www.thestatetheatre.com [M] E. Falls Church.*

Performing Arts

Suburban Virginia is home to a number of outstanding performance venues offering Shakespeare, opera, dance, popular music, and more. Arlington's Signature Theatre stages some of the best musical productions in the area and is only a short trip from downtown Washington, while Synetic Theatre, made nationally famous by its production of Silent Hamlet, is but a Metro stop away in Crystal City. If you're looking for something farther afield, head to The Birchmere to enjoy an array of country, folk, and popular music nightly.

MAJOR VENUES

George Mason University Center for the Arts

ARTS CENTERS | This state-of-the-art performance complex on the suburban Virginia campus of George Mason University satisfies music, ballet, and drama patrons with regular performances in its 1,900-seat concert hall, the 500-seat proscenium Harris Theater, and an intimate 150-seat black-box theater. The 9,500-seat Patriot Center, venue for pop acts and sporting events, is also on campus. *✉ George Mason University, 4400 University Dr., MS 2F5, Fairfax*

☏ *703/993–8888, 888/945–2468* ⊕ *cfa. gmu.edu.*

Wolf Trap National Park for the Performing Arts

ARTS CENTERS | At the only national park dedicated to the performing arts, the 7,000-seat outdoor Filene Center hosts more than 80 performances from June through September. They range from pop and jazz concerts to dance and musical theater productions. The National Symphony Orchestra is based here in summer, and the Children's Theatre-in-the-Woods delivers 70 free performances. During the colder months the intimate, indoor Barns at Wolf Trap fill with the sounds of musicians playing folk, country, and chamber music, along with many other styles. The park is just off the Dulles Toll Road, about 20 miles from downtown Washington. Wolf Trap provides round-trip bus service from the West Falls Church Metro stop during events. ✉ *1645 Trap Rd., Vienna* ☏ *703/255–1900, 703/255–1868 Barns at Wolf Trap* ⊕ *www.wolftrap.org* Ⓜ *W. Falls Church–VT/UVA.*

THEATER
Signature Theatre
THEATER | Led by artistic director Eric Schaeffer, the Tony Award–winning Signature has earned national acclaim for its presentation of contemporary plays and groundbreaking American musicals, especially those of Stephen Sondheim. The company performs in a dramatic facility with two performance spaces, the 299-seat MAX and the 99-seat ARK. ✉ *4200 Campbell Ave., Arlington* ☏ *703/820–9771 box office* ⊕ *www. sigtheatre.org.*

Synetic Theatre
THEATER | FAMILY | One of the most distinctive performing arts groups in the Washington area uses music, dance, high energy, acting, and athleticism to transform the works of Shakespeare, Dante, Edgar Allan Poe, and Robert Louis Stevenson into visual theatrics that are guaranteed to leave audiences fascinated. The award-winning theater is tucked away in Virginia's Crystal City, a short Metro ride away from downtown Washington. ✉ *1800 S. Bell St., Arlington* ☏ *866/811–4111* ⊕ *synetictheater.org* Ⓜ *Crystal City.*

Chapter 14

SIDE TRIPS FROM WASHINGTON, D.C.

Updated by
Sabrina Medora
and Laura Rodini

⊙ Sights	🍴 Restaurants	🛏 Hotels	🛍 Shopping	🍸 Nightlife
★★★★★	★★★★☆	★★★★☆	★★★☆☆	★★★☆☆

WELCOME TO SIDE TRIPS FROM WASHINGTON, D.C.

TOP REASONS TO GO

★ **Walk in Washington's shadow:** The minute you step onto the grounds of Mount Vernon, you'll be transported back in time to colonial America.

★ **Travel back in time:** Delve into colonial history in Old Town Alexandria, then fast-forward to the 21st century with funky shops, artists' galleries, hot restaurants, boutiques, and bars. Don't miss Alexandria's farmers' market, held every Saturday year-round from 7 am to noon. Believe it or not, it has been around since George Washington's produce was sold here.

★ **Feast on some crabs:** Head east to Annapolis on the Chesapeake Bay and enjoy a Maryland specialty: blue crabs by the bushel (the bib is optional).

With just a bit of planning, any one of these trips can be done in a day or even an afternoon.

1 Alexandria, Virginia. Alexandria is across the Potomac and 7 miles downstream from Washington. As a commercial port, it competed with Georgetown in the days before Washington was a city. It's now a big small town loaded with historic homes, shops, and restaurants.

2 Mount Vernon, Woodlawn, and Gunston Hall, Virginia. Three splendid examples of plantation architecture remain on the Virginia side of the Potomac. Sixteen miles south of D.C. is George Washington's beautifully preserved Mount Vernon, the most visited historic house in America; Woodlawn was the estate of Martha Washington's granddaughter; and Gunston Hall was the residence of George Mason, a patriot and author of the document on which the Bill of Rights was based.

3 Great Falls, Virginia, and C&O Canal National Historic Park, Maryland. A short drive yet worlds apart from the Capital gridlock, both the Virginia and Maryland sides of the

Potomac River feature dramatic waterfalls of varying sizes, picnic areas and bike paths.

4 National Harbor, Maryland. Washington's newest entertainment destination is just a water taxi ride away from the National Mall. Shopping and dining successfully mixes big names with family-owned businesses, but the biggest draw is the new MGM National Harbor

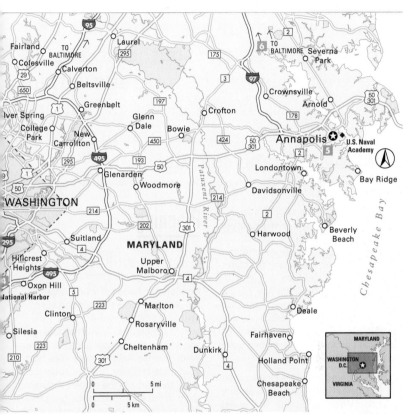

Hotel and Casino, which already accounts for more than 40% of Maryland's total gaming revenue.

5 Annapolis, Maryland. Maryland's capital is a popular destination for seafood lovers and boating fans. Warm, sunny days bring many boats to the City Dock, where they're moored against a background of waterfront shops and restaurants. The city's nautical reputation is enhanced by the presence of the U.S. Naval Academy. It also has one of the country's largest assemblages of 18th-century architecture.

6 Baltimore, Maryland. Thirty-nine miles north of Washington—a trip made easy by the MARC commuter rail's new weekend Penn Line service ($7 each way)—Baltimore's burgeoning restaurant scene has earned national acclaim. But crabs and Old Bay aren't the only things on the menu. A world of fine flavors, Afghan, Indian, Italian, Japanese, Korean, Spanish and other cuisines, from standout chefs such as Spike Gjerde, Cindy Wolf, and most recently, Andrew Carmellini, makes it a choice destination for foodies—at outside-the-Beltway prices.

The District of Columbia was carved out of Maryland and Virginia in July 1790 and borders both states, with Virginia to the west and southwest, and Maryland to the north, east, and southeast. The entire region is very historic, and within an hour of D.C. are getaway destinations connected to the nation's first president, naval history, and colonial events.

In Virginia, Alexandria was once a bustling colonial port, and its Old Town preserves this flavor with cobblestone streets, historic taverns, and a busy waterfront. Cycle 7 miles downriver along the banks of the Potomac to get here, or hop on the Metro for a quick 30-minute ride. Mount Vernon, George Washington's plantation, is 8 miles south of Alexandria. Make a day of it, and visit two other interesting plantation homes—Woodlawn and Gunston Hall—that are nearby.

In Maryland, you can visit a historic canal that was begun in the early 18th century to connect Washington, D.C., to Cumberland, MD. Another option is to get out on the water in Annapolis, a major center for boating and home to the U.S. Naval Academy. Feast on Chesapeake Bay's famous crabs, then watch the midshipmen parade on campus at the academy. Or you can visit the booming city of Baltimore.

Planning

Traveling with Kids

No matter the ages of your children or the weather, Mount Vernon can keep everyone amused with activities that delight the senses. See where George and Martha Washington and their slaves lived, hear the Revolutionary rifles fired in animated movies, taste hoecakes, and smell the herbs in the garden. A dress-up room in the education center gives children the chance to look like colonial kids.

In Annapolis, find out what it takes to become a midshipman at the **U.S. Naval Academy** 's exhibit in the visitor center.

■ TIP→ **Even kids who don't "dig" history might like sifting through dirt for artifacts in Alexandria during Family Dig Days at the archaeology museum in the Torpedo Factory.**

To Get To ...	By Car:	By Public Transit:
Alexandria	George Washington Memorial Pkwy. or Jefferson Davis Hwy. (Rte. 1) south from Arlington (10 mins)	The Blue or Yellow Line to the King St.–Old Town Metro stop (25 mins from Metro Center)
Mount Vernon	Exit 1 off the Beltway; follow signs to George Washington Memorial Pkwy. southbound (30 mins)	The Yellow Line to the Huntington Metro stop, then Fairfax County Connector Bus No. 101, 151, or 159 (45–50 mins); ferry from Pier 4 (90 minutes)
Woodlawn	Rte. 1 southwest to the second Rte. 235 intersection; entrance is on the right at the traffic light (40 mins)	Bus No. 101, 151, or 159 from Huntington Metro station (45–50 mins)
Gunston Hall	Rte. 1 south to Rte. 242; turn left and go 3½ miles to entrance (30 mins)	No Metro or bus
Annapolis	U.S. 50 east to the Rowe Blvd. Exit (35–45 mins, except during weekday rush hour when it may take twice as long)	Amtrak from Union Station to BWI; MTA Light Rail from BWI to Patapsco Light Rail Station; transfer to Bus No. 14 (2 hrs)
C&O Canal	George Washington Memorial Pkwy. northwest 15.1 miles (30 mins)	No Metro or bus
National Harbor	I–295 South 10 miles (30 mins)	Water taxi from The Wharf (45 mins)
Baltimore	Baltimore-Washington Pkwy. 39 miles (1 hr)	MARC Penn Line or Amtrak train from Union Station (28–60 mins)

Alexandria, Virginia

A short drive (or bike ride) from Washington, Alexandria provides a welcome break from the monuments and hustle and bustle of the District. Here you encounter America's colonial heritage. Founded in 1749 by Scottish merchants eager to capitalize on the booming tobacco trade, Alexandria became one of the most important colonial ports and has been associated with the most significant personages of the colonial, Revolutionary, and Civil War periods. In Old Town this colorful past is revived through restored 18th- and 19th-century homes, churches, and taverns; on the cobblestone streets; and on the revitalized waterfront, where clipper ships docked and artisans displayed their wares. Alexandria also has a wide variety of small- to medium-size restaurants and pubs, plus a wealth of boutiques and antiques dealers vying for your time and money.

GETTING HERE AND AROUND

Take either the George Washington Memorial Parkway or Jefferson Davis Highway (Route 1) south from Arlington to reach Alexandria. ■TIP➔ **Stop at the Alexandria Visitor Center at Ramsay House (221 King Street) to get oriented.**

The King Street–Old Town Metro stop (about 25 minutes from Metro Center) is right next to the Masonic Memorial and a 10-block walk on King Street from the

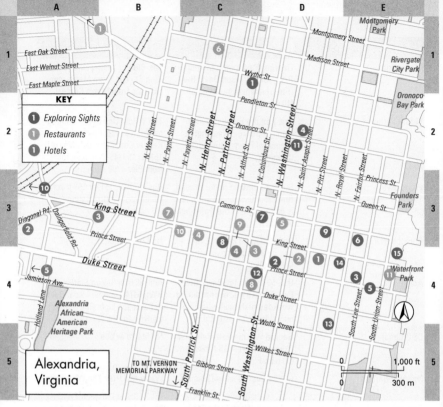

Alexandria, Virginia

center of Old Town. ■TIP→ **A free King Street trolley runs daily between the King Street Metrorail station and the Potomac River Waterfront. Hours are 10 am to 10:15 pm Sunday–Wednesday and 10 am to midnight Thursday–Saturday.**

TOURS

A great way to learn more about Alexandria's fascinating history is on a walking tour with Alexandria Colonial Tours, Footsteps to the Past, or Old Town Experience. All tours depart from the Alexandria Visitor Center at Ramsay House.

Alexandria Colonial Tours

WALKING TOURS | FAMILY | Some of America's most historic moments have happened on the streets of Alexandria. Relive and explore them through historical tours or—for the more adventurous—ghost tours. You can opt for private tours or group tours for up to 20 people. ⊠ *201 King St., No. 3, Old Town* ☎ *703/519–1749* ⊕ *www.alexcolonialtours.com* 🎫 *$13.*

Footsteps to the Past

WALKING TOURS | FAMILY | Want to see where George Washington trained his troops, influenced politics, dined, and danced? Join costumed guides for an hour-long walking History Tour. Or you can learn about life in the city during the Civil War, while it was under military occupation and thousands of wounded soldiers were treated here. If you'd rather hunt for Alexandria's resident ghosts using actual paranormal investigation equipment, sign up for a Historical Haunt Tour. ⊠ *15 Chester St., Front Royale, Old Town* ☎ *703/683–3451* ⊕ *www.footstepstothepast.com* 🎫 *From $10.*

Old Town Experience

WALKING TOURS | FAMILY | Explore the history, legends, and folklore of Alexandria on a 90-minute walking tour. You'll visit the Carlyle House, Gadsby's Tavern, Christ Church, Captain's Row, and Old Presbyterian Meeting House, among others. ⊠ *507 Prince St., Old Town*

☎ *703/836–0694* ⊕ *www.oldtowntour-alexandriava.com* 🎫 *$15* Ⓜ *King St.–Old Town.*

VISITOR INFORMATION

CONTACTS Alexandria Visitor Center ✉ *Ramsay House, 221 King St., Old Town* ☎ *703/838–5005* ⊕ *www.visitalexandriava.com.*

Sights

Founded in 1749, Alexandria is known for well-preserved architecture dating back to before George Washington considered it his "adopted' home town. Alexandria, now a nationally designated historic district, is easily walkable with a new historic site to discover on every street. Most of the sights are free, though some have a nominal fee. Alexandria is a warm and welcoming place, ideal for anyone from solo travelers to families with small children and pets.

Alexandria Black History Museum

MUSEUM | This collection, devoted to the history of African Americans in Alexandria and Virginia, is housed in part in the Robert H. Robinson Library, a building constructed in the wake of a landmark 1939 sit-in protesting the segregation of Alexandria libraries. The Watson Reading Room, next to the museum, holds a vast collection of books, periodicals, videos, and historical documents detailing the social, economic, and cultural contributions of African Americans who helped shape the city's growth since its establishment in 1749. The federal census of 1790 recorded 52 free African Americans living in the city, but the port town was one of the largest slave-exporting points in the South, with at least two highly active slave markets. ⊠ *902 Wythe St., Old Town* ☎ *703/746–4356* ⊕ *www.alexblackhistory.org* 🎫 *$2* ☉ *Closed Sun. and Mon.* Ⓜ *King St.–Old Town.*

Appomattox Confederate Statue

PUBLIC ART | FAMILY | In 1861, when Alexandria was occupied by Union forces, the 800 soldiers of the city's garrison marched out of town to join the Confederate Army. In the middle of South Washington and Prince Streets stands a statue marking the point where they assembled. In 1885 Confederate veterans proposed a memorial to honor their fallen comrades. This statue, based on John A. Elder's painting *Appomattox,* is of a lone soldier glumly surveying the battlefields after General Robert E. Lee's surrender. The names of 100 Alexandria Confederate dead are carved on the base. ⊠ *S. Washington and Prince Sts., Old Town* Ⓜ *King St.–Old Town.*

Athenaeum

MUSEUM | One of the most noteworthy structures in Alexandria, this striking Greek Revival edifice at the corner of Prince and Lee Streets stands out from its many redbrick Federal neighbors. Built in 1852 as a bank (Robert E. Lee had an account here) and later used as a Union commissary headquarters, then as a talcum powder factory for the Stabler-Leadbeater Apothecary, the Athenaeum now houses the gallery of the Northern Virginia Fine Arts Association, which hosts free rotating art exhibitions, classes, and receptions throughout the year. This block of Prince Street between Fairfax and Lee Streets is known as **Gentry Row,** after the 18th- and 19th-century inhabitants of its imposing three-story houses. ⊠ *201 Prince St., Old Town* ☎ *703/548–0035* ⊕ *www.nvfaa.org* 🖭 *Free* 🕙 *Closed Mon.–Wed.* Ⓜ *King St.–Old Town.*

Boyhood Home of Robert E. Lee

HOUSE | This childhood home of the commander of the Confederate forces of Virginia is a fine example of a 19th-century Federal town house. The house is privately owned and not open to visitors. ⊠ *607 Oronoco St., Old Town* Ⓜ *King St.–Old Town.*

Captain's Row

NEIGHBORHOOD | Many of Alexandria's sea captains once lived on this block, which gives visitors the truest sense of

what the city looked like in the 1800s. The houses are now all private residences and reflect the style of the Federal period. While the cobblestone pavement is a replica, it accurately represents the original which, according to local folklore, was laid down by Hessian soldiers taken prisoner in the Revolutionary War. Captain's Row is one of only two streets in Alexandria that is paved with cobblestones. ⊠ *Prince St., between Lee and Union Sts., Old Town* Ⓜ *King St.–Old Town.*

Carlyle House Historic Park

HOUSE | **FAMILY** | Alexandria forefather and Scottish merchant John Carlyle built this grand house, which was completed in 1753 and modeled on a country manor in the old country. Students of the French and Indian War will want to know that the dwelling served as General Braddock's headquarters. The house retains its original 18th-century woodwork and contains Chippendale furniture and Chinese porcelain. An architectural exhibit on the second floor explains how the house was built; outside there's an attractive garden of colonial-era plants. ⊠ *121 N. Fairfax St., Old Town* ☎ *703/549–2997* ⊕ *www.novaparks.com/*

parks/carlyle-house-historic-park ✉ $5 ☉ Closed Mon. Ⓜ King St.–Old Town.

Christ Church

RELIGIOUS SITE | FAMILY | George Washington and Robert E. Lee were pewholders in this Episcopal church, which remains in nearly original condition. (Washington paid quite a lot of money for pews 59 and 60.) Built in 1773, it's a fine example of an English Georgian country-style church with its Palladian window, interior balcony, and English wrought-brass-and-crystal chandelier. Docents give tours during visiting hours. ✉ 118 N. Washington St., Old Town ☎ 703/549–1450 ⊕ www. historicchristchurch.org ✉ $5 donation suggested Ⓜ King St.–Old Town.

Friendship Firehouse

MUSEUM | FAMILY | Alexandria's showcase firehouse dates from 1855 and is filled with typical 19th-century implements, but the resident Friendship Fire Company was established in 1774 and bought its first engine in 1775. Among early fire engines on display is a hand pumper built in Philadelphia in 1851. Most everything can be seen through the windows even when the firehouse is closed. ✉ 107 S. Alfred St., Old Town ☎ 703/746–3891 ✉ $2 ☉ Closed weekdays Ⓜ King St.–Old Town.

Gadsby's Tavern Museum

MUSEUM | FAMILY | The museum consists of two buildings—a circa-1785 tavern and the 1792 City Hotel. These were the centers of political and social life. Notable patrons included John Adams, James Madison, Thomas Jefferson, and even George Washington (who celebrated two of his birthdays in the ballroom). They now form a museum in which the taproom, dining room, assembly room, ballroom, and communal bedrooms have been restored to their original appearances. Special events include costumed reenactments, balls, afternoon teas, and free tours on President's Day, Mother's Day, and Father's Day. Opt for a self-guided or group tour, or enjoy an after-hours

lantern tour with a costumed guide. ✉ 134 N. Royal St., Old Town ⊹ Take the free King St. trolley (runs every 15 mins) to King and Royal Sts., then walk ☎ 703/746–4242 ⊕ www.gadsbystavern. org ✉ $5 ☉ Closed Mon. and Tues. Nov.– Mar. Ⓜ King St.–Old Town.

George Washington Masonic National Memorial

MEMORIAL | FAMILY | Because Alexandria, like Washington, D.C., has no really tall buildings, the spire of this memorial dominates the surroundings and is visible for miles. The building overlooks King and Duke Streets, Alexandria's major east–west arteries. Reaching the memorial requires a respectable uphill climb from the King Street Metrorail and bus stations. From the ninth-floor observation deck (reached by elevator) you get a spectacular view of Alexandria and Washington, but access above the first two floors is by guided tour only. The building contains furnishings from the first Masonic lodge in Alexandria. George Washington became a Mason in 1752 in Fredericksburg, and became Charter Master of the Alexandria lodge when it was chartered in 1788, remaining active in Masonic affairs during his tenure as president, from 1789 to 1797. Daily guided tours are included with admission. ✉ 101 Callahan Dr., Old Town ☎ 703/683–2007 ⊕ www.gwmemorial. org ✉ $15 Ⓜ King St.–Old Town.

Lee-Fendall House Museum and Garden

HOUSE | FAMILY | Built in 1785 at historic Lee Corner, the Lee-Fendall House was, over the course of the next 118 years, home to 37 members of the Lee family and also served as a Union hospital. The house and its furnishings, of the 1850–70 period, present an intimate study of 19th-century family life. Highlights include a splendid collection of Lee heirlooms, period pieces produced by Alexandria manufacturers, and the beautifully restored, award-winning garden, which can be visited without buying a ticket for the museum. ✉ *614 Oronoco St., Old Town* ☎ *703/548–1789* ⊕ *www. leefendallhouse.org* ⊑ *$5* ⊙ *Closed Mon. and Tues.* Ⓜ *King St.–Old Town.*

The Lyceum: Alexandria's History Museum
MUSEUM | FAMILY | Built in 1839 and one of Alexandria's best examples of Greek Revival design, the Lyceum is also a local history museum. Restored in the 1970s for the Bicentennial, it has an impressive collection, including examples of 18th- and 19th-century silver, tools, stoneware, and Civil War photographs taken by Mathew Brady. Over the years the building has served as the Alexandria Library, a Civil War hospital, a residence, and offices. ✉ *201 S. Washington St., Old Town* ☎ *703/838–4994* ⊕ *www. alexandriava.gov/Lyceum* ⊑ *$2* Ⓜ *King St.–Old Town.*

Old Presbyterian Meeting House
RELIGIOUS SITE | Except from 1899 through 1949, the Old Presbyterian Meeting House has been the site of an active Presbyterian congregation since 1772. Scottish pioneers founded the church, and Scottish patriots used it as a gathering place during the Revolution. Four memorial services were held for George Washington here. The tomb of an unknown soldier of the American Revolution lies in a corner of the small churchyard, where many prominent Alexandrians—including Dr. James Craik, physician and best friend to Washington, and merchant John Carlyle—are interred. The original sanctuary was rebuilt after a lightning strike and fire in 1835. The interior is appropriately plain; if you'd like to visit the sanctuary you can borrow a key in the church office at 323 South Fairfax Street, or just peek through the many wide windows along both sides. ✉ *323 S. Fairfax St., Old Town* ☎ *703/549–6670* ⊕ *www.opmh.org* ⊑ *Free* Ⓜ *King St.–Old Town.*

Stabler-Leadbeater Apothecary Museum
MUSEUM | Once patronized by Martha Washington and the Lee family, the

Stabler-Leadbeater Apothecary is among the oldest apothecaries in the country (the reputed oldest is in Bethlehem, Pennsylvania). The shop now houses a museum of apothecary memorabilia, including one of the finest collections of apothecary bottles in the country. In fact, they have so many of these original bottles that it took six years to process them all. Tours include discussions of Alexandria life and medicine, as well as the history of the family that owned and ran the shop for 141 years. ✉ *105–107 S. Fairfax St., Old Town* ☎ *703/746–3852* ⊕ *www.apothecarymuseum.org* ⊑ *$5* ⊙ *Closed Mon. and Tues. Nov.–Mar.* Ⓜ *King St.–Old Town.*

Torpedo Factory Art Center
MUSEUM | FAMILY | Torpedoes were manufactured here by the U.S. Navy during World War II, but now the building houses six galleries, as well as the studios and workshops of about 160 artists and artisans. You can observe printmakers, jewelers, sculptors, painters, potters, textile artists, and glass makers as they create original work in their studios. The Torpedo Factory also houses the Alexandria Archaeology Museum, which displays artifacts such as plates, cups, pipes, and coins from an early tavern, and Civil War soldiers' equipment. If archaeological activities interest you, call to sign up for the well-attended public digs (offered monthly from June through September and occasionally in October). ✉ *105 N. Union St., Old Town* ⊹ *Take free King St. trolley to Old Town waterfront. The Torpedo Factory is about 100 feet from final stop (King and Union Sts.)* ☎ *703/838–4565, 703/746–4399 Archaeology Museum* ⊕ *www.torpedofactory. org* ⊑ *Free* Ⓜ *King St.–Old Town.*

🍴 Restaurants

For centuries, the founding fathers and other international dignitaries have dined in Alexandria. Today, you can choose from more than 200 restaurants in all price

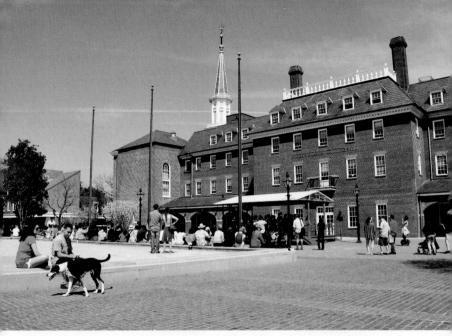

King Street is the heart of historic Old Town Alexandria, Virginia, with lively restaurants and shops.

ranges. During Alexandria's biannual restaurant weeks in January and August, dozens of establishments offer either a $35 three-course meal or dinner for two, and several also offer lunch specials.

Cheesetique

$ | **AMERICAN** | Fans of cheese and wine will fall in love with this quirky shop-cum-restaurant. With more than 200 cheeses from local and domestic creameries, a large selection of less available wines, and an extensive menu that covers every fan favorite from grilled cheese to mac 'n' cheese, visitors will find themselves in cheese heaven. **Known for:** wide variety of both domestic and international cheeses; great wine selections; cheese boards with wine pairings. $ *Average main: $15 ⊠ 2411 Mount Vernon Ave.* ☎ *703/706–5300* ⊕ *www. cheesetique.com.*

Columbia Firehouse

$$ | **AMERICAN** | **FAMILY** | Built in 1883 and used as an actual firehouse in the heart of Old Town, the historic building now just off bustling King Street houses a popular brasserie with a barroom, atrium, and outdoor patio. There's a menu of comfort food, small plates, steaks, and an excellent seafood section, including a good raw bar. **Known for:** good staples like fish-and-chips, beef bourguignonne, and steak frites; beautiful interior; separate bar menu of seafood and sandwiches. $ *Average main: $24 ⊠ 109 St. Asaph St., Old Town* ☎ *703/683–1776* ⊕ *colum-biafirehouse.com.*

Don Taco

$ | **MEXICAN FUSION** | As its name suggests, tacos of every variety are the specialty at this lively spot in the heart of Alexandria's busy King Street. From tacos to rice bowls, burritos, and small plates for sharing, Don Taco's menu will make you crave more than just one item. **Known for:** late-night happy hour (until 2 am); large tequila menu; excellent desserts. $ *Average main: $12 ⊠ 808 King St., Old Town* ☎ *703/518–8800* ⊕ *www. dontacova.com.*

★ Hank's Oyster Bar Old Town

$$ | **AMERICAN** | **FAMILY** | This classic raw bar is consistently busy thanks to a nice mix of locals and visitors. No doubt it's because the oysters, clams, and lobster rolls are incredibly fresh, not to mention the great wine list. **Known for:** amazing oysters, duh; non-seafood dinner specials; daily raw bar deals. [$] *Average main: $25* ✉ *1026 King St., Old Town* ☎ *703/739–4265* 🌐 *www.hanksoysterbar.com.*

Le Refuge

$$$ | **FRENCH** | At this local favorite, run by Jean François Chaufour and his wife, Françoise, for more than 30 years, lovingly prepared French country fare is served with beaucoup flavor. Popular selections include trout, bouillabaisse, garlicky rack of lamb, frogs' legs, and beef Wellington. **Known for:** authentic French cuisine with no pretension; three-course prix-fixe lunch and dinner options; tasty profiteroles for dessert. [$] *Average main: $30* ✉ *127 N. Washington St., Old Town* ☎ *703/548–4661* 🌐 *www.lerefugealexandria.com* 🕒 *Closed Sun.* [M] *King St.–Old Town.*

★ Mason Social

$$ | **CONTEMPORARY** | The depth of Mason Social's seasonal menu made it a hit right from the get-go. Adventurous eaters will relish options like the marrow burger while those happier with more traditional staples will be delighted with the fried green tomatoes or jumbo lump crab cakes. **Known for:** adventurous comfort food; long list of craft cocktails; bone marrow burger. [$] *Average main: $24* ✉ *728 N. Henry St., Old Town* ☎ *703/548–8800* 🌐 *www.mason-social.com* [M] *Braddock Rd.*

Nasime

$$$$ | **JAPANESE FUSION** | A tiny gem in the area, Nasime serves an exquisite five-course tasting menu of both traditional and contemporary Japanese flavors. The selections change frequently based on the season and availability of products, but always include a wonderful blend of raw, grilled, fried, and baked dishes, plus dessert. **Known for:** stunning, artlike dishes; revolving menu of fresh sushi; intimate seating. [$] *Average main: $48* ✉ *1209 King St., Old Town* ☎ *703/548–1848* 🌐 *www.nasimerestaurant.com* 🕒 *Closed Mon.*

Society Fair

$$ | **AMERICAN** | **FAMILY** | Among the many hidden and historical gems of Old Town lies a glitzy, upbeat, market-theme restaurant that is starkly different from its neighbors. Diners will be enthralled by the vibrant interior—inspired by *carnivale* flair—and a bold, seasonal menu with such favorites as seafood stew, chicken-and-sausage gumbo, and roasted half chicken. **Known for:** prix-fixe meals in the Demo Kitchen; excellent charcuterie; good desserts, including Big Ass Chocolate Cake. [$] *Average main: $19* ✉ *277 S. Washington St., Old Town* ☎ *703/683–3247* 🌐 *www.societyfair.net.*

Taverna Cretekou

$$ | **MODERN GREEK** | Whitewashed stucco walls and colorful macramé tapestries bring a bit of the Mediterranean to the center of Old Town. The menu takes diners on a trip around Greece—each dish identifies its region of origin, and the whole country is represented. **Known for:** extensive Greek-only wine list; live music on Thursday; romantic canopied garden. [$] *Average main: $22* ✉ *818 King St., Old Town* ☎ *703/548–8688* 🌐 *www.tavernacretekou.com* 🕒 *Closed Mon.* [M] *King St.–Old Town.*

★ Vermilion

$$$ | **MODERN AMERICAN** | Be sure to make reservations because foodies flock here for a taste of chef Thomas Cardarelli's's award-winning modern American menu. Morris favors locally sourced, sustainable ingredients, though quality trumps local here, so you may find a Scottish salmon alongside a Shenandoah beef fillet on this mid-Atlantic menu. **Known for:** casual, hip interior with exposed brick and gas

lamps; popular weekend brunch; house-made pastas. $ *Average main: $32* ⊠ *1120 King St., Old Town* ☎ *703/684–9669* ⊕ *www.vermilionrestaurant.com* ⊘ *No lunch Tues.* Ⓜ *King St.–Old Town.*

Virtue Feed & Grain

$$ | **AMERICAN** | Housed in what was once a feed house in the 1800s (now beautifully restored with reclaimed wood, antique bricks, and glass panes), this rustic American tavern serves an all-day menu and weekend brunch. You can sample a wide variety of selections with a seasonal bent, from duck meat loaf and pasta puttanesca to a grilled chicken BLT or a gem lettuce salad. **Known for:** classic farm-to-table cuisine with some spice; fried chicken and waffles for brunch; late-night menu. $ *Average main: $20* ⊠ *106 S. Union St., Old Town* ☎ *571/970–3669* ⊕ *www.virtuefeedgrain.com.*

Hotels

A short train-ride away from Washington, D.C., Alexandria is an excellent option for those who want a quieter stay near the District. Choose from dozens of larger hotel groups or boutique hotels, all ranking highly for ambience and service.

The Alexandrian Autograph Collection

$$ | **HOTEL** | **FAMILY** | If you're looking to stay right in the heart of Old Town Alexandria, the Alexandrian, now a Marriott Autograph Collection member, is the place to be. **Pros:** indoor pool; pet-friendly; self-parking (expensive) available. **Cons:** no outdoor pool; breakfast not included; Wi-Fi costs extra if you're not a Marriott Rewards member. $ *Rooms from: $219* ⊠ *480 King St., Old Town* ⊹ *Take free trolley toward waterfront from anywhere on King St. starting at King St.–Old Town Metro* ☎ *703/549–6080* ⊕ *thealexandrian.com* ⊸ *241 rooms* ⦿*No meals* Ⓜ *King St.–Old Town.*

Embassy Suites Alexandria–Old Town

$$ | **HOTEL** | **FAMILY** | A location across from the Metro station makes this all-suites hotel a convenient base for city exploration. **Pros:** large rooms; good breakfast; complimentary fitness center. **Cons:** small indoor pool is often crowded; parking is expensive; popular with school groups. $ *Rooms from: $270* ⊠ *1900 Diagonal Rd., Old Town* ☎ *703/684–5900, 800/362–2779* ⊕ *embassysuites3.hilton.com* ⊸ *288 rooms* ⦿*Free Breakfast.*

Kimpton Lorien Hotel & Spa

$$$ | **HOTEL** | Service is top-notch at this casually elegant boutique hotel in the heart of Old Town Alexandria. **Pros:** central to Old Town sights; full-service spa (only one in town); free use of bikes; well-appointed fitness center. **Cons:** no pool; daily fee for valet-only parking; some rooms are small. $ *Rooms from: $339* ⊠ *1600 King St., Old Town* ☎ *703/894–3434, 703/894–3434* ⊕ *www.lorienhotelandspa.com* ⊸ *107 rooms* ⦿*No meals* Ⓜ *King St.–Old Town.*

Morrison House, Autograph Collection

$$$ | **HOTEL** | In a charming brick manor-style home a half block off bustling King Street, this Marriott Autograph Collections hotel is a quiet escape for couples and business travelers. **Pros:** in the heart of Old Town; delightful literary theme, including on-site library; modern building with historic charm. **Cons:** about a 15-minute walk from Metro and train stations; daily fee for valet-only parking; fee for in-room Wi-Fi. $ *Rooms from: $329* ⊠ *116 S. Alfred St., Old Town* ☎ *703/838–8000, 888/236–2427* ⊕ *www.marriott.com* ⊸ *45 rooms* ⦿*No meals* Ⓜ *King St.–Old Town.*

The Westin Alexandria

$$ | **HOTEL** | **FAMILY** | The staff seems genuinely happy to see you come through the door at this hotel just 1½ miles from the cobbled streets of Old Town Alexandria, and if you don't need or want to be in D.C.—only 20–25 minutes away by Metro—you'll get more for your travel dollar here. Decorated in blues, wood tones, and imported Jerusalem stone, the lobby and public areas have something of a

Frank Lloyd Wright feel. **Pros:** indoor heated pool and 24-hour gym are complimentary; free shuttle service to waterfront and Old Town Alexandria; close to airport (but there's no shuttle). **Cons:** outside the city; half-hour walk to waterfront; fee for in-room Wi-Fi. Ⓢ *Rooms from: $283* ✉ *400 Courthouse Sq.* ☎ *703/253–8600* ⊕ *www.westin.com/alexandria* ⤵ *319 rooms* ⦿| *No meals* Ⓜ *Eisenhower Ave.*

Nightlife

Alexandria is not without nightlife options, including a few good bars and places to hear live music.

★ The Birchmere

MUSIC CLUBS | A legend in the D.C. area, the Birchmere is one of the best places outside the Blue Ridge Mountains to hear acoustic folk, country, and bluegrass. Enthusiastic crowds regularly enjoy table-side service while taking in performances by artists such as Judy Collins, Don McLean, Bela Fleck, and Emmylou Harris. But the club is also a draw for some of the country's best jazz and R&B artists (Rachelle Farrell, Sheila E., Angie Stone). ✉ *3701 Mt. Vernon Ave.* ☎ *703/549–7500* ⊕ *www.birchmere.com.*

Fishmarket

BARS/PUBS | There's something different in just about every section of this multilevel, multiroom space, though the nightlife centers on the sports-focused Anchor Bar. The thirty- and fortysomething crowd watching local televised games is boisterous. If you really like beer, order a "Schooner" size; at 32 ounces, it's a glass big enough to put your face in. Or make it an innocent night out at the adjacent Pop's Old Fashioned Ice Cream Co. ✉ *105 King St., Old Town* ☎ *703/836–5676* ⊕ *www.fishmarketva.com* Ⓜ *King St.–Old Town.*

PX

BARS/PUBS | Reservations are accepted for this swanky, small speakeasy featuring artisanal libations by Todd Thrasher, but if the blue light is lit that's the sign there's room for some walk-ins. It's hard to say what's the best part—the intimate setting, the attentive service, or the otherworldly drinks. PX asks its patrons to dress up—no baseball caps, T-shirts or jeans—and to refrain from wearing anything that shows too much skin, from tank tops to shorts and flip-flops. ✉ *728 King St., Old Town* ⊹ *Above Eamonn's A Dublin Chipper* ☎ *703/299–8385* ⊕ *www.barpx.com* Ⓜ *King St.–Old Town.*

Activities

An asphalt bicycle path leads from the Virginia side of Key Bridge (across from Georgetown), past Ronald Reagan National Airport, and through Alexandria all the way to Mount Vernon. Bikers in moderately good condition can make the 16-mile trip in less than two hours. You can rent bicycles as well as sailboats, paddleboards, and kayaks in Alexandria. A great place to rent is the Washington Sailing Marina, which is beside the Mount Vernon Bike Trail just past the airport. A 12-mile ride south will take you right up to the front doors of Mount Vernon.

Washington Sailing Marina

BICYCLING | FAMILY | A great place to rent a bike is the Washington Sailing Marina, which is beside the Mount Vernon Bike Trail just past the airport. A 12-mile ride south will take you right up to the front doors of Mount Vernon. Cruiser bikes rent for $8.50 per hour or $30 per day. You can also rent kayaks ($16 per hour), small sailboats ($17 to $25 per hour), and paddleboards ($22 per hour). The marina is open 9–5 daily. ✉ *1 Marina Dr.* ☎ *703/548–9027* ⊕ *www.washingtonsailingmarina.com.*

C&O Canal and Great Falls Parks

In the 18th and early 19th centuries, the Potomac River was the main transportation route between Cumberland, Maryland, an important port on the nation's frontier, and the seaports of the Chesapeake Bay. Coal, tobacco, grain, whiskey, furs, iron ore, and timber were sent down the Potomac to Georgetown and Alexandria, which served as major distribution points for both domestic and international markets.

Although it was a vital link with the country's western territories, rapids and waterfalls along the 185 miles between Cumberland and Washington originally made it impossible for traders to travel the entire distance by boat. Just a few miles upstream from Washington, the Potomac cascades through two such barriers: the breathtakingly beautiful Great Falls and the less dramatic but equally impassable Little Falls.

Upon completion in 1850, the Chesapeake & Ohio Canal, with its 74 locks, provided an economical and practical way for traders to move goods through the Washington area to the lower Chesapeake, but floods and competition from the B&O Railroad would end traffic less than a century later. The railroad transferred ownership of the canal to the federal government in 1938 to settle a $2 million debt. Since 1971 the canal has been a national park, providing a window into the past and a marvelous place to enjoy the outdoors.

C&O Canal National Historic Park, Maryland

Extends 13 miles west from Georgetown, including Great Falls Tavern.

C&O Canal National Historic Park originates in Georgetown and encloses a 184.5-mile towpath that ends in Cumberland, Maryland. This relic of America's canal-building era and a few structures are still there.

GETTING HERE AND AROUND

C&O Canal National Historic Park is along the Maryland side of the Potomac and is accessible by taking Canal Road or MacArthur Boulevard from Georgetown or by taking Exit 41 off the Beltway and then following the signs to Carderock. There are several roadside stops accessible from the southbound lanes of Canal Road where you can park and visit restored canal locks and lock houses.

SIGHTS

Clara Barton National Historic Site

HOUSE | Beside Glen Echo Park's parking lot is this monument to the founder of the American Red Cross. Barton first used the structure, built by the founders of Glen Echo village, to store Red Cross supplies; later it became both her home and the organization's headquarters. Today the building is furnished with period artifacts and many of her possessions. Access is by a 45-minute guided tour only, typically offered only on Friday and Saturday. Check the park's website to plan your visit. ✉ *5801 Oxford Rd., Glen Echo* ☎ *301/320–1410* ⊕ *www.nps. gov/clba* ☒ *Free* ⊗ *Closed Sun.–Thurs.*

Great Falls Tavern Visitor Center

INFO CENTER | Headquarters for the Palisades area of C&O Canal National Historic Park, this visitor center has displays of canal history and photographs that show how high the river can rise. A platform on Olmsted Island, accessible from near the tavern, provides a spectacular view of the falls. On the lock walls are grooves worn by decades of friction from boat towlines. Interpretive ranger programs are offered year-round (in winter the schedule is limited), including hikes, nature walks, demonstrations, and lectures. Themed canal-boat rides are available in spring, summer, and fall, and the schedule varies depending on the month. Ongoing efforts to repair and restore locks can result in temporary towpath closures; call the visitor center for the exact schedule on the day of your visit. ✉ *11710 MacArthur Blvd., Potomac* ☎ *301/767–3714* ⊕ *www. nps.gov/choh* ✉ *$10 per vehicle or $5 per person without vehicle; good for 3 days at both Great Falls Park and C&O Canal National Historic Park.*

ACTIVITIES

The C&O Canal National Historic Park and its towpath are favorites of walkers, joggers, bikers, and canoeists. The path has a slight grade, which makes for a leisurely ride or hike. Most recreational bikers consider the 13 miles from Georgetown to Great Falls Tavern an easy ride; you need to carry your bike for only one short stretch of rocky ground near Great Falls. You can also take a bike path that parallels MacArthur Boulevard and runs from Georgetown to Great Falls Tavern. Storm damage has left parts of the canal dry, but many segments remain intact and navigable by canoe.

BOAT TOURS
C&O Canal Barges

BOAT TOURS | FAMILY | During one-hour rides on mule-drawn barges along the C&O Canal at Great Falls, costumed guides and volunteers explain the history of the waterway. Run by the National Park Service, the barge rides depart from its visitor center on weekends, from April through October. Tours were suspended while the locks were being repaired but will resume in summer 2019. ✉ *Great Falls Tavern Visitor Center, 11710 MacArthur Blvd., Potomac* ☎ *301/739–4200* ⊕ *www.nps.gov/choh* ✉ *$8.*

Great Falls Park, Virginia

23 miles northwest of Georgetown.

Part of the National Park System, Great Falls Park is on the Virginia side of the Potomac, across the river from C&O Canal National Historic Park.

GETTING HERE AND AROUND

To reach Great Falls Park, take the scenic and winding Route 193 (Exit 13 off Route 495, the Beltway) to Route 738 (Old Dominion Drive), and follow the signs. It takes about 25 minutes to drive to the park from the Beltway.

SIGHTS
★ **Great Falls Park**

NATIONAL/STATE PARK | FAMILY | Facing the C&O Canal National Historical Park across the Potomac River on the Virginia side, this is where the steep, jagged falls of the Potomac roar into the narrow Mather Gorge, the rocky narrows that make the Potomac churn. No matter the time of year, the views of the falls and river are spectacular, and more than 150 species of birds make their home in and around the 800-acre park. Great Falls Park is a favorite for outings; here you can follow trails past the old Patowmack Canal and among the boulders and forests lining the edge of the falls. There are three overlooks in the park, two of which are handicap accessible. Camping and alcoholic beverages are not allowed, but you can fish (a Virginia or Maryland license is required), climb rocks (climbers must register first at the visitor center or lower parking lot), or—if you're an experienced boater with your own equipment—go white-water kayaking (*below* the falls only). ⚠ **As is true all along this stretch of the river, the currents are deadly. Despite frequent signs and warnings, there are those who occasionally dare the water and drown.** Staff members conduct special tours and walks year-round. ✉ *9200 Old Dominion Dr., McLean* ☎ *703/757–3101* ⊕ *www.nps.gov/grfa* ✉ *$10 per vehicle;*

$5 for entry on foot, horse, or bicycle; admission good for 3 days.

National Harbor

12 miles south of Downtown Washington, D.C., 2 miles west of Oxon Hill.

National Harbor sprawls across 350 acres of previously abandoned banks of the Potomac River, across from Old Town Alexandria. It's about a 25-minute water taxi ride from the National Mall and provides an alternative if you're D.C.-bound and don't mind commuting. While only one-quarter as tall as the London Eye, the Capital Wheel's 42 glass-enclosed gondolas soar 180 feet above the Potomac River, affording breathtaking views over the District.

Shopping and dining is a mix of big names and successful family-owned businesses. Some of the finest white-linen-napkin options are helmed by local celebrity chefs (José Andrés and the Voltaggio brothers) with several restaurants under their belts.

The new MGM National Harbor Hotel and Casino brings Las Vegas–style entertainment inside the Beltway, while its upscale boutiques and shops, including Sarah Jessica Parker's eponymous shoe store, aim for mass appeal.

GETTING HERE AND AROUND

The easiest way to reach National Harbor is by car via Interstate 295, Interstate 95, or Interstate 495, but keep in mind that neither street nor garage parking is free. Water taxis from Old Town Alexandria, the National Mall, or Georgetown are also convenient. Once in National Harbor, the National Harbor Circulator shuttle provides easy transport along Waterfront Street and between the Tanger Outlets, Gaylord National Resort, and MGM National Harbor Hotel for a onetime cost of $5, good for all-day riding.

TOURS

★ Potomac Riverboat Company

BOAT TOURS | Jump aboard a cruise ship from National Harbor's dock for a water tour of Mount Vernon, Alexandria, or Washington's monuments and memorials. The trip to Mount Vernon includes admission to the grounds. The company also operates water taxis across the Potomac to even more sightseeing, shopping, and dining options in Alexandria, Georgetown (transfer at Alexandria), The Wharf, or the National Mall. ✉ *Commercial Pier* ☎ *703/684–0580, 877/511–2628* ⊕ *www.potomacriverboat-co.com* ⛴ *From $16.*

◉ Sights

The Awakening

PUBLIC ART | This sculpture, created by J. Seward Johnson, depicts a 70-foot giant struggling to free himself from the earth and is actually five separate pieces buried in the ground. The statue was originally at Hains Point in Washington, but was moved to National Harbor in 2008. Feel free to climb all over the giant; everyone else does. ✉ *National Plaza.*

★ The Capital Wheel

VIEWPOINT | Stunning at sunset, the nearly 200-foot ascent on this giant Ferris wheel affords views of Alexandria's Masonic Temple, the Washington Monument, and the U.S. Capitol, lasting approximately 15 minutes. Glass-enclosed gondolas are climate-controlled and wheelchair-accessible. Landlubbers can enjoy drinks and Potomac vistas from the Flight Deck bar at the base of the wheel since admission tickets are not required. ✉ *141 American Way* ☎ *301/842–8650* ⊕ *thecapitalwheel.com* ⏲ *$15.*

🍴 Restaurants

Elevation Burger

$ | BURGER | One of the few restaurants in National Harbor without waiter service, this burger joint is known for its grass-fed organic beef and heaping servings of skinny fries. The original Elevation Burger comes with two patties, while a Half-the-Guilt burger consists of one beef patty and one veggie patty. **Known for:** organic, grass-fed, free-range burgers; french fries cooked in olive oil; thick shakes, including chocolate mixed with black cherry. Ⓢ *Average main: $12* ✉ *108 Waterfront St.* ☎ *301/567–9290* ⊕ *www. elevationburger.com* ▭ *No credit cards.*

★ Fish by José Andrés

$$$$ | SEAFOOD | The acclaimed Spanish-American chef's restaurant inside the MGM National Harbor serves seafood with his signature global flair—and the results are delicious. Try the lobster jambalaya or the crab mac and cheese made with vermicelli noodles. **Known for:** live scallop and sea urchin appetizers; airy, sea-inspired design; fine dining in the heart of the casino. Ⓢ *Average main: $40* ✉ *MGM National Harbor, 101 MGM National Harbor Ave.* ☎ *301/971–6050* ⊕ *www.mgmnationalharbor.com* ⊘ *Closed Tues.*

★ Old Hickory Steakhouse

$$$$ | STEAKHOUSE | The signature restaurant of the Gaylord National Resort, Old Hickory is perfect for a romantic meal watching the sun set over the harbor or for an expense-account evening of cocktails and fine cigars out on the terrace. The signature 24-ounce porterhouse comes with four sauce choices: béarnaise, bordelaise, green peppercorn, and blue cheese. **Known for:** prime cuts of meat; waterfront views; excellent cheese courses. Ⓢ *Average main: $55* ✉ *Gaylord National Resort & Convention Center, 201 Waterfront St.* ☎ *301/965–4000* ⊕ *www.oldhickoryrestaurant.com* ⊘ *No lunch.*

The Walrus Oyster & Ale House

$$$ | SEAFOOD | FAMILY | Come here for a crab cake sandwich or select from the list of fresh, briny Chesapeake oysters in a casual, modern pub setting. The Walrus proudly partners with Maryland's Oyster Recovery Partnership, which recycles shells and builds reefs for the area's once-declining bivalve population. **Known for:** all things oysters; patio seating; friendly service. Ⓢ *Average main: $30* ✉ *152 Waterfront St.* ☎ *301/567–6100* ⊕ *www.walrusoysterandale.com.*

Hotels

AC Hotel National Harbor

$ | HOTEL | Loftlike spaces, dramatic art, and lounge seating in the second-floor lobby create a minimalistic atmosphere more like a nightclub than your standard Marriott hotel. **Pros:** outdoor patio and fantastic views of the Capital Wheel and Potomac River; free in-room Wi-Fi; more affordable than most of the other hotels in National Harbor. **Cons:** small closets; expensive valet parking on-site or cheaper off-site self-parking; small fitness room. Ⓢ *Rooms from: $179* ✉ *156 Waterfront St.* ☎ *301/749–2299* ⊕ *www. marriott.com* ⤶ *192 rooms* ¶◯¶ *No meals.*

Gaylord National Resort and Convention Center

$$ | HOTEL | FAMILY | Guests at this larger-than-life resort can dine, shop, get pampered, and even go clubbing without ever leaving the property, which anchors the National Harbor waterfront, and with about a 25-minute ride to the National Mall, it provides an alternative to the more expensive options downtown. **Pros:** waterfront location; water taxi to Alexandria and National Mall; full-service spa, fitness center, and indoor pool. **Cons:** downtown D.C. is fairly far; extra per-day resort fee; resort might be too big for some. Ⓢ *Rooms from: $233* ✉ *201 Waterfront St.* ☎ *301/965–4000, 301/965–2000* ⊕ *www.marriott.com* ⤶ *1996 rooms* ¶◯¶ *No meals.*

★ MGM National Harbor

$$ | HOTEL | The newest addition to the Potomac waterfront at National Harbor is the ultramodern MGM. **Pros:** great restaurants by some of the nation's most celebrated chefs; awesome views from many of the public spaces and rooms; Maryland's most popular gambling venue. **Cons:** might be too overwhelming for some travelers; room rates are high; expensive nightly resort fee. $ *Rooms from: $259* ⊠ *101 MGM National Ave.* ☎ *844/646–6847* ⊕ *www.mgmnational-harbor.com* ⟿ *308 rooms* ⦿ *No meals.*

Mount Vernon, Woodlawn, and Gunston Hall

Long before Washington, D.C., was planned, wealthy traders and gentlemen farmers had parceled the shores of the Potomac into plantations. Most traces of the colonial era were obliterated as the capital grew in the 19th century, but several splendid examples of plantation architecture remain on the Virginia side of the Potomac, 15 miles or so south of D.C. In one day you can easily visit three such mansions: Mount Vernon, the home of George Washington and one of the most popular sites in the area; Woodlawn, the estate of Martha Washington's granddaughter; and Gunston Hall, the home of George Mason, author of the document on which the Bill of Rights was based. Set on hillsides overlooking the river, these estates offer magnificent vistas and bring back to vivid life the more palatable aspects of the 18th century.

Mount Vernon, Virginia

16 miles southeast of Washington, D.C., 8 miles south of Alexandria.

Once a vibrant plantation in the 18th century, Mount Vernon is an enduring reminder of the life and legacy of George Washington. This historic site features an authentically interpreted 18th-century home, lush gardens and grounds, captivating museum galleries, and immersive educational programs.

GETTING HERE AND AROUND
To reach Mount Vernon by car from the Capital Beltway (Route 495), take Exit 1 and follow the signs to George Washington Memorial Parkway southbound. Mount Vernon is about 8½ miles south. From downtown Washington, cross into Arlington on Key Bridge, Memorial Bridge, or the 14th Street Bridge and drive south on the George Washington Memorial Parkway past Ronald Reagan National Airport through Alexandria straight to Mount Vernon. The trip from D.C. takes about a half hour.

Getting to Mount Vernon by public transportation requires that you take both the Metro and a bus. Begin by taking the Yellow Line train to the Huntington Metro station. From here, take Fairfax County Connector Bus No. 101 ($1.75 cash or $1.25 with SmarTrip card). Buses on each route leave about once an hour—more often during rush hour—and operate weekdays from about 5 am to 9:15 pm, weekends from about 6:30 am to 7 pm.

CONTACTS Fairfax County Connector ☎ *703/339–7200* ⊕ *www.fairfaxconnector.com.* **Washington Metro Area Transit Authority** ☎ *202/637–7000* ⊕ *www. wmata.com.*

TOURS
Gray Line
BUS TOURS | Gray Line runs a nine-hour Mount Vernon and Arlington National Cemetery tour, Friday through Sunday from January through mid-March and daily mid-March through December. Priced at $90, it includes admission to the mansion and grounds, the tour departs at 8 am from Union Station. ⊠ *Washington* ☎ *202/779–9894 weekdays 8:30 am–6:30 pm* ⊕ *www.graylinedc.com.*

Spirit of Mount Vernon
BOAT TOURS | **FAMILY** | You can enjoy a Potomac River cruise and explore George

Washington's famous grounds in one trip. *Spirit of Mount Vernon* is the only cruise option that provides a narrated sightseeing round-trip from the Washington, D.C., Waterfront area to Mount Vernon and back. The boats dock directly at Mount Vernon, and it's a short walk up the hill to the estate. Admission to the grounds of Mount Vernon is included in the fare. Cruise goers have three hours to explore Mount Vernon grounds and gardens before embarking back to their original destination. Cruises are offered from March through October and start at $49.95. ⊠ *580 Water St., Pier 4, Southwest* ☎ *866/302–2469 boat reservations* ⊕ *www.spiritcruises.com* Ⓜ *Waterfront-SEU.*

◉ Sights

Whether you're visiting for the day or spending a few days in Mount Vernon, there is much to see and do. George Washington's estate is one of the most popular historic estates in the country, averaging over 1 million guests each year. Despite this, there is an air of consistent tranquility, between the vast grounds and a well-organized programming schedule. Take a room-by-room tour of our founding father's mansion followed by a stroll through his grounds and gardens. Travel back in time by exploring the various outbuildings where all the estate operations took place, including blacksmithing, laundry, and cooking. You can also explore the estate by way of interactive shows, tours, tributes, and exhibitions. Mount Vernon also provides a variety of dining options that are suitable for families, large groups, and fine dining alike.

George Washington's Gristmill and Distillery
HISTORIC SITE | George Washington's Gristmill and Distillery—both reproductions—operate on their original sites near Mount Vernon estate. In 1799, the distillery was the largest American whiskey producer. Today, using the same recipe and processes thanks to the excellent records

kept by Washington, small batches of his whiskey are made and sold here. During guided tours, led by costumed interpreters, you'll meet an 18th-century miller and watch the water-powered wheel grind grain into cornmeal and watch the grains being distilled. The mill and distillery are 3 miles from Mount Vernon on Route 235 toward U.S. 1, almost to Woodlawn. General-admission tickets to Mount Vernon include the gristmill and distillery. ⊠ *5429 Grist Mill Woods Way* ☎ *703/780–3383* ⊕ *www.mountvernon.org* ☞ *$20 ($18 if booked online), includes admission to Mount Vernon estate* ⊗ *Closed Nov.–Mar.*

★ George Washington's Mount Vernon
HISTORIC SITE | FAMILY | This plantation and the surrounding lands (some 8,000 acres with five operating farms) had been in the Washington family for nearly 70 years by the time the future president inherited it all in 1743. Washington, using the inheritance of his widowed bride, Martha, oversaw the transformation of the main house from an ordinary farm dwelling into what was, for the time, a grand mansion. The red-roof main house is elegant though understated, with quite ornate first-floor rooms, especially the formal large dining room, with a molded ceiling decorated with agricultural motifs. You can stroll around the estate's 500 acres and three gardens, visiting workshops, kitchen, carriage house, greenhouse, slave quarters, and, down the hill, the tomb of George and Martha Washington. There's also a pioneer farmer site, a 4-acre hands-on exhibit with a reconstructed barn as its centerpiece. But some of the most memorable experiences at Mount Vernon, particularly for kids, are in the Museum and Education Center's interactive displays. Actors in period dress who portray General Washington and his wife welcome visitors at special occasions throughout the year, including President's Day, Mother's and Father's Day, and July 4. Evening candlelight tours are offered weekend evenings in late November and early

The exterior of the plantation house at Mount Vernon may look as if it's built of stone, but it's not. It's rusticated pine with sand thrown into the wet paint to give it the rough look of sandstone blocks.

December. ✉ *3200 George Washington Pkwy.* ⚲ *Southern end of George Washington Pkwy.* ☎ *703/780–2000* ⊕ *www.mountvernon.org* ✉ *$20 ($18 if booked online), includes admission to distillery and gristmill.*

Woodlawn, Virginia

3 miles west of Mount Vernon, 15 miles south of Washington, D.C.

Woodlawn was once part of the Mount Vernon estate, and from here you can still see the trees of the bowling green that fronted Washington's home. The mansion was built for Martha Washington's granddaughter, Nelly Custis, who married George Washington's nephew, Lawrence Lewis. Also on the grounds of Woodlawn is one of Frank Lloyd Wright's "Usonian" homes, the **Pope-Leighey House.** The structure, which belongs to the National Trust for Historic Preservation, was completed in 1941 at a cost of $7,000 and is one of only three homes in Virginia designed by Wright.

GETTING HERE AND AROUND

To drive to Woodlawn, travel southwest on Route 1 to the second Route 235 intersection (the first leads to Mount Vernon). The entrance to Woodlawn is on the right at the traffic light. From Mount Vernon, travel northwest on Route 235 to the Route 1 intersection; Woodlawn is straight ahead through the intersection.

To use public transportation, take Bus No. 101, 151, or 159 ($1.75 cash or $1.25 with SmarTrip card) from Huntington Metro station. Buses returning to the station have the same numbers but are marked Huntington.

Sights

The Woodlawn Plantation is a two-part manor that consists of a home as well as a farm complex. It was recognized on the National Register of Historic Places in 2005 and is worth the short trip from Alexandria or Washington, D.C.

Woodlawn and Pope-Leighey House
HOUSE | FAMILY | Completed in 1805, Woodlawn was designed by William

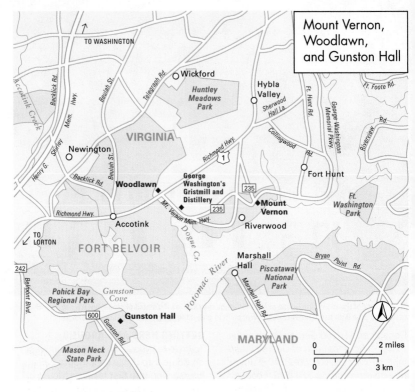

Thornton, a physician and amateur architect who drew up the original plans for the U.S. Capitol. Built on a site selected by George Washington, the mansion has commanding views of the surrounding countryside and the Potomac River. It was once an estate where more than 100 people, most of them slaves, lived and worked. Guides explain how the family entertained and architectural details of the house. The modest and sparsely furnished Pope-Leighey House, designed by Frank Lloyd Wright, provides a stark contrast to Woodlawn. It was moved here from Falls Church, Virginia, in 1964, to save it from destruction during the building of Route 66. Built to bring nature inside, the 1,200-square-foot, two-bedroom, one-bath home features Tidewater red cypress, brick, a flat roof, and tall glass windows and doors. Even

the furniture was designed by Wright. The home was commissioned by journalist Lauren Pope and his wife, Charlotte, and they lived here for six years, selling the house in 1946 to Robert and Marjorie Leighey. ✉ *9000 Richmond Hwy., Alexandria* ☎ *703/570–6902* ⊕ *www.woodlawn-popeleighey.org* 💳 *From $10* ⊙ *Closed Tues.–Thurs.*

Gunston Hall, Virginia

12 miles south of Woodlawn, 25 miles south of Washington, D.C.

Down the Potomac from Mount Vernon is the home of another important George. Gentleman-farmer George Mason was a colonel of the Virginia militia and author of the Virginia Declaration of Rights, the model for the U.S. Bill of Rights, which called for freedom of the press, tolerance of religion, and other fundamental democratic principles. Mason was a framer of the Constitution but refused to sign the final document because it didn't stop the importation of slaves, adequately restrain the powers of the federal government, or include a bill of rights. Mason's objections spurred the movement for the inclusion of the Bill of Rights into the Constitution. This 18th-century Georgian mansion was located at the center of a 5,500-acre plantation. You can tour the home and grounds of Gunston Hall, a National Historic Landmark.

GETTING HERE AND AROUND

You'll have to use a car to get to Gunston Hall because there is no bus stop within walking distance. Travel south on Route 1, 9 miles past Woodlawn to Route 242; turn left there and go 3½ miles to the plantation entrance.

 Sights

Not far from George Washington's home lies Gunston Hall, a mansion built in the 18th century for founding father George Mason. Many well-known historical figures have set foot on this land. The mansion is now known for its association with Mason as well as its intricate, unique architecture and interior design. It serves as a museum and is open to the general public.

★ George Mason's Gunston Hall

HOUSE | FAMILY | The Georgian-style mansion has some of the finest hand-carved ornamented interiors in the country and is the handiwork of the 18th-century's foremost architect, William Buckland, originally an indentured servant from England. Construction of Gunston Hall took place between 1755 and 1759. Buckland went on to design several notable buildings in Virginia and Maryland, including the Hammond-Harwood and Chase-Lloyd houses in Annapolis. It is believed he worked closely with another indentured servant, William Bernard Sears, to complete the house. Unlike other Virginia colonial homes which tended to be very simple, Gunston Hall was the only house known to have had chinoiserie decoration. The interior and the outbuildings have been meticulously restored.

The formal gardens, excavated by a team of archaeologists, are famous for their boxwoods—some were planted during George Mason's time, making them among the oldest in the country. The Potomac is visible past the expansive deer park, and Mason's landing road to the river has been found. Guided tours are offered daily every half hour between 9:30 am and 4:30 pm, with longer tours on Monday morning and Thursday afternoon (see the website for specific times). ⊠ 10709 Gunston Rd., Mason Neck ☎ 703/550–9220 ⊕ www.gunstonhall. org ⊠ $10.

★ National Museum of the Marine Corps

MUSEUM | FAMILY | The glassy atrium of this 118,000-square-foot homage to the military's finest soars into the sky next to the Marine Corps Base Quantico. The design was inspired by the iconic photograph of Marines lifting the American flag on Iwo Jima. Inside the museum, visitors are able to see the flag itself, as well as experience the life of a Marine. The museum is completely interactive and also has a staggering collection of tanks, aircraft, rocket launchers, and other weapons. There is even a rifle range simulator, where guests of all ages can learn how to hold a laser rifle and practice hitting targets. Family Day at the Museum is held the second Saturday of the month with activities and crafts. There also are gallery hunts for children ages 4–10 that encourage exploration of the museum. ⊠ 18900 Jefferson Davis Hwy., Triangle ☎ 877/635–1775 ⊕ www. usmcmuseum.org ⊠ Free.

Annapolis, Maryland

32 miles east of Washington, D.C.

This beautiful city, the capital of Maryland, offers something for everyone. Whether you spend one or several days here, you'll discover fascinating history; exciting sporting, visual, and performing arts events; great dining, shopping, and nightlife; and dozens of recreation activities. There are more 18th-century brick homes in Annapolis than in any other city in the nation, and, because the city is so walkable, it is truly a walk down memory lane. It's also a popular boating destination and on warm sunny days, the waters off City Dock become center stage for boats of all sizes. If you love the water, the Chesapeake Bay, and the area's winding inlets, creeks, and rivers provide wonderful opportunities for paddleboarding, kayaking, sailing, or fishing. One of Annapolis's longest-standing institutions is the U.S. Naval Academy, which has been training officers for the U.S. Navy and Marine Corps since 1845. As you stroll through downtown, you'll often see uniformed midshipmen in their crisp white uniforms in summer and navy blue in winter. A visit to the Naval Academy campus, to learn about its lengthy and proud history and get a close-up look at what life as a midshipman is like, is a must.

GETTING HERE AND AROUND

The drive (east on U.S. 50 to the Rowe Boulevard exit) normally takes 35–45 minutes from Washington. During rush hour (weekdays 3:30–6:30 pm), however, it takes about twice as long. Also, beware of Navy football Saturdays.

Parking spots on the historic downtown streets of Annapolis are scarce, but there are some parking meters for $2 an hour (maximum two hours). You can park on some residential streets for free for two hours. The public parking garage adjacent to the Annapolis Visitors Center charges $2 per hour with a daily maximum of $15. The Annapolis Circulator offers free trolley transportation within the historic area. On Sunday morning from 6 am to 1 pm, most parking is free.

TOURS

Walking tours are a great way to see the historic district, and Discover Annapolis Tours and Watermark run historical and ghost tours. Watermark and Schooner *Woodwind* Cruises offer boat trips.

Discover Annapolis Tours

BUS TOURS | Narrated trolley tours, departing from the visitor center, introduce you to the history and architecture of Annapolis. ⊠ *26 West St.* ☎ *410/266–3392* ⊕ *www.townetransport.com/tours* 🚌 *From $18.*

Schooner Woodwind Cruises

BOAT TOURS | Two 74-foot sailboats, *Woodwind* and *Woodwind II,* make daily trips and overnight excursions. ⊠ *Annapolis Waterfront Hotel dock, 80 Compromise St.* ☎ *410/263–7837, 410/263–7837* ⊕ *www.schoonerwoodwind.com* 🚌 *From $43.*

★ Watermark

WALKING TOURS | Tour guides wearing colonial-style dress take you to the State House, St. John's College, and the Naval Academy on their very popular twice-daily, 2¼-hour "Four Centuries Walking Tour." There's also a "Historic Ghost Walk" on weekends. Watermark also runs boat tours, lasting from 40 minutes to 7½ hours, going as far as St. Michael's on the Eastern Shore where there's a maritime museum as well as dining and boutiques. ⊠ *1 Dock St.* ☎ *410/268–7601* ⊕ *www.watermarkjourney.com* 🚌 *From $20.*

VISITOR INFORMATION

CONTACTS Visit Annapolis & Anne Arundel County ⊠ *26 West St.* ☎ *410/280–0445, 888/302–2852* ⊕ *www.visitannapolis.org.* **Visitor Information Booth** ⊠ *Ego Alley, Dock St.* ☎ *410/280–0445.*

Sights

Banneker-Douglass Museum

MUSEUM | FAMILY | This museum of African American heritage is named in honor of abolitionist Frederick Douglass and scientist Benjamin Banneker. This former church and its next-door neighbor make up a museum that tells the stories of African Americans in Maryland through performances, lectures, educational programs, and both permanent and changing exhibits. ✉ *84 Franklin St.* ☎ *410/216–6180* ⊕ *bdmuseum.maryland. gov* 🎫 *Free* ⊘ *Closed Sun. and Mon.*

Hammond-Harwood House

HOUSE | Based on the Villa Pisani in Montagnana, Italy, this 1774 home was considered America's greatest colonial high-style residence. Called the architectural "Jewel of Annapolis," the residence was greatly admired by Thomas Jefferson when he sketched the house in 1783. The wood carvings surrounding the front door and enriching the dining room are some of the best surviving of their kind in America. The site today exhibits famous colonial art by Charles Willson Peale and Rembrandt Peale as well as a decorative arts collection covering everything from Chinese-export porcelain to Georgian-period silver. The property's Colonial Revival garden is lovely. ✉ *19 Maryland Ave.* ☎ *410/263–4683* ⊕ *www.hammondhar-woodhouse.org* 🎫 *$10* ⊘ *Closed Tues. By appointment only Jan.–Mar.*

Historic Annapolis Museum

MUSEUM | Light-filled and modern, this little museum occupies a historic building that once held supplies for the Continental Army during the Revolutionary War. The current exhibit, *Freedom Bound: Runaways of the Chesapeake,* tells the stories of individuals who resisted servitude during the 1760s–1860s, through artifacts and displays, video, and hands-on activities. The Museum Store sells a wonderful array of history books, beautiful ceramic pieces, crafts made by local artisans, and nautical gifts. Nearby, the Historic Annapolis Waterfront Warehouse at 4 Pinkney Street, which was used in the early 19th century to store tobacco before it was shipped to England, serves as a great orientation site for historic Annapolis properties with its detailed diorama of Annapolis during the 1790s. ✉ *99 Main St.* ☎ *410/267–7619* ⊕ *www. annapolis.org* 🎫 *Free.*

Historic London Town and Gardens

HISTORIC SITE | The 17th-century tobacco port of London, on the South River a short car ride from Annapolis, was made up of 40 dwellings, shops, and taverns. London all but disappeared in the 18th century, its buildings abandoned and left to decay, but one of the few remaining original colonial structures is a three-story brick house, built by William Brown between 1758 and 1764, with dramatic river views. Newly reconstructed buildings include a tenement for lower-class workers, a carpenter's shop, and a barn. Walk around on your own or take a 30-minute docent-led tour; allow more time to wander the house grounds, woodland gardens, and a visitor center with an interactive exhibit on the area's archaeology and history. ✉ *839 London-town Rd., Edgewater* ☎ *410/222–1919* ⊕ *www.historiclondontown.org* 🎫 *$12* ⊘ *Closed Mon. and Tues.*

Kunta Kinte–Alex Haley Memorial

MEMORIAL | *The Story Wall,* comprising 10 plaques along the waterfront, recounts the story of African Americans in Maryland. These granite-framed markers lead to a sculpture group depicting Alex Haley, famed author of *Roots,* reading to a group of children. Here you'll also see a plaque that commemorates the 1767 arrival of the African slave Kunta Kinte, who was immortalized in Haley's novel. Across the street is "The Compass Rose," a 14-foot-diameter inlaid bronze map of the world oriented to true north with Annapolis in the center. ✉ *Sidewalk at City Dock* ⊕ *www.annapolis.gov.*

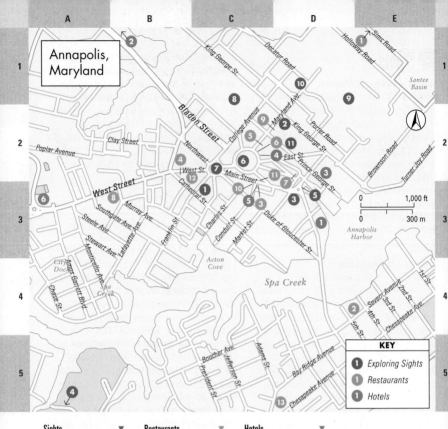

Annapolis, Maryland

Sights ▼

1 Banneker-Douglass Museum **C3**
2 Hammond-Harwood House **D2**
3 Historic Annapolis Museum **D3**
4 Historic London Town and Gardens **A5**
5 Kunta Kinte-Alex Haley Memorial **C2**
6 Maryland State House .. **C2**
7 St. Anne's Episcopal Church **C2**
8 St. John's College **C1**
9 United States Naval Academy **D1**
10 US Naval Academy Museum **D1**
11 William Paca House and Garden **D2**

Restaurants ▼

1 Cantler's Riverside Inn .. **E1**
2 Carrol's Creek Cafe **D4**
3 Chick & Ruth's Delly **C3**
4 49 West Coffeehouse, Winebar and Gallery **B2**
5 Galway Bay Irish Restaurant and Pub **C2**
6 Harry Browne's **C2**
7 Iron Rooster **D3**
8 Metropolitan Kitchen & Lounge **B3**
9 Old Fox Books and Coffeehouse **D2**
10 Osteria 177 .... **C3**
11 Preserve **C3**
12 Rams Head Tavern **C2**
13 Vin 909 Winecafe **D5**

Hotels ▼

1 Annapolis Waterfront Hotel, Autograph Collection **D3**
2 Country Inn & Suites by Radisson, Annapolis, MD **B1**
3 Gibson's Lodging sof Annapolis **D2**
4 Historic Inns of Annapolis **C2**
5 Scotlaur Inn **C3**
6 The Westin Annapolis **A3**

Maryland State House

GOVERNMENT BUILDING | Originally constructed between 1772 and 1780, the State House is the oldest state capitol in continuous legislative use; it's also the only one in which the U.S. Congress has sat (1783–84). General George Washington resigned as commander in chief of the Continental Army here in 1783 and the Treaty of Paris was ratified in 1784, ending the Revolutionary War. Both events took place in the Old Senate Chamber. Visit the Office of Interpretation on the first floor to pick up self-guided tour information. You must have a photo ID to enter the State House. In the State House Square is the **Thurgood Marshall Memorial,** an 8-foot statue of Thurgood Marshall as a young lawyer, benches with images of students for whom he fought for integration, and plaques commemorating his achievements. Born in Baltimore, Marshall (1908–93) was the first African American Supreme Court justice. He won the decision in 1954's *Brown v. Board of Education,* in which the court overturned the doctrine of "separate but equal." ⊠ *100 State Circle* ⊕ *www.msa. maryland.gov* ⊠ *Free.*

St. Anne's Episcopal Church

RELIGIOUS SITE | In the center of one of the historic area's busy circles, this brick building is one of the city's most prominent places of worship. King William III donated the communion silver when the parish was founded in 1692, but the first St. Anne's Church wasn't completed until 1704. The second church burned in 1858, but parts of its walls survived and were incorporated into the present structure, which was built the following year. Free guided tours are offered the first and third Monday of every month at 10 and every Wednesday at 12:30.

The churchyard contains the grave of the last colonial governor, Sir Robert Eden. ⊠ *Church Circle* ☎ *410/267–9333* ⊕ *www.stannes-annapolis.org* ⊠ *Free.*

St. John's College

COLLEGE | St. John's is the third-oldest college in the country (after Harvard and William and Mary) and adheres to a Great Books program: all students follow the same four-year, liberal-arts curriculum, which includes philosophy, mathematics, music, science, Greek, and French. Students are immersed in the classics through small classes conducted as discussions rather than lectures. Start a visit here by climbing the slope of the long, brick-paved path to the cupola of McDowell Hall.

Down King George Street toward the water is the **Carroll-Barrister House,** now the college admissions office. Once home to Charles Carroll (not the signer of the Declaration but his cousin), the house was built in 1722 at Main and Conduit Streets and moved onto campus in 1955. The **Elizabeth Myers Mitchell Art Gallery,** on the east side of Mellon Hall, presents world-class exhibits and special programs that relate to the fine arts. ⊠ *60 College Ave.* ☎ *410/263–2371* ⊕ *www.sjc.edu* ⌚ *Mitchell Gallery closed Mon.*

★ United States Naval Academy

COLLEGE | Probably the most interesting and important site in Annapolis, the Naval Academy, established in 1845, occupies 328 waterfront acres along the Severn River. The midshipmen (the term used for both women and men) go to classes, conduct military drills, and practice or compete in intercollegiate and intramural sports. Your visit to "The Yard" (as the USNA grounds are nicknamed) will start at the **Armel-Leftwich Visitor Center.** The visitor center features an exhibit, *The Quarter Deck,* which introduces visitors to the Academy's mission, including a 13-minute film, "The Call to Serve," and a well-stocked gift shop. From here you can join one of the hour-long guided walking tours of the Academy. The centerpiece of the campus is the bright copper-clad dome of the interdenominational

Did You Know?

The Navy's Blue Angels fly over each graduating class at the U.S. Naval Academy in Annapolis to celebrate their accomplishments.

U.S. Naval Academy Chapel, beneath which is buried Revolutionary War naval hero John Paul Jones. You can go inside Bancroft Hall (one of the world's largest dormitories) and see a sample room and the glorious Memorial Hall. ■ **TIP→ You can have lunch on campus either at Drydock in Dahlgren Hall or the Naval Academy Club.** ✉ *121 Blake Rd.* ✥ *All visitors 18 years and older must have a government-issued photo ID to be admitted. You cannot park on campus; enter on foot through the Visitor Access Center at Gate 1* ☎ *410/293–8687* 🌐 *www.usna.edu* 🎫 *Free.*

U.S. Naval Academy Museum

MUSEUM | FAMILY | Displays of model ships and memorabilia from naval heroes and fighting vessels tell the story of the U.S. Navy. The Rogers Ship Model Collection has nearly 80 models of sailing ships built for the British Admiralty, the largest display of 17th- and 18th-century ship models in North America. Kids of all ages will enjoy watching the restoration and building of model ships on the ground level and might even learn a few tricks of the trade should they wish to purchase a model ship kit to build when they get home. ✉ *Preble Hall, 118 Maryland Ave.* ✥ *On campus, so a government-issued photo ID is required if you are 18 or over* ☎ *410/293–2108* 🌐 *www.usna.edu* 🎫 *Free.*

William Paca House and Garden

HOUSE | A signer of the Declaration of Independence, Paca (pronounced "PAY-cuh") was a Maryland governor from 1782 to 1785. His house was built from 1763 through 1765, and its original garden was finished by 1772. The main floor (furnished with 18th-century antiques) retains its original Prussian blue and soft gray color scheme and the second floor houses more 18th-century pieces. The adjacent 2-acre garden provides a longer perspective on the back of the house, plus worthwhile sights of its own: upper terraces, a Chinese Chippendale bridge, a pond, a wilderness area, and formal arrangements. An inn, Carvel Hall, once stood in the gardens, now planted with 18th-century perennials. You can take a self-guided tour of the garden, but to see the house you must go on the docent-led tour, which leaves every hour at half past the hour. The last tour leaves 1½ hours before closing. ✉ *186 Prince George St.* ☎ *410/990–4543* 🌐 *www.annapolis.org/contact/william-paca-house-garden* 🎫 *$10* 🕓 *Closed Jan. and Feb.*

🍴 Restaurants

In the beginning, there was crab: crab cakes, crab soup, whole crabs to crack. This Chesapeake Bay specialty is still found in abundance, but Annapolis has broadened its horizons to include eateries—many in the historic district—that offer many sorts of cuisines. Ask for a restaurant guide at the visitor center.

★ Cantler's Riverside Inn

$$$ | SEAFOOD | Jimmy Cantler, a native Marylander who worked as a waterman on Chesapeake Bay, founded this local institution 40 years ago. The no-nonsense interior has nautical items laminated beneath tabletops, and steamed mussels, clams, and shrimp as well as a tomato-based Maryland crab soup, seafood sandwiches, crab cakes, and much more. **Known for:** seasonal outdoor dining right next to the water; steamed crabs served on a "tablecloth" of brown paper; a classic casual Maryland seafood experience. [$] *Average main: $32* ✉ *458 Forest Beach Rd.* ☎ *410/757–1311* 🌐 *www.cantlers.com.*

Carrol's Creek Cafe

$$$ | AMERICAN | You can walk, catch a water taxi from City Dock, or drive over the Spa Creek drawbridge to this local favorite in Eastport. Whether you dine indoors or out, the view of historic Annapolis and its harbor is spectacular. **Known for:** à la carte Sunday brunch; upscale (but not too pricey) seafood specialties; amazing city and harbor views. $ *Average main: $34* ✉ *410 Severn Ave.* ☎ *410/263–8102* ⊕ *www. carrolscreek.com.*

Chick and Ruth's Delly

$ | **AMERICAN** | Deli sandwiches (many named after local politicians), burgers, subs, crab cakes, and milk shakes are the fare at this very busy counter-and-booth institution. Baltimoreans Ruth and Chick Levitt purchased the building, built in 1899, in 1965. **Known for:** giant milk shakes (including a 6-pounder); patriotic decor and a daily recitation of the Pledge of Allegiance; homemade pies and breads. $ *Average main: $9* ✉ *165 Main St.* ☎ *410/269–6737* ⊕ *www.chickandruths.com.*

49 West Coffeehouse, Winebar and Gallery

$$ | **ECLECTIC** | In what was once a hardware store, this casual eatery has one interior wall of exposed brick and another of exposed plaster; both are used to hang art for sale by local artists. Daily specials are chalked on a blackboard and include a large cheese-and-pâté plate, flatbread pizzas, deli sandwiches, espresso, waffles, soups, and salads. **Known for:** live music every night; eclectic coffeehouse vibe; flatbread pizzas, deli sandwiches, and coffee galore. $ *Average main: $17* ✉ *49 West St.* ☎ *410/626–9796* ⊕ *49westcoffeehouse.com.*

★ Galway Bay Irish Restaurant and Pub

$ | **IRISH** | Step inside this Irish pub and you'll be welcomed like a member of the family. As you would expect, the corned beef and cabbage and other traditional Irish menu items (along with classic Annapolis bar food like crab and oysters) are fantastic. **Known for:** traditional Irish grub and hospitality; authentic housemade corned-beef hash; Sunday brunch with live music. $ *Average main: $12* ✉ *63 Maryland Ave.* ☎ *301/263–8333* ⊕ *www.galwaybaymd.com.*

Harry Browne's

$$$ | **AMERICAN** | In the shadow of the State House, this understated establishment has long held a reputation for quality food and attentive service that ensures bustle year-round, especially during the busy days of the legislative session (early January into early April) and special weekend events at the Naval Academy. The menu clearly reflects the city's maritime culture, but also has seasonal specialties. **Known for:** political clientele; tasty homemade desserts, such as Oreo cheesecake; champagne brunch on Sunday. $ *Average main: $35* ✉ *66 State Circle* ☎ *410/263–4332* ⊕ *www.harrybrownes.com.*

★ Iron Rooster

$ | **AMERICAN** | There's often a line of hungry diners waiting for a table at this comfort-food haven located on the city dock, where the portions are generous and service first-rate. You can enjoy breakfast all day—Benedicts and omelets are top sellers, as are the chicken and waffles and the shrimp and grits. **Known for:** daily homemade pop-tart specials; Southern-inspired all-day breakfast (including amazingly light and fluffy biscuits); long lines. $ *Average main: $15* ✉ *12 Market Space* ☎ *410/990–1600* ⊕ *www.ironroosterallday.com.*

Metropolitan Kitchen & Lounge

$$ | **MEDITERRANEAN** | One of the few restaurants in the city with a rooftop, this establishment co-owned by Annapolis mayor Gavin Buckley, takes full advantage of its lovely perch and features live music most evenings. The menu satisfies global palates in a town otherwise known for Old Bay and crab cakes, bringing in a bit of Australia flair from the mayor's homeland. **Known for:** lamb burgers and traditional Greek salad; one of the few rooftop bars in town; craft cocktails. $ *Average main: $24* ✉ *175 West St.* ☎ *410/280–5160* ⊕ *www.metropolitanannapolis.com.*

Old Fox Books and Coffeehouse
$ | **BAKERY** | More than just a bookstore, the café here is a local favorite spot for an espresso drink, freshly baked pastry, soup, or sandwich. After a bite, head outside to see the charming Fairy Garden and book house, which is literally made of books. **Known for:** popular meeting spot for locals; coffee drinks made with beans from local roaster, Ceremony Coffee; free Wi-Fi. [$] *Average main: $4* ✉ *35 Maryland Ave.* ☎ *410/626–2020* 🌐 *oldfoxbooks.com.*

★ **Osteria 177**
$$$$ | **MODERN ITALIAN** | This might be the only local Italian restaurant that doesn't offer pizza or spaghetti. Instead, Osteria serves seafood from all over the world, meat, and pasta made on the premises. **Known for:** politicians and lobbyists at lunchtime; authentic coastal Italian cuisine; unique pastas. [$] *Average main: $38* ✉ *177 Main St.* ☎ *410/267–7700* 🌐 *www.osteria177.com.*

Preserve
$$$ | **AMERICAN** | Jars of pickled chard stems and radishes, preserved lemons, and pepper jelly line the shelves at this lively spot on Main Street run by a husband-and-wife team who both have impressive culinary resumes and a shared passion for pickling, fermenting, and preserving. The chef's roots in the Pennsylvania Dutch country shine through with chicken potpie, pork and sauerkraut, and a Dutch hash and liverwurst sandwich. **Known for:** varied dishes that highlight unique preservation methods; kimchi and sauerkraut galore; lots of seasonal veggies. [$] *Average main: $29* ✉ *164 Main St.* ☎ *443/598–6920* 🌐 *www.preserve-eats.com* 🕒 *Closed Mon.*

Rams Head Tavern
$ | **BRITISH** | This traditional English-style pub serves better-than-usual tavern fare, as well as more than 100 beers—30 on tap—including five Fordham beers and others from around the world. Brunch is served on Sunday, and nationally known folk, rock, jazz, country, and bluegrass artists perform most nights. **Known for:** Maryland cream of crab soup; massive beer menu; live music. [$] *Average main: $15* ✉ *33 West St.* ☎ *410/268–4545* 🌐 *www.ramsheadtavern.com.*

Vin 909 Winecafe
$ | **AMERICAN** | If it wasn't for the sign out front, you might think you're at someone's Eastport home given the charming front porch and well-tended gardens. But walk through the doors and you'll discover a casually hip and always crowded restaurant serving organic, sustainable, and seasonally focused food that's simply fantastic. **Known for:** crispy pizza with farm-to-table toppings; huge wine menu by the glass and bottle; diverse selection of beers. [$] *Average main: $16* ✉ *909 Bay Ridge Ave.* ☎ *410/990–1846* 🌐 *www.vin909.com* 🕒 *Closed Mon.*

🛏 Hotels

There are many places to stay near the heart of the city, as well as bed-and-breakfasts and chain motels a few miles outside town. Prices vary considerably. They rise astronomically for "Commissioning Week" at the Naval Academy (late May), the week of July 4, and during the sailboat and powerboat shows in October.

Annapolis Waterfront Hotel, Autograph Collection
$$$ | **HOTEL** | **FAMILY** | You can practically fish from your room at the city's only waterfront hotel (now part of Marriott's Autograph Collection), where rooms have either balconies over the water or large windows with views of the harbor or the historic district. **Pros:** "pure room" available for the allergy sensitive; accessible for travelers with disabilities; complimentary Wi-Fi throughout. **Cons:** some rooms have no waterfront view, some have only partial views; chain hotel lacks charm; parking is pricey. [$] *Rooms from: $299* ✉ *80 Compromise*

St. ☎ *410/268–7555* 🌐 *www.annapoliswaterfront.com* 🍴 *No meals.*

Country Inn & Suites by Radisson, Annapolis, MD
$ | **HOTEL** | Although this hotel is 5 miles from the historic Annapolis waterfront, there's a free shuttle, and the two-room suites with pullout sofas are perfect for families. **Pros:** reliable and inexpensive option; free shuttle services; complimentary Wi-Fi. **Cons:** distance from the dock; tiny gym; small indoor heated pool can be crowded at times. [$] *Rooms from: $125* ✉ *2600 Housely Rd.* ☎ *410/571–6700, 800/456–4000* 🌐 *www.countryinns.com* 🛏 *100 rooms* 🍴 *Free Breakfast.*

Gibson's Lodgings of Annapolis
$ | **HOTEL** | Just half a block from the water, the three detached houses that form this hotel come from three centuries—1780, 1890, and 1980—and all the guest rooms are furnished with pre-1900 antiques. **Pros:** conveniently located between the Naval Academy and downtown; free parking in the courtyards; free continental breakfast. **Cons:** cannot accommodate children under the age of eight; two of the rooms share a bathroom; no elevator, although three rooms are on the ground floor. [$] *Rooms from: $146* ✉ *110 Prince George St.* ☎ *410/268–5555, 877/330–0057* 🌐 *www.gibsonslodgings.com* 🛏 *20 rooms* 🍴 *Free Breakfast.*

★ **Historic Inns of Annapolis**
$ | **B&B/INN** | Three 18th-century properties in the historic district—the Governor Calvert House, Robert Johnson House, and Maryland Inn—are grouped as one inn, all offering guest rooms individually decorated with antiques and reproductions. **Pros:** beautifully renovated historic properties; within walking distance of activities; lemonade or spiced cider served daily in the Calvert House. **Cons:** prices vary greatly; some rooms are small; all parking at Robert Johnson house. [$] *Rooms from: $129* ✉ *58 State Circle* ☎ *410/263–2641, 800/847–8882* 🌐 *www.historicinnsofannapolis.com* 🛏 *124 rooms* 🍴 *No meals.*

Scotlaur Inn
$ | **B&B/INN** | On the two floors above Chick and Ruth's Delly in the heart of the historic district, this family-owned B&B is cozy and characterful. **Pros:** a chance to stay above one of Annapolis's landmarks; half off in nearby parking garage; literally in the heart of town. **Cons:** not for those who prefer modern style and don't like chintz; rooms are on the small side; no elevator. [$] *Rooms from: $100* ✉ *165 Main St.* ☎ *410/268–5665* 🌐 *www.scotlaurinn.com* 🛏 *10 rooms* 🍴 *Free Breakfast.*

The Westin Annapolis
$$ | **HOTEL** | **FAMILY** | About a mile and a half from City Dock, in a rapidly gentrifying neighborhood, this hotel is the centerpiece of a European-themed planned community, complete with restaurants, shops, and condominiums. **Pros:** comfy "heavenly beds"; modern hotel with many amenities; spacious guest rooms. **Cons:** distance from the City Dock; Wi-Fi only free in public areas; lacking charm found in other historic properties. [$] *Rooms from: $249* ✉ *100 Westgate Circle* ☎ *410/972–4300* 🌐 *www.marriott.com/hotels/hotel-rooms/bwiwa-the-westin-annapolis/* 🛏 *225 rooms* 🍴 *No meals.*

Baltimore

39 miles northeast of Washington, D.C.

Baltimore is a city of distinct neighborhoods. While stellar downtown attractions such as the National Aquarium and the Inner Harbor draw torrents of tourists each year, much of the city's character can be found in bergs like Hampden (the "p" is silent) and Federal Hill. One of the largest cities in early America, Baltimore's protected harbor gave the city a strategic advantage.

Tourism grew dramatically in the early 1980s with the completion of the Harborplace shopping plaza and its crown jewel, the National Aquarium. Further development of the Inner Harbor, including Oriole Park at Camden Yards and M&T Bank Stadium, continued to fuel the city's resurgence.

GETTING HERE AND AROUND

If you are going to Baltimore by car, it's about an hour from Washington, D.C. Parking in the Inner Harbor area, where most tourist attractions are, can be expensive. Fell's Point is usually cheaper.

It's usually easier and faster (and cheaper, considering the cost of parking) to get to Baltimore from D.C. by train. MARC Penn Line trains run from Union Station to Baltimore's Penn Station several times a day, including weekends, taking about 45 minutes and costing $7. You can also take Amtrak from Union Station to Baltimore Penn Station, but it's about twice as expensive. The Camden Line runs only during commuting hours on weekdays and takes a bit longer, but takes you to Camden Station, which is more convenient to the Inner Harbor sights. You can also take a bus from Union Station, but it generally takes longer.

Once in Baltimore, you can take the free Charm City Circulator shuttle (four bus lines plus a harbor ferry), or, if you are in a hurry, jump in a taxi or ride-share.

CONTACTS Charm City Circulator
☎ 410/545–1956 ⊕ www.charmcitycirculator.com **Maryland Transit Administration** ☎ 800/325–7245, 410/539–5000 ⊕ www.mta.maryland.gov.

VISITOR INFORMATION

CONTACTS Baltimore Visitor Center ✉ 401 Light St., Inner Harbor ☎ 877/225–8466 ⊕ baltimore.org.

◉ Sights

Most of the major sights in Baltimore are in the Inner Harbor area or nearby, but you may also want to visit some sights that are further out, all of which are on one of the Charm City Connector routes.

★ American Visionary Art Museum

MUSEUM | The nation's primary museum and education center for self-taught or "outsider" art has won great acclaim by both museum experts and those who don't even consider themselves art aficionados. Seven galleries exhibit the quirky creations—paintings, sculptures, relief works, and pieces that defy easy classification—of untrained "visionary" artists working outside the mainstream art world. In addition to the visual stimulation of amazingly intricate or refreshingly inventive works, reading the short bios of artists will give you insight to their often-moving spiritual and expressive motivations. The museum's unusual, playful philosophy extends outside its walls, with large exhibits installed in a former whiskey warehouse, an outdoor movie theater, and a 55-foot whirligig twirling in the museum's plaza. ✉ 800 Key Hwy., Federal Hill ☎ 410/244–1900 ⊕ www.avam.org ⌂ $10.

★ Baltimore Museum of Art

MUSEUM | Works by Matisse, Picasso, Cézanne, Gauguin, van Gogh, and Monet are among the 90,000 paintings, sculptures, and decorative arts on exhibit at this impressive museum near Johns Hopkins University. Particular strengths include an encyclopedic collection of postimpressionist paintings donated to the museum by the Cone sisters, Baltimore natives who were pioneer collectors of early-20th-century art. The museum also owns the world's second-largest collection of Andy Warhol works, and many pieces of 18th- and 19th-century American painting and decorative arts. The museum's neoclassical main building was designed by John Russell Pope,

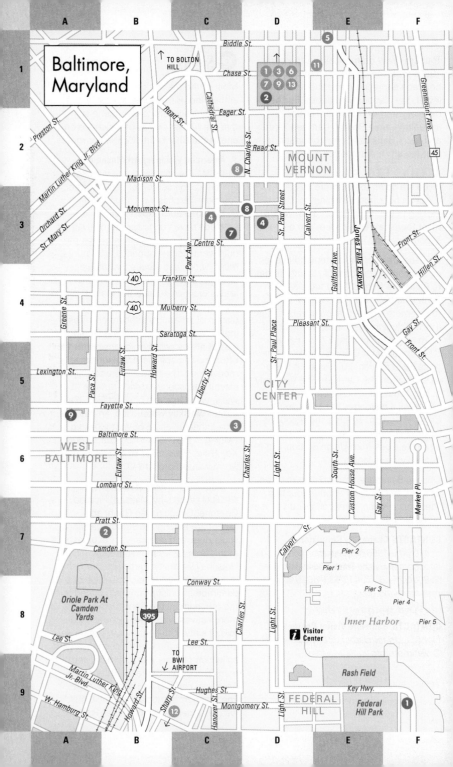

14

Sights ▼

1 American Visionary
Art Museum **F9**
2 Baltimore Museum of Art......... **D1**
3 Fort McHenry National Monument
and Historic Shrine **G9**
4 George Peabody Library.......... **D3**
5 The National Great Blacks
In Wax Museum **J1**
6 Oriole Park at Camden Yards..... **G8**
7 Walters Art Museum............... **C3**
8 Washington Monument........... **D3**
9 Westminster Burying Ground and
Catacombs **A5**

Restaurants ▼

1 Ambassador Dining Room........ **D1**
2 Azumi............................... **G8**
3 Bottega **D1**
4 Charleston........................... **H8**
5 Cinghiale........................... **G8**
6 The Food Market.................. **D1**
7 Gertrude's **D1**
8 The Helmand **C2**
9 La Cuchara **D1**
10 Ouzo Bay.......................... **H8**
11 The Prime Rib **E1**
12 Rye Street Tavern................ **B9**
13 Woodberry Kitchen............... **D1**

Hotels ▼

1 Four Seasons Baltimore **G9**
2 Hilton Baltimore................... **B7**
3 Hotel Monaco Baltimore.......... **C6**
4 Hotel Revival **C3**
5 The Ivy Hotel **E1**
6 Marriott Baltimore Waterfront... **G8**
7 Sagamore Pendry Baltimore **J9**

the architect of the National Gallery in Washington. A $28-million renovation resulted in a new, interactive exhibition space, a renovated visitor's entrance, and a completely reworked contemporary wing. From Gertrude's, the museum restaurant, you can look out at 20th-century sculpture displayed in two landscaped gardens. ⊠ *10 Art Museum Dr., Charles Village* ☎ *443/573–1700* ⊕ *www.artbma. org* ⊠ *Free* ☉ *Closed Mon. and Tues.*

★ Fort McHenry National Monument and Historic Shrine

MILITARY SITE | This star-shaped brick fort is forever associated with Francis Scott Key and "The Star-Spangled Banner," which Key penned while watching the British bombardment of Baltimore during the War of 1812. Through the next day and night, as the battle raged, Key strained to be sure, through the smoke and haze, that the flag still flew above Fort McHenry—indicating that Baltimore's defenders held firm. "By the dawn's early light" of September 14, 1814, he saw the 30- by 42-foot "Star-Spangled Banner" still aloft and was inspired to pen the words to a poem (set to the tune of an old English drinking song). The flag that flew above Fort McHenry that day had 15 stars and 15 stripes, and was hand-sewn for the fort. A visit to the fort includes a 15-minute history film, guided tour, and frequent living-history displays on summer weekends. To see how the formidable fortifications might have appeared to the bombarding British, catch a water taxi from the Inner Harbor to the fort instead of driving. ⊠ *E. Fort Ave., Locust Point* ✛ *From Light St., take Key Hwy. for 1½ miles and follow signs* ☎ *410/962–4290* ⊕ *www. nps.gov/fomc* ⊠ *$15.*

George Peabody Library

LIBRARY | Known as a "cathedral of books," the five-story reading room is consistently listed among the world's most beautiful libraries. Designed by Edmund Lind, it opened to the public in 1878. Its gilded framework of cast iron and gold showcases more than 300,000 volumes printed from the 15th to the 19th centuries in the areas of archaeology, architecture, history, literature, travel, and art. ⊠ *17 E. Mt. Vernon Pl., Mount Vernon* ☎ *410/234–4943* ⊕ *peabodyevents.library.jhu.edu.*

The National Great Blacks in Wax Museum

MUSEUM | FAMILY | Though not as convincing as the likenesses at a Madame Tussauds, the more than 100 wax figures on display here do a good job of recounting the triumphs and trials of Africans and African Americans. The wax figures are accompanied by text and audio. Baltimoreans honored include Frederick Douglass, who as a youth lived and worked in Fells Point; singer Billie Holiday; and jazz composer Eubie Blake. To get here from Mount Vernon, take Charles Street north and turn left at North Avenue. ⊠ *1601 E. North Ave., East Baltimore* ☎ *410/563–3404* ⊕ *www.greatblacksinwax.org* ⊠ *$15* ☉ *Closed Mon.*

★ Oriole Park at Camden Yards

SPORTS VENUE | FAMILY | Home of the Baltimore Orioles, Camden Yards and the nearby area bustle on game days. Since it opened in 1992, this nostalgically designed baseball stadium has inspired other cities to emulate its neotraditional architecture and amenities. The Eutaw Street promenade, between the warehouse and the field, has a view of the stadium; look for the brass baseballs embedded in the sidewalk that mark where home runs have cleared the fence, or visit the Orioles Hall of Fame display and the monuments to retired Orioles. Daily 90-minute tours take you to nearly every section of the ballpark, from the massive, JumboTron scoreboard to the dugout to the state-of-the-art beer-delivery system. ⊠ *333 W. Camden St., Downtown* ☎ *410/685–9800 general information, 410/547–6234 tour times, 888/848–2473 tickets to Orioles home games* 🌐 *www.theorioles.com* 🎟 *Eutaw St. promenade free; tour $9.*

★ Walters Art Museum

MUSEUM | The Walters' prodigious collection of more than 30,000 artworks provides an organized overview of human history over 5,500 years, from the 3rd millennium BC to the early 20th century. The museum houses major collections of Renaissance, baroque, and Asian art as well as one of the nation's best collections of Egyptian, Greek, Roman, Byzantine, and Ethiopian art. It also houses medieval armor and artifacts, jewelry and decorative works, a gift shop, a family activities and arts center on the lower-level, and a café. ✉ *600 N. Charles St., Mount Vernon* ☎ *410/547–9000* 🌐 *www.thewalters.org* 🎟 *Free* 🕓 *Closed Mon. and Tues.*

★ Washington Monument

MEMORIAL | **FAMILY** | Completed on July 4, 1829, the impressive monument was the first one dedicated to the nation's first president. An 18-foot statue depicting Washington caps the 160-foot white marble tower. The tower was designed and built by Robert Mills, the first architect born and educated in the United States; 19 years after completing Baltimore's Washington Monument, Mills designed and erected the national Washington Monument in D.C. After extensive restorations, the monument's lower-level museum has reopened; visitors can climb the 227-step circular staircase to the top and enjoy stunning bird's-eye vistas over downtown. ✉ *Mt. Vernon Pl., Mount Vernon* 🌐 *mvpconservancy.org/the-monument* 🎟 *$6* 🕓 *Closed Mon. and Tues.*

Westminster Burying Ground and Catacombs

CEMETERY | The city's oldest cemetery is the final resting place of Edgar Allan Poe and other famous Marylanders, including 15 generals from the American Revolution and the War of 1812. Dating from 1786, the cemetery was originally known as the Old Western Burying Grounds. In the early 1850s a city ordinance demanded that burial grounds be part of a church, so a building was constructed above the cemetery, creating catacombs beneath it. In the 1930s the schoolchildren of Baltimore collected pennies to raise the necessary funds for Poe's monument. Tours of Westminster Hall (which include the Burying Ground and Catacombs) are offered from April through November every first and third Friday and 6:30 pm and every Saturday at 10 am. ✉ *University of Maryland, Westminster Hall, 519 W. Fayette St., Downtown* ☎ *410/706–2072 tour information and reservations* 🌐 *baltimore.org/listings/historic-sites/westminster-hall-burying-ground* 🎟 *Cemetery free; tours $5.*

🍴 Restaurants

Baltimore cuisine is not all crabs. The city has a wide range of good restaurants.

Ambassador Dining Room

$$ | **INDIAN** | A Tudor-style dining room in a 1930s apartment building is the setting for superb Indian fare. Go for the classics such as chicken *tikka masala* (grilled chicken in a sauce of red pepper, ginger, garlic, and yogurt) or *alu gobi* (spicy potatoes and cauliflower). **Known for:** outdoor dining in the lovely garden; excellent service; traditional Indian desserts. [$] *Average main: $26* ✉ *3811 Canterbury Rd., Tuscany-Canterbury* ☎ *410/366–1484* 🌐 *www.ambassadordining.com.*

Azumi

$$$ | **JAPANESE** | In a town known for its local catch, Azumi's chef flies his fish in daily from Tokyo's famous fish market. Creative takes on Maryland specialties are sure to delight, such as the crab starter, made with tiny Sawagani crabs, which are fried whole and pop in your mouth like buttered popcorn. **Known for:** excellent sashimi, including fresh hamachi; extensive list of Japanese whiskeys; beautiful waterfront views in

a luxury hotel setting. $ *Average main: $31 ✉ Four Seasons Hotel Baltimore, 725 Aliceanna St., Harbor East ☎ 443/220–0477 🌐 www.azumirestaurant.com.*

Bottega

$$ | **TUSCAN** | Conveniently situated near Penn Station, by the Charles Theater and the new Parkway Film Center, chef Sandy Smith's cozy restaurant relocated to this space, which formerly housed the restaurant Cosette, from Maryland Avenue in 2017, offering the same Tuscan comfort food in a larger venue. The menu changes daily, utilizing the freshest ingredients and simplest Tuscan culinary techniques. **Known for:** heavenly handmade pastas and gnocchi; seasonal specialties; a BYOB establishment (so bring your favorite bottle). $ *Average main: $24 ✉ 1709 N. Charles St., Midtown ☎ 443/835–2945 🌐 www.bottega1729.com.*

★ Charleston

$$$$ | **SOUTHERN** | Chef-owner Cindy Wolf's cuisine has a South Carolina Low Country accent with French roots—and the results are unparalleled. Inside the glowingly lit dining room, classics like she-crab soup and shrimp and grits complement more elegant fare, such as a lobster bisque spiced with curry, and wild salmon with avocado. **Known for:** decadent desserts; excellent service; the city's most elegant dining room. $ *Average main: $79 ✉ 1000 Lancaster St., Harbor East ☎ 410/332–7373 🌐 www.charlestonrestaurant.com ⏲ Closed Sun. 👔 Jacket and tie.*

Cinghiale

$$ | **ITALIAN** | The spotlight is on wine at Cinghiale (pronounced "ching-GYAH-lay"), an open, inviting space with tall, wide windows. Enjoy hand-cut pastas such as tagliatelle with tender chicken, greens, and walnuts, or lasagna with veal ragù. **Known for:** northern Italian fare; vast wine list of more than 600 bottles; sharp and unpretentious service. $ *Average main: $22 ✉ 822 Lancaster St., Harbor East ☎ 410/547–8282 🌐 www.cgeno.com ⏲ No lunch.*

The Food Market

$$$$ | **FUSION** | **FAMILY** | In the heart of Hampden, on "The Avenue" (36th Street), chef Chad Gauss presents some of Baltimore's most consistently excellent dining with a global reach. Try the Amish soft pretzels with cheddar-cheese dipping sauce as a starter, then move on to coconut green curry or the lamb with spaetzle. **Known for:** convivial atmosphere; popular Sunday brunch with huge pours; desserts like Heath bar bread pudding. $ *Average main: $36 ✉ 1017 W. 36th St., Hampden ☎ 410/366–0606 🌐 www.thefoodmarketbaltimore.com ⏲ No lunch weekdays.*

Gertrude's

$$ | **AMERICAN** | In the Baltimore Museum of Art, this casual yet classy spot cooks up creative Maryland specialties. Crab cakes, served with a variety of tasty sauces, are one option, as is the Parmesan-crusted salmon. **Known for:** lovely outdoor terrace overlooking the sculpture garden; a commitment to sustainable Chesapeake cuisine; Sunday jazz brunch. $ *Average main: $22 ✉ Baltimore Museum of Art, 10 Art Museum Dr., Charles Village ☎ 410/889–3399 🌐 www.gertrudesbaltimore.com ⏲ Closed Mon.*

The Helmand

$ | **AFGHAN** | Owned by Hamid Kharzai's brother, Qayum Karzai, Helmand serves outstanding Afghan fare in a casual yet elegant space. Beautiful woven textiles and traditional dresses adorn the walls, adding color to the simple white table settings. **Known for:** outstanding lamb dishes ; vegetarian ; the unforgettable appetizer. $ *Average main: $13 ✉ 806 N. Charles St., Mount Vernon ☎ 410/752–0311 🌐 www.helmand.com ⏲ No lunch.*

La Cuchara

$$$$ | **BASQUE** | Authentic Basque cuisine is on full display at this lovely restaurant located in the Meadow Mill building:

pinxtos like ham croquettes with Gruyère cheese, sardines in oil, and fingerling potatoes with garlic aioli are perfect for sharing. The vast space is anchored by a 40-foot chestnut bar, behind which sits a wood-fired grill. **Known for:** duck breast with a honey-Banyuis reduction; house-made breads; friendly service. [$] *Average main: $38* ✉ *3600 Clipper Mill Rd., Hampden* ✥ *Turn into mill complex, crossing wooden bridge, which spans Jones Falls (expressway is overhead). Note: only one car can cross bridge at a time* ☎ *443/708–3838* 🌐 *www.lacucharabaltimore.com* 🕑 *No lunch weekdays.*

Ouzo Bay

$$$ | **MEDITERRANEAN** | Blink, and you may think you're in South Beach: this trendy restaurant has quickly become the city's most popular, where the suit-and-tie crowd sidles up to the elevated bar or takes a seat on the cushy outdoor terrace. Try the grilled octopus starter, tossed with lemon juice and capers, or the charcoal-grilled whole fish, be it wild sea bass, sole, or snapper. **Known for:** laid-back, sexy vibe; Mediterranean-style seafood; grilled lamp chops. [$] *Average main: $35* ✉ *1000 Lancaster St., Harbor East* ☎ *443/708–5818* 🌐 *www.ouzobay.com.*

The Prime Rib

$$$$ | **STEAKHOUSE** | Bustling and crowded, this luxuriously dark dining room is just north of Mount Vernon Square and a five-minute drive from the Inner Harbor. The leopard-print carpet and live pianist lend a swanky 1960s feel to a place that seems untouched by time, including the meat-heavy menu of steak-house classics. **Known for:** superb prime rib and an even better filet mignon; jumbo lump crab cakes; good but predominately U.S. wine list. [$] *Average main: $41* ✉ *1101 N. Calvert St., Mount Vernon* ☎ *410/539–1804* 🌐 *www.theprimerib.com* 🕑 *No lunch.*

★ Rye Street Tavern

$$$ | **SOUTHERN** | **FAMILY** | Baltimore's best new restaurant is located in the rapidly developing—and hotly contested—Port Covington neighborhood, a waterfront destination just south of Federal Hill off Interstate 95. Here New York celebrity-chef Andrew Carmellini spotlights Southern flavors, such as whiskey grilled ribs, bacon-wrapped trout, and crab-stuffed deviled eggs. **Known for:** seafood bakes; gorgeous Tidewater-style construction with waterfront views; craft cocktails made with locally distilled Sagamore Spirit rye. [$] *Average main: $33* ✉ *225 E. Cromwell St., Federal Hill* ☎ *443/662–8000* 🌐 *www.ryestreettavern.com.*

★ Woodberry Kitchen

$$$$ | **AMERICAN** | In an old flour mill, Woodberry Kitchen has a cozy, relaxed atmosphere and a menu that harkens back to a simpler era. The best items are often the most basic since chef and owner Spike Gjerde is committed to sourcing the finest local ingredients. **Known for:** cast-iron chicken and biscuits with carrots and string beans; homemade ice cream with hot fudge and peanuts; lovely outdoor garden terrace. [$] *Average main: $36* ✉ *2010 Clipper Park Rd., Suite 126, Hampden* ☎ *410/464–8000* 🌐 *www.woodberrykitchen.com* 🕑 *No lunch weekdays.*

Hotels

There's plenty to see and do in Baltimore for a long weekend. Should you wish to spend one or more nights, there are a lot of options in Baltimore.

★ Four Seasons Baltimore

$$$$ | **HOTEL** | The 18-story glass tower rises above the harbor, commanding prime views from each plush and comfortable (albeit minimalist) guest room. **Pros:** hands down, Baltimore's most luxurious hotel; impeccable service; within walking distance to the Inner Harbor and Fell's

Point. **Cons:** room rates are steep, even in the off-season; expensive valet parking; ongoing construction around Harbor East can be noisy. [$] *Rooms from: $499* ✉ *200 International Dr., Harbor East* ☎ *410/576–5800* 🌐 *www.fourseasons.com/baltimore* 🛏 *255 rooms* 🍴 *No meals.*

Hilton Baltimore

$ | **HOTEL** | The towering Hilton has an unparalleled view of Camden Yards and a skywalk that connects to the city's convention center. **Pros:** connected to the convention center; excellent ballpark views; on-site Coffee Bean & Tea Leaf. **Cons:** rooms are considerably smaller than those at similarly priced hotels in town; it's a chain hotel, albeit a nice one; busy convention hotel generates crowds. [$] *Rooms from: $194* ✉ *401 W. Pratt St., Inner Harbor* ☎ *443/573–8700* 🌐 *www.hilton.com* 🛏 *757 rooms* 🍴 *No meals.*

Hotel Revival

$ | **HOTEL** | **FAMILY** | Joie de Vivre hotel group has made a splash in town with its rehab of a historic apartment building, right across from the Washington Monument, offering rooms with wood-laminate floors, brightly colored fabrics, and art reflecting the surrounding neighborhood. **Pros:** free Wi-Fi throughout; historical accents that instill a sense of place; location near the BSO and the Walters Art Museum. **Cons:** area can feel forlorn at night; expensive valet parking; residential-style guest rooms curiously lack desks. [$] *Rooms from: $159* ✉ *101 W. Monument St., Mount Vernon* ☎ *410/727–7101* 🌐 *www.jdvhotels.com* 🛏 *107 rooms* 🍴 *No meals.*

The Ivy Hotel

$$$$ | **HOTEL** | Nestled in a century-old brownstone, just a few blocks from Penn Station, this 18-room boutique hotel features luxurious appointments such as original art and antiques, a library, billiards room and private interior courtyard, Frette linens atop the beds, gas fireplaces in the guest rooms, heated floors and large soaking tubs in the bathrooms. **Pros:** small but noteworthy spa on-site; attentive staff ensures every need is met; each layout is different; some suites feature multiple levels. **Cons:** very expensive; limited privacy in a historic home setting; area can be dicey at night. [$] *Rooms from: $650* ✉ *205 E. Biddle St., Mount Vernon* ☎ *410/514–6500* 🌐 *www.theivybaltimore.com* 🛏 *10 rooms, 8 suites* 🍴 *Free Breakfast.*

Hotel Monaco Baltimore

$ | **HOTEL** | **FAMILY** | This boutique hotel is in the historic headquarters of the B&O Railroad—just 2½ blocks from the Inner Harbor and within easy walking distance of Oriole Park at Camden Yards. **Pros:** a posh downtown hotel at family-friendly prices; amenities include rooms with bunk beds, Xbox video-game systems; free bike-share program complete with a map of the best downtown routes. **Cons:** the reception area is on the building's second floor; ongoing construction project across the street (former Mechanic Theater); expensive valet parking. [$] *Rooms from: $179* ✉ *2 N. Charles St., Downtown* ☎ *410/692–6170* 🌐 *www.monaco-baltimore.com* 🛏 *202 rooms* 🍴 *No meals.*

Marriott Baltimore Waterfront

$$ | **HOTEL** | The city's tallest hotel and one of a handful directly on the Inner Harbor, this 31-story Marriott has a neoclassical interior that uses multihue marbles, rich jewel-tone walls, and photographs of Baltimore architectural landmarks. **Pros:** nice amenities; great location and view; water taxi stop right out front. **Cons:** pricey compared to nearby hotels in the same category; expensive valet parking; room renovation still has yet to happen. [$] *Rooms from: $239* ✉ *700 Aliceanna St., Harbor East* ☎ *410/385–3000* 🌐 *www.marriott.com* 🛏 *751 rooms* 🍴 *No meals.*

Sagamore Pendry Baltimore

$$$ | **HOTEL** | **FAMILY** | The cornerstone of Fells Point has long been the Rec Pier building, once an immigration hub, then later the setting for the TV series *Homicide: Life on the Street*, and now a 128-room boutique gem that has inspired a neighborhood-wide renaissance. **Pros:** stunning infinity pool overlooking the harbor and Domino Sugar Factory; gorgeous circa-1914 ballroom with original windows and state-of-the-art technology; free Wi-Fi throughout. **Cons:** expensive valet parking; no spa; service can be pretentious. $ *Rooms from: $319* ✉ *1715 Thames St., Fells Point* ☎ *443/552–1400* ⊕ *www.pendryhotels.com* ⤵ *128 rooms* ⊙ *No meals.*

320

Index

Photo Credits

Front Cover: Gavin Hellier / AWL Images [Description: Statue of Iwo Jima U S Marine Corps Memorial at Arlington National Cemetery, Washington DC, USA.] Back cover, from left to right: Timothy Michael Morgan/Shutterstock; SurangaWeeratunga/Shutterstock; graham s. klotz/Shutterstock. Spine: Orhancam | Dreamstime.com. Interior, from left to right: Smithsonian Institution and the National Museum of African American History and Culture (1). Spencer Grant / age fotostock (2-3). Smithsonian Institute (5). **Chapter 1**: Experience Washington, D.C.: Lunamarina | Dreamstime.com (6-7). Steve Heap/Shutterstock (8-9). Lewis Tse Pui Lung / Shutterstock (9). Orhan Cam/Shutterstock (9). Orhan Cam/Shutterstock (10). Konstantin L/Shutterstock (10). Sgoodwin4813 | Dreamstime.com (10). Courtesy of washington.org (10). travelview/Shutterstock (11). Walleyelj | Dreamstime.com (11). Rena Schild/Shutterstock (12). Gary Blakeley/Shutterstock (12). cdrin / Shutterstock (12). Bob Pool/Shutterstock (12). Albert Pego/Shutterstock (13). Lissandra Melo / Shutterstock (13). DavidNNP/Shutterstock (13). Sean Pavone / Shutterstock (13). Orhan Cam/Shutterstock (14). Avmedved | Dreamstime.com (14). Orhan Cam/Shutterstock (15). Maria Bryk/Newseum (16). Sean Pavone/Shutterstock (16). stock_photo_world / Shutterstock (16). Courtesy of washington.org (16). Steve Heap/Shutterstock (17). Sean Pavone / Shutterstock (17). The White House Historical Association (20). Courtesy of Kramerbooks & Afterwords Cafe (21). f11photo/Shutterstock (22). Sean Pavone / Shutterstock (22). Afagundes | Dreamstime.com (22). Mandritoiu | Dreamstime.com (23). Tupungato/Shutterstock (23). Stephen Bobb Photography (24). Freer Gallery of Art, Smithsonian (24). Courtesy of The Phillips Collection, Washington, DC./Lee Stalsworth(24). Romiana Lee/Shutterstock (24). Clewisleake | Dreamstime.com (25). Jon Bilous/Shutterstock (25). Nicole S Glass/Shutterstock (25). Andrei Medvedev/Shutterstock (25). David Tran Photo / Shutterstock (26). MarkSweep/Wikipedia.org (26). Rudi Riet/Wikimedia.org (26). Jwblinn | Dreamstime.com (27). Alankolnik | Dreamstime.com (27). **Chapter 3**: The National Mall: Orhan Cam/Shutterstock (59). Getty Images (66). tomwachs (68). Phototake Inc. / Alamy (69). Wikipedia.org (70). Popperfoto / Alamy (71). Tramonto / age fotostock (71). Wikipedia.org (71). Dennis MacDonald / age fotostock (72). Douglas Litchfield/Shutterstock (72). Chuck Pefley / Alamy (72). Dennis MacDonald / age fotostock (73). Stock Connection Distribution / Alamy (73). Gordon Logue/Shutterstock (73). Smithsonian Institution (73). P_R_/Flickr, [CC BY-ND 2.0]. (73). David R. Frazier Photolibrary, Inc. / Alamy (73). Sandra Baker / Alamy (73). Franko Khoury National Museum of African Art Smithsonian Institution (73). United States Holocaust Memorial Museum (73). Smithsonian Institution (74). DC St. Patrick's Day/Parade Photographers (76). National Cherry Blossom Festival (76). William S. Kuta / Alamy (76). San Rostro / age fotostock (76). Visions of America, LLC / Alamy (76). Lee Foster / Alamy (77). Smithsonian Institution and the National Museum of African American History and Culture (80). Crimestudio | Dreamstime.com (87). Orhan Cam/Shutterstock (88). **Chapter 4**: Downtown, Chinatown, and Penn Quarter: Emily Haight, NMWA (93). Prakash Patel (97). Courtesy of the Smithsonian's National Portrait Gallery (101). Groovysoup | Dreamstime.com (103). **Chapter 5**: Capitol Hill and Northeast: Shawn Miller/Library of Congress (121 Bartomeu Amengual / age fotostock (129). SuperStock / age fotostock (129). kimberlyfaye/Flickr (129). Library of Congress Prints & Photographs Division (130). Classic Vision / age fotostock (130). Library of Congress Prints & Photographs Division (130). Prints and Photographs Division Library of Congress (130). Architect of the Capitol (131). Jose Fuste Raga (131). Architect of the Capitol (131). U.S. Capitol Visitor Center (132). Wadester (133). MShades/Flickr, [CC BY-ND 2.0] (134). Wikipedia.org (134). Wikipedia.orgk (136). DCstockphoto.com / Alamy (136). SCPhotos / Alamy (136). United States Congress (136). Gary Blakeley/Shutterstock (138). Courtesy US Botanic Garden (141). **Chapter 6**: Foggy Bottom: Andrea Izzotti/Shutterstock (247). Sepavo | Dreamstime.com (161). **Chapter 7**: Georgetown: Tupungato/Shutterstock (171). **Chapter 8**: Dupont Circle and Kalorama: Courtesy of The Phillips Collection, Washington, DC./Max Hirshfeld (187). Sarah Sampsel/Flckr [CC BY-ND 2.0]. (194). **Chapter 9**: Adams Morgan: Avmedved | Dreamstime.com (203). **Chapter 10**: U Street Corridor and Shaw: Carol M. Highsmith/Flckr [CC BY-ND 2.0]. (213). Destination DC (216). **Chapter 11**: Upper Northwest: Jon Bilous/Shutterstock (235). **Chapter 12**: DC Waterfront: Romiana Lee/Shutterstock (247). **Chapter 13**: Arlington: Hang Dinh/Shutterstock (261). SuperStock / age fotostock (267). Condor 36/Shutterstock (268). Scott S. Warren/Aurora Photos (269). Dennis Brack/Aurora Photos (269). Vario images GmbH & Co.KG / Alamy (269). Jeremy R. Smith Sr/Shutterstock (270). Ken Hackett / Alamy (272). National Archives and Records Administration (272). Rough Guides / Alamy (272). William S. Kuta / Alamy (273). Jeremy R. Smith/Shutterstock (273). Chris A Crumley / Alamy (273). Vacclav | Dreamstime.com (275). **Chapter 14**: Side Trips From DC: Appalachianviews | Dreamstime.com (279). Lee Snider Photo Images / Shutterstock (289). Orhan Cam/Shutterstock (299). vittorio sciosia / age fotostock (306).` About Our Writers: All photos are courtesy of the writers except for the following: Mike Lillis, Courtesy of Greg Nash.

Notes

Notes

Notes

Notes

Notes

Notes

Fodor's WASHINGTON, D.C.

Editorial: Douglas Stallings, *Editorial Director*; Margaret Kelly, Jacinta O'Halloran, *Senior Editors*; Kayla Becker, Alexis Kelly, Amanda Sadlowski, *Editors*; Teddy Minford, *Content Editor*; Rachael Roth, *Content Manager*

Design: Tina Malaney, *Design and Production Director*; Jessica Gonzalez, *Production Designer*

Photography: Jill Krueger, *Senior Photo Editor*

Maps: Rebecca Baer, *Senior Map Editor*; David Lindroth, Mark Stroud (Moon Street Cartography), *Cartographers*

Production: Jennifer DePrima, *Editorial Production Manager*; Carrie Parker, *Senior Production Editor*; Elyse Rozelle, *Production Editor*

Business & Operations: Chuck Hoover, *Chief Marketing Officer*; Robert Ames, *Vice President and General Manager*; Stephen Horowitz, *Director of Business Development and Revenue Operations*; Tara McCrillis, *Director of Publishing Operations*

Public Relations and Marketing: Joe Ewaskiw, *Manager*; Esther Su, *Marketing Manager*

Writers: Bob Carden, Barbara Noe Kennedy, Mike Lillis, Sabrina Medora, Laura Rodini, Alison Thoet, Celia Wexler

Editor: Douglas Stallings

Production Editor: Carrie Parker

Production Design: Liliana Guia

24th Edition

ISBN 978-1-64097-144-8

ISSN 0743–9741

Library of Congress Control Number 2018914616

SPECIAL SALES

This book is available at special discounts for bulk purchases for sales promotions or premiums. For more information, e-mail SpecialMarkets@fodors.com.

PRINTED IN THE UNITED STATES OF AMERICA

10 9 8 7 6 5 4 3 2 1

About Our Writers

Bob Carden is a business and travel writer whose work appears frequently in the *Washington Post, Philadelphia Inquirer, Chicago Tribune,* and others. He has had a long and varied journalism career and has worked as a correspondent for CNN in Washington, D.C., PBS in Tokyo, and as a newspaper writer for the *Philadelphia Daily News.* Mr. Carden has produced four PBS documentaries dealing with International business and investment fraud. He lives in Bethesda, MD, with his wife. He updated Downtown, Penn Quarter, and Chinatown; and Upper Northwest.

After many years as senior editor with NatGeo Travel Publishing, **Barbara Noe Kennedy** left in 2015 to fly solo as a freelance travel writer and editor, focusing on destinations, art, culture, food, and adventure around the world. She's watched D.C. grow up into a global city, though her favorite activity remains running on its leafy paths. Her website is barbaranoekennedy.com. She updated Foggy Bottom, the West End, and the White House; Experience Washington, D.C.; and Travel Smart.

Born and raised in Virginia, **Mike Lillis** now lives in Washington, D.C., where he covers politics for *The Hill* newspaper. Many weekends find him in a canoe, paddling the rocky streams of the region. He updated Capitol Hill and Northeast D.C.

After several years as a digital marketing specialist, **Sabrina Medora** quit her job in advertising to pursue a career as a food writer. Today, she is the founder and editor of Unplated, a national multimedia platform dedicated to celebrating the little known stories of people working in the restaurant industry.

In her spare time, Sabrina enjoys napping, practicing yoga, watching competitive cooking shows, and rereading Harry Potter books. Sabrina and her husband live in Virginia with Albus, their golden doodle. She updated Arlington and Northern Virginia and Virginia side-trips.

Laura Rodini believes that happiness is a tank full of gas and a road you've never been down. She has worked on more than 90 destination and luxury hotel guides around the world, but her heart belongs to Baltimore—a surprise discovery made on assignment 10 years ago. Her perfect day includes brunch in Hampden, an Orioles game, and walking her dog, Monty Python, around Fort McHenry. She updated Georgetown and Maryland side-trips.

Alison Thoet is a freelance travel writer and reporter based in the District. She has written for the *Washington Post* and covered museum events and exhibitions for the PBS NewsHour. She began her career as an intern at *The Hill,* covering politics and whip lists, continuing to the *National Journal's* online team before moving to ABC News in New York City. She updated The National Mall and Federal Triangle; U Street Corridor, Logan Circle, and Columbia Heights; and Waterfront and Southeast.

Celia Viggo Wexler is an award-winning journalist who has lived and worked in the Washington, DC area since 1996. Her work has appeared in *The New York Times, The Washington Post,* the *San Francisco Chronicle,* the *Pittsburgh Post-Gazette, The Nation,* and *Columbia Journalism Review.* She's also written two books. She and her spouse are based in Alexandria, Virginia, and are seasoned travelers. She updated Dupont Circle and Kalorama.